Table of Contents

KW-222-420

Section 2: Text-Related Resources

Section 3: Organizations

Philosophy in
Cyberspace

2nd *edition*

@ Guide to Philosophy
Related Resources
on the Internet

Edited by
Dey Alexander

RELATED PUBLICATIONS:

Directory of American Philosophers, 1998-1999, Nineteenth Edition,
ISBN 0-912632-74-7, ISSN 0070-508X

International Directory of Philosophy and Philosophers 1997-1998,
Tenth Edition, ISBN 0-912632-69-0

The Philosopher's Phone and E-mail Directory, 1998 Edition,
ISBN 0-912632-63-1

Guidebook for Publishing Philosophy, 1997 Edition, ISBN 0-912632-62-3

Published by Philosophy Documentation Center
Bowling Green State University
Bowling Green, OH 43403-0189 USA

Phone: 419-372-2419
Fax: 419-372-6987
e-mail: pdc@mailserver.bgsu.edu
web site: http://www.bgsu.edu/pdc/

ISBN   1-889680-00-1

Section 4: Discussion Forums

Section 5: Miscellaneous

Introduction

*H*ello and welcome to the second edition of *Philosophy in Cyberspace*. I am delighted to note that since the first print edition of the guide, there has been a phenomenal growth in the number of resources available on the Internet. The World Wide Web was then in its infancy, but today is the focus of the net—seemingly everyone has their own home page, and even some cats and dogs appear to have gotten in on the act!

This growth means that the Web is now a rich source of philosophical resources. The problem is, of course, how to find quality resources as quickly as possible. Searches on philosophy topics using the various search engines on the net are time-consuming and do not always produce the results you are hoping for. Trying to track down philosophy discussion lists on topics of interest can be even more difficult.

The aim of this guide is to increase your chances of finding the resources that will assist you in your teaching, research, study, or general interest in philosophy, without you having to waste precious time wading through thousands of results produced by online search engines. At a glance, you can see what resources are available and assess their suitability to your needs. *Philosophy in Cyberspace* annotates and indexes more than 1500 web sites, more than 300 mailing lists, and approximately 60 newsgroups. The resources are divided into five sub-sections and catalogued in more than 50 categories for ease of use.

I established the first version of *Philosophy in Cyberspace* in late 1993. It was the result of the rather incidental documentation of the various philosophy sites I'd found while surfing the net, a pastime which was becoming increasingly time-consuming—no doubt due to the psychological state often referred to as 'thesis-avoidance'. The guide was first compiled using a number of resource lists already available on the net, but it was based in particular on two lists of resources (primarily mailing lists, as the web sites were few in those days), one by Peter Morville with Stephen Clark and the other, the Ferhmann philosophy and ethics list. My intention, originally, was to find resources in the areas of philosophy in which I was interested—feminism and political philosophy—areas which were not well covered by the earlier guides.

In a short period of time I'd amassed an enormous collection of resources which I initially compiled and distributed via ftp and gopher in text file format. Dan Brickley of the University of Bristol was enthused enough about *Philosophy in Cyberspace* to volunteer to convert it to html for viewing on the web. When was that Dan? In any case, we believe this was the first, and if not it was certainly among the first, philosophy guide on the Web (now there are probably several hundred). The difficulties of keeping the text and html versions simultaneously up-to-date proved problematic, so I began to produce the guide in html format myself. Dan now works on the WWW Virtual Library's Guide to Philosophy.

The first print edition of *Philosophy in Cyberspace* was published by the Philosophy Documentation Center in 1995. The resources available online at the time were primarily mailing lists, gopher sites, a few ftp sites, and some web pages. Web pages now dominate, though there are still some gopher, ftp, and telnet sites listed in the guide. The layout and organization of the second print edition conform to the arrangement of materials on the Web site.

Section 1 indexes sites by philosophical topic—metaphysics and epistemology, ethics, or philosophy of mind, for example. The resources listed in each area are those which I believe someone working in that field might find valuable. They are primarily philosophical in orientation, but not all are strictly philosophy sites. The miscellaneous division in this section lists those sites for which there were too few on any one topic to necessitate creating a separate index.

Section 2 lists sites which are, roughly speaking, text-oriented. Here you will find bibliographies, libraries, preprints, reviews, journals, electronic texts, publishers, magazines, and related resources. Indexes listed as 'directories' provide information on 'meta sites', resources which are themselves guides or indexes of information.

Section 3 brings together organizational resources. Here you will find links to philosophy departments worldwide, as well as links to various philosophical organizations, associations, projects, and centers.

Section 4 is a guide to the vast number of mailing lists and newsgroups which might be of relevance to philosophers. As in Section 1, this section is divided into topical areas— logic, feminism, philosophy of law, and so on. A 'how to' to guide you in the use of mailing lists and newsgroups can also be found.

Section 5 brings together a listing of the remaining miscellaneous resources. Here you will find information on job vacancies for philosophers, conferences and calls for papers, syllabi and other teaching resources, resources for students, and even some sites which provide a little philosophical humor.

To keep you completely abreast of changes to the sites listed in the guide, updates are available on the Web. The main site for *Philosophy in Cyberspace* is located in Australia on the Monash University web server, at:

> http://www-personal.monash.edu.au/~dey/phil/

Mirror sites are located in the United States at:

> *http://www.geocities.com/Athens/Acropolis/4393/*

and in Europe at:

> *http://lgxserver.uniba.it/lei/alexander/index.htm*

I welcome suggestions for additions to the guide, as well as updated information on any of the resources currently listed.

NOTE: Early in 1998, I was invited to join in a new and exciting online venture called Hippias. Hippias is a 'limited area search engine', and has some major advantages, over the larger, more general search engines which produce extremely long, and sometimes useless results when searching on philosophical terms. Hippias is designed to search only those sites selected by a team of associate editors. This will save you time, and produce results that are more useful and relevant to philosophy. Hippias can be accessed directly from the *Philosophy in Cyberspace* websites, or at its own location at:

http://hippias.evansville.edu/

Dey Alexander
dey@silas.cc.monash.edu.au
http://www-personal.monash.edu.au/~dey/

User Guide

W ith all the talk of the Internet in the media, as well as in our professional and everyday lives, I have assumed that readers are aware of at least some of the basic concepts of the Internet, particularly the world wide web and web pages. In the first edition of *Philosophy in Cyberspace*, I gave a brief outline of the nature of various Internet tools and protocols: gopher, telnet, ftp, and so on. With the advent of new web browsers (such as Netscape and Internet Explorer), accessing these resources is as easy as accessing web pages—you simply type the address of the site into the location field of your browser, press enter, and the browser makes the connection for you. There seems then, little need to explain how these protocols work.

In any case, to provide any truly useful or comprehensive beginner's guide to the use of Internet resources is beyond the scope of this project. There are, however, numerous guides already in existence, both in print and online. Print guides are readily available in bookstores, and you can access a number of online guides at:

gopher://nic.merit.edu:70/1/.introducing.the.internet

Throughout this guide, the address (or URL, short for Uniform Resource Locator) of each site appears immediately below the title of the site. (Note: URLs need to be entered in exactly the same format as they appear—don't add any spaces, remember they are case-sensitive, and don't add linebreaks to the long URLs that were split to make them fit the page width.) The exception to this layout is in the electronic journals and mailing lists sections.

Where possible, I have included the name and email address of the person responsible for the site so that you can contact them directly if you are having any difficulties connecting to the site (sites often move, servers break down, and so forth), or if you are seeking more information.

For those interested in online discussion forums, there is information on accessing and using newsgroups and mailing lists in the Discussion Forum section of this guide.

Section 1: Philosophy Topics

Aesthetics

Aesthetics Online

http://www.indiana.edu/~asanl/

Aesthetics Online from Dominic Lopes dlopes@indiana.edu is the official web site of the American Society for Aesthetics, and contains articles in aesthetics and philosophy of art, book reviews, conference announcements and calls for papers, and links to aesthetics-related net resources.

Aesthetics Teaching Materials

http://www.indiana.edu/~asanl/teaching/syllabi.html

This site, from Dominic Lopes dlopes@indiana.edu, provides links to materials useful for those teaching aesthetics. It includes online courses, syllabi, and miscellaneous aesthetics resources.

African Art: Aesthetics and Meaning

http://www.lib.virginia.edu/dic/exhib/93.ray.aa/Introduction.html

This site gives an introduction to an exhibition of African artifacts, placing them in the context of African aesthetic principles and related moral and religious values.

British Society for Aesthetics

http://www.indiana.edu/~asanl/asa/bsa-info.html

This site provides information on the Society, plus contact details and membership application information. The Society can be contacted via Richard Woodfield woodfra@innotts.co.uk.

Canadian Society for Aesthetics

http://tornade.ere.umontreal.ca/~guedon/AE/ae.html

Available in both French and English, this page provides information on the Society's conference program, its journal, and links to other aesthetics organizations on the web. It is maintained by allegre@ere.umontreal.ca.

Center for Cognitive Issues in the Arts

http://www.bris.ac.uk/Depts/Philosophy/confad.html

Located at the University of Bristol, the Center's page announces forthcoming conferences and other events relevant to aesthetics. The site is maintained by Andrew Harrison Andrew.Harrison@bris.ac.uk.

Center for the Cognitive Science of Metaphor

http://metaphor.uoregon.edu/metaphor.html

This site, maintained by Tim Rohrer rohrer@darkwing.uoregon.edu, provides access to a range of resources including an annotated bibliography of work on metaphor, master metaphor list, and links to other metaphor resources.

Center for Research in Philosophy and Literature

http://www.warwick.ac.uk/fac/soc/Philosophy/CRPL/CRPL.html

The University of Warwick's Center for Research in Philosophy & Literature exists to promote a wide variety of interdisciplinary research activity—lectures, colloquia, and major international conferences. The annual programme of events is supplemented by the contributions of distinguished Visiting Scholars, among whom have been John Sallis, Paul Ricouer, Jean-Francois Lyotard, Julia Kristeva, Gianni Vattimo, Frank Kermode, Christopher Norris, David Krell, Manfred Frank, Stanley Cavell, Geoffrey Hartman, Jaques Derrida, and Edward Saïd. This site provides information on the activities of the Center, its staff and, participating departments. The maintainer of the site can be contacted at PYRBL@snow.csv.warwick. ac.uk.

Christianity and Aesthetics

http://members.aol.com/evassembly/aesth.htm

This site features a selection of papers on the intersection between aesthetics and christianity. The site is maintained by Jim Rovira evassembly@aol.com.

Cognitive Science and the Arts: A Collaborative Bibliography

http://www.hfac.uh.edu/cogsci/Bibliography.html

This site, maintained by Cynthia Freeland cfreeland@uh.edu, provides an online bibliography with sections including: visual arts, film, literature, linguistics, music, and more.

Committee on Aesthetics and Higher Education

http://www.csulb.edu/~philos/asa.html

This site provides information on the activities of the committee, and access to the Committee's annual reports is also available. The page is maintained by Julie Van Camp jvancamp@csulb.edu.

Dutch Association of Aesthetics

http://www.phil.ruu.nl/esthetica/

This page, in Dutch only, provides information on the activities of the Association.

El Mundo Ensombrecido

http://www.redestb.es/personal/fanfrio/

This is the personal home page of Francisco Caja fanfrio@redestb.es. It includes a selection of his essays on aesthetics and photography. Currently the essays are presented in Spanish only, but English versions are forthcoming.

European Society for the Cognitive Sciences of Music

http://www.mus.cam.ac.uk/ESCOM/

This site, which will soon be in French and English, provides information on events and activities of the Society. The Society's newsletters are available online, and links are provided to sites related to the cognitive science of music. The Society's secretariat can be contacted at i.deliege@ulg.ac.be.

Film and Philosophy

http://www.hanover.edu/philos/film/home.htm

This site, from John Ahrens ahrens@hanover.edu, provides access to the articles from the journal *Film and Philosophy*, a publication of the Society for the Philosophic Study of the Contemporary Visual Arts. The Society's newsletters can also be accessed from this site.

The Film Studies Site

http://www.inform.umd.edu/filmweb/

The Film Studies Site is dedicated to scholarship in screen textualities. Film, television, and computer screens are the subject of the site, and works that use the multi- and hypermedia potentials of the Web are invited for consideration.

International Association of Empirical Aesthetics

http://www.ume.maine.edu/~iaea/

This site, maintained by Colin Martindale rpy383@maine.maine.edu, provides information about the activities of the Association, and links to other aesthetics-related resources on the net.

International Society for the Empirical Study of Literature

http://www.ualberta.ca/ARTS/RICL/riclseal.html

This site provides information on the aims and activities of the Society, and access to a downloadable bibliography.

Sydney Society of Literature and Aesthetics

http://centrum.arts.su.edu.au/Arts/departs/philos/ssla/

This site, maintained by Paul Redding paul.redding@philosophy.su.edu.au, provides information on the activities of the Society, and links to related resources.

Ancient Philosophy & Classical Thought

The 4th Tetralogy

http://plato.evansville.edu/

"The 4th Tetralogy: Exploring Plato's Middle Dialogues," is dedicated to examining Plato's *Republic*, *Phaedrus*, *Symposium*, and *Phaedo*, and was recently put online for the general public. The site features the texts of Plato, hyperlinked to several search engines (with appropriate cross-links to Perseus), a new forum for scholarly exchange, and an on-going Internet discussion group that examines the four dialogues continually in fourteen week cycles. Membership in the discussion group is open to anyone with a serious interest in the study of Plato. The general editor of the site is Anthony F. Beavers tb2@evansville.edu.

The American Classical League

http://www.umich.edu/~acleague/

This page provides access to a range of classics-related resources, including texts, teaching tools, professional resources, journals and publications, and classical art and architecture. The ACL can be contacted at a.c.l@umich.edu.

Ancient Greece

http://www.wsu.edu:8080/~dee/GREECE/GREECE.HTM

This site provides access to a variety of resources relevant to scholars of Ancient Greece, and includes a section on philosophy comprising Pre-Socratic Philosophy, Socrates, Plato, Aristotle, and Hellenistic Philosophy. It is maintained by Richard Hooker dee@mail.wsu.edu.

Ancient Greek (Hellenic) Sites on the WWW

http://www.webcom.com/shownet/medea/grklink.html

This site provides a range of links to Ancient Greek resources online, including: authors and texts, art and images, maps and geography, and essential sites. The site is maintained by shownet@webcom.com.

Ancient Philosophy Home Page

http://www.ic.nanzan-u.ac.jp/~kaneko/

This page aims to provide information and resources to scholars who study ancient Greek philosophy and related topics. It currently provides links to the Perseus Project, primary texts, English translations, lexicons, and Greek-English texts of Plato and Aristotle. It is maintained by Y. Kaneko kaneko@ic.nanzan-u.ac.jp.

Argos

http://argos.evansville.edu/

Argos is a limited area search engine, specialising in indexing resources in ancient and medieval studies. This is a very useful site, limiting search results to quality sites selected by Argos' associate editors.

Aristotle

http://www.ilt.columbia.edu/academic/digitexts/aristotle/bio_aristotle.html

Part of the ILTWeb site webmaster@ilt.columbia.edu, this page provides biographical information on Aristotle, as well as links to Aristotle texts.

Aristotle

http://www.ultranet.com/~rsarkiss/ARISTOT.HTM

This site provides a short biography, selected quotations, and links to online texts. It is maintained by Robert Sarkissian rsarkissian@smtp.microcom.com.

Marcus Aurelius

http://www.ultranet.com/~rsarkiss/AURELIUS.HTM

This site provides a short biography, selected quotations, and links to online texts. It is maintained by Robert Sarkissian rsarkissian@smtp.microcom.com.

The Marcus Aurelius Think Page

http://ucsu.colorado.edu/~biggus/Marcus/Marcus.html

This page, from Jeff Biggus biggus@colorado.edu, presents excerpts from the *Meditations*, with links to full translations of the text.

The Cicero Homepage

http://www.utexas.edu/depts/classics/documents/Cic.html

Links from this page provide access to Cicero texts, a Cicero chronology, a bibliography, images of Cicero, and Cicero's biography (according to Plutarch [trans. Dryden]). The page is maintained by ariggsby@utxvms.cc.utexas.edu.

Classics Collections Page

http://nervm.nerdc.ufl.edu/~blaland/Class.html

Produced by Blake Landor blaland@nervm.nerdc.ufl.edu, this site houses a large collection of links to classics resources including: bibliographies, journals, texts, databases, online guides to classics resources, discussion groups, art and archaeology, instructional resources, and more.

Classics Resources

http://www.artsci.wustl.edu/~cwconrad/classics.html

Maintained by Carl Conrad cwconrad@artsci.wustl.edu, this page provides links to a vast range of classics resources including: Greek and Latin language resources, Greek and Latin authors and texts, classics associations, classics departments, electronic journals in classics, classics publishers, and general classics sites.

Diogenes of Sinope

http://www.halcyon.com/colinp/diogenes.htm

This page, produced by Colin Pringle colinp@halcyon.com, provides a short biography and overview of the thought of the Cynics, plus links to related resources.

Diotima: Women and Gender in the Ancient World

http://www.uky.edu/ArtsSciences/Classics/gender.html

This site offers a range of research materials for the study of women and gender in the ancient world. It includes course materials, a bibliography, an anthology, essays, and more. The site is maintained by Ross Scaife scaife@pop.uky.edu and Suzanne Bonefas bonefas@hippokrene.colleges.org.

Electronic Fora: Classical Resources

http://www.utexas.edu/depts/classics/links.html

From the Classics Department at the University of Texas, Austin, this site provides links to a range of classics resources including discussion lists, course materials, and journals.

Electronic Resources for Classicists: The Second Generation

http://www.tlg.uci.edu/~tlg/index/resources.html

This site is part of the Thesaurus Linguae Graecae project (see below) and is located at the University of California, Irvine. This page, maintained by Maria Pantelia mcpantel@uci.edu, provides access to electronic text archives, bibliographies, electronic publications, images, and a range of other useful classics resources.

Epicurus and Epicurean Philosophy

http://www.creative.net/~epicurus/

This page, from Vincent Cook epicurus@creative.net, provides an overview of Epicureanism (Epicurean beliefs, Epicurus and his school, how Epicureanism relates to other philosophy), as well as links to other Epicurean resources.

Greek Philosophy Archive

http://iris.dissvcs.uga.edu/~archive/Greek.html

This site, maintained by David Knox dknox@uga.cc.uga.edu, provides access to the works of Greek philosophers, links to Greek Philosophy and classics sites, and the Sculpture Garden, where you can view Greek architecture, ceramics, and sculptures.

History of Ancient Philosophy

http://weber.u.washington.edu/~smcohen/phil320.htm

This site, from S. Marc Cohen smcohen@u.washington.edu, is intended as a guide for students of his History of Ancient Philosophy class, but it is an excellent resource for anyone interested in the area. Included are lecture notes, links to electronic texts, and links to other ancient philosophy resources.

International Association for Greek Philosophy

http://www.hri.org/iagp/

This site, part of the Hellenic Resources Network *http://www.hri.org/*, provides information on the activities of the Association, including forthcoming conferences, and books published. It also links to the International Center for Greek Philosophy and Culture.

International Center for Greek Philosophy and Culture

http://www.hri.org/iagp/icgpc.html

The International Center for Greek Philosophy and Culture (ICGPC) is a non-profit academic, research and cultural Institution which was formed in 1987 and established by law in 1990. The ICGPC has its seat in Samos (Pythagorion), land of Ionia, which is also the birthplace of philosophy. The aim of the ICGPC is to promote international research into Greek philosophy, and to coordinate and develop the research carried out by specialists in Greek philosophy, and Greek Culture. The web site is fairly basic at this point in time.

The Internet Classics Archive

http://webatomics.com/Classics/

A beautifully-presented, searchable collection of almost 400 classical Greek and Roman texts (in English translation) with user-provided commentary is provided at this site. The maintainer can be contacted at classics@webatomics.com.

Perseus Project

http://medusa.perseus.tufts.edu/

Perseus is an evolving digital library which currently focuses upon the ancient Greek world. Current areas of development include ancient Science, evaluation of Perseus as a learning tool, and developing more sophisticated electronic tools for the study of Greek. Planning has also begun to expand Perseus into Roman materials. The site is managed by the Classics Department, Tufts University, and overseen by Gregory Crane. Enquiries about the page should be directed to webmaster@perseus.tufts.edu.

Philosophy Garden

http://www.cluon.com/~ea/garden.html

This page is dedicated to the spirit of life pioneered by Epicurus and Lucretius, and includes resources and discussion of epicureanism, information on an epicureanism discussion group, and links to related topics. Maintained by ea@cluon.com.

Plato

htp://www.ultranet.com/~rsarkiss/PLATO.HTM

This site provides a short biography, selected quotations, and links to online texts. It is maintained by Robert Sarkissian rsarkissian@smtp.microcom.com.

Plato

http://www.2xtreme.net/dstorm/plato/

This beautifully-designed site, from D. Anthony Storm dstorm@2xtreme.net, is devoted to the writings and writing method of Plato. To that end "A Commentary On Plato's Writings" with links to the works of Plato online has been constructed. Also provided is an introduction to Plato's thought and his method of composition, a bibliography, and links to other relevant sites.

Plato and His Dialogues

http://phd.evansville.edu/plato.htm

Maintained by Bernard Suzanne bfsuzan@ibm.net, this site provides an overview of Plato's life and main philosophical theories, plus links to Plato resources.

Project Archelogos

http://www.archelogos.phil.ed.ac.uk/

This site houses an ambitious and exciting project which is currently under construction. Project Archelogos is the creation of an electronic database for the recording of all the philosophical arguments that can be extracted from the texts of the Ancient Greek philosophers. Through the use of hypertext, Archelogos will interconnect the arguments, sub-arguments and the alternative interpretations of the Ancient Greek philosophical texts, all linked to the original Greek texts and translations. The project was initiated and is managed by Dr. Theodore Scaltsas Scaltsas@ed.ac.uk.

Rome Project

http://www.dalton.org/groups/rome/

This site provides access to a collection of resources of value to anyone doing research or study on ancient Rome. Maintained by Neil Goldberg neil@dalton.org, the site's resources are divided into the following categories: philosophy, political, religion, drama, archaelogy, maps, literature, military, and general resources.

Society for Ancient Greek Philosophy

http://philosophy.adm.binghamton.edu/ssips/sagpnews.html

The SAGP web page provides information on the aims and activities of the Society, and is maintained by Tony Preus apreus@bingvmb.cc.binghampton.edu.

Society for Bioethics & Classical Philosophy

http://www.pitt.edu/~caj3/sbcp/

The society is interested in facilitating and promoting the study of bioethics informed by classical philosophy, and the cross-fertilisation of ideas that results from the interchange of these two areas. This site provides information on the aims and activities of the Society, and is maintained by Mark Kuczewski mak7+@pitt.edu.

Socrates: Philosophy's Martyr

http://www.btinternet.com/~socratic/

This site contains substantial excerpts from *Socrates: Philosophy's Martyr*, a brief book for the general reader by Anthony Gottlieb socratic@btinternet.com.

Stoicism

http://www.evansville.edu/~ecoleweb/articles/stoicism.html

This page, part of the Ecole Initiative, provides an article on stoicism, together with a list of primary and secondary works in the field.

Stoicism on the Web

http://www.cs.latrobe.edu.au/~doug/generic/links.html

This site provides links to a range of Stoic resources, as well as to the New Stoa: Generic Theory Project, a resource authored by D. J. Huntington Moore doug@latcs1.lat.oz.au.

Stoic Registry

http://members.aol.com/cyberstoic/index.html

The purpose of the Stoic Registry is to bring together all those who are Stoics and who wish to be known by the commitment they have made. The site provides a list of past and present Stoics, and provides an overview of Stoic philosophy. The maintainer of the site can be contacted at cyberstoic@aol.com.

Thesaurus Lingae Graecae

http://www.uci.edu/~tlg/

The Thesaurus Linguae Graecae (TLG) is an electronic data bank of ancient Greek literature from Homer (8th century B.C.) to 600 A.D. with historiographical, lexicographical, and scholastic texts from the period between 600 and 1453 A.D. The TLG project is located at the University of California, Irvine, and the web page is maintained by Maria Pantelia mcpantel@uci.edu.

Women's Life in Greece and Rome

http://www.uky.edu/ArtsSciences/Classics/wlgr/wlgr-index.html

This site is an online version (selected excerpts only) of the book of the same name by Mary R. Lefkowitz and Maureen B. Fant. The online version is maintained by Suzanne Bonefas sbonefa@emory.edu and Ross Scaife scaife@pop.uky.edu, and includes a section on the role of women as seen in the works of ancient philosophers.

Atheism & Humanism

African Americans for Humanism

http://www.SecularHumanism.org/aah/index.html

"The need for critical thinking skills and a humanistic outlook in our world is great. This is no less true in the Black community than in others. Many African Americans have been engulfed by religious irrationality, conned by self-serving "faith healers", and swayed by dogmatic revisionist historians. Many others, however, have escaped the oppression of such delusions, and live happy and upstanding lives free of superstition. African Americans for Humanism (AAH) exists to bring these secular humanists together, to provide a forum for communication, and to facilitate coordinated action. In an irrational world, those who stand for reason must stand together." This site provides information on the goals and activities of AAH, and is maintained by David Noelle admin@SecularHumanism.org.

Alliance of Secular Humanist Societies

http://www.secularhumanism.org/ashs/

The Alliance of Secular Humanist Societies is a network created for mutual support among local and/or regional societies of secular humanists. This web site provides information on the activities of ASHS and is maintained by David Noelle admin@SecularHumanism.org.

alt.atheism FAQ

http://www.cs.ruu.nl/wais/html/na-bng/alt.atheism.html

This is the Frequently Asked Questions archive from the newsgroup alt.atheism. The FAQ provides an overview of atheism and the nature of atheism arguments, information on constructing a logical argument, an overview for new readers, and lists of atheist resources.

American Atheists

http://www.atheists.org/

American Atheists is a nationwide movement founded by Dr. Madalyn Murray O' Hair for the advancement of Atheism, and the total, absolute separation of government and religion. The web site provides information on the history of the organization, its aims, and various discussions of atheism vs. theism. The association can be contacted at info@atheists.org.

Atheism Page

http://www.ed.ac.uk/~humphrys/Personal/atheism.html

This site from Mark Humphrys M.Humphrys@ed.ac.uk, provides extensive resources including an overview of atheism, constructing a logical argument, a variety of essays and articles on atheism, links to other atheist resources, feedback pages, FAQs, and more.

The Atheism Web

http://www.infidels.org/news/atheism/

This site, maintained by Jeff Lowder jlowder@frii.com, provides extensive and well-organised information and resources, as well as links to newsgroups, for those who are interested in atheism and related topics.

CAA Atheists' Contact Page

http://www.sdsmt.edu/caa-bin/contact?none?noback

This page provides contact details for atheists all over the world. Individuals can add themselves to the database. The page is maintained by Ben Sutter bsutter@pobox.com.

Fredrik Benz' Atheist Links

http://www.update.uu.se/~fbendz/atheism/athlinks.htm

This site, maintained by Fredrick Benz fbendz@update.uu.se, provides a range of links to resources including: freethought organizations, humanist organizations, atheist 'religions', freethought resources, evolutionary science sites, individuals' atheist pages, FAQs, and more.

Freethought, Atheism and Evolution Links

http://www.california.com/~rpcman/FREEDOM.HTM

A range of links to resources on atheism and evolution can be found on this site. Resources include quotations, articles and essays, books to order online, bibliographies, and links to other related sites. The maintainer of the site can be contacted at rpcman@california.com.

The Freethought Page

http://www.eskimo.com/~pmoon/Homepage/freethot.html

This site, maintained by Phillip Moon pmoon@eskimo.com, provides links to freethought and atheist organizations, individuals' pages, books and magazines, and other resources.

Humanism

http://www.etla.net/~willey/personal/humanism.html

This site by Mark Willey willey@etla.net provides an overview of humanism, as well as links to humanist organizations and newsgroups, mailing lists, and home pages devoted to the topic.

Humanist Association of Canada

http://magi.com/~hac/hac.html

This site, maintained by Galen Thurber godfree2@atheist.com, provides information on the activities of the Association, and links to humanist resources.

International Academy of Humanism

http://www.SecularHumanism.org/academy.html

The International Academy of Humanism was established to recognise distinguished humanists and to disseminate humanistic ideals and beliefs. This web site provides information on the aims and activities of the Academy, and is maintained by David Noelle admin@SecularHumanism.org.

Is Objectivity Faith: A Reconciliation of Science and Religion

http://pages.prodigy.com/TX/science/religion.html

This site is a summary of a book by Bill McKee ptjh80a@prodigy.com and describes a conventional experiment designed to challenge the realist assumptions of the scientific method, and replace them with the mystics paradigm.

Prometheus Books

http://www.hutch.demon.co.uk/prom/

Prometheus Books specialises in a range of atheist and humanist publications and claims to be the premier publisher to challenge the claims of paranormal believers. Their catalogue can be viewed online, or delivered via email or snail mail.

Secular Humanism on the Web

http://www.SecularHumanism.org/home.html

This page provides information on the activities of the Council of Secular Humanism and also acts as a general educational resource on secular humanism. It includes links to press releases, conferences and events, articles, the humanist manifesto, and a range of secular humanist resources. The site is maintained by David Noelle admin@SecularHumanism.org.

The Secular Web

http://www.infidels.org/

This site, maintained by Internet Infidels infidels@infidels.org, provides access to a collection of 'freethought' literature, as well as various online magazines, including: Free Inquiry—a secular humanist magazine founded in 1980 to challenge the forces of fundamentalism. It also provides access to a variety of organizations, including: Agnostic and Atheist Student Group, and the Skeptics Society, and to a variety of resources including the Dead Sea Scrolls, Project Gutenberg master index of electronic texts, and the WWW Bible Gateway—plus a whole lot more.

Society of Humanist Philosophers

http://www.SecularHumanism.org/philosophers.html

This site, maintained by David Noelle admin@SecularHumanism.org, provides information on the aims and activities of the Society.

Sources of Sceptical Information on the Internet

http://www.primenet.com/~lippard/skeptical.html

This page provides an extensive range of resources including links to scepticism magazines, publishers, organizations, FAQs, newsgroups, and important parapsychology papers. It is an excellent resource, maintained by lippard@primenet.com.

Stanford Humanists

http://www-leland.stanford.edu/group/Humanists/

This page, maintained by Mark Willey willey@etla.net, provides information on the aims and activities of SH, as well as links to humanist resources.

Swedish Humanist Foundation

http://www.unicom.se/humanetik.html

This page provides information on the SHF—in Swedish only.

Yahoo: Atheism

http://www.yahoo.com/Society_and_Culture/Religion/Atheism/

This is the Yahoo net directory's list of atheist resources online.

Yahoo: Humanism

http://www.yahoo.com/Society_and_Culture/Religion/Humanism/

This is the Yahoo net directory's list of humanist resources online.

Critical & Cultural Theory

alt.postmodern FAQ

http://ftp.tuwien.ac.at/faqs/newfaqs/alt.postmodern/Alt.Postmodern_FAQ

This is a Frequently Asked Questions archive from the newsgroup alt.postmodern and provides a host of general information on postmodernism.

The Bakhtin Center: University of Sheffield

http://www.shef.ac.uk/uni/academic/A-C/bakh/bakhtin.html

The Center's purpose is to promote multi-and inter-disciplinary research on the work of the Russian philosopher and theorist Mikhail Bakhtin and the Bakhtin Circle, and on related areas of cultural, critical, linguistic, and literary theory. The Center's website provides an analytical database of work by and about the Bakhtin circle. Visitors are able to search or make contributions to the database. Information is provided on seminars, conferences, and other activities of the Center, and on Bakhtin studies elsewhere. The site is maintained by Carol Adlam c.a.adlam@shef.ac.uk.

Cambridge Center for Hermeneutic and Analytic Philosophy

http://www.anglia.ac.uk/hae/phil/CHRAP.Htm

The Center is a joint activity of the Philosophy Division of Anglia Polytechnic University, and the Department of History and Philosophy of Science of Cambridge University. Its aim is to encourage contacts between the various continental traditions of philosophy and mainstream Anglo-Americal approaches. This page provides information on the activities of the center. Further information can be obtained from Neil Gascoigne ngascoigne@bridge.anglia.ac.uk.

Center for Advanced Research in Phenomenology

http://www.fau.edu/carp/

This site provides information on the activities of the Center, which aims to foster, extend, and deepen phenomenology and kindred continental thought in philosophy, the social sciences, and the humanities wherever it can. The website is currently maintained by John Drabinski jdrabinski@fau.edu.

Contemporary Philosophy, Critical Theory, and Postmodern Thought

http://www.cudenver.edu/~mryder/itc_data/postmodern.html

A well-organized and comprehensive site maitained by Martin Ryder mryder@www.cudenver.edu, which houses a collection of resources on a host of critical and postmodern theorists and schools of thought.

Continental Philosophy

http://www.augustana.ab.ca/~janzb/continental.htm

From Bruce Janz janzb@augustana.ab.ca, this site collects an extensive range of links to information on all aspects of continental philosophy: thinkers, issues, conferences, societies, journals, and more.

Continental Philosophy

http://ourworld.compuserve.com/homepages/michaelpat/

From Mark Paterson michaelpat@compuserve.com this page provides information on a range of thinkers from the continental philosophical tradition, including: Heidegger, Nietzsche, Kant, Foucault, and Derrida. It also provides introductory materials on existentialism and phenomenology, and links to related sites.

Cultural and Critical Theory

http://www.ksu.edu/english/theory

From Gregory Eiselein eiselei@ksu.edu, this page is a collection of links to resources in critical and cultural theory.

Cultural Studies & Critical Theory

http://eng.hss.cmu.edu/theory/

This page, part of the English Server and maintained by Geoffrey Sauer webmaster@ english.hss.cmu.edu, provides a series of articles and essays which introduce the issues and concerns raised by the field of cultural theory.

Cyberspace and Critical Theory

http://www.stg.brown.edu:80/projects/hypertext/landow/cpace/cspaceov.html

From Brown University, this site collects a huge array of resources relevant to various aspects of critical theory, including visual arts, literature, politics, economics, philosophy, and more.

Deconstruction on the Net

http://www.lake.de/home/lake/hydra/jd.html

This site by Peter Krapp derrida@hydra.lake.de, provides links to a range of resources relevant to Derrida and deconstruction. If this is too slow, you can try the US mirror site at *http://www.hydra.umn.edu/derrida/*.

Deconstruction on the Net

http://www.tezcat.com/~ksbrooks/deconstruction.html

Although there is not much here at present, apart from archived selections from a discussion list on Derrida, Kevin Brooks ksbrooks@tezcat.com intends to expand the page, adding a site devoted to the work of Paul de Man.

Deleuze & Guattari Internet Resources

http://jefferson.village.Virginia.EDU/~spoons/d-g_html/d-g.html

From Jon Beasley-Murray jpb8@acpub.duke.edu, this site links to a wide range of resources including bibliographies, conference information, electronic texts and more.

Deleuze & Guattari on the Web

http://www.uta.edu/english/apt/d&g/d&gweb.html

This site provides a list of links to works about and by Gilles Deleuze and Félix Guattari compiled by Alan Taylor apt6083@utarlg.uta.edu.

Deleuze & Guattari Web Resources

http://www.langlab.wayne.edu/romance/FreDeleuze.html

From Charles Stivale C_Stivale@wayne.edu, this site provides links to a range of resources relevant to critical theory, in particular to the work of Deleuze and Guattari, including essays, discussion lists, journals, and conferences.

A Few References to Michel Foucault

http://www.synaptic.bc.ca/ejournal/foucault.htm

This site, maintained by Patrick Jennings patrick@synaptic.bc.ca, provides links to a range of Foucault resources.

Foucault Pages at CSUN

http://www.csun.edu:80/~hfspc002/foucault.home.html

This site, by Ben Attias hfspc002@csun.edu, provides a genealogy of Foucault, information on Foucault discussion lists, links to other Foucault resources, calls for participation for Foucault Scholars, and online essays by, about, or influenced by Foucault.

Illuminations

http://www.uta.edu/huma/illuminations

Illuminations: The Critical Theory Website is a research resource for those interested in the critical theory project. Firmly based in the Frankfurt School of theory, this site maintains a collection of articles, excerpts, and chapters from many contemporary writers of and about critical theory. Additional submissions from graduate students and others are also available, as are links to other websites and related sources. The site is maintained by Douglas Brown Quisp@utarlg.uta.edu and Douglas Kellner kellner@ccwf.cc.utexas.edu.

Kid A in Alphabet Land

http://www.freedonia.com/~carl/kida/kida_index.html

This site provides access to the electronic edition of Kid A In Alphabet Land, "an abecedarian roller coaster ride through the phallocentric obscurantism of Jacques Lacan." Kid A In Alphabet Land was originally designed as a tangible trading card set, intended to be an introduction to Lacanian concepts and cultural references. The page's author, Carl Steadman carl@freedonia.com, has also commenced writing Lacan for Beginners, with the first chapter linked to this page.

The Notebook for Contemporary Continental Philosophy

http://www.baylor.edu/~Scott_Moore/Continental.html

From Scott Moore ScottMoore@baylor.edu, this site presents an impressive array of links to information on continental philosophers and philosophy.

Panic Encyclopedia: The Definitive Guide to the Postmodern Scene

http://www.freedonia.com/panic/

This site houses a fairly eclectic collection of what might best be described as resources inspired by postmodern culture. Offering commentaries on various aspects of personal and social life, politics, and culture, the site is maintained by Arthur Kroker, Marilouise Kroker, and David Cook kroker@vax2.concordia.ca, who invite readers to add their own submissions to the growing collection.

The Phenomenology Page

http://www.connect.net/ron/phenom.html

This page, from Ron Turner ron@connect.net, provides a summary of phenomenology, especially as it is informed by the work of Husserl and Heidegger.

Philosophy: Your Guide to the Wonderful World of (Post)modern Thinking

http://www.sci.fi/~phinnweb/links/philosophy.html

This site provides a collection of links to resources in the postmodern philosophical tradition. It is maintained by Erkki Rautio trerra@uta.fi.

Postmodern and Cyberculture

http://www.academic.marist.edu/1/postmod.htm

This site, maintained by Tom Goldpaugh jzk5@maristb.marist.edu, provides a collection of links to sites providing postmodernist and related resources.

Postmodern Philosophy

http://http.tamu.edu:8000/~gkp1982/pomo.html

On this page, from G.K Parish-Philp dionysos@tamu.edu, you will find links to modern, phenomenological, Marxist, hermeneutical, deconstructive, structuralist, and related philosophical resources.

Soundsite

http://sysx.apana.org.au/soundsite/

This site is concerned with sound theory, philosophy of sound, and sound art. Sound theory is a discipline that is a hybrid of cultural theory, philosophy, and modern communications courses. Writers studied in this discipline range from Nietzsche to Deleuze and Barthes, as well as various film theorists. The maintainer of the site can be contacted at soundsite@sysx.apana.org.au.

The Structural Years

http://www.france.diplomatie.fr/culture/france/biblio/folio/philo2/index.html

This French-language site provides a study of "the structural years and the rebellious years of French Philosophy." Philosophers considered in this study include Derrida, Althusser, Deleuze, and others. The site is maintained by Michel Deverge deverge @imaginet.fr.

UC Irvine Critical Theory Resource

http://sun3.lib.uci.edu/~scctr/online.html

This resource features a large number of the scholarly bibliographies prepared by UC Irvine Library's Special Collections Bibliographer, Eddie Yeghiayan eyeghiay@uci.edu.

WWW Resources for Gilles Deleuze and Félix Guattari

http://www.stg.brown.edu:80/projects/hypertext/landow/cpace/theory/deleuze.html

Part of a larger Critical Theory resource, this site provides access to a range of Deleuze and Guattari links.

Early Modern to 19th Century Philosophy

18th Century Resources

http://www.english.upenn.edu/~jlynch/18th/index.html

This site, maintained by Jack Lynch jlynch@english.upenn.edu, provides a searchable catalogue of links to resources on 18th century culture and thought in the following categories: Art, Architecture, Landscape Gardening; History; Literature (and Electronic Texts); Music; Philosophy; Religion and Theology; Science and Mathematics. It also provides links to professional resources and journals (including calls for papers), and links to home pages of people working in the area of eighteenth century study.

18th Century Studies

http://english-www.hss.cmu.edu/18th/

This collection archives works of the eighteenth century from the perspectives of literary and cultural studies. Novels, plays, memoirs, treatises, and poems of the period are kept here (in some cases, influential texts from before 1700 or after 1800 as well), along with modern criticism.

19th Century Philosophy

http://www-philosophy.ucdavis.edu/phi151/phi151.htm

This site was created by GJ Mattey gjmattey@ucdavis.edu, for a course offered at UC Davis. It contains resources relating to key 19th century thinkers, including Schopenhauer, Hegel, Marx, Kierkegaard, Nietzsche, and Dostoyevski.

Clandestine Etexts from the 18th Century
http://www.vc.unipmn.it/~mori/e-texts/

French clandestine manuscripts are one of the most interesting phenomena of early Enlightenment. A great number of texts have been discovered and studied since Gustave Lanson's (1912) and Ira O. Wade's (1938) pioneer studies. Offered here is a limited but representative selection of texts which will be increased in the future. The site is maintained by Gianluca Mori moveon@dada.it.

Early Modern Philosophy
http://jhunix.hcf.jhu.edu/~deschene/earlymod/earlymod.html

This site, maintained by Dennis Des Chene deschene@jhunix.hcf.jhu.edu, intends to become an encyclopedia of early modern philosophy—Western European philosophy from 1550 to 1700. At the moment it includes pages devoted to eight canonical figures, to one important movement (Aristotelianism), and to natural philosophy.

Historians and Philosophers
http://dorit.ihi.ku.dk/~peterr/histphil.html

As part of a larger history-oriented project, Peter Ravn Rasmussen peterr@dorit.ihi.ku.dk has created this page which provides links to other sources of information on historians and philosophers, grouped according to historical period: classical, medieval and renaissance, early modern, and modern. Peter's history page is located at *http://dorit.ihi.ku.dk/~peterr/history.html* and provides information and links to other sources on various historical periods.

Mathematicians of the 17th and 18th Centuries
http://www.maths.tcd.ie/pub/HistMath/People/RBallHist.html

This site, from David Wilkins dwilkins@maths.tcd.ie, provides accounts of the lives and works of seventeenth and eighteenth century mathematicians (and some other scientists), adapted from *A Short Account of the History of Mathematics* by W. W. Rouse Ball (4th Edition, 1908).

Eastern Philosophy

14 Lectures on the Intercommunication between Chinese and Western Philosophy
http://www.nevada.edu/home/15/chancl/html/14lects.html

The lectures on this site were given by Prof. Mou Tsung-san, and present a Chinese interpretation on Kant to the West. According to Mou, Kant is the greatest and the most difficult philosopher in the West and is also the bridge between Chinese and Western philosophy.

Berkeley Buddhist Research Center
http://socrates.berkeley.edu/~yaoming/

This is the the Home Page of the Group in Buddhist Studies at the University of California at Berkeley and the Berkeley Buddhist Research Center. The page provides access to numerous Buddhist resources, including electronic publications, conferences, and related sites of interest. The site is maintained by Yao-ming Tsai yaoming@socrates.berkeley.edu.

Buddhist Studies

http://www.ciolek.com/WWWVL-Buddhism.html

This site, part of the WWW Virtual Library series, and edited by T. Matthew Ciolek tmciolek@coombs.anu.edu.au and John C. Powers, provides access to hundreds of Buddhist-related links and resources including: files, graphics, and Buddhist organizations. An extensive list of religious studies resources is also included.

Center for Buddhist Studies

http://ccbs.ntu.edu.tw/e-CBS.htm

This page is provided by the Center for Buddhist Studies, College of Liberal Arts, National Taiwan University. It maintains links to an extensive range of resources including: Buddhist libraries, online texts, Buddhist sutras, Sanskrit, Pali and Tibetan lessons, Buddhist institutes, and more. A Chinese version of the page is also available.

Chad Hansen's Daoist Home Page

http://hkusuc.hku.hk/philodep/ch/

This page provides interpretations of Chinese Philosophy, particularly Daoism (Taoism) and Classical Chinese theories of language and mind. Translations and essays will be added as Chad hrxahac@hkuxa.hku.hk finishes and prepares them for his comparative philosophy classes at the University of Hong Kong.

Chinese Classics

http://www.cnd.org:8010/Classics/

This site provides access to Chinese classics texts, in Chinese and English translations. The maintainers of the site cnd-ib@cnd.org aim at collecting as much Chinese classic literature as possible for the benefit of the Internet community.

Chinese Philosophy Page

http://www-personal.monash.edu.au/~sab

This page, by Stephen A Brown sab@silas.cc.monash.edu.au, provides access to an impressive array of information and resources on Confucian, Daoist and other schools of thought, Chinese philosophical texts and mailing list, and other resources.

DharmaNet International: Gateways to Buddhism

http://www.dharmanet.org/

This site provides a wealth of information on Buddhism and links to Buddhist resources, both for practicising Buddhists and those interested in learning more about Buddhist thought. The maintainer of the page can be contacted at dharma@dharmanet.org.

Daoism Depot

http://www.edepot.com/taoism.html

A range of Daoist resources are offered at this site, maintained by Po-Han Lin phlin @ix.netcom.com, including scriptures, mailing and discussion lists, art gallery, humor, and links to related sites.

East Asian Buddhist Studies: A Reference Guide

http://www.humnet.ucla.edu/humnet/ealc/refguide.htm

This site provides access to a bibliography of East Asian Buddhist Studies, and is compiled in the following sections: scriptural collections, catalogues of scriptural collections, Asian translations of the scriptures, Buddhist dictionaries, methodology and history of Buddhist Studies, encyclopedias, non-Buddhist Asian language dictionaries, bibliographies, concordances, and indexes.

Graduate Programs in Asian Philosophy and Religion

http://www2.gol.com/users/acmuller/GradStudies.htm

Maintained by A. Charles Muller acmuller@gol.com, this site provides information regarding graduate studies programs in the field of Asian philosophy and religion (including Buddhism, Hinduism, Confucianism, or Taoism).

Indian Philosophy

http://jhunix.hcf.jhu.edu/~js8/philosophy/

"Philosophy has a long history in India. And for almost all that time it has had a strong relationship with religion. Philosophy questions and clarifies modes of behavior while religion is the application of the philosophical ideas in ones life. Mere philosophy starts with doubts and ends with arid speculation. Mere religion leads but to dogma and blind ritual. A philosophic religion is supposed to remove doubts and avoid dogma." This page, from Jagannathan Shrikanth shrikant@chow.mat.jhu.edu, provides an overview of Indian philosophy, with links to related resources.

Links Pitaka: Buddhist Resources

http://www.ville-ge.ch/musinfo/ethg/ducor/intro.htm

A page providing an extensive range of links to both general and academic Buddhist resources. Maintained by Jérôme Ducor jerome.ducor@ville-ge.ch.

Mysticism in World Religions

http://www.digiserve.com/mystic

This site by Deb Platt mystic@digiserve.com, presents the mystical traditions of Judaism, Christianity, Islam, Buddhism, Hinduism, and Taoism. You can compare and contrast these six religions by going directly to the World Index, or you can look at each religion individually by going to that religion's particular index.

The Philosophy of Upanishads

http://www.ee.memphis.edu/~sreedhar/Upanisad/upanisad.html

From Sreedhar Chintalapaty sreedhar@lear.csp.ee.memphis.edu, this site discusses Indian philosophy through a focus on the upanishads and the vedas.

Resources for Indian Philosophy & Buddist Studies

http://iris.ioc.u-tokyo.ac.jp/suzuki/resources.html

From Takayasu Suzuki suzuki@ioc.u-tokyo.ac.jp, this page provides a collection of links to Eastern Philosophy.

Resources for the Study of Buddhism, Confucianism and Taoism

http://www2.gol.com/users/acmuller/index.html

Maintained by A. Charles Muller acmuller@gol.com, this site has four main sections. Section I is devoted to direct references to Muller's own electronically-published texts and other reference works; Section II is a directory of online CJKE-texts (scriptural texts from Buddhist, Confucian, and Taoist Studies); Section III is a selected, annotated listing of some of the more significant scholarly Buddhist resources; and Section IV contains substantial scholarly Web resources in Confucianism and Taoism. This directory is not intended to be a comprehensive listing of all resources in these fields; instead, the focus is on sites which contain significant research tools and/or information.

Shin Darma Net

http://www.aloha.net/~albloom/sdn/

The purpose of this page is to share information concerning Shin Buddhist Tradition and Pure Land Buddhism as it is presently practiced and interpreted by Shin communities in the West and Japan. Research materials will be made available and questions from respondents will be entertained. Links to Buddhist resources are also provided at this site.

Su Tzu's Chinese Philosophy Page

http://mars.superlink.net/user/fsu/philo.html

A beautifully-designed page maintained by Francisco S. Su fsu@worldnet.att.net, providing links to a range of Chinese philosophy resources on the net.

The Taoism Information Page

http://www.clas.ufl.edu/users/gthursby/taoism/

Maintained by Gene Thursby gthursby@religion.ufl.edu, this page provides an introduction to Taoism and access to Taoist texts online. It also discusses Taoism and modernity, Taoism and alchemy, Taoism and martial arts, and includes links to other online Taoist resources.

Taoist Resource Center

http://members.aol.com/gr8tao/index.html

This page provides a complete guide to taoist resources, and is updated monthly. The maintainer of the site can be contacted at Gr8tao@aol.com.

The Temple of the Immortal Spirit: The Western Taoist

http://www.thetemple.com/

Maintained by Steven Ericsson Zenith steven@thetemple.com, this page provides information on Taoism, but is particularly aimed at exploring the meaning of Taoist mystical and spiritual philosophies in the context of Western culture.

Wesleyan Confucian Etext Project

http://www.wesleyan.edu/~sangle/etext/index.html

This site hosts an ongoing project to convert Confucian and Confucian-inspired texts from the 11th century C.E. to the present into electronic format for viewing online. Several texts are already online, but the site will grow over time. It is currently maintained by Stephen C. Angle sangle@wesleyan.edu.

White Path Temple: Shin Buddhism

http://www.mew.com/shin/

This site by provides an enormous range of information relating to Buddhism generally, and also to Shin Buddhism. It is maintained by Claude Huss claude@trc.mew.co.jp, and promises to grow to encompass an even greater range of links.

WWW Database of Chinese Buddhist Texts

http://www.gwdg.de/~cwitter/can2/ind/canwww.htm

This site provides access to a comprehensive list of Chinese Buddhist texts. It currently contains 4375 texts by 1349 authors. Buddhist texts exist in many languages and cultural environments. Currently, this list contains only texts in Chinese, authored by people from the countries that use(d) Chinese characters. The site is maintained by Chris Wittern cwitter@gwdg.de.

Environmental Philosophy

Center for Environmental Philosophy

http://www.cep.unt.edu/centerfo.html

The homepage for the Center for Environmental Philosophy includes links to the Center's journal *Environmental Ethics*, information on workshops, conferences, and the operation of the Center. The Center can be contacted at cep@unt.edu, and the page is maintained by Eugene Hargrove hargrove@unt.edu.

Earth Pledge Foundation

http://www.earthpledge.org/

The Earth Pledge Foundation (EPF) promotes the principles and practices of sustainable development—the need to balance the desire for economic growth with the necessity of environmental protection. EPF is a non-profit foundation which recognises appropriate intersections between business interests and environmental, social, and cultural concerns. This web page provides links to the United Nations Environment Program, Enviroweb, EcoNet, as well as reviews of books on sustainable development.

Ecofeminism: An Introductory Bibliography

gopher://silo.adp.wisc.edu:70/00/.uwlibs/.womenstudies/.bibs/.ecofem

A selective and annotated bibliography on sources concerning political activism within womens groups on the environment and surrounding issues. Part of a series of bibliographies published by the University of Wisconsin System Women's Studies Librarian's Office.

Ecological Philosophy

http://www.geocities.com/Athens/Acropolis/5147/

Maintained by David Large davidlarge@hotmail.com, this site offers an introduction to ecological philosophy in the hope that it will act as a conduit for more detailed discussion of the subject.

EcoNet

http://www.igc.org/igc/econet/index.html

EcoNet is part of the Institute for Global Communications at *http://www.igc.apc.org/* and provides extensive information on environmental issues, including environmental justice and law, activism, and more. IGC's web manager can be contacted at webweaver@igc.org.

Ecopsychology Web

http://www.scotweb.co.uk/Environment/ecopsyweb/

This evolving site brings together a variety of Internet resources and contacts relating to our psychological relationship with nature. Maintained by Brendan Hill brendan@clan.com, it includes an introduction to ecopsychology, a discussion of ecopsychology's origins and antecendents, as well as links to relevant and related resources and organizations on the web.

Environmental Ethics

http://www.cep.unt.edu/

Located at the University of North Texas, and part of the Center for Environmental Philosophy, this page is dedicated to providing access to Internet resources throughout the world which pertain to or focus on environmental ethics and environmental philosophy. It includes links to graduate programs, associations, publications, and other relevant sites. The site is maintained by Eugene Hargrove hargrove@unt.edu.

Environmental Ethics Graduate Programs

http://www.cep.unt.edu/other.html

This page provides links to a range of graduate programs offered in the US, UK, and Australia. It is part of the Center for Environmental Philosophy site, maintained by Eugene Hargrove hargrove@unt.edu.

Environmental Ethics, University of Gothenburg

http://www.phil.gu.se/environment.html

This page, maintained by Helge Malmgren helge.malmgren@phil.gu.se at the Philosophy Department at Gothenburg, provides information related to philosophical discussion of the preconditions for a good environment and sustainable development.

EnviroLink

http://envirolink.org/

EnviroLink is a non-profit organization, a grassroots online community that unites hundreds of organizations and volunteers around the world with millions of people in over 130 countries. EnviroLink is dedicated to providing the most comprehensive, up-to-date environmental resources available. EnviroLink can be contacted at info@envirolink.org.

Guide to Philosophy and the Environment

http://www.lancs.ac.uk/users/philosophy/mave/Guide_1.htm

This page provides a consideration of some issues in environmental philosophy, including: the world as family, the world as ours to exploit, looking after human interests, science's role in the domination of nature, "Deep Ecology", environmental issues and the Third World, ecofeminism, environmental economics, the phenomenological perpective, aesthetics and the environment, and the perspectives of other cultures and of our own past. Maintained by the Philosophy Department at Lancaster philweb @lancaster.ac.uk.

International Society for Environmental Ethics

http://www.cep.unt.edu/ISEE.html

This page provides information on the Society and membership. It also provides links to a bibliography and books of relevance to environmental ethics. Part of the Center for Environmental Ethics, the site is maintained by Eugene Hargrove hargrove@unt.edu.

International Society for Environmental Ethics Comprehensive Bibliography

http://www.phil.unt.edu/bib/

This bibliography is an ongoing project of the International Society for Environmental Ethics. It contains all the bibliographic entries from the Newsletter of the Society, as well as articles and abstracts from the journals *Environmental Ethics*, *Environmental Values*, and the *Journal of Agricultural and Environmental Ethics*. The maintainer of the site can be contacted at rolston@lamar.colostate.edu.

Towards An Ecology of Mind

http://www.networld.it/oikos/psicen.htm

"There exists a very close connection between the activities of the human species and the natural environment in which we witness the occurence of these activities: to the degree that human intelligence is able to profoundly change Nature it has also created the conditions in which our cognitive activity has evolved. At the present moment in which the ecological crisis coincides with the collapse of human social values and of the certainties upon which are based industrial and post-industrial society—having extreme effects upon the individual and collective experience of living—all ecologists are obliged to evolve a precise and profound model of reflection and analysis upon the nature of the processes which accompany change, and which includes the analysis of subjects like ethology, epistemology, and the study of complex systems." On this web site, maintained by Vincent Kenny kenny@networld.it, the user will find bibliographical references, instruments of investigation and inquiry, articles and commentaries, and links to other relevant web sites.

Ethics & Bioethics

Academic Dialogue on Applied Ethics

http://www.lcl.cmu.edu/CAAE/Home/Forum/ethics.html

This site hosts online discussions by invited academics on various topics in applied ethics, including abortion, pornography, and euthanasia. Discussions occur over a specified period of time and then move on to a new topic with new participants, but all are archived for ongoing access. The site is maintained by Robert Cavalier rc2z@andrew.cmu.edu and Charles Ess cess@andrew.cmu.edu.

American Society of Law, Medicine & Ethics

http://lawlib.slu.edu/aslme/

The mission of the American Society of Law, Medicine & Ethics (ASLME) is to provide high-quality scholarship, debate, and critical thought to the community of professionals at the intersection of law, health care, policy, and ethics. This web page provides information on the activities of the Society and is maintained by webmaster@lawlib.slu.edu.

Animal Rights Resource Site

http://envirolink.org/arrs/index.html

This site provides FAQs, reference materials, essays, guides, journals and leaflets, links to other animal-rights resources sites, an animal rights chat room, and more. It is maintained by Allen Schubert alathome@clark.net.

Applied Ethics Resources

http://www.ethics.ubc.ca/resources/

Maintained by Chris MacDonald chrismac@ethics.ubc.ca, this site provides links to resources in biomedical, business, computer and information, professional, and science and technology ethics.

Applied Research Ethics National Association (ARENA)

http://www.anes.hmc.psu.edu/ArenaFolder/ArenaHome.html

ARENA is a membership organization for those involved in the day-to-day application of ethical principles, governmental regulations, and other policies regarding research and clinical practice. The web site provides information on the aims, services, and activities of the Association, and is maintained by PRIMR@Delphi.com.

Ariadne's Thread: Experiments in Critical Thinking

http://www.lm.com/~jdehullu/

Ariadne's Thread is concerned with arguments related to politically-significant ethical issues like abortion. The arguments are mainly ethical rather than legal or political. The purpose of this site is not to promote any particular answer to any particular question. It is rather to help each of us to critically analyse, to practice a kind of moral reasoning, and to develop reasoned views of our own. The current discussion topic is on abortion. The site is maintained by James DeHullu jdehullu@telerama.lm.com.

Bibliography of Bioethics

http://www.ncgr.org/gpi/grn/edures/elsi.tc.html

This page, hosted and maintained by the National Center for Genome Resources ncgr@ncgr.org, provides access to a large and well-organized, searchable bibliography edited by LeRoy Walters and Tamar Joy Kahn of the Kennedy Institute of Ethics, Georgetown University. A list of related journals, and a glossary of genetic terms are also linked to this site.

Big Dummies Guide to Theology, Philosophy, and Ethics

http://www.teleport.com/~oro/bdintro.html

By Orrin R. Onken oro@teleport.com, this page serves as a somewhat humorous introduction to philosophy, theology, and ethics.

Bioethics Discussion Pages

http://www-hsc.usc.edu/~mbernste/

This site includes a discussion on physician-assisted suicide, polls on various ethical issues including harvesting of organs for transplantation, and links to bioethics resources. It is maintained by Maurice Bernstein, M.D. doktormo@aol.com.

Bioethics Website

http://www.csu.edu.au/faculty/arts/humss/bioethic/bioethic.htm

This site was developed for bioethics students at Charles Sturt University in Australia, but its resources are available to the electronic community at large. Featuring information on the ethical dilemmas posed by issues such as Jenner's smallpox vaccination research and the medical experimentation exposed in the Nuremberg trials, this site provides comprehensive and well-designed information for students of bioethics.

Biomedical Ethics Bookmarks

http://www.cariboo.bc.ca/ae/php/phil/mclaughl/COURSES/ETHICS/BIOETH/BIOMARK.HTM

This site provides links to a range of sources on the net for biomedical ethics. The site is maintained by Jeff McLaughlin.

Biomedical Ethics: Readings on the Internet

http://www.uwc.edu/fonddulac/faculty/rrigteri/biomed.htm

This site, maintained by Roger J. Rigterink rrigteri@uwc.edu, provides access to a range of papers in biomedical ethics. While this page was created for use within an undergraduate biomedical ethics course, none of the linked readings require an extensive philosophical or medical background. Thus, anyone with an active curiosity concerning the topics covered might find this page of interest.

British Society for Ethical Theory

http://www.gla.ac.uk/Acad/Philosophy/Lenman/bset.html

Information on the Society, and links to its mailing list and ethics-related resources can be found at this site, which is maintained by Jimmy Lenman j.lenman@philosophy.arts.gla.ac.uk. A mirror of the site is located at *http://www.keele.ac.uk/depts/pi/ethics/index.htm* and maintained by David McNaughton pia02@keele.ac.uk.

Center for Advancement of Applied Ethics

http://www.lcl.cmu.edu/CAAE/Home/CAAE.html

The CAAE, located at Carnegie Mellon University, is a research and development environment that focuses on teaching people practical methods for analysing and responding to real ethical problems. The Center's members combine knowledge and experience from different areas: interactive multimedia, business and professional ethics, and conflict resolution. This site, maintained by Robert Cavalier rc2z@andrew.cmu.edu, includes links to Project Theoria, discussion on firearms policy, conflict resolution, and more.

Center for Applied Ethics

http://www.ethics.ubc.ca/

This site, located at the University of British Columbia and maintained by Chris MacDonald chrismac@ethics.ubc.ca, provides general information on the workings of the Center, plus links to a range of applied ethics resources, and information on the research projects of the Center.

Center for Bioethics, University of Pennsylvania

http://www.med.upenn.edu/~bioethic/

This site, overseen by Glenn McGee mcgee@mail.med.upenn.edu, provides information on the Center, plus links to a bioethics library and other related materials.

Center for Research Ethics

http://www.cre.gu.se/Homepage

Information on the activities of the Center, its current research projects, and links to related material can be found at this site, located at Göteborg in Sweden and maintained by cmunthe@cre.gu.se.

Center for the Study of Ethics in the Professions

http://www.iit.edu/~csep/

The Center for the Study of Ethics in the Profession at the Illinois Institute of Technology was established in 1976 for the purpose of promoting education and scholarship relating to the professions. The Center is currently developing a code of ethics database, accessible online. Links to the Center's newsletters and library are also available, and the Center can be contacted at csep@charlie.cns.iit.edu.

Computer Ethics

http://www.seas.upenn.edu/~mengwong/comp.ethics.html

As computer technology grows increasingly ubiquitous, ethical considerations in the computer environment become paramount. This site provides a collection of links to information relating to ethics and computing. It is maintained by Meng Weng Wong mengwong@pobox.com.

Consortium Ethics Program

http://www.pitt.edu/~caj3/CEP.html

The Consortium Ethics Program is co-sponsored by the University of Pittsburgh's Center for Medical Ethics, and the Hospital Council of Western Pennsylvania. This site, maintained by Alan Joyce caj3+@pitt.edu, provides links to the Community Ethics Electronic Newsletter, guide to membership, and links to online ethics resources.

DeathNet

http://www.islandnet.com/~deathnet/

DeathNet specialises in "end-of-life" issues. It was created by John Hofsess, Executive Director of The Right to Die Society of Canada, in collaboration with Derek Humphry, founder of the National Hemlock Society in 1980, author of the international best-seller Final Exit in 1991, and currently President of ERGO! (Euthanasia Research and Guidance Organization) in Eugene, Oregon. DeathNet offers a large collection of "right to die" materials and services. It gathers together a wide array of information dealing with specific illnesses and severe disabilities—especially those of a life-threatening nature. It provides connecting links to medical libraries and other online services dealing with bereavement, caregiving, emotional support, and counselling. DeathNet also provides advice on "living wills," palliative care, and all aspects of assisted suicide and euthanasia. The maintainers of the site can be contacted at rights@rights.org.

Engineering Ethics

http://www.ece.utexas.edu/~tillerso/eeint.html

Ethics in engineering is a very important aspect of the field that is often overlooked by new students. This page provides a collection of links to information on ethics in engineering, and is maintained by Robert Tillerson rtillerson@mail.utexas.edu.

Environmental Ethics Graduate Programs

http://www.cep.unt.edu/other.html

This page provides links to a range of graduate programs offered in the US, UK, and Australia. It is part of the Center for Environmental Philosophy site, maintained by Eugene Hargrove hargrove@unt.edu.

Ethical Issues of Animal Research

http://www.indiana.edu/~poynter/animals.html

This site provides information relating to both the 1996 and 1997 Conferences on Ethics and Animal Research. The page is maintained by pimple@indiana.edu.

Ethics and Genetics: A Global Conversation

http://www.med.upenn.edu/~bioethic/genetics.html

What do you think about genetic testing, genetic enhancement, gene therapy, genetic engineering? This "electric conversation" lets you post your comments instantly and engage in live conversation with any of the hundreds who visit our site every week. Ten researchers in the field serve as discussants, posting remarks, papers, and comments upon which visitors can comment. The site is maintained by Glenn McGee mcgee@mail.med.upenn.edu.

Ethics Center for Engineering and Science

http://web.mit.edu/ethics/www/

Located at MIT, the Center aims to provide engineers, scientists, science and engineering students with resources useful for understanding and addressing ethically significant problems that arise in their work life. The Center is also intended to serve teachers of engineering and science students who want to include discussion of ethical problems closely related to technical subject as a part of science and engineering courses, or in free-standing subjects in professional ethics or in research ethics for such students. This site provides access to a range of resources including essays, ethical codes and guidelines, instructional resources, links to research-related materials, and much more. It is maintained by students at MIT, and is also available in a Spanish version.

Ethics Connection

http://scuish.scu.edu/Ethics/homepage.html

This page is provided by the Markkula Center for Applied Ethics at Santa Clara University. The site has the feel of an online zine, providing short online papers on ethical issues, a link to the Center's quarterly online publication, and a database of links to ethics-related resources on the net.

Ethics in Science

http://www.chem.vt.edu/ethics/ethics.html

This site provides a range of resources including a science-ethics bibliography—an extensive list of publications that pertain to ethics and misconduct in science, plus selected essays on ethics in science, and links to related sites. It is maintained by Brian Tissue tissue@vt.edu.

Ethics, Law, and Computing Resource Site

http://www.cs.ccsu.ctstateu.edu/~boconnel/

This site was designed to provide resources for students studying ethics and legal issues relating to computing. It includes links to a range of ethics, law, and computing resources, and resources which consider issues relating to a combination of the three. It is maintained by Brian O'Connell oconnell@cris.com.

Ethics on the World Wide Web

http://commfaculty.fullerton.edu/lester/ethics/ethics_list.html

This site, maintained by Paul Martin Lester <u>lester@fullerton.edu</u>, links to resources in the following areas: courses in ethics, mailing lists, associations, business ethics, legal ethics, science ethics, media ethics, sports ethics, ethics in TV and movies, and more.

Ethics Resources on the Net

http://condor.depaul.edu/ethics/resource.html

This page provides links to ethics resources including journals, newsletters, teaching resources, ethics institutes, and general ethics links. The site is maintained by <u>lpincus@wppost.depaul.edu</u> and <u>swalton@wppost.depaul.edu</u>.

Ethics Updates

http://ethics.acusd.edu/index.html

This is a site primarily intended for those teaching ethics courses, and for students of ethics. It is divided into three sections—ethical theory, issues in applied ethics, and additional resources. It offers numerous resources including bibliographical essays, summaries of recent articles, links to online texts in ethics, and links to discussion groups and other ethics-related resources. Additions to the site should be mailed to its author, Lawrence Hinman <u>hinman@acusd.edu</u>.

Euroethics

http://www.spri.se/spriline/sokforie.htm

Euroethics is a European database on medical ethics, ethics in health professions, and in health care. It provides means to facilitate a professionally-organized exchange of information across the borders of individual European countries, the realization of a European consensus (e.g. Bioethics Convention of the Council of Europe), and the comparison and analysis of different ethical viewpoints and standards between European countries. The database is maintained in English, German, Dutch, and French by Ute Elsner and Ute Meinecke <u>UTE@ethik.med.uni-goettingen.de</u>.

Euthanasia

http://www.netlink.co.uk/users/vess/fastaccs.html

An impressive collection of resources from around the world on euthanasia is provided at this site, maintained by Chris Docker <u>vessj@euthanasia.org</u>. Resources include case histories, living wills, a bibliography, mailing lists and magazines, and links to related sites.

Gaia's Friends

http://www.gaiafriends.com/

This is the site of the Ethics Information Center, providing information on ethically-sound goods and services, as well as links to a library of applied ethics resources and the Center's own online discussion group. The site is maintained by <u>webmaster@wholecatalog.com</u>.

Genetics and Ethics

http://www.ethics.ubc.ca/brynw/

Maintained by Bryn Williams-Jones brynw@ethics.ubc.ca, this site provides extensive resources on genetics and ethics with sections on the Human Genome Project/ELSI, public action groups, journals and ejournals, professors studying genetics and ethics, discussion groups, genetics and the law, biotechnology/biodiversity resources, news and bulletins, miscellaneous and general philosophy resources.

Hedonist's HomePage

http://www.geocities.com/Athens/Acropolis/2743/index.html

This page provides an overview and discussion of neoepicurean hedonism, and a link to an online chat with others logged into the page. A java-capable browser is required to participate in the live chat. Maintained by Garrett Gecewicz garrettof99th@juno.com.

The Hedonistic Imperative

http://www.pavilion.co.uk/david-pearce/hedonist.htm

In the Hedonistic Imperative, David Pearce davidp@pavilion.co.uk outlines an ambitious, wildly implausible but technically feasible long-term species project to abolish the biological substrates of aversive experience in organic life forms.

Information Ethics

http://www.wolfson.ox.ac.uk/~floridi/ie.htm

From Luciano Floridi luciano.floridi@philosophy.oxford.ac.uk, this site provides a short webliography on computer ethics, information on research in recent years in the fields of philosophy and computing, a reading list on the philosophy of computer ethics, and a paper by Dr Floridi titled "Information Ethics: On the Philosophical Foundation of Computer Ethics."

Institute for Business and Professional Ethics

http://condor.depaul.edu/ethics/

The Institute for Business and Professional Ethics was established in 1985 by a joint effort of the Colleges of Liberal Arts and Sciences and Commerce at DePaul University. The Institute is one of the first ethics-related resources to pioneer a hypertext linked ethics network throughout the Internet. The Mission of the Institute is to foster ethical behavior. This site provides information about the activities and programs of the Institute, as well as links to a range of ethics-related resources. It is maintained by S. Walton swalton@wppost.depaul.edu.

Institute for Global Ethics

http://www.globalethics.org/

The Institute for Global Ethics wethics@globalethics.org is an independent, non-sectarian, and non-political organization dedicated to elevating public awareness and promoting the discussion of ethics in a global context. This non-profit think tank is an international, membership-based organization focusing on ethical activities for corporations, educators, professionals, and communities. This site provides information on the Institute's mission, activities, and products. It also presents a monthly dilemma and calls for participation in solving it. Results are then published in the following month.

Institute for the Study of Applied and Professional Ethics

http://www.dartmouth.edu/artsci/ethics-inst/

This site, maintained by Barbara J. Hillinger ethics.institute@dartmouth.edu, provides information on the activities of the Institute which is located at Dartmouth College.

International Business Ethics Forum

http://www.pitt.edu/~ethics/

This site was put together from resources gathered by MBA students at the Joseph M. Katz Graduate School of Business at the University of Pittsburgh. It contains information pertaining to the business ethics climate in a number of countries in every region of the world.

KPMG Business Ethics

http://www.us.kpmg.com/ethics/

Accounting Firm KPMG Peat Marwick provides this site which presents an archive of 'interative ethical dilemmas' in the business environment, plus access to archives of the KPMG Business Ethics Institute's newsletter "Integrity."

Lawrence Berkeley National Laboratory's ELSI Project

http://www.lbl.gov/Education/ELSI/ELSI.html

Lawrence Berkeley National Laboratory's Ethical, Legal, and Social Issues in Science program is a pilot project designed to stimulate discussions on the implications of selected areas of scientific research. Aimed at high school students, the project makes materials available to assist educators in designing programs for students to explore social, legal and ethical issues in science.

Maclean Center for Clinical Medical Ethics

http://ccme-mac4.bsd.uchicago.edu/CCMEHomePage.html

The MacLean Center for Clinical Medical Ethics at the University of Chicago consists of an interdisciplinary group of professionals who study and teach about practical ethical concerns confronting patients and health professionals. The Center's core faculty of physicians, nurses, legal scholars, philosophers, and social scientists, direct medical ethics education at the University of Chicago, and provide ethics consultation to the University of Chicago Hospitals, area hospitals, and the media. This site provides information on the activities of the Center, as well as links to a vast range of online bioethics-related resources. The site is maintained by kerielam@midway.uchicago.edu.

Medical College of Wisconsin, Bioethics Online Service

http://www.mcw.edu/bioethics/

This site, maintained by Arthur Derse, M.D. aderse@post.its.mcw.edu, provides access to bioethics bulletins, texts, news alerts, and a bioethics database.

MedWeb: Bioethics

http://www.gen.emory.edu/medweb/medweb.bioethics.html

This site provides extensive links to bioethics-related information on the net. MedWeb links are maintained by Steve Foote, Andy Kogelnik, and Bill Davis.

The Poynter Center

http://www.indiana.edu/~poynter/index.html

The Poynter Center for the Study of Ethics and American Institutions is an endowed center at Indiana University, charged with fostering the examination and discussion of ethical issues in American society. This site, maintained by Kenneth D. Pimple pimple@indiana.edu, provides information on the activities of the Center.

San Francisco Epicureans

http://www.epicureans.org/

This site, maintained by Jeff Diehl jdiehl@activa.net, provides information on Epicureanism and the San Francisco Epicureans, a private, non-academic cultural organization in the San Francisco Bay Area, founded for the sake of discussing the philosophy of the Ancient Greek Epicurus, and how his philosophic insights apply to modern living.

Society for Bioethics and Classical Philosophy

http://www.pitt.edu/~caj3/sbcp/

The Society is interested in facilitating and promoting the study of bioethics informed by classical philosophy, and the cross-fertilisation of ideas that results from the interchange of these two areas. This site provides information on the aims and activities of the Society, and is maintained by Mark Kuczewski mak7+@pitt.edu.

Society for Ethics

http://www-rohan.sdsu.edu/faculty/corlett/se.html

Established in 1995, The Society for Ethics (SE) serves the purpose of promoting philosophical research in ethics, broadly construed, including areas such as (but not limited to) ethical theory, moral, social and political philosophy, as well as areas of applied ethics such as (but not limited to) legal, business and medical ethics. The Society's page is maintained by J. Angelo Corlett corlett@rohan.sdsu.edu.

Values, Ethics, and Justice Specialty Group

http://pollux.geog.ucsb.edu/vejsg/

Practical and theoretical questions of values, ethics, and justice arise across the spectrum of geographical research, and are central to the professional conduct of geographers. The Values, Ethics, and Justice Specialty Group of The Association of American Geographers exists to further inquiry in normative issues of relevance to geography. This page provides information on the activities of the Group, plus links to relevant resources. The site is maintained by Jim Proctor jproctor@mailhost.geog.ucsb.edu.

Wharton Ethics Program

http://rider.wharton.upenn.edu/~ethics/

This site, maintained by Anita Zelinski zelinskia@wharton.upenn.edu, provides access to descriptions and syllabi for Wharton's business ethics courses, including a range of hypothetical ethics dilemmas for consideration, and links to ethics-related resources.

Existentialism

Albert Camus

http://www.levity.com/corduroy/camus.htm

This site, part of a larger site called Bohemian Ink *http://www.levity.com/corduroy/index.htm* and maintained by Christopher Ritter corduroy@earthlink.net, provides links to biographies, bibliographies, essays, articles, and reviews on the work of Camus.

Albert Camus

http://members.aol.com/KatharenaE/private/Philo/Camus/camus.html

This page, maintained by Katharena Eiermann KatharenaE@aol.com, provides access to biographical details, essays, and links to other pages of information on Camus. It is part of the Realm of Existentialism site.

A Page About Albert Camus

http://www.clark.net/pub/samg/camus.html

Maintained by Sam Gallagher samg@clark.net, this well-designed page includes a biography, bibliography, links to essays online, and links to other pages on Camus.

Simone de Beauvoir

http://www.bvx.ca/RobeNoire/Beauvoir/Beauvoir.html

This page, in French and by Mélanie Garneau, gives biographical details, a bibliography of de Beavoir's writings, and provides a short review of selected titles.

Simone de Beauvoir

http://Userzweb.lightspeed.net/~tameri/debeauv.html

This page, maintained by Christopher Scott Wyatt tameri@lightspeed.net, provides a biography, chronology, list of works, and commentaries on existentialist and feminist philosopher, Simone de Beauvoir.

Ereignis: Heidegger Links

http://www.webcom.com/~paf/ereignis.html

Access archives of Heidegger mailing lists, reference lists, abstracts of papers by others on the works of Heidegger, and a bibliography which are linked to this site. Maintained by Pete paf@netcom.com.

Existentialism

http://www.connect.net/ron/exist.html

A simple page from Ron Turner ron@connect.net, giving a summary of existentialist thought by focusing on its major themes.

Existentialism and Beyond

http://Userzweb.lightspeed.net/~tameri/tframes.html

This page, maintained by Christopher Scott Wyatt tameri@lightspeed.net, is a growing resource on information relating to existentialism and existentialist thinkers, taking an historical perspective on the development of this school of thought.

The Existentialism Hideout

http://www.geocities.com/Athens/6510/index1.htm

A very well-designed page comprising of articles on existentialist topics by the maintainer, Mikael Siirilä mscore@spider.compart.fi, as well as links to other existentialist resources.

Existential Psychology

http://oldsci.eiu.edu/psychology/Spencer/Existential.html

A fairly basic site providing a short description of existential psychology and its founders.

Franz Kafka Home Page

http://www.fairhavenuhs.k12.vt.us/TheCastle

This site, maintained by C.M. Wisniewski wisniewsc@fairhavenuhs.k12.vt.us, provides a chronology of Kafka's life, a bibliography on Kafka-related works, Kafka texts, essays on Kafka, and a list of Kafka-related links.

Kierkegaard on the Internet

http://www.webcom.com/sk/

An excellent page by Lindso Larsen lindsoe@po.ia.dk providing an introduction to Kierkegaard, his collected works on the web, other web resources, the Kierkegaard web library, news and announcements, and the Kierkegaard discussion forum.

Lectures on Heidegger's Being and Time
http://caae.phil.cmu.edu/CAAE/80254/Heidegger/SZHomePage.html

These lectures, developed and delivered over several courses at different schools, represent an attempt to guide the reader through the work in a thoughtful and careful manner. It is best to use these notes in conjunction with the Macquarrie & Robinson translation. A list of selected secondary sources is also provided. Lectures are by Robert Cavalier rc2z@andrew.cmu.edu at Carnegie Mellon University.

Karl Jaspers

http://Userzweb.lightspeed.net/~tameri/jaspers.html

This page offers information on the life and work of existentialist philosopher, Karl Jaspers. It is maintained by Christopher Scott Wyatt <u>tameri@lightspeed.net</u>.

Soren Kierkegaard

http://www.2xtreme.net/dstorm/sk/

A beautifully-designed page by D. Anthony Storm <u>dstorm@2xtreme.net</u>, providing a range of Kierkegaard resources.

Realm of Existentialism

http://members.aol.com/KatharenaE/private/Philo/philo.html

This site by Katharena Eiermann <u>KatharenaE@aol.com</u>, provides an overview of existentialism and phenomenology, and includes resources and information on existentialist writers and philosophers including: Karl Barth, Simone de Beauvoir, Martin Buber, Albert Camus, Fyodor Mikhailovich Dostoyevsky, Martin Heidegger, Karl Jaspers, Franz Kafka, Soren Aabye Kierkegaard, Andre Malraux, Gabriel Marcel, Friedrich Wilhelm Nietzsche, Jose Ortega y Gasset, Blaise Pascal, Maurice Merleau-Ponty, Rainer Maria Rilke, Jean Paul Sartre, Paul Tillich, Miguel de Unamuno, and Eliezer Wiesel.

Jean-Paul Sartre

http://members.aol.com/KatharenaE/private/Philo/Sartre/sartre.html

This page, part of the Realm of Existentialism site maintained by Katharena Eiermann <u>KatharenaE@aol.com</u>, is an excellent page on Sartre with links to essays, commentaries and summaries of Sartre's work, and links to related pages.

Jean-Paul Sartre

http://www.knuten.liu.se/~bjoch509/philosophers/sar.html

This page, part of Bjorn's Guide to Philosophy and maintained by Bjorn Christensson <u>bjoch509@knuten.liu.se</u>, provides an extensive biography on Sartre, a list of his works, and links to the ThinkNet Sartre mailing list.

Jean-Paul Sartre

http://www.lcl.cmu.edu/CAAE/80254/Sartre/Sartre.html

This page, maintained by Robert Cavalier <u>rc2z@andrew.cmu.edu</u> as a resource for his students, and which will be further developed over time, attempts to define and spell out the key concepts in existentialist thought.

Feminism & Women's Studies

Activism & Policy

Australian Institute for Women's Research and Policy

http://www.gu.edu.au/gwis/aiwrap/AIWRAP.home.html

Formed in 1991, AIWRAP focuses on the links between academics, government, industry, and the wider community in developing policies affecting women or gender issues. In addition to providing information on AIWRAP, this page provides links to women's resources on the net, and access to a database of Australian women researchers. The page is maintained by J.Greder J.Greder@hum.gu.edu.au.

Feminists for Animal Rights WWW Page

http://envirolink.org/arrs/far/home.html

The site, maintained by Kelly Marbury klmarbury@envirolink.org, includes basic information about FAR, all of the 1994 newsletters, and an art gallery containing the drawings of Sudie Rakusin, the FAR Newsletter artist.

National Organization for Women (NOW)

http://www.now.org/

The National Organization for Women in commemoration of the 175th birthday of suffragist Susan B. Anthony, has its own homepage on the Web. NOW believes an Internet presence will allow it to reach a wider public audience, and facilitate an exchange of information and resources between feminists, activists, and organizations around the world. This page provides information on NOW, NOW news and events, how to join, NOW chapters, and links to feminist-related information.

National Women's Justice Commission

http://www.ozemail.com.au/~nwjc/

NWJC is a lobbying and networking organization which aims to promote women's equality before the law. Formed in 1995, it consists of over 30 national women's peak organizations. This site, maintained by Marian Sheridan nwjc@ozemail.com.au, provides information on the NWJC, information on legal assistance for women, and access to the NWJC journal.

Virtual Sisterhood

http://www.igc.apc.org/vsister/

Virtual Sisterhood vsister@igc.apc.org is a global women's electronic support network, offering a range of support services and information for women online. It is available in a variety of languages, including Chinese, French, German, Japanese, Russian, and Spanish.

Women's Electoral Lobby, Australia

http://www.pcug.org.au/other/wel/

WEL is a feminist political organization founded in 1972 as a women's political lobby. This site provides information on WEL offerings and activities, announcements, WEL newsletter, Australian political issues, conferences, calls for papers/submissions, book reviews, and general information. The WEL webpage is maintained by Val Thomson val@pcug.org.au.

General Resources

FeMiNa

http://www.femina.com/

FeMiNa was created by A. Sherman cybergrrl@cgim.com to provide women with a comprehensive, searchable directory of links to sites and information of interest to women and feminists. The site continues to be updated regularly and includes links to women's studies resources, education, arts and humanities, as well as more general women-oriented links.

feminist.com

http://feminist.com/

This site, like FeMiNa, provides links to a wide range of feminist resources, but also includes a section on women's studies and feminist theory. The maintainers of the site can be contacted at feminist@feminist.com.

Feminist Majority Foundation Online

http://www.feminist.org/

This excellent site, maintained by Jessica Haney haney@feminist.org, provides feminist news and events, information on feminist university networks, the UN Women's Conference, Feminist Research Center, and links to a range of feminist educational and research resources.

Full Circle Books

http://www.bookgrrls.com/fcb/

Full Circle Books carries books of interest to women, including a large selection of non-sexist, non-racist books for children of all ages. They also feature books on women and technology, cybergrrls, women and computing, the interface of technology and women's lives, and more. This site is maintained by dorothy@bookgrrls.com.

International Association of Women Philosophers

http://web.bu.edu/WCP/IAPH/

This site provides information on the 8th Symposium of the International Association of Women Philosophers, to be held at the World Congress in 1998.

Women's Resource Page

http://www.mit.edu:8001/people/sorokin/women/index.html

This site houses a collection of online writings and resources by, for, or about women, as well as links to resources including: Women in Computer Science and Engineering; Women's Studies Programs and Women's Centers; General and Sexuality; Women in Academia and Industry; Women's Health and Women in the Health Care Industry; Feminism and Political Activism; Women, Feminism, and Religion; and more. The page is maintained by Jessie Stickgold-Sarah sorokin@mit.edu.

Women's Resource Project

http://sunsite.unc.edu/cheryb/women/

This site, maintained by Cheryl Friedman cheryb@sunsite.unc.edu and others, provides links to a wide range of women's studies and feminist resources, as well as more general women's resources.

WWWomen: the Premier Search Directory for Women Online

http://www.wwwomen.com/

A searchable database of feminist and women's studies links including women in history, women and government, women's education, women in business, women in computing, publications, and much more. Enquiries about the site can be made to webmeister@wwwomen.com.

Research & Professional Sites

APA Directory of Women Philosophers

http://www.ruf.rice.edu/~krist/APA/

This site houses a database developed by the Committee on the Status of Women of the American Philosophical Association. Search online for women working in philosophy by name or specialisation.

Bibliography on Feminism and World Politics

gopher://csf.Colorado.EDU:70/00/feminist/bibliography/women.world.politics.bibliography

This extensive bibliography is oriented towards the study of feminism and international relations theory. It is based on a bibliography by V. Spike Petersons with supplementary materials supplied by Lev Gonick.

Canadian Society for Women in Philosophy (C-SWIP)

http://sbrennan.philosophy.arts.uwo.ca/cswip/

The Canadian Society for Women in Philosophy aims to foster philosophical scholarship and teaching in the area of feminist studies as a legitimate area of interest within philosophic inquiry; to provide support and encouragement for the professional work of women philosophers; and to work toward eliminating discrimination against women in philosophy. This site provides information on the activities of the Society, access to its newsletter, conference information, and notification of job vacancies in philosophy. The site is maintained by Samantha Brennan sbrennan@julian.uwo.ca.

Center for Advanced Feminist Studies

http://rhetoric.agoff.umn.edu/~cafs//

Located at the University of Minnesota, CAFS' mission is to create and coordinate a coherent, integrated curriculum for graduate students specialising in feminist studies, and to foster intellectual community and collaborative research among feminist scholars within and outside the University of Minnesota.

Collaborative Bibliography of Women in Philosophy

http://billyboy.ius.indiana.edu/WomeninPhilosophy/WomeninPhilo.html

The work on this site is an attempt to produce a first rate, comprehensive, and continually updated bibliography of works in philosophy published by women. The bibliography is arranged in alphabetical order. Additions or comments can be mailed to Noël Parish Hutchings nhutchin@ius.indiana.edu.

DIANA: International Human Rights Database

http://www.law-lib.utoronto.ca/diana/

This site houses extensive women's human rights information including links to sites for legal research, links to documents, conventions, reports, bibliographies, and more. It is maintained by Anne Johnstone annej@istar.ca.

Diotima: Women and Gender in the Ancient World

http://www.uky.edu/ArtsSciences/Classics/gender.html

This site offers a range of research materials for the study of women and gender in the ancient world. It includes course materials, a bibliography, an anthology, essays, and more. The site is maintained by Ross Scaife scaife@pop.uky.edu and Suzanne Bonefas bonefas@hippokrene.colleges.org.

Distinguished Women of Past and Present

http://www.netsrq.com:80/~dbois/

This site houses a collection of biographies of distinguished women. The collection is searchable by field of activity (politics, astronomy, physics, etc.), or by name, and provides some useful preliminary research materials. It is maintained by Danuta Bois dbois@netsrq.com.

Ecofeminism: An Introductory Bibliography

gopher://silo.adp.wisc.edu:70/00/.uwlibs/.womenstudies/.bibs/.ecofem

A selective and annotated bibliography on sources concerning political activism within women's groups on the environment and surrounding issues. Part of a series of bibliographies published by the University of Wisconsin System Women's Studies Librarian's Office.

Feminist Curricular Resources Clearinghouse

http://www.law.indiana.edu/fcrc/fcrc.html

The Clearinghouse provides access to a number of resources related to teaching about feminism and law. It offers syllabi, reading lists and bibliographies from courses taught in law schools and other departments. All materials deal with legal or jurisprudential issues of concern to women. The site is maintained by Susan Williams SusanWilliams@law. indiana.edu.

Feminist Law Website

http://www.geocities.com/capitolhill/2995

Resources on feminism and law, with links to feminist organizations, and a range of feminist and women's studies material can be found at this site, maintained by Kim Goforth kimgo@u.washington.edu.

Feminist Theory and Feminist Jurisprudence on the WWW

http://lark.cc.ukans.edu/~akdclass/femlit/femjur.html

This site is a collection of links to sites providing materials on feminist theory and feminist jurisprudence. It is maintained by Kim Dayton kdayton@falcon.cc.ukans.edu.

Feminist Theory: University of Iowa Library, Women's Studies Series

http://bailwick.lib.uiowa.edu/wstudies/theory.html

This page provides reviews of books in feminist theory, a locally maintained French Feminists page, links to journals, and other resources. Enquiries about the page can be directed to gateway@uiowa.edu.

Feminist Theory Website

http://www.utc.edu/~kswitala/Feminism/

The Feminist Theory Website is designed to provide research materials for students and scholars interested in Feminist Theory. It is a collaborative project, involving submissions of material from women around the world, maintained by Kristin Switala KristinSwitala@utc.edu.

Institute for Research on Women and Gender

http://www-leland.stanford.edu/group/IRWG/

The Institute is located at Stanford University. Its primary mission is to support research on women and gender and to organize programs that will make such work accessible to a broader public. By providing thoughtful and in-depth analyses, these programs have contributed to policy making on issues with enormous importance for women and their families. This site provides information on the activities of the institute and its programs and publications. It also provides links to related resources.

International Association of Women Philosophers

http://web.bu.edu/WCP/IAPH/

This is the homepage of the International Association of Women Philosophers, which at present, contains only conference information.

National Women's Studies Association

http://www.feminist.com/nwsa.htm

The National Women's Studies Association (NWSA) is a professional organization designed "to further the social, political and professional development of women's studies throughout the country and the world, at every educational level and in every educational setting." NWSA membership includes scholars, educators, students, women's centers and activists interested in pursuing these common goals. This site provides information on the activities of the Association, as well as links to feminist and women's studies resources.

The Society for Women in Philosophy (SWIP)

http://www.uh.edu/~cfreelan/SWIP/

The Society for Women in Philosophy aims to promote and support women in philosophy. SWIP holds divisional meetings, meetings in conjunction with the meetings of the American Philosophical Association, and it publishes newsletters. This site provides information on the activities of the Society, as well as links to feminist and philosophy resources.

Women's Studies Librarian's Office

http://www.library.wisc.edu/libraries/WomensStudies/

Located at the University of Wisconsin and provided primarily for its students, faculty, librarians, and administrators, this page provides a vast array of resources including bibliographies, lists of women's studies books, links to websites on women and gender, and more. Enquiries about the page can be directed to wiswsl@doit.wisc.edu.

Women's Studies Resources

http://www.inform.umd.edu/EdRes/Topic/WomensStudies/

This women's studies database provides resources for those interested in the women's studies, both professionally and in general. The database contains collections of conference announcements, calls for papers, bibliographies, online texts, employment opportunities, as well as a picture gallery, a significant number of government documents, and much more. The site is maintained by Megan L. Hollmann megan@info.umd.edu.

Women's Studies/Women's Issues Resource Site

http://www-unix.umbc.edu/~korenman/wmst/links.html

This page provides a compilation of links to a vast range of women's studies resources on the net, including a frequently updated list of mailing lists. Maintained by Joan Korenman korenman@umbc2.umbc.edu, the site is updated regularly.

Great Thinkers: A to Z

Abelard

http://www.nd.edu/Departments/Maritain/etext/abelard.htm

This page presents a biographical essay on Abelard by William Turner.

Theodor W. Adorno

http://www2.rz.hu-berlin.de/~h0444pjf/Adorno.html

From Ken Kubota h0444pjf@rz.hu-berlin.de, this page presents a range of links to information on the life and work of Adorno.

Apollonius

http://magna.com.au/~prfbrown/a_tyana0.html

This page provides extensive information on the life and work of Apollonius of Tyana. Selected articles are from the English translation of F. C. Conybeare, the Loeb Classical Library, Edition 1912. The site is maintained by P. Brown prfbrown@magna.com.au.

Aquinas

http://www.epas.utoronto.ca:8080/~loughlin/index.html

Part of Stephen Loughlin's loughlin@chass.utoronto.ca home page, this page provides biographical details on Aquinas, as well as links to Aquinas' works.

St. Thomas Aquinas

http://www.ultranet.com/~rsarkiss/AQUINAS.HTM

This site provides a short biography, selected quotations and links to online texts. It is maintained by Robert Sarkissian rsarkisssian@smtp.microcom.com.

St. Thomas Aquinas Five Ways

http://members.aol.com/plweiss1/aquinas.htm

Maintained by Patricia Weiss patricia-w@worldnet.att.net, this web page details Aquinas' arguments for the existence of God and provides a link to a page on Paley's Teleological Argument.

Thomistic Philosophy Page

http://members.aol.com/jmageema/index.html

This site includes essays on the main points in Thomistic Philosophy, links to lists of works by Thomas Aquinas, a list of works about Thomistic Philosophy arranged by subject, links to sites with relevant information for those interested in Thomistic philosophy (including biographies of Aquinas, scholars engaged in Thomistic studies, and links to online versions of some of his works). This page is maintained by Joseph Magee jmagee@basil. stthom.edu.

Archimedes of Syracuse

http://www-groups.dcs.st-and.ac.uk/~history/Mathematicians/Archimedes.html

An excellent overview of the life and work of Archimedes, including links to resources elsewhere on the net. This site is part of the Mac Tutor History of Mathematics archive at *http://www-groups.dcs.st-and.ac.uk/~history/index.html* and is maintained by John J. O'Connor joc@st-andrews.ac.uk and Edmund F. Robertson efr@st-andrews.ac.uk.

Aristotle

http://www.ilt.columbia.edu/academic/digitexts/aristotle/bio_aristotle.html

Part of the ILTWeb site webmaster@ilt.columbia.edu, this page provides biographical information on Aristotle, as well as links to Aristotle texts.

Aristotle

http://www.ultranet.com/~rsarkiss/ARISTOT.HTM

This site provides a short biography, selected quotations, and links to online texts. It is maintained by Robert Sarkissian rsarkissian@smtp.microcom.com.

Augustine

http://ccat.sas.upenn.edu/jod/augustine.html

Maintained by James O'Donnell jod@ccat.sas.upenn.edu, this site provides access to electronic texts and translations, commentaries, research materials and essays, and other miscellaneous Augustine resources.

St. Augustine

http://www.ultranet.com/~rsarkiss/AUGUST.HTM

This site provides a short biography, selected quotations, and links to online texts. It is maintained by Robert Sarkissian rsarkissian@smtp.microcom.com.

Marcus Aurelius

http://www.ultranet.com/~rsarkiss/AURELIUS.HTM

This site provides a short biography, selected quotations, and links to online texts. It is maintained by Robert Sarkissian rsarkissian@smtp.microcom.com.

The Marcus Aurelius Think Page

http://ucsu.colorado.edu/~biggus/Marcus/Marcus.html

This page, from Jeff Biggus biggus@colorado.edu, presents excerpts from the *Meditations*, with links to full translations of the text.

Francis Bacon

http://www.knuten.liu.se/~bjoch509/philosophers/bac.html

This page provides a biography and links to the works of Francis Bacon. It is part of Bjorn's Guide to Philosophy, maintained by Bjorn Christensson bjoch509@knuten.liu.se.

The Bakhtin Center: University of Sheffield

http://www.shef.ac.uk/uni/academic/A-C/bakh/bakhtin.html

The Center's purpose is to promote multi-and inter-disciplinary research on the work of the Russian philosopher and theorist Mikhail Bakhtin and the Bakhtin Circle, and on related areas of cultural, critical, linguistic and literary theory. The Center's website provides an analytical database of work by and about the Bakhtin circle. Visitors are able to search or make contributions to the database. Information is provided on seminars, conferences, and other activities of the Center, and on Bakhtin studies e lsewhere. The site is maintained by Carol Adlam c.a.adlam@shef.ac.uk.

Michael Bakunin

http://www.pitzer.edu/~dward/Anarchist_Archives/bakunin/Bakuninarchive.html

This site is part of the Anarchist Archives *http://www.pitzer.edu/~dward/Anarchist_Archives/ anarchy.html* maintained by Dana Ward dward@pitzer.edu, and provides a biography, links to collected works, a bibliography, commentaries, and graphics of Bakunin.

Karl Barth

http://members.aol.com/KatharenaE/private/Philo/Barth/barth.html

This page by Katharena Eiermann KatharenaE@aol.com, provides information on the life and work of theologian, Karl Barth.

Baudrillard Resources on the Web

http://www.netspace.org/~erica/Mobius/links.html

This page, maintained by Erica J. Seidel erica@netspace.org, provides a range of links to Baudrillard-related resources.

Pierre Bayle Home Page

http://www.cisi.unito.it/progetti/bayle/

The Bayle home page, maintained by Gianluca Mori moveon@mbox.vol.it, includes a bibliography, Bayle's Dictionary, Bayle on toleration, and links to related sites.

The Bentham Project

http://www.ucl.ac.uk/Bentham-Project/index.htm

The Bentham Project aims to produce a new edition of the works of influential utilitarian thinker, Jeremy Bentham. Information about the project, and about Bentham, is available on this page, maintained by Johnathan Harris j.harris@ucl.ac.uk.

Berdyaev, The Thinker

http://www.maine.com/yfa/philosophy/fedotov.html

This site provides a biography of Berdyaev by Georgii P. Fedotov and translated by Fr. Stephen Janos.

George Berkeley

http://www.knuten.liu.se/~bjoch509/philosophers/ber.html

This page, maintained by Bjorn Christensson bjoch509@knuten.liu.se, provides a biography, list of works, and links to other Berkeley-related information on the net.

Jacob Boehme

http://www.augustana.ab.ca/~janzb/boehme.htm

An extensive range of Boehme-related resources are collected on this site, maintained by Bruce Janz janzb@Corelli.Augustana.AB.CA.

Jakob Boehme

http://www.erols.com/nbeach/boehme.html

This site, created by Edward A. Beach nb6@evansville.edu, provides biographical details and a summary of Boehme's principal philosophical and theological ideas.

Boethius

http://ccat.sas.upenn.edu/jod/boethius.html

This page was created for the 1994 Boethius Internet seminar at University of Pennsylvania and is an index to the materials for that course. The page will continue to be maintained as a resource for students and scholars. For further information contact James O'Donnell jod@ccat.sas.upenn.edu.

Martin Buber

http://www.uni-karlsruhe.de/~uneu/buber.htm

This site (in German, but with a link to an abridged version in English) is devoted to an exploration of the life and work of Jewish philosopher, Martin Buber. It is maintained by Andreas Schmidt uneu@rz.uni-karlsruhe.de.

Edmund Burke

http://odur.let.rug.nl/~usa/B/burke.htm

This site, maintained by George Welling welling@let.rug.nl and part of an American history project called From Revolution to Reconstruction *http://grid.let.rug.nl/~welling/usa/revolution.html*, provides Burke's biographical details, the text of one of his speeches, an essay, and links to works cited in the essay.

Noam Chomsky, Libertarian Socialist

http://www.tigerden.com/~berios/chomsky.html

This page by Jamal Hannah jah@iww.org, provides links to a variety of Chomsky resources.

The Cicero Homepage

http://www.utexas.edu/depts/classics/documents/Cic.html

Links from this page provide access to Cicero texts, a Cicero chronology, a bibliography, images of Cicero, and Cicero's biography (according to Plutarch [trans. Dryden]). The page is maintained by Andrew Riggsby ariggsby@utxvms.cc.utexas.edu.

Emile Mihai Cioran

http://www.olympic.net/~taylor/cioran/

This page, from Donald Taylor taylor@olympic.net, provides information on the work of Romanian thinker, EM Cioran.

Auguste Comte and Positivism

http://www.mygale.org/04/clotilde/

This page, primarily in French but being translated into English, provides detailed information and links relating to Comte's thought and work, plus a range of information and resources on positivist thought. The page is maintained by Eric Dupuis edupuis@FranceNet.fr.

Marquis de Condorcet

http://www-groups.dcs.st-and.ac.uk:80/~history/Mathematicians/Condorcet.html

An overview of the life and work of Condorcet is available at this site which is part of the the Mac Tutor History of Mathematics archive at *http://www-groups.dcs.st-and.ac.uk/~history/index.html* and is maintained by John J. O'Connor joc@st-andrews.ac.uk and Edmund F. Robertson efr@st-andrews.ac.uk.

Confucius

gopher://gopher.vt.edu:10010/11/66

This gopher site provides links to the Confucian Analects, the Doctrine Of The Mean, and the Great Learning.

Nicolaus Copernicus

http://www-groups.dcs.st-and.ac.uk:80/~history/Mathematicians/Copernicus.html

The page provides an overview of the life and work of Copernicus, including references and links to other Copernicus sites. This site is part of the Mac Tutor History of Mathematics archive at *http://www-groups.dcs.st-and.ac.uk/~history/index.html* and is maintained by John J. O'Connor joc@st-andrews.ac.uk and Edmund F. Robertson efr@st-andrews.ac.uk.

Charles Darwin

http://www.nobunaga.demon.co.uk/htm/darwin.htm

This site, from Shino and Ian Jordan ian@amgmps.com provides a brief chronology of Darwin's life, plus links to other Darwin materials online.

Donald Davidson

http://www.geocities.com/athens/oracle/3841/davidson.html

Vladimir Kalugin kaluginv@jetlink.net has produced this page which provides an overview of Davidson's main philosophical views, plus links to Davidson quotations, a bibliography, an interview with Davidson, and links to other related sites.

Donald Davidson on the Internet

http://www.philosophie.uni-bielefeld.de/Benutzer/Meurer/english/Davidson/index.htm

This site, from Volker Meurer vmeurer@philosophie.uni-bielefeld.de, provides an excellent resource for those interested in the philosophy of Donald Davidson. It includes an extensive bibliography, plus links to a range of Davidson-related materials, and is available online in German as well.

Simone de Beauvoir

http://www.bvx.ca/RobeNoire/Beauvoir/Beauvoir.html

This page, in French and by Mélanie Garneau, gives biographical details, a bibliography of de Beavoir's writings, and provides a short review of selected titles.

Simone de Beauvoir

http://Userzweb.lightspeed.net/~tameri/debeauv.html

This page, maintained by Christopher Scott Wyatt tameri@lightspeed.net, provides a biography, chronology, list of works and commentaries on existentialist and feminist philosopher, Simone de Beauvoir.

Deleuze & Guattari Internet Resources

http://jefferson.village.Virginia.EDU/~spoons/d-g_html/d-g.html

From Jon Beasley-Murray jpb8@acpub.duke.edu, this site links to a wide range of resources including bibliographies, conference information, electronic texts and more.

Deleuze & Guattari on the Web

http://www.uta.edu/english/apt/d&g/d&gweb.html

This site provides a list of links to works about and by Gilles Deleuze and Félix Guattari compiled by Alan Taylor apt6083@utarlg.uta.edu.

Deleuze & Guattari Web Resources

http://www.langlab.wayne.edu/romance/FreDeleuze.html

From Charles Stivale CStivale@wayne.edu, this site provides links to a range of resources relevant to critical theory, in particular to the work of Deleuze and Guattari, including essays, discussion lists, journals, and conferences.

WWW Resources for Gilles Deleuze and Félix Guattari

http://www.stg.brown.edu:80/projects/hypertext/landow/cpace/theory/deleuze.html

Part of a larger critical Theory resource, this site provides access to a range of Deleuze and Guattari links.

Daniel Dennett

http://www.webconn.com/~maiers/dennett/home.html

This page, maintained by Martin Maiers maiers@cs.umn.edu, provides links to Dennett-related resources including essays, reviews, and an archive of the Dennett mailing list.

Jacques Derrida Online: Deconstruction on the Net

http://www.lake.de/home/lake/hydra/jd.html

This site by Peter Krapp derrida@hydra.lake.de, provides links to a range of resources relevant to Derrida and deconstruction. If this is too slow, you can try the US mirror site at: *http://www.hydra.umn.edu/derrida/.*

Descartes

http://www.france.diplomatie.fr/culture/france/biblio/folio/descartes/index.html

This is a beautifully-designed French-language site with extensive information of the life and work of René Descartes, maintained by Michel Deverge deverge@imaginet.fr.

Descartes

http://www-phil.philengl.dundee.ac.uk/staff/gs/descartes/

This is an online version of a course on Descartes from the University of Dundee, covering issues from his *Discourse of Method* and the *Meditations*. The site is maintained by Alistair Lyall a.m.lyall@dundee.ac.uk and Seonaid Woodburn s.h.woodburn@dundee.ac.uk.

Descartes: Discourse on Method

http://www.wsu.edu:8080/~wldciv/world_civ_reader/world_civ_reader_2/descartes.html

This page provides an excerpt from *Reading About the World*, Volume 2, edited by Paul Brians, Mary Gallwey, Douglas Hughes, Michael Myers, Michael Neville, Roger Schlesinger, Alice Spitzer, and Susan Swan and published by American Heritage Custom Books. The site is maintained by Paul Brians brians@wsu.edu.

Descartes' "Meditations on First Philosophy"

http://philos.wright.edu/Descartes/Meditations.html

This site provides a trilingual version of the *Meditations* in English, French, and Latin. It is maintained by Charles Taylor and David Manley manley@checkov.hm.udayton.edu.

René Descartes

http://www-groups.dcs.st-and.ac.uk:80/~history/Mathematicians/Descartes.html

Part of the Mac Tutor History of Mathematics archive at *http://www-groups.dcs.st-and.ac.uk/~history/index.html* maintained by John J. O'Connor joc@st-andrews.ac.uk and Edmund F. Robertson efr@st-andrews.ac.uk, this site provides an excellent overview of the life and work of the philosopher, Descartes, plus references and links to related sites.

Center for Dewey Studies

http://www.siu.edu/~deweyctr/

The Center for Dewey Studies at Southern Illinois University at Carbondale was established in 1961 as the "Dewey Project." In the course of collecting and editing Dewey's works, the Center amassed a wealth of source materials for the study of America's quintessential philosopher-educator, John Dewey. By virtue of its publications and research, the

Center has become the international focal point for research on Dewey's life and work, and its location at the University makes it possible for visitors to take advantage of the resources and professional expertise of the faculty and staff of the Department of Philosophy, the College of Education, Special Collections in Morris Library, and the Southern Illinois University Press. The site is maintained by Dr. Larry Hickman lhickman@siu.edu.

John Dewey

http://www.ilt.columbia.edu/academic/texts/dewey/d_e/contents.html

Access the text of Dewey's *Democracy and Education*, plus a short biography, on this site. Enquiries about the site can be directed to webmaster@ilt.columbia.edu.

Diogenes of Sinope

http://www.halcyon.com/colinp/diogenes.htm

This page, produced by Colin Pringle colinp@halcyon.com, provides a short biography and overview of the thought of the Cynics, plus links to related resources.

The Durkheim Pages

http://eddie.cso.uiuc.edu/Durkheim/

This well-presented site by Robert Alun Jones rajones@uiuc.edu provides access to a range of resources including a biography, timeline, bibliography, glossary, texts, lectures, and more.

Epicurus and Epicurean Philosophy

http://www.creative.net/~epicurus/

This page, from Vincent Cook epicurus@creative.net, provides an overview of Epicureanism (Epicurean beliefs, Epicurus and his school, how Epicureanism relates to other philosophy), as well as links to other Epicurean resources.

Euclid of Alexandria

http://www-groups.dcs.st-and.ac.uk/~history/Mathematicians/Euclid.html

This site provides an excellent overview of the life and work of Euclid, plus links to other related sites on the net. It is part of the the Mac Tutor History of Mathematics archive at *http://www-groups.dcs.st-and.ac.uk/~history/index.html* and is maintained by John J. O'Connor joc@st-andrews.ac.uk and Edmund F. Robertson efr@st-andrews.ac.uk.

Foucault Pages at CSUN

http://www.csun.edu:80/~hfspc002/foucault.home.html

This site, by Ben Attias hfspc002@csun.edu, provides a genealogy of Foucault, information on Foucault discussion lists, links to other Foucault resources, calls for participation for Foucault Scholars, and online essays by, about, or influenced by Foucault.

Foucault

http://www.synaptic.bc.ca/ejournal/foucault.htm

This site, maintained by Patrick Jennings feedback@synaptic.bc.ca, provides links to an interesting range of Foucault resources.

Joseph Fourier

http://www-groups.dcs.st-and.ac.uk:80/~history/Mathematicians/Fourier.html

This site provides an excellent summary of the life and work of mathematician Joseph Fourier. It includes references and links to related sites. It is part of the the Mac Tutor History of Mathematics archive at *http://www-groups.dcs.st-and.ac.uk/~history/index.html* and is maintained by John J. O'Connor joc@st-andrews.ac.uk and Edmund F. Robertson efr@st-andrews.ac.uk.

Gottlob Frege

http://mally.stanford.edu/frege.html

This page, part of the Metaphysics Research Lab site at *http://mally.stanford.edu/index.html* maintained by Edward N. Zalta zalta@mally.stanford.edu, provides a short biography, a discussion of Frege's advances in logic, a list of his principal works, and suggestions for further reading.

Freud Archives

http://plaza.interport.net/nypsan/freudarc.html

This site, maintained by the Abraham Brill Library of the New York Psychoanalytic Institute brill@interport.net, provides extensive links to biographical and other material on Sigmund Freud.

Sigmund Freud on the Web

http://www.strangelove.com/marc/freudhm.html

This page, by Marc Fonda mfonda@magmacom.com, provides access to an annotated bibliography of certain volumes of editor James Strachey's "The Standard Edition of the Collected Psychological Works of Sigmund Freud." Annotations of other volumes are promised. Two essays on Freud are also accessible here, as well as links to Freud-related resources. The site is mirrored at: *http://www.clas.ufl.edu/users/gthursby/fonda/ freudhm.html*.

Jakob Friedrich Fries

http://www.friesian.com/fries.htm

This site by Kelley Ross kross@friesian.com, provides an overview of Friedrich's work, links to his essays, and links to related texts and thinkers. A German version of the page is also available from this link.

Gadamer Home Page

http://www.ms.kuki.sut.ac.jp:80/KMSLab/makita/gadamerd.html

In German and Japanese, this page provides access to a range of Gadamer resources and is maintained by Etsuro Makita <u>makita@ms.kuki.sut.ac.jp</u>.

Galileo Galilei

http://www-groups.dcs.st-and.ac.uk:80/~history/Mathematicians/Galileo.html

From the Mac Tutor History of Mathematics archive at *http://www-groups.dcs.st-and.ac.uk/ ~history/index.html* maintained by John J. O'Connor <u>joc@st-andrews.ac.uk</u> and Edmund F. Robertson <u>efr@st-andrews.ac.uk</u>, this page provides a summary of the life and work of Galileo, plus references and links to related sites.

Mahatma Gandhi

http://www.engagedpage.com/gandhi.html

This site provides a short biography, "Death before Prayers" by Louis Fisher on Ghandi's death, and links to vegetarian resources. It is maintained by <u>engaged@maui.net</u>.

William Godwin Archive

http://www.pitzer.edu/~dward/Anarchist_Archives/godwin/Godwinarchive.html

This site is part of the Anarchist Archives *http://www.pitzer.edu/~dward/Anarchist_Archives/ anarchy.html* maintained by Dana Ward <u>dward@pitzer.edu</u>, and provides a biography, links to collected works, a bibliography, commentaries, and graphics of Godwin.

Christian Goldbach

http://www-groups.dcs.st-and.ac.uk:80/~history/Mathematicians/Goldbach.html

Remember Goldbach's conjecture? Here's a web page that provides more detail on Goldbach's life and work on prime numbers. It is from the Mac Tutor History of Mathematics archive at *http://www-groups.dcs.st-and.ac.uk/~history/index.html* and is maintained by John J. O'Connor <u>joc@st-andrews.ac.uk</u> and Edmund F. Robertson <u>efr@st-andrews.ac.uk</u>.

Emma Goldman

http://www.pitzer.edu/~dward/Anarchist_Archives/goldman/Goldmanarchive.html

This page, part of the Anarchist Archives *http://www.pitzer.edu/~dward/Anarchist_Archives/ anarchy.html* maintained by Dana Ward <u>dward@pitzer.edu</u>, provides a biography, links to collected works, a bibliography, commentaries, and graphics of anarchist thinker and activist, Emma Goldman.

The Emma Goldman Papers

http://sunsite.berkeley.edu/Goldman/

From the Berkeley Digital Library, this excellent site presents electronic resources from the Emma Goldman Papers Project, including selections from Goldman's writing.

Resources on Antonio Gramsci

http://www.soc.qc.edu/gramsci/

This site provides links to a searchable complete Gramsci bibliography, an introduction and appendices to the bibliography, International Gramsci Society Newsletters, and the Fondazione Istituto Gramsci.

Gregory of Nyssa Homepage

http://www.ucc.uconn.edu/~das93006/nyssa.html

This is a page which provides links to English translations of Gregory's work, as well as general introductions, bibliographies, and other references. It is maintained by David A. Salomon das93006@uconnvm.uconn.edu.

The Friedrich Hayek Scholars Page

http://members.aol.com/gregransom/hayekpage.htm

This page, from Greg Ransom gbransom@aol.com, provides access to select links related to Friedrich Hayek and his work, a bibliography of Hayek's publications, a bibliography of writings discussing Hayek and his work, book reviews, and more.

Georg Wilhelm Freidrich Hegel

http://www.ultranet.com/~rsarkiss/HEGEL.HTM

This site provides a short biography, selected quotations, and links to online texts. It is maintained by Robert Sarkissian rsarkissian@smtp.microcom.com.

Georg Wilhelm Freidrich Hegel: An Introduction

http://www.geocities.com/Athens/5079/hegel.html

This page includes a short bio, an overview of Hegelian thought, Hegelian history of philosophy, impacts of Hegel's thought, a section on American Hegelians, and links to other Hegel-related resources. This well-designed site is maintained by hamilto@students.wisc.edu.

GWF Hegel

http://www2.rz.hu-berlin.de/~h0444pjf/Hegel.html

From Ken Kubota h0444pjf@rz.hu-berlin.de, this page presents a range of links to information on the life and work of Hegel.

Hegel

http://xyz.uchicago.edu/users/bmdelane/hegel.htm

This page features a collection of Hegel links including biographies and graphics. The page is maintained by Brian Manning Delaney bmdelane@uchicago.edu, who also includes some of his work on Hegel.

Hegel by Hypertext

http://www.werple.net.au/~andy/index.htm

This site provides an impressive array of Hegelian texts, Marx and Engels on Hegel, and Marxist texts and resources. It is maintained by andy@werple.mira.net.au.

Lectures on Heidegger's Being and Time

http://www.lcl.cmu.edu/CAAE/80254/Heidegger/SZHomePage.html

These lectures, developed and delivered over several courses at different schools, represent an attempt to guide the reader through the work in a thoughtful and careful manner. It is best to use these notes in conjunction with the Macquarrie & Robinson translation. A list of selected secondary sources is also provided. Lectures are by Robert Cavalier rc2z @andrew.cmu.edu at Carnegie Mellon University.

Ereignis: Heidegger Links

http://www.webcom.com/~paf/ereignis.html

Access archives of Heidegger mailing lists, reference lists, abstracts of papers by others on the works of Heidegger, and a bibliography which are linked to this site. Maintained by Pete paf@netcom.com.

Thomas Hobbes

http://www-groups.dcs.st-and.ac.uk:80/~history/Mathematicians/Hobbes.html

From the Mac Tutor History of Mathematics archive at *http://www-groups.dcs.st-and.ac.uk/ ~history/index.html* maintained by John J. O'Connor joc@st-andrews.ac.uk and Edmund F. Robertson efr@st-andrews.ac.uk, this page provides an overview of the life and work of philosopher, Thomas Hobbes.

Thomas Hobbes

http://www.ultranet.com/~rsarkiss/HOBBES.HTM

This site provides a short biography, selected quotations and links to online texts. It is maintained by Robert Sarkissian rsarkissian@smtp.microcom.com.

Edwin Hubble

http://www-groups.dcs.st-and.ac.uk:80/~history/Mathematicians/Hubble.html

Another page from the Mac Tutor History of Mathematics archive at *http://www-groups. dcs.st-and.ac.uk/~history/index.html* maintained by John J. O'Connor joc@st-andrews.ac.uk and Edmund F Robertson efr@st-andrews.ac.uk, this time on the life and work of Edwin Hubble.

Hume Archives

http://www.utm.edu:80/research/hume/hume.html

This site, maintained by Jim Fieser jfieser@utm.edu is a repository of texts by and about David Hume. It includes all Hume texts, early commentaries, 18th century reviews of Hume's writing, and early biographies.

Ty's David Hume Page

http://www.geocities.com/Athens/3067/hume.html

This page, maintained by D. Tycerium Lightner tycerium@geocities.com, provides links to a Hume bibliography, a bibiography of secondary sources on Hume, Hume events, and information on the Hume mailing list.

Edmund Husserl

http://Userzweb.lightspeed.net/~tameri/husserl.html

This page, by Christopher Scott Wyatt tameri@lightspeed.net, provides information on the life and work of Edmund Husserl.

The Husserl Page

http://www.mesa.colorado.edu/~bobsand/husserl.html

This page provides links to a biography, chronological bibliography, announcements, and Husserl-related resources. It is maintained by Bob Sandmeyer bobsand@mesa5.mesa.colorado.edu.

Hypatia of Alexandria

http://www-groups.dcs.st-and.ac.uk:80/~history/Mathematicians/Hypatia.html

An excellent page giving an overview of the life and work of Hypatia, and linking to other pages on this mathematician/astronomer. This site is part of the Mac Tutor History of Mathematics archive at *http://www-groups.dcs.st-and.ac.uk/~history/index.html* and is maintained by John J. O'Connor joc@st-andrews.ac.uk and Edmund F. Robertson efr@st-andrews.ac.uk.

Hypatia of Alexandria

http://cosmopolis.com/people/hypatia.html

This page, maintained by David Fideler as part of a larger project—Philosophy and Cosmological Studies at *http://cosmopolis.com/philosophy/index.html* which is under construction—provides an overview of the life of Hypatia, mathematician, astronomer, and Platonic philosopher, and includes links to various works which detail her life and work.

The Webbing of William James

http://www.strangelove.com/marc/james.html

This page, by Marc Fonda mfonda@magmacom.com, provides links to resources on James' life and writings, including two annotated essays. The site is mirrored at *http://www.clas.ufl.edu/users/gthursby/fonda/james.html.*

Karl Jaspers

http://Userzweb.lightspeed.net/~tameri/jaspers.html

This page offers information on the life and work of existentialist philosopher, Karl Jaspers. It is maintained by Christopher Scott Wyatt tameri@lightspeed.net.

Thomas Jefferson On Politics and Government

http://etext.virginia.edu/jefferson/quotations/

This page is primarily a large selection (over 2100) of quotations from the work of Jefferson, though it does include links to recommended collections of Jefferson's writings, other sites for information on Thomas Jefferson and for sources related to the philosophy of liberty, and discussion groups for issues related to liberty. The site is maintained by Eyler Coates eyler.coates@worldnet.att.net.

The CG Jung Index

http://www.arches.uga.edu/~nautis/

This impressive site provides links to an enormous array of Jungian materials including: an introduction to Jung; Jungian glossary; articles, essays, and interviews; a Jungian journal index; links to other Jung homepages; and much more, including the ability to add your own material to the site. Maintained by Matthew Clapp nautis@arches.uga.edu, this site is certainly worth a visit.

Notes on CG Jung

http://www.strangelove.com/marc/jung01.html

This page, by Marc Fonda mfonda@magmacom.com, provides links to information about Jung's life, his thought, and some publications. The site is mirrored at: *http://www.clas. ufl.edu/users/gthursby/fonda/james.html*.

Kant

http://www.chez.com/kant/

This French-language site provides an introduction to the philosophy of Immanuel Kant, and includes a biography and bibliography. It is maintained by Emmanuel Salé kant@chez.com.

Kant

http://home.t-online.de/home/Winfried.Krauss/kant.htm

This site, from Winfried Krauss Winfried.Krauss@t-online.de and available in German and English, provides links to a range of Kant-related resources.

Immanuel Kant

http://www.fb03.uni-marburg.de/~kant/welcome.htm

This German site, which promises to be an extensive resource on Kant's life and work, is a joint project of the Universities of Marburg, Milan, and Rome. The site's maintainers can be contacted at kantinfo@ps0304.Fb03.Uni-Marburg.DE.

Immanuel Kant

http://www.nobunaga.demon.co.uk/htm/kant.htm

This site, from Shino and Ian Jordan ian@amgmps.com provides links to Kant-related information online.

Immanuel Kant

http://www.ultranet.com/~rsarkiss/KANT.HTM

This site provides a short biography, selected quotations, and links to online texts. It is maintained by Robert Sarkissian rsarkissian@smtp.microcom.com.

Kant on the Web

http://www.hkbu.edu.hk/~ppp/Kant.html

This comprehensive site provides Kant's texts in electronic format, plus lexical aids and articles and books on Kant by Stephen Palmquist, graphical images of Kant, and links to other Kantian resources. It is maintained by StevePq@hkbu.edu.hk.

John Maynard Keynes

http://www-groups.dcs.st-and.ac.uk:80/~history/Mathematicians/Keynes.html

From the Mac Tutor History of Mathematics archive at *http://www-groups.dcs.st-and.ac.uk/ ~history/index.html* maintained by John J O'Connor joc@st-andrews.ac.uk and Edmund F. Robertson efr@st-andrews.ac.uk, this page provides a summary of the life and work of economist, John Maynard Keynes.

Omar Khayyam

http://www-groups.dcs.st-and.ac.uk:80/~history/Mathematicians/Khayyam.html

This page provides an overview of the life and work of poet and mathematician, Omar Khayyam. It is part of the Metaphysics Research Lab site at *http://mally.stanford.edu/ index.html* maintained by Edward N. Zalta zalta@mally.stanford.edu.

Kierkegaard on the Internet

http://www.webcom.com/sk/

An excellent page by Lindso Larsen lindsoe@po.ia.dk providing an introduction to Kierkegaard, his collected works on the web, other web resources, the Kierkegaard web library, news and announcements, and the Kierkegaard discussion forum.

Søren Kierkegaard

http://www.2xtreme.net/dstorm/sk/

A beautifully designed page by D. Anthony Storm dstorm@2xtreme.net, providing a range of Kierkegaard resources.

Søren Kierkegaard

http://www.ultranet.com/~rsarkiss/KIERKE.HTM

This site provides a short biography, selected quotations and links to online texts. It is maintained by Robert Sarkissian *rsarkissian@smtp.microcom.com*.

Kierkegaard Societies & Institutions Worldwide

http://www.utas.edu.au/docs/humsoc/kierkegaard/institutions.html

This site, maintained by Julia Watkin julia.watkin@human.utas.edu.au, provides links to Kierkegaard resources, teaching centers, and societies all over the world.

UG Krishnamurti

http://www.well.com/user/jct/

This page provides extensive resources, including full texts, of the works of Indian thinker UG Krishnamurti, plus articles, texts, and video clips for downloading.

Peter Kropotkin

http://www.pitzer.edu/~dward/Anarchist_Archives/kropotkin/Kropotkinarchive.html

This page, part of the Anarchist Archives *http://www.pitzer.edu/~dward/Anarchist_Archives/anarchy.html* maintained by Dana Ward dward@pitzer.edu, provides a biography, links to collected works, a bibliography, commentaries and graphics of the 'anarchist prince', Peter Kropotkin.

Thomas Kuhn

http://www-elec-eng.scu.edu/kuhn.html

This site from Tim Healy provides a brief overview of Kuhn's work and its effect on our thinking about science.

Corliss Lamont

http://www.corliss-lamont.org/

This site is devoted to the life and work of author, philosopher, and civil libertarian, Corliss Lamont. Included on this site is a copy of Lamont's "The Philosophy of Humanism" for download, plus several multimedia files. The page is maintained by webmaster@ corliss-lamont.org.

Gottfried Wilhelm Leibniz

http://mally.stanford.edu/leibniz.html

This page, part of the Metaphysics Research Lab site at *http://mally.stanford.edu/index.html* maintained by Edward N. Zalta zalta@mally.stanford.edu, provides an overview of the life and work of Liebniz, plus suggestions for further reading.

Gottfried Wilhelm von Leibniz

http://www-groups.dcs.st-and.ac.uk/~history/Mathematicians/Leibniz.html

An excellent page introducing the life and work of Leibniz, this page is part of a larger site—the Mac Tutor History of Mathematics archive at *http://www-groups.dcs.st-and.ac.uk/~history/index.html* and is maintained by John J. O'Connor joc@st-andrews.ac.uk and Edmund F. Robertson efr@st-andrews.ac.uk.

Emmanuel Levinas

http://pw1.netcom.com/~cyberink/lev.html

From Peter Atterton atterton@rohan.sdsu.edu, this page presents a biography and bibliography, plus links to other Levinas resources.

John Locke

http://daemon.ilt.columbia.edu/academic/digitexts/locke/bio_JL.html

From the ILTWeb project at *http://daemon.ilt.columbia.edu/*, this page provides an overview of the life and work of British empiricist John Locke, plus access to an html version of "Of the Conduct of the Understanding," and text versions of Second "Treatise on Civil Government," "A Letter concerning Toleration," "An Essay Concerning Human Understanding," and "Concerning Civil Government, Second Essay."

John Locke

http://www.nobunaga.demon.co.uk/htm/locke.htm

This site, from Shino and Ian Jordan ian@amgmps.com provides a general overview of Locke's ideas and links to Locke materials online.

John Locke

http://www.ultranet.com/~rsarkiss/LOCKE.HTM

This site provides a short biography, selected quotations and links to online texts. It is maintained by Robert Sarkissian rsarkissian@smtp.microcom.com.

Los Angeles Lonergan Center

http://www.concentric.net/~Mmorelli/

The Los Angeles Lonergan Center makes available in a single location a range of research materials for use by visiting scholars. Its web page, maintained by Mark Morelli MMorelli@lmumail.lmu.edu, provides access to numerous Lonergan resources, including: Primary Sources—the Center's collection of published philosophical and theological works, Latin works and English translations, economics manuscripts, course outlines, course transcriptions, transcriptions of lectures, tape recordings and much more; Secondary Materials—lists the Center's holdings including journals, theses and dissertations, books and other reference materials; a link to the Lonergan Philosophical Society, and *Method: Journal of Lonergan Studies*. An excellent site of great value to Lonergan scholars.

The Lonergan Website

http://www.lonergan.on.ca/index.htm

The Lonergan Web Site aims to facilitate Internet-based collaboration among Lonergan scholars and those interested in the work of Jesuit philosopher and theologian, Bernard Longergan. The site offers a comprehensive range of Lonergan-related resources, including primary texts, commentary and book reviews, as well as links to other Lonergan or related sites. Beautifully designed, the site is administered by Paul Allen and Peter L. Monette administrator@lonergan.on.ca.

Niccolo Machiavelli

http://daemon.ilt.columbia.edu/academic/digitexts/machiavelli/bio_machiavelli.html

This page, part of the ILTWeb project at *http://daemon.ilt.columbia.edu/* provides a short summary of the life and work of Machiavelli, plus a hypertext version of his famous work, *The Prince.*

Ernst Mally

http://mally.stanford.edu/mally.html

This page, part of the Metaphysics Research Lab site at *http://mally.stanford.edu/index.html* maintained by Edward N. Zalta zalta@mally.stanford.edu, provides an overview of the life and work of Austrian philosopher, Ernst Mally.

Jacques Maritain Center

http://www.nd.edu/Departments/Maritain/ndjmc.htm

This site provides access to an overview of the work of Maritain, the French Catholic philosopher, plus links to Maritain's works, and various papers, dissertations, and books related to Maritain. The Center can be contacted at Maritain.1@nd.edu.

Karl Marx

http://www.lake.de/home/lake/hydra/marx.html

This page presents links to works by Marx, as well as commentaries and essays. It is maintained by Peter Krapp marx@hydra.lake.de.

Karl Marx

http://www2.rz.hu-berlin.de/~h0444pjf/Marx.html

From Ken Kubota h0444pjf@rz.hu-berlin.de, this page presents a range of links to information on the life and work of Marx.

Marx/Engels Archive

http://csf.colorado.edu/psn/marx/

This site, maintained by Ken Campbell kcampbel@colorado.edu, provides links to electronic texts as well as a photo gallery and biographical information on Marx and Engels.

Alexius Meinong

http://mally.stanford.edu/meinong.html

This page, from the Metaphysics Research Lab site at *http://mally.stanford.edu/index.html* maintained by Edward N. Zalta zalta@mally.stanford.edu, presents information on the life and work of the Austrian philosopher, Alexius Meinong.

Maurice Merleau-Ponty

http://Userzweb.lightspeed.net/~tameri/merleau.html

This page presents information on the life and work of existentialist philosopher, Merleau-Ponty, with links to other existentialist philosophers. It is maintained by Christopher Wyatt tameri@lightspeed.net.

Maurice Merleau-Ponty

http://members.aol.com/KatharenaE/private/Philo/Ponty/ponty.html

This page, part of the Realm of Existentialism site maintained by Katharena Eiermann KatharenaE@aol.com, provides a biography and bibliography, as well as links to related resources.

John Stuart Mill

http://www.cpm.ll.ehime-u.ac.jp/AkamacHomePage/Akamac_E-text_Links/Mill.html

This site gives details of Mill's career and publications, plus links to his autobiography, a bibliography on related works, the texts of *On Liberty*, *The Subjection of Women*, *Utilitarianism*, and others.

Leonard Nelson

http://www.friesian.com/nelson.htm

Maintained by Kelley Ross kross@friesian.com, this site provides information on the life and work of Friesian philosopher, Leonard Nelson.

Friedrich Wilhelm Nietzsche

http://Userzweb.lightspeed.net/~tameri/nietz.html

This page, maintained by Christopher Wyatt tameri@lightspeed.net, provides information on the life and work of influential philosopher Friedrich Nietzsche.

Nietzsche Page

http://www.usc.edu/dept/annenberg/thomas/nietzsche.html

This page, maintained by Douglas Thomas douglast@almaak.usc.edu, provides an online reference for contemporary scholarship about the works of Nietzsche, including: bibliography of Nietzsche's writings, in English and German, Nietzsche societies and organizations, selected writings on Nietzsche, and book reviews.

Rudolph Otto

http://www.netrax.net/~galles/

An excellent resource on the life and work of Rudolph Otto, this page, maintained by Gregory D. Alles galles@ns1.wmc.car.md.us, provides bibliographical materials, selected works, and more.

Rudolph Otto

http://www.friesian.com/otto.htm

Maintained by Kelley Ross kross@friesian.com, this site provides information on the work of Friesian philosopher, Rudolph Otto.

Parmenides

http://home.ican.net/~arandall/Parmenides/

From Allan Randall arandall@ican.net, this page provides a translation of Parmenides' On Nature, a commentary, and references.

Blaise Pascal

http://members.aol.com/KatharenaE/private/Philo/Pascal/pascal.html

This page, part of the Realm of Existentialism site maintained by Katharena Eiermann KatharenaE@aol.com, provides a short biography, links to Pascal's text, and links to other Pacal sources on the net.

Blaise Pascal

http://www.ultranet.com/~rsarkiss/PASCAL.HTM

This site provides a short biography, selected quotations and links to online texts. It is maintained by Robert Sarkissian rsarkissian@smtp.microcom.com.

Jan Patocka

http://www.univie.ac.at/iwm/patocka.htm

Jan Patocka, born in 1907, was a student of Edmund Husserl and Martin Heidegger. He is, along with Thomas Garrigue Masaryk, one of the most important Czech philosophers of this century. This site, from the Institute for Human Sciences, Vienna iwm@iwm. univie.ac.at, provides information on Patocka publications and the Jan Patocka Junior Visiting Fellowships.

risbe: the International Peirce Telecommunity

http://www.door.net/arisbe/

The Peirce Telecommunity Project was established to form a single "place" where everyone in the world who is interested in Peirce or in Peirce-related matters could "go." This site provides access to a number of resources relating to the philosophy of Charles S Peirce, including: biographical information on C. S. Peirce, abstracts of dissertations on Peirce, access to the Peirce-l mailing list and archives, access to other Peirce materials, and access to the Dewey-l mailing list and archives. The site is maintained by Joseph Ransdell ransdell@door.net.

Charles S. Peirce Studies on the Internet

http://www.peirce.org/

This site provides access to hypertext editions of Peirce's works, as well as access to other Peirce resources. Enquiries about the site can be directed to webmaster@peirce.org.

Walker Percy Project

http://sunsite.unc.edu/wpercy/

This site provides access to Percy's biography, essays, scholarly resources and bibliographies, new books on Percy, and the Walker Percy Society.

Plato

http://www.2xtreme.net/dstorm/plato/

This beautifully-designed site, from D. Anthony Storm <u>dstorm@2xtreme.net</u>, is devoted to the writings and writing method of Plato. To that end "A Commentary On Plato's Writings" with links to the works of Plato online has been constructed. Also provided is an introduction to Plato's thought and his method of composition, a bibliography and links to other relevant sites.

Plato

http://www.ultranet.com/~rsarkiss/PLATO.HTM

This site provides a short biography, selected quotations and links to online texts. It is maintained by Robert Sarkissian <u>rsarkissian@smtp.microcom.com</u>.

Plato and His Dialogues

http://phd.evansville.edu/plato.htm

Maintained by Bernard Suzanne <u>bfsuzan@ibm.net</u>, this site provides an overview of Plato's life and main philosophical theories, plus links to Plato resources.

Karl Popper Web

http://www.eeng.dcu.ie/~tkpw/

This is an excellent page providing links to Popper resources including the Popper Newsletter, conference announcements, journals, and more. The page is maintained by Ray Scott Percival <u>100525.373@compuserve.com</u>.

Pierre-Joseph Proudhon

http://www.pitzer.edu/~dward/Anarchist_Archives/proudhon/ Proudhonarchive.html

This site is part of the Anarchist Archives *http://www.pitzer.edu/~dwardAnarchist_Archives/anarchy.html* maintained by Dana Ward <u>dward@pitzer.edu</u>, and provides a biography, links to collected works, a bibliography, commentaries, and graphics of anarchist philosopher, Proudhon.

Willard van Orman Quine

http://users.aol.com/drquine/wv-quine.html

This is a comprehensive page giving a summary of Quine's work, news announcements, and links to a host of Quine-related resources. It is maintained by Douglas Quine <u>drquine@aol.com</u>.

Objectivism and Ayn Rand

http://www.vix.com/pub/objectivism/

This site, currently maintained by Jeff Schachter Schachter@pfc.mit.edu, provides links to FAQs, bibliographies, mailing lists and newsgroups, objectivist organizations, electronic texts, and news and events.

The Objectivists' Ring

http://www.geocities.com/Athens/6234/index.html

The Objectivists' Ring is a collection of web pages authored by various individuals with a focus on objectivism and the philosophy of Ayn Rand. Over fifty individual sites are linked to the ring which is co-ordinated by Timothy D. Chase tchase@shadow.sjcsf.edu.

The Reid Project

http://www.abdn.ac.uk/philosophy/reidstu.htm

The Reid Project aims to stimulate, coordinate, and support interest in Thomas Reid and the Philosophy of Common Sense, their place within the history of philosophy, and their relevance to contemporary philosophical discussion. The project and website are located at the University of Aberdeen, which houses a repository of virutally all of Reid's surviving manuscripts.

Jean Jacques Rousseau

http://daemon.ilt.columbia.edu/academic/digitexts/rousseau/bio_rousseau.html

This site, from the ILTWeb project at *http://daemon.ilt.columbia.edu/* provides a summary of the life and work of Rousseau, a link to a text version of his Confessions, and promises an html version of *Emile* in the near future.

Bertrand Russell Archives

http://www.mcmaster.ca/russdocs/russell.htm

This site provides information on book catalogues, online catalogues, Russell's writings, Russell editorial project, favourite quotations from Russell's work, and courses on Russell's philosophy. Kenneth Blackwell blackwk@mcmaster.ca maintains this site.

George Santayana Home Page

http://members.aol.com/santayana/index.htm

From TP Davis santayana@aol.com, this page provides access to a range of resources including a collection of quotations from the works of George Santayana on recurring themes in his philosophy, electronic versions of Santayana's writings and descriptions of works available in print, items of historical interest, and more.

Jean-Paul Sartre

http://members.aol.com/KatharenaE/private/Philo/Sartre/sartre.html

This page, part of the Realm of Existentialism site maintained by Katharena Eiermann

KatharenaE@aol.com, is by far the best page on Sartre, with links to essays, commentaries and summaries of Sartre's work, and links to related pages.

Jean-Paul Sartre

http://www.knuten.liu.se/~bjoch509/philosophers/sar.html

This page, part of Bjorn's Guide to Philosophy and maintained by Bjorn Christensson bjoch509@knuten.liu.se, provides an extensive biography on Sartre, a list of his works, and links to the ThinkNet Sartre mailing list.

Jean-Paul Sartre

http://www.lcl.cmu.edu/CAAE/80254/Sartre/Sartre.html

This page, maintained by Robert Cavalier rc2z@andrew.cmu.edu as a resource for his students, and which will be further developed over the next year, attempts to define and spell out the key concepts in existentialist thought.

Arthur Schopenhauer

http://www.ultranet.com/~rsarkiss/SCHOPEN.HTM

This site provides a short biography, selected quotations, and links to online texts. It is maintained by Robert Sarkissian rsarkissian@smtp.microcom.com.

Problems from Wilfred Sellars

http://csmaclab-www.uchicago.edu/philosophyProject/sellars/sellars.html

This site is both a moderated forum for discussion and an archive of works by and on Wilfrid Sellars. It is maintained by Andrew Chrucky andchrucky@aol.com.

Adam Smith Page

http://www.efr.hw.ac.uk/EDC/edinburghers/adam-smith.html

This page provides a short biography of Adam Smith.

Socrates: Philosophy's Martyr

http://www.btinternet.com/~socratic/

This site contains substantial excerpts from *Socrates: Philosophy's Martyr*, a brief book for the general reader by Anthony Gottlieb socratic@btinternet.com.

Spinoza

http://www.dircon.co.uk/meta4/spinoza/

This is a beautifully designed site offering an introduction to the life and work of the Dutch philosopher Benedict de Spinoza. The information is divided into three areas: life, philosophy and work, and is maintained by Ian Martin ian@meta4.co.uk.

Spinoza's Insights

http://www.erols.com/jyselman/index.htm

From Joseph B. Yesselman jyselman@erols.com, this site is devoted to the exploration of Spinoza's writings, offering links to electronic texts, a glossary and index of key terms, and links to other Spinoza sites.

Studia Spinoziana

http://frank.mtsu.edu/~rbombard/RB/spinoza.new.html

An excellent page maintained by Ron Bombardi rbombard@frank.mtsu.edu, providing links to Spinoza's Ethics, a logical index to Spinoza's Ethica, a Spinoza chronology, a reading list, and more.

Spinoza Web

http://www.stg.brown.edu/~santiago/SpinozaWeb/

Maintained by Santiago Barona santiago@stg.brown.edu, this page is an excellent resource for those interested in the life and work of Baruch Spinoza. It provides a biography, links to Spinoza's works, and links to other web-based resources.

Introducing Rudolph Steiner

http://www.io.com/~lefty/SteinerIntro.html

This page, from Lefty@apple.com, presents a short biographical essay on Steiner by Owen Barfield.

Max Stirner Web Page

http://www.math.uio.no/~solan/Stirner/stirner-netscape.html

This page, by Svein Olav Nyberg, provides links to resources relating to the work of egoist, Max Stirner. Svein is currently residing in Edingburgh and his Stirner page can also be accessed at *http://www.maths.ed.ac.uk/~solan/stirner/main.html*.

Swedenborg-Oz

http://www.ozemail.com.au/~sllandec/

This is a page devoted to the theological teachings of Emmanuel Swedenborg and offering a biography, as well overviews of various areas of Swedenborg's work. Enquiries about the page can be made to sllandec@swedenborg.com.au.

Henry David Thoreau

http://miso.wwa.com/~jej/1thorea.html

This excellent page from Lorella Thomas FamousUUs@aol.com brings together a biography, portrait and graphics, links to Thoreau's works, analysis and commentary, and links to related information.

Alan Turing

http://www.wadham.ox.ac.uk/~ahodges/Turing.html

A comprehensive site featuring an illustrated biography, a chronology of Turing's life, an annotated bibliography, notes on archives of Turing's manuscripts, and links to many resources related to the work of the famous computer scientist, maintained by Andrew Hodges andrew.hodges@wadh.ox.ac.uk, author of "Alan Turing: The Enigma."

Giambattista Vico Home Page

http://www.connix.com/~gapinton/

From Giorgio A. Pinton gapinton@connix.com, this site includes a biography and chronology of the life of Italian philosopher, Vico, plus overviews and bibliographies relating to each of his major works.

Voltaire

http://www.geocities.com/Athens/7308/

This page provides information on the life and work of Voltaire, with links to a variety of sources on the net. It is maintained by F. DeVenuto.

Simone Weil

http://www.rivertext.com/simone_weil.shtml

This site provides a biographical overview of the life and work of Simone Weil, a contemporary of feminist philosopher Simone de Beauvoir. It is maintained by cafe@rivertext.com.

Otto Weininger on the Internet

http://www.ozemail.com.au/~ksolway/ottow.html

This site provides a reading list and information on the life of Otto Weininger.

Alfred North Whitehead for Dummies

http://www.well.com/user/rcl/wthd.long.html

Its name no doubt inspired by the 'for dummies' series computer books, this site from Richard Lubbock rcl@well.com, aims to introduce readers to the work of Whitehead and process philosophy. Links to mailing lists and process philosophy resources are also included.

Wittgenstein Archives

http://www.hd.uib.no/wab/

The goal of The Wittgenstein Archives at the University of Bergen is to make the complete writings of Wittgenstein available in the form of electronic facsimile and transcriptions. The archives, housed at the University of Bergen, provide an extensive range of Wittgenstein-related resources in addition to transcriptions of his work. The maintainer of the archives can be contacted at wab@hd.uib.no.

Wittgenstein Think Page

http://ucsu.colorado.edu/~biggus/ludwig/

This page, from Jeff Biggus biggus@colorado.edu, presents excerpts from Wittgensten's writings.

Ludwig Wittgenstein

http://www.seanet.com/~john7/wittgenstein/

This site, from John Siebenbaum webmaster@seanet.com, provides an overview of Wittgenstein's writings and a forum for the discussion of Wittgenstein-related philosophical problems. It also includes an archive of LW quotations submitted by visitors, a list of graduate schools with a Wittgensteinian focus, and a list of Wittgenstein scholars.

Ludwig Wittgenstein

http://www.nobunaga.demon.co.uk/htm/witt.htm

This site, from Shino and Ian Jordan ian@amgmps.com, provides links to a range of Wittgenstein information on the net, and will soon include Shino's BA dissertation on Wittgenstein and colour.

Ludwig Wittgenstein

http://www.ultranet.com/~rsarkiss/WITTGEN.HTM

This site provides a short biography, selected quotations, and links to online texts. It is maintained by Robert Sarkissian rsarkissian@smtp.microcom.com.

Arthur M. Young

http://www.arthuryoung.com

This page is devoted to the thought of Arthur Young, inventor of the Bell Helicopter, cosmologist, philosopher, and author of *The Reflexive Universe* and *The Geometry of Meaning*. Young's work addresses issues in physics, mathematics, consciousness and evolution. The site is maintained by Arthur Bloch ab@hypersphere.com.

Great Thinkers: Directories

Anarchist Archive

http://www.pitzer.edu/~dward/Anarchist_Archives/archivehome.html

This site, maintained by Dana Ward dward@pitzer.edu, provides information on key anarchist thinkers, as well as on anarchist movements and history.

Anarchists & Left Libertarians

http://www.tigerden.com/~berios/libertarians.html

This page provides information on left libertarian and anarchist thinkers, "all individuals who have distinguished themselves in the past and present by opposing various forms of coercion, authority and injustice, political and economic, in true libertarian tradition." It is maintained by Jamal Hannah jah@iww.org.

Assembled Philosophers

http://people.delphi.com/gkemerling/ph/

From Garth Kemerling gkemerling@delphi.com, this site contains summaries of the life and work of thirty-seven major figures in Western philosophy, with links to available electronic texts and to other sources of online information.

Celebrities in Cognitive Science

http://carbon.cudenver.edu/~mryder/itc_data/cogsci.html

Maintained by Martin Ryder mryder@www.cudenver.edu, this excellent resource provides links to information (profiles, abstracts, articles, interviews, etc.) on a number of prominent figures—authors, critics, and philosophers—in the field of cognitive science.

DynaWeb's Philosophy Aide

http://www.geocities.com/Athens/4753/

This site specialises in links to particular thinkers, including Plato, Descartes, Locke, Hume, and Freud. It is a small project at present, with plans to expand and include more philosophers.

Everything You Need to Know About History of Philosophy

http://www.arts.ubc.ca/~irvine/eyntk1.html

Compiled by Andrew Irvine irvine@unixg.ubc.ca, this page provides an insight into earlier thinkers by linking select quotations on thinkers from ancient, medieval, renaissance, early and late modern periods.

Everything You Need to Know About Contemporary Philosophy

http://www.arts.ubc.ca/~irvine/eyntk2.html

Compiled by Andrew Irvine irvine@unixg.ubc.ca, this page provides an insight into the thoughts of contemporary philosophers—including Dewey, Whitehead, Russell, Einstein, Neurath, Weyl, Wittgenstein, Popper, Sartre, Arendt, Austin, Godel, Quine, Warnock, Armstrong, and Cartwright—by providing select quotations from each of them.

Great Thinkers and Visionaries

http://www.lucifer.com/~sasha/thinkers.html

This page by Alexander Chislenko sasha1@netcom.com, provides links to web pages and news on a host of 'great thinkers' in a variety of fields including philosophy, science, and literature.

Here Madam

http://tqd.advanced.org/3075/

This site gives a brief overview of some of the major philosophical schools of thought, historical periods, and thinkers. It also provides some links to further resources on particular thinkers.

Historians and Philosophers

http://dorit.ihi.ku.dk/~peterr/histphil.html

This page, from Peter Ravn Rasmussen peterr@dorit.ihi.ku.dk, provides links to biographical and related information, and to electronic texts of historians and philosophers from the classical period through to the modern period.

Hyper-Weirdness by World Wide Web: Philosophy Page

http://www.physics.wisc.edu/~shalizi/hyper-weird/philosophy.html

A hypertext version by shalizi@phenxa.physics.wisc.edu, of Mitchell Porter's High Weirdness by E-Mail. Provides links primarily to electronic texts covering a vast range of philosophers including Aristotle, Plato and the Ancients, Descartes, Hobbes, Locke, Marx, Mill, and more contemporary philosophers.

Living Philosophers

http://www.rpi.edu/~cearls/real.philosophers.html

This page by Sean Cearley cearls@rpi.edu, provides links to pages and information on living philosophers.

MacTutor History of Mathematics Archive: Great Mathematicians

http://www-groups.dcs.st-and.ac.uk:80/~history/BiogIndex.html

This site provides biographies as well as links to further information on a number of great thinkers in the field of mathematics. The information can be searched alphabetically or chronologically.

Philosopher's Almanac

http://www.muohio.edu/~phlcwis/philosophers/

This site provides a range of resources on philosophers including Aquinas, Aristotle,

Augustine, Berkeley, Boethius, Descartes, Epictetus, Frege, Heidegger, Hobbes, Hume, Kant, Leibniz, Locke, Marx, Mill, Nietzsche, Peirce, Plato, Plotinus, and Russell. This site is currently maintained by Shannon Sullivan sullivs@muohio.edu.

Philosophers' Gallery

http://watarts.uwaterloo.ca/PHIL/cpshelle/Gallery/gallery.html

Sure, you've read their books, but what did they look like? Now you can see your favourite philosopher's mug shot. This site is maintained by cpshelle@watarts.uwaterloo.ca.

Philosophers' Home Pages

http://users.ox.ac.uk/~worc0337/phil_pages.html

This site brings together a collection of home pages of philosophers, including academics, philosophy graduates, and even undergraduates. It is maintained by Peter King peter.king@philosophy.ox.ac.uk.

Prominent Anarchists and Left-Libertarians

http://tigerden.com/~berios/libertarians.html

This page lists mainly biographical information, but provides some links to further information on a range of anarchist thinkers. It is maintained by jah@iww.org.

The Window: Philosophy on the Internet

http://www.trincoll.edu/~phil/philo/

This site, maintained by Chris Marvin cmarvin@trincoll.edu, provides links to philosophy resources, particularly biographical information on dozens of major philosophers.

History of Philosophy & Ideas

African and African-American History of Ideas

http://home.sn.no/~tadesse/

Melaku Tadesse tadesse@sn.no has created this page which focuses on African and African-American philosophies with sections on logic, metaphysics and epistemology, and links to various resources including a bibliography.

British Society for the History of Philosophy

http://www.leeds.ac.uk/philosophy/bshp/bshp.htm

The British Society for the History of Philosophy (BSHP), launched in 1984, exists to promote and foster all aspects of the study and teaching of the history of philosophy. This website provides information on the aims and activities of the Society, its newsletter, and conference information. The site is maintained by Mike Beaney m.a.beaney@leeds.ac.uk.

Everything You Need to Know About History of Philosophy

http://www.arts.ubc.ca/~irvine/eynyk1.htm

Compiled by Andrew Irvine irvine@unixg.ubc.ca, this page provides an insight into earlier thinkers by linking select quotations on thinkers from ancient, medieval, renaissance, early and late modern periods.

Historians and Philosophers

http://dorit.ihi.ku.dk/~peterr/histphil.html

As part of a larger history-oriented project, Peter Ravn Rasmussen peterr@dorit.ihi.ku.dk has created this page which provides links to other sources of information on historians and philosophers, grouped according to historical period: classical, medieval and renaissance, early modern, and modern. Peter's history page is located at *http://dorit.ihi.ku.dk/~peterr/history.html* and provides information and links to other sources on various historical periods.

History of Ancient Philosophy

http://weber.u.washington.edu/~smcohen/phil320.htm

This site, from S. Marc Cohen smcohen@u.washington.edu, is intended as a guide for students of his History of Ancient Philosophy class, but it is an excellent resource for anyone interested in the area. Included are lecture notes, links to electronic texts, and links to other ancient philosophy resources.

History of Economic Thought

http://socserv2.socsci.mcmaster.ca:80/~econ/ugcm/3ll3/index.html

This site provides an overview of thinkers in the history of economic thought, including: Marx, Mill, Godwin, Locke, Rousseau, and more. It is maintained by Rod Hay hay@sscl.uwo.ca, and mirrored at: *http://melbecon.unimelb.edu.au/het/* and also at: *http://www.ecn.bris.ac.uk/het/index.htm*.

History of Economics Internet Resources

http://cfec.vub.ac.be/cfec/hope.htm

This site, from Bert Mosselmans bmosselm@vnet3.vub.ac.be, includes an extensive range of links to resources relating to the history of economics, political economy, and related fields. Resources are grouped into the following areas: general references, classical political economy, Marxism, neoclassical economics, Keynesianism, specific topics, organizations, forthcoming conferences, and interdisciplinary issues.

History of Western Philosophy

http://people.delphi.com/gkemerling/hy/

From Garth Kemerling gkemerling@delphi.com, this site offers a narrative survey of the historical development of Western philosophy, from ancient, through medieval, to modern philosophy.

Philosophy

http://www.geocities.com/Athens/Acropolis/4349/philos.htm

This page, by Anjoum Noorani anj@ooh.dircon.co.uk, gives a brief overview of the history of philosophy in an attempt to explain what philosophy is.

A Timeline of Western Philosophers

http://people.delphi.com/gkemerling/dy/zt.htm

Beginning with Thales, Anaximander & Anaximenes, and continuing to the present day to Dennett and Singer, this timeline of western philosophy, from Garth Kemerling gkemerling@delphi.com, provides students with an overview of the evolution of philosophical thought.

Logic & Philosophy of Science

12th Century Logic HomePage

http://iwakuma.ecn.fpu.ac.jp/

This page, maintained by IWAKUMA Yukio yukio@fpu.ac.jp, provides access to various papers and resources in Medieval Logic.

Advances in Modal Logic

http://turing.wins.uva.nl/~mdr/AiML/

This page contains general information on the Advances in Modal Logic initiative, a bi-annual book and workshop series held at various locations throughout the world. The page is maintained by Maarten de Rijke mdr@wins.uva.nl.

Association for Symbolic Logic

http://www.math.uiuc.edu/~asl/

This site provides information on the Association, as well as meetings, conferences and announcements, and a link to the *Bulletin of Symbolic Logic*. The site is maintained by adam@math.uiuc.edu.

Association for the Foundations of Science

http://pespmc1.vub.ac.be/AFOS/

AFOS afos@plearn.edu.pl is an international professional association of working scientists, theorists of science, linguists, and logicians that was founded in 1993. This site provides detailed information on AFOS and links to its mailing list.

Australian Logic Home Page

http://www.cse.unsw.edu.au/~ksg/AusLogic/

This site, maintained by Maurice Pagnucco morri@cse.unsw.edu.au provides links to a variety of logic resources, and information on Australian events for logicians and students of logic.

Beginner's Guide to Research in the History of Science

http://www.kaiwan.com/~lucknow/horus/guide/tp1.html

From Ronald Tobey lucknow@kaiwan.com, this is an online version of a book published in 1995, and provides information and advice for students of the history of science.

Bertrand

http://www.humnet.ucla.edu/humnet/phil/grads/herzberg/Bertrand.html

Bertrand is symbolic logic software for the Macintosh, which may be downloaded from this site. Using a decomposition/instantiation algorithm inspired by the "consistency tree" method found in Leblanc and Wisdom's textbook *Deductive Logic*, Bertrand solves sets of first-order symbolic logic statements (subject-identity supported) for satisfiability (consistency), validity, and equivalence. It also checks single statements for "logical truth" and "logical falsity," and produces truth-tables for single truth-functional statements. The site is maintained by Larry Herzberg herzberg@humnet.ucla.edu.

British Logic Colloquim

http://www-theory.dcs.st-and.ac.uk/~rd/blc/

The BLC aims to advance the education of the public within Great Britain and Northern Ireland in the study of formal or mathematical logic and other subjects in so far as they relate to such logic. This web site provides information on the activities of the BLC, links to logic-related resources, and is maintained by Roy Dyckhoff rd@dcs.st-and.ac.uk.

British Society for Philosophy of Science

http://www.dur.ac.uk/~dfl0www/bsps/BSPSHome.html

This site provides information on the activities of the BSPS which publishes the *British Journal for Philosophy of Science*. This page is maintained by Ginny Watkins.

Category Theory

http://math.rutgers.edu/~mauri/categories.html

This site, maintained by Luca Mauri mauri@math.rutgers.edu, provides resources and information on category theory including links to *Theory and Applications of Categories* (an electronic journal) American Mathematical Society preprint server for category theory, abstracts and papers, events relevant to the topic, mailing list information, links to people and departments working on category theory, and links to other pages with relevant information.

Christian Gottschall's Gateway to Logic

http://logik.phl.univie.ac.at/~chris/formular-uk.html

This page, in German and English versions, provides access to logic software including a proof checker, proof builder and client and server side processors which handle Parse trees, alpha graphs (Peirce), Begriffsschrift notation (Frege), Polish notation, truth tables, normal forms, miscellaneous operations in classical propositional logic and some multi-valued logics. Christian can be contacted at chris@logik.phl.univie.ac.at.

Computational Logic, St. Andrews

http://www-theory.dcs.st-and.ac.uk/Groups/logic.html

This research project, headed by Roy Dyckhoff rd@dcs.st-and.ac.uk, comprises the development of proof assistants and theorem-provers for various logics. The site lists recent publications of the project staff, and provides access to logic software, the Logic Work Bench Project at Bern, the AI repository as CMU, and the Computational Logic Network.

Critical Thinking Core Concepts

http://www.kcmetro.cc.mo.us/longview/ctac/corenotes.htm

From Longview Community College, this site provides an excellent introduction to basic logic, including a short history of logic, a discussion of symbolic vs. informal logic, and an introduction to logical vocabulary.

Description Logics

http://www.ida.liu.se/labs/iislab/people/patla/DL/index.html

This site provides access to resources for those interested in or doing research in description logics. The site is maintained by Patrick Lambrix patla@ida.liu.se.

Ethics & Genetics: A Global Conversation

http://www.med.upenn.edu/~bioethic/genetics.html

What do you think about genetic testing, genetic enhancement, gene therapy, genetic engineering? This "electric conversation" lets you post your comments instantly and engage in live conversation with any of the hundreds who visit our site every week. Ten researchers in the field serve as discussants, posting remarks, papers, and comments upon which visitors can comment. The site is maintained by Glenn McGee mcgee@ mail.med.upenn.edu.

Evolution, Complexity & Philosophy

http://www.sepa.tudelft.nl/webstaf/hanss/evolu.htm

This site provides links to resources in biological evolutionary and ecological theory, artificial intelligence, chaos theory, memetics, and related areas of philosophy. It is maintained by Hans-Cees A.M. Speel hanss@sepa.tudelft.nl.

FoLLI: The European Association for Logic, Language, and Information

http://www.wins.uva.nl/research/folli/

FoLLI was founded in 1991 to advance the practising of research and education on the interfaces between Logic, Linguistics, Computer Science and Cognitive Science, and related disciplines in Europe. The website provides information on the activities of the Association, including its newsletter, journal, summer schools and conferences.

Fuzzy Logic FAQ

http://www.cs.cmu.edu/Web/Groups/AI/html/faqs/ai/fuzzy/part1/faq.html

From the newsgroup com.ai.fuzzy, this list of Frequently Asked Questions (and their answers), provides an extensive source of information on fuzzy logic.

History of Science Society

http://weber.u.washington.edu/~hssexec/index.html

This site provides information on the Society's activities, meetings, and membership, and provides links to research tools, information on employment and research opportunities, and various competitions. The Executive of HSS can be contacted at hssexec@u.washington.edu.

History of Science, Technology, and Medicine

http://www.asap.unimelb.edu.au/hstm/hstm_ove.htm

This page which is part of the WWW Virtual Library series, contains a range of information including: bibliographies, organizations and conferences, specialised collections and documents, women scientists, biographical dictionary, historical directory of scientific institutions and organizations, museums, exhibitions and images, electronic journals, email discussion lists and, news groups. The page is maintained by Tim Sherratt Tim.Sherratt@asap.unimelb.edu.au.

Hypertext Bibliography of Measures of Complexity

http://www.fmb.mmu.ac.uk/~bruce/combib

This is a bibliography produced by Bruce Edmonds B.Edmonds@mmu.ac.uk covering some of the philosophical and practical references to the concept and measurement of Complexity. It does not attempt to cover all the new sciences that might come under the "Complexity" banner, unless they are relevant to the idea of Complexity per se.

Indiana University: Program in Pure and Applied Logic

http://www.phil.indiana.edu/~iulg/iulg.html

Information about the IU course in pure and applied logic can be found at this site. Enquiries can be directed to iulg@phil.indiana.edu.

Informal Fallacies

http:www.drury.edu/faculty/Ess/Logic/Informal/Overview.html

From Charles Ess DRU001D@vma.smsu.edu, this site provides a guide to logical fallacies, grouped into three sections: fallacies of relevance, fallacies of presumption, and additional fallacies, and written as a guide for undergraduate students.

Institute for Logic, Language, and Computation

http://www.fwi.uva.nl/research/illc/

The Institute illc@fwi.uva.nl is located at the University of Amsterdam and its web page provides information on courses and syllabi, research conducted at the Institute, newsletters and publications, and information on forthcoming events relevant to the work of the Institute.

Kurt Goedel Society

http://www.logic.tuwien.ac.at/kgs/home.html

An international organization for the promotion and research in all areas of logic, in philosophy, and in history of mathematics. Access information about the activities of the Society, and information on membership. The Society can be contacted through its secretary Karin Horwein karin@logic.tuwien.ac.at.

Laboratory for Applied Logic

http://lal.cs.byu.edu/

The Laboratory for Applied Logic is a research unit of the Department of Computer Science at Brigham Young University. The laboratory specialises in applying mathematical methods to problems in computer dependability. This page includes section on formal methods, research projects (modelling abstract hardware components, verified computer systems, and WWW technologies), papers, and technical reports. The site is maintained by Paul Black black@cs.byu.edu.

Linear Logic

http://www.csl.sri.com/linear/sri-csl-ll.html

This site, maintained by Patrick Lincoln Lincoln@csl.sri.com, provides an introduction to linear logic, and papers, bibliographies, and course materials for those researching or teaching linear logic.

Logic

http://people.delphi.com/gkemerling/lg/

The treatment of elementary logic on this site, from Garth Kemerling gkemerling@ delphi.com, closely follows the structure, content, and nomenclature of Copi and Cohen's, *Introduction to Logic* (9th Ed.) (New York: Macmillan, 1994). It includes discussion of: Logical Arguments, Language and Logic, Informal Fallacies, Definition and Meaning, Categorical Propositions, Categorical Syllogisms, Syllogistic in Ordinary Language, Symbolic Representation, Proving Validity and Invalidity, Quantification Theory, Analogical Argument, Causal Reasoning, Scientific Explanation, and Probability.

LogicAL: Logic, Philosophy, and Artificial Life Resources

http://uu-gna.mit.edu:8001/~napoli/LAMBDA/logical.html

A comprehensive site with links to resources divided into the following categories: Logic through History, Logic and Philosophy, Logic and Education, Logic and Mathematics, Logic and Computation, Fuzzy Logic, Automata and Systems, and Meetings and Conferences. The site is maintained by S. Kritikos napoli@sturgeon.mit.edu.

The Logic Daemon

http://logic.tamu.edu/

Enter a sequent to prove, then enter your proof, press a button, and watch the Colin Allen's colin-allen@tamu.edu logic daemon do its thing checking the validity of your proofs. This site will no doubt be of enormous help to logic students. An alternative service via email to logic@tam2000.tamu.edu is also offered.

Logic Group Preprint Series

http://www.phil.ruu.nl:80/home/marco/preprints.html

This page, maintained at the University of Utrecht Philosophy Department by Marco Hollenberg hollenb@phil.ruu.nl, provides access to a series of preprints in logic.

Logic, Language, and Reasoning Web

http://medlar.doc.ic.ac.uk/

The Logic, Language, and Reasoning Web page is sponsored by the research group on Language and Reasoning Agents whose active research interests include logics of practical reasoning, natural language processing, and multi-agent systems. Enquiries about the page can be directed to rjc@doc.ic.ac.uk.

Logic Notation on the Web

http://www.earlham.edu/~peters/writing/logicsym.htm

So far HTML does not support most of the symbols which make up standard logic notation. On this page, Peter Suber peters@earlham.edu, provides links to information about the development of HTML to support logic notation, and pages which provide alternative solutions.

Logic Puzzles

http://einstein.et.tudelft.nl/~arlet/puzzles/logic.html

From Arlet Ottins arlet@dutecai.et.tudelft.nl, this page provides some fun logic puzzles and their solutions.

Logic Server

http://logik.phl.univie.ac.at/

The logic server, maintained by Christian Gottschall chris@logik.phl.univie.ac.at, is a collection of logic-related resources including an introductory text on logic, exercises for the beginner logician, and access to a range of logic-related software.

MacTutor History of Mathematics Archive: Great Mathematicians

http://www-groups.dcs.st-and.ac.uk:80/~history/BiogIndex.html

This site provides biographies as well as links to further information on a number of great thinkers in the field of mathematics. The information can be searched alphabetically or chronologically. The sites creators are John O'Connor joc@st-andrews.ac.uk and Edmund Robertson efr@st-andrews.ac.uk.

Mathematical Logic Around the World

http://www.uni-bonn.de/logic/world.html

This site, created by Boris Piwinger 3.14@Uni-Bonn.de, links to logic resources, projects and teaching at various universities and centers around the world. The site also provides a logic preprint service.

Medieval Logic and Philosophy

http://www.phil.indiana.edu/~spade/

This page, from Paul Vincent Spade spade@indiana.edu, provides links to resources in medieval logic and philosophy. It includes email addresses of others working in this field, a section called 'Questions and Requests' where Paul provides a place to post requests for information so that others visiting the site might offer assistance, the obligatory page of links, and a variety of papers which can be downloaded and read with the Adobe Acrobat reader.

Minnesota Center for Philosophy of Science

http://www.umn.edu/mcps/center/mcps.html

The University of Minnesota houses the Minnesota Center for Philosophy of Science (MCPS)—the oldest center for philosophy of science in the world. Founded by Herbert Feigl in 1953 the Center is a research unit whose members include faculty from a variety of units on the Twin Cities campus. It is the source of the series *Minnesota Studies in the Philosophy of Science*, published by the University of Minnesota Press. Overall, the Minnesota Center for Philosophy of Science represents one the world's largest co ncentrations of resources for the study of philosophy of science. This site, maintained by Steve Lelchuk mcps@maroon.tc.umn.edu, provides information on the activities of the Center and links to resources in philosophy of science.

New Foundations

http://math.idbsu.edu/~holmes/holmes/nf.html

This page, by Randall Holmes holmes@math.idbsu.edu, provides information and resources related to the set theory "New Foundations," first introduced by W. V. O. Quine in 1937.

Paul Wong's Logic Page

http://www.sfu.ca/philosophy/paulwong.htm#Logic

Paul Wong's wongas@arp.anu.edu.au page provides extensive links to logic and related resources, as well as more general philosophy links. The page can also be found at *http://arp.anu.edu.au/~wongas/#Logic*.

Philosophy of Science & Information Technology: A Tribute to Thomas Kuhn

http://www.brint.com/kuhn.htm

This site is a collection of online papers influenced by the work of Thomas Kuhn.

Philosophy of Science and Mathematics: Events in Britain

http://www.herts.ac.uk/humanities/philosophy/philsci.html

From this site, maintained by Brendan Larvor B.P.Larvor@HERTS.AC.UK, visitors can access information on events in philosophy of science in Britain and abroad. Access to information pertaining to the British Society for Philosophy of Science, the

British Society for Philosophy of Mathematics, and lists of philosophy of science re-sources is also provided.

Philosophy of Science Association

http://scistud.umkc.edu/psa/

This site, maintained by George Gale ggale@cctr.umkc.edu and Elam O'Renick eorenick@umkc.edu, provides links to the association's mailing list, journal, and newsletter.

Philosophy of Science Society, Japan

http://cogsci.l.chiba-u.ac.jp/PSSJ/pssj.html

This site provides access to the Society's mailing list and journal (in Japanese), as well as links to philosophy of science resources.

Paradoxes, Valdosta State University

gopher://catfish.valdosta.peachnet.edu:70/11/ccr/subjv/phi/paradoxes

From this gopher site, you can access a variety of puzzles and Paradoxes including: logic puzzles, induction puzzles, black hole paradox, and Newcomb paradox. Enquiries about the site can be made to Ron Barnette rbarnett@grits.valdosta.peachnet.edu.

Quadralay's Fuzzy Logic Archive

http://www.quadralay.com/Fuzzy

This site, provided by Quadralay WebMistress@quadralay.com, provides access to fuzzy logic FAQs, brief course in fuzzy logic, fuzzy logic for beginners, fuzzy logic international, Erick Horskotte on fuzzy logic, and the fuzzy email server.

Stephen's Guide to Logical Fallacies

http://www.assiniboinec.mb.ca/user/downes/fallacy/fall.htm

The point of an argument is to give reasons in support of some conclusion. An argument commits a fallacy when the reasons offered do not support the conclusion. These pages, by Stephen Downes downes@adminnet.assiniboinec.mb.ca, describe the known logical falla-cies, and are an excellent teaching resource.

Medieval Thought & Philosophy

12th Century Logic HomePage

http://iwakuma.ecn.fpu.ac.jp/

This page, maintained by IWAKUMA Yukio yukio@fpu.ac.jp, provides access to various papers and resources in Medieval Logic.

Aquinas

http://www.epas.utoronto.ca:8080/~loughlin/index.html

Part of Stephen Loughlin's loughlin@chass.utoronto.ca home page, this page provides biographical details on Aquinas, as well as links to Aquinas' works.

St. Thomas Aquinas

http://www.ultranet.com/~rsarkiss/AQUINAS.HTM

This site provides a short biography, selected quotations and links to online texts. It is maintained by Robert Sarkissian rsarkissian@smtp.microcom.com.

St. Thomas Aquinas Five Ways

http://members.aol.com/plweiss1/aquinas.htm

Maintained by Patricia Weiss patricia-w@worldnet.att.net, this web page details Aquinas' arguments for the existence of God and provides a link to a page on Paley's Teleological Argument.

Argos

http://argos.evansville.edu/

Argos is a limited area search engine, specialising in indexing resources in ancient and medieval studies.

Augustine

http://ccat.sas.upenn.edu/jod/augustine.html

Maintained by James O'Donnell jod@ccat.sas.upenn.edu, this site provides access to electronic texts and translations, commentaries, research materials and essays, and other miscellaneous Augustine resources.

St. Augustine

http://www.ultranet.com/~rsarkiss/AUGUST.HTM

This site provides a short biography, selected quotations and links to online texts. It is maintained by Robert Sarkissian rsarkissian@smtp.microcom.com.

Boethius

http://ccat.sas.upenn.edu/jod/boethius.html

This page was created for the 1994 Boethius Internet seminar at University of Pennsylvania and is an index to the materials for that course. The page will continue to be maintained as a resource for students and scholars. For further information contact James O'Donnell jod@ccat.sas.upenn.edu.

The Labyrinth: WWW Server for Medieval Studies

http://www.georgetown.edu/labyrinth/

This comprehensive site, sponsored by Georgetown University, includes a library of electronic texts, bibliographies, pedagogical resources, and Medieval Studies text, image, and archival databases.

Late Medieval and Early Modern Intellectual History

http://www.mq.edu.au/~ockham/

Maintained by R. J. Kilcullen john.kilcullen@mq.edu.au, this site provides access to electronic texts, commentaries, and lectures from his Late Medieval philosophy class, covering the thought of Scotus, Ockham, Wyclif, Buridan, and Grotius.

The Library of the Medieval Institute

http://www.nd.edu/~medvllib/

From the University of Notre Dame comes this electronic sampling of the vast resources of the Library of the Medieval Institute. The page is under construction by Marina Smyth Marina.B.Smyth.2@nd.edu, but promises much more in the future.

Medieval and Later Medieval Philosophy

http://www.mq.edu.au/~ockham/0pge5260.html

This page provides access to transcripts of lectures from courses in Medieval and Late Medieval Philosophy by R. J. Kilcullen john.kilcullen@mq.edu.au of Macquarie University, Australia. The courses cover the works of thinkers including: Boethius, Anselm, Abelard, Aquinas, Scotus, and Ockham.

Medieval Logic and Philosophy

http://www.phil.indiana.edu/~spade/

This page, from Paul Vincent Spade spade@indiana.edu, provides links to resources in medieval logic and philosophy. It includes email addresses of others working in this field, a section called 'Questions and Requests' where Paul provides a place to post requests for information so that others visiting the site might offer assistance, the obligatory page of links, and a variety of papers which can be downloaded and read with the Adobe Acrobat reader.

Medieval Studies Institute: University of Fribourg (Switzerland)

http://www.unifr.ch/iem/welcome.html

The Medieval Studies Institute of the University of Fribourg is part of the Arts Faculty. It endeavours to promote and coordinate research and teaching in all fields related to the study of medieval civilization. This site provides information on the research projects currently undertaken at the Institute, as well as providing links to other medieval resources. The page is available in French and German language versions, and is maintained by Alain Nadeau alain.nadeau@unifr.ch.

Medieval Studies Resources

http://info.ox.ac.uk/departments/humanities/med.html

Part of the Humbul Gateway series, this site provides links to a range of medieval resources, and is maintained by Chris Stephens christopher.stephens@oucs.ox.ac.uk.

Medieval Women

http://www.millersv.edu/~resound/women.html

This is an excellent site providing access to an extensive range of information on women and women's issues in medieval times. Maintained by Bonnie Duncan bduncan@ marauder.millersv.edu, there is also an extensive list of links to other medieval sites.

Netserf: The Internet Connection for Medieval Resources

http://www.cua.edu/www/hist/netserf/

This is a beautifully-designed (but slow-loading) page which provides a searchable list of medieval resources including sections on medieval architecture, drama, art, culture, history, archaeology, and more. It is maintained by Beau A.C. Harbin 59harbin@cua.edu.

Online Medieval and Classical Library

http://sunsite.berkeley.edu/OMACL/

The Online Medieval and Classical Library (OMACL) is a collection of some of the most important literary works of Classical and Medieval civilization. The Library can be searched by keywords, and browsing by author, genre, or language is supported. Douglas B. Killings DeTroyes@EnterAct.Com is responsible for the project.

ORB: Online Reference Book for Medieval Studies

http://orb.rhodes.edu/

This site provides an array of references including the ORB Encyclopedia: An index of original essays, arranged by topic, the Online Medieval Sourcebook which provides resources for teaching, and the ORB reference shelf. Enquiries about ORB should be directed to Caroline Schriber schriber@rhodes.edu.

Websites Relevant to Medieval Studies

http://orb.rhodes.edu/websites.html

Maintained by Douglas B. Killings DeTroyes@EnterAct.COM, this site provides links to an impressive range of medieval studies resources including conference information, databases, general resources, graphics, journals and newsletters, language resources, libraries and museums, literature and manuscripts, maps and cartography, university medieval studies departments, and various miscellaneous resources.

WWW Medieval Resources

http://ebbs.english.vt.edu/medieval/medieval.ebbs.html

Access is provided to a host of medieval sites including discussion lists, texts, databases, archives of medieval art and other resources, medieval science sites, and a variety of miscellaneous medieval information. The site is maintained by Dan Mosser Dan.Mosser@vt.edu.

Yahoo: Medieval Studies

http://www.yahoo.com/Arts/Humanities/History/Medieval_Studies/

This is the Yahoo net directory's list of medieval studies resources.

Metaphysics & Epistemology

Actualism

http://www.csulb.edu/~pmartin/research.html

This page presents some issues relating to modal actualism, the view that there neither are nor could have been any objects that don't exist: it's necessary that everything whatever exists. Maintained by Paul Martin pmartin@csulb.edu, the page promised to grow to include topics such as: actualism and Kripke semantics, actualism and quantification, actualism and iterated modalities, serious actualism, and the demon existentialism.

Brock's Philosophy Page: Metaphysics

http://www.magibox.net/~brock/philosophy/

This page, maintained by Carl Brock Sides cbks@magibox.net, provides a range of papers written on metaphysics-related topics.

Center for Meaning and Metaphysical Studies

http://www.herts.ac.uk/humanities/Res-hum-philcentre.html

The Center for Meaning and Metaphysical Studies, located at the University of Hertfordshire, promotes and encourages quality research into the philosophical study of any aspect of meaning, metaphysics or the relation (or lack thereof) between the two. Although the Center's concerns are philosophical, it encourages collaborative and interdisciplinary discussion. This site, maintained by T. Welling t.d.welling@herts.ac.uk, provides information on the activities of the Center.

Metaphysics: Multiple Meanings

http://websyte.com/alan/metamul.htm

This site, maintained by Alan Anderson caa@gis.net, explains—with links to additional online resources—the difference between popular and academic conceptions of metaphysics.

Metaphysics Research Lab at CSLI

http://mally.stanford.edu/

The Metaphysics Research Lab is located in the Center for the Study of Language and Information at Stanford University. The Web server provides information about the research conducted in the lab, and in particular, about the axiomatic theory of abstract objects being developed there. The site is maintained by Edward N. Zalta zalta@mally. stanford.edu.

Monorealism: Philosophy of the Real World

http://www.onthenet.com.au/~thinker/

Maintained by Robin Craig thinker@onthenet.com.au, this site provides extensive information on monorealism "which is much like Ayn Rand's Objectivism."

Non-Linear Philosophy

http://home.fia.net/~n4bz/Nonlinhm.htm

Linear philosophy—the idea that everything that exists is connected through cause and effect to everything else that exists—came into its own with Descartes in the seventeenth century. But it is an assumption. Non-linear philosophy simply sets that assumption aside and examines the universe as connected through complex organization. This page provides online access to the published writings of Wallace H. Provost Jnr n4bz@fia.net, and invites comment and criticism from readers, which will be placed online for others to view.

Ontologies and Knowledge Sharing

http://www-ksl.stanford.edu/kst/ontology-sources.html

This page, maintained by Adam Farquhar afarquhar@ksl.stanford.edu, provides an extensive range of links to resources on ontology. It includes links to specific ontological projects, general resources, sources for implemented ontologies, and workshops and conferences.

Ontology: SUNY at Buffalo

http://wings.buffalo.edu/philosophy/ontology/

The SUNY ontology site contains information on ontology, on the history of ontology, and on contemporary ontology and its applications. It also provides links to other ontology sites and announcements of relevant conferences and publications. This well-designed site is maintained by Barry Smith phismith@acsu.buffalo.edu.

Ontology

http://mnemosyne.itc.it:1024/ontology.html

This site provides an exhaustive list of projects, people, conferences, and specific resources on ontology and related fields. It is maintained by Enrico Franconi franconi@irst.itc.it.

Ontology: A Resource Page

http://www.csi.uottawa.ca/dept/Ontology/

Maintained by Doug Skuce doug@csi.uottawa.ca, this page provides links to a range of resources on ontology including workshops and conferences, research groups, specific ontologies, and related resource pages.

Perspectivism

http://www.stud.his.no/~onar/Ess/Perspectivism.html

This page by Onar Am onar@hsr.no, is an essay describing perspectivism, and provides links to explanatory resources.

Sensation and Perception Links

http://www.guam.net/home/bmarmie/sandp.html

From William R. Marmie bmarmie@kuentos.guam.net, this site houses a collection of links on sensation and perception including: 3D pictures, optical illusions; tutorials on receptive fields and Fourier analysis and synthesis; an extensive collection of auditory samples to demonstrate things like auditory science analysis, pitch perception, and Shepard scales; and a philosophical essay on the history of the epistemological problem posed by the Necker Cube.

Philosophy of Mind, AI, & Cognitive Science

Artificial Intelligence

http://www.cs.reading.ac.uk/people/dwc/ai.html

This site provides information on research sites and projects on AI, newsgroups, programming languages, journals, commercial sites and products, and links to a range of information on AI. It is maintained by D.W. Corne D.W.Corne@reading.ac.uk.

Artificial Life Online

http://alife.santafe.edu/

This site, located at the Santa Fe Institute, provides links to artificial life information and software, John von Neumann Universal Constructor, genetic algorithms, genetic programming, neural nets, FAQs, and more. This online service is an experiment by MIT Press in electronic distribution of scientific information. It is a supplement to the *Artificial Life Journal*. The page's editor can be contacted at www-editor@alife.santafe.edu.

Association for the Scientific Study of Consciousness

http://www.phil.vt.edu/ASSC/

ASSC promotes rigorous analytic research on consciousness. The official purpose of the organization is to encourage research within cognitive science, neuroscience, philosophy, and other relevant disciplines in the sciences and humanities, directed toward understanding the nature, function, and underlying mechanisms of consciousness. Any solid research on consciousness falls within ASSC's area of interest. This site, maintained by Valerie Gray Hardcastle valerie@vt.edu, provides information on the Society's by-laws, membership, and links to relevant research materials.

Automated Reasoning Project, ANU

http://arp.anu.edu.au/home.html

This page provides information on research staff and students, as well as access to software developed by the project team, including: FINDER (Finite Domain Enumerator), MaGIC (Matrix Generator for Implication Connectives), Kripke (A theorem prover for the relevant logic LR). Enquiries about the site can be directed to its head, John Slaney John.Slaney@anu.edu.au.

The Brain Project: Consciousness Studies

http://www.merlin.com.au/brain_proj/prog.htm

This web site, maintained by Stephen Jones sjones@merlin.com.au, is a continuing development project attempting to provide background briefings, summaries of the main issues raised at the Towards a Science of Consciousness Conference (held in Tuscon, Arizona in 1996), as well as offer opinion and discussion of those issues and perhaps to synthesise some sort of overall suggestions towards a theory of consciousness. The site presently includes: background notes on historical ideas of the brain and the mind; some papers by Stephen Jones; and papers by other authors.

The Brain Project: Links on Consciousness

http://www.merlin.com.au/brain_proj/links.htm

This web site, maintained by Stephen Jones sjones@merlin.com.au, is a collection of links to help track down articles of interest in the following areas: neuro-physiology, philosophy of mind, quantum consciousness, neural nets, and computational brain.

Celebrities in Cognitive Science

http://carbon.cudenver.edu/~mryder/itc_data/cogsci.html

Maintained by Martin Ryder mryder@www.cudenver.edu, this excellent resource provides links to information (profiles, abstracts, articles, interviews, etc.) on a number of prominent figures—authors, critics, and philosophers—in the field of cognitive science.

Center for the Cognitive Science of Metaphor

http://metaphor.uoregon.edu/metaphor.html

This site, maintained by Tim Rohrer rohrer@darkwing.uoregon.edu, provides access to a range of resources including an annotated bibliography of work on metaphor, master metaphor list, and links to other metaphor resources.

Center for the Mind

http://www.anu.edu.au/mind/

The Center for the Mind is a think-tank at the Australian National University that acts as a catalyst for interdisciplinary scientific research into the mind. Its goals are to foster a culture of ideas and inquiry into the sciences of the mind and to bring hard science to bear on questions of central importance to the community as a whole. It crosses academic boundaries and considers questions about the mind not normally dealt with by the traditional disciplines. This site, maintained by Ian Gold ian.gold@mind.anu.edu.au, provides information on the activities of the Center, and on conferences, workshops, and other events relevant to this field of enquiry.

Center for Research on Concepts and Cognition, Indiana University

http://www.cogsci.indiana.edu/

An interdisciplinary center for research in cognitive science, directed by Douglas Hofstadter. Provides links to cognitive science resources, information on researchers at CRCC, access to cognitive science papers, access to Copycat, a computer program modelling the interplay between concepts and perception in the course of analogy-making. Papers produced at the Center can accessed via its ftp archive at *ftp://ftp.cogsci.indiana.edu/pub*. The site is maintained by gem@cogsci.indiana.edu.

Cognitive and Psychological Sciences on the Internet

http://dawww.essex.ac.uk/~roehl/PsycIndex/

This resource is maintained by Ruediger Oehlmann oehlmann@essex.ac.uk, and provides links to academic programs, organizations and conferences, newsgroups, journals and magazines, and mailing lists relevant to the cognitive and psychological sciences. A mirror of this site is accessible at *http://matia.stanford.edu/cogsci.html.*

Cognitive Science Initiative

http://www.hfac.uh.edu/cogsci/

This site provides information on the CSI, an interdisciplinary project at the University of Houston. The site includes links to a range of cognitive science-related information, and is maintained by Cynthia Freeland cfreeland@uh.edu.

Cognitive Science Society

http://www1.pitt.edu/~cogsci95/

News and information for society members, and details of the Society's conferences can be obtained from this site maintained by Alan Lesgold al@pop.pitt.edu.

Complexity Related Links

http://www.cpm.mmu.ac.uk/~bruce/complink.html

This page by Bruce Edmonds B.Edmonds@mmu.ac.uk, presents an impressive collection of links related to complex systems.

Computational Epistemology Lab

http://cogsci.uwaterloo.ca/

Located at the Philosophy Department, University of Waterloo, this site provides information on research in the field of cognitive science, including coherence, analogy, visual mental imagery, and scientific hypothesis-generation. The site is maintained by Cameron Shelley cpshelle@watarts.uwaterloo.ca.

Computer-Aided Theory of Consciousness

http://www.inm.de/kip/

This site, from Gerd Doeben-Henisch doeb@inm.de, is an online philosophical and scientific exploration in the art of digital modelling of the human consciousness. Based on modern philosophy of science, "mixed up with the phenomenological tradition," the author is attempting "to develop formal models of consciousness which can truly learn concepts and arbitrary languages."

Conceptual Metaphor Home Page

http://cogsci.berkeley.edu/MetaphorHome.html

This server is a research tool for cognitive scientists and others interested in the study of conceptual metaphor systems. Ongoing work in the metaphor system of English and other languages is made available here using a hypertext format which allows the reader to trace links between metaphors and thus get a better idea of the structure of the system. The site is maintained by Alan Schwartz metaphor@cogsci.berkeley.edu.

The Consciousness in the Natural World Project

http://www.stir.ac.uk/philosophy/cnw/webpage1.htm

The Consciousness in the Natural World project is based in the Philosophy Department at the University of Stirling. It aims to bring together philosophers from the Scottish Universities and beyond to allow concerted and collective progress to be made on one of the central problems in the philosophy of mind—the problem of explaining the place of conscious psychological life within the natural world. This page is maintained by Fiona Macpherson fem1@stir.ac.uk.

Dictionary of Philosophy of Mind

http://www.artsci.wustl.edu/~philos/MindDict/

The page provides access to a dictionary of terms used in philosophy of mind. It is compiled by Chris Eliasmith chris@twinearth.wustl.edu, who welcomes suggestions for additions to help expand the usefulness of the site. A search engine facilitates ease of use and quality is ensured via a blind peer-reviewed editorial policy and advisory boards.

Imagination, Mental Imagery, Consciousness, and Cognition

http://web.calstatela.edu/faculty/nthomas/index.htm

A resource for the study of imagination and mental images and their relevance to the understanding of consciousness and cognition, as approached primarily through the methods of analytical philosophy, experimental psychology, cognitive science, and the history of ideas/intellectual history. This site is maintained by Nigel J.T. Thomas NJTThomas @aol.com. It is mirrored at: *http://members.aol.com/njtthomas/.*

Links on Consciousness

http://www.merlin.com.au/brain_proj/links.htm

Part of Stephen Jones' sjones@merlin.com.au Brain Project site, this page provides links to a range of consciousness-related materials, divided into these categories: neuro-physiology, philosophy of mind, quantum consciousness, and neural nets and computational brain.

LogicAL: Logic, Philosophy, and Artificial Life Resources

http://uu-gna.mit.edu:8001/~napoli/LAMBDA/logical.html

A comprehensive site with links to resources divided into the following categories: Logic through History, Logic and Philosophy, Logic and Education, Logic and Mathematics, Logic and Computation, Fuzzy Logic, Automata and Systems, and Meetings and Conferences. The site is maintained by S. Kritikos napoli@sturgeon.mit.edu.

Mind and Body: René Descartes to William James

http://serendip.brynmawr.edu/Mind/Table.html

This site, maintained by Robert Wozniak rwozniak@brynmawr.edu, provides an outline on the rise of experimental psychology as it occurred at the interface between philosophical analyses of the mind/world relationship and physiological conceptions of the nervous system as a sensory-motor device mediating between the mind and the world. The site focuses not only on European but on early and often overlooked American contributions.

Mind and Consciousness

http://www.cs.latrobe.edu.au/~doug/generic/mind.html

Links to a range of articles on mind matter unification, consciousness, and language of thought hypothesis can be found at this site created by D.J.Huntington Moore doug@latcs1.lat.oz.au.

Mind/Brain Resources: A Research Aid

http://mind.phil.vt.edu/www/mind.html

This site, maintained by Valerie Gray Hardcastle valerie@vt.edu, provides links to a list of resources that researchers in cognitive science or philosophy of mind might find useful. It includes links to journals, technical reports and research papers, cognitive science and AI links, and more.

Music, Mind, Machine

http://www.nici.kun.nl/mmm/

This site is dedicated to research in the computational modeling of temporal structure in musical knowledge and music cognition. It describes the research, and contains papers with sound examples, quicktime animations, and other material. Those responsible for the research can be contacted at mmm@psych.kun.nl.

Non-Cartesian Cognitive Science

http://www.cogs.susx.ac.uk/users/ronaldl/noncartesian.html

Traditional Cognitive Science is Cartesian in the sense that it takes as fundamental the distinction between the mental and the physical, the mind and the world, the subject and the object. It is this Cartesianism which leads to such claims as that cognition must be representational and that what sets cognisers apart is the fact that they exhibit "aboutness." It is the aim of this page to bring together non-Cartesian approaches to the study of cognition—the main point which holds this page together is the idea that mind and body form a unity, not a union. This site is maintained by Ronald Lemmen ronaldl@cogs.susx.ac.uk.

Ohio State Neuroprose Archive

ftp://archive.cis.ohio-state.edu/pub/neuroprose

This ftp site, maintained by Jordan Pollack pollack@cs.brandeis.edu, contains technical reports as a public service to the connectionist and neural network scientific community. Researchers are able to add preprints to the directory, the contents of which may be viewed by reading the Index file. A file providing abstracts of the papers is also available.

Philosophy, Neuroscience, Psychology Archive

http://www.artsci.wustl.edu/~philos/pnp/archive.html

This site archives technical reports for the PNP Program at Washington University in St. Louis. Reports are available in a number of areas of cognitive science and philosophy of mind, and an index of abstracts of papers in the archive is included. It is maintained by Bill Bechtel bill@twinearth.wustl.edu.

Philosophy Neuroscience Psychology Program

http://www.artsci.wustl.edu/~philos/pnp/

This site provides information about the PNP Program at Washington University in St. Louis. The site also provides links to relevant Internet resources, and to an archive of papers and technical reports produced by participants in the program (see above).

Philosophy of Mind Homepage

http://www.trinity.edu/~cbrown/mind/

This page, created by Curtis Brown cbrown@trinity.edu, contains links to philosophy of mind resources, and to materials for his Philosophy of Mind class at Trinity.

Research Project on Cognitive Musicology

http://www.jyu.fi/~louhivuo/

This site charts the progress of those involved in a research project between cognitive musicologists and philosophers. Questions being considered include: How does the physically implemented mind make holistic musical experience and action possible? How is music, or some of its subdomains, such as timbre or pitch, represented by the brain? How can temporal-sequential mental processes be explained by connectionism?

Social Cognition Paper Archive and Information Center

http://www.psych.purdue.edu/~esmith/scarch.html

Maintained by Eliot R. Smith esmith@psych.purdue.edu, this site houses a collection of abstracts of papers or presentations and links to information about active researchers in the area of social cognition. It also provides links to journals and resource collections.

Society for Philosophy and Psychology

http://www.hfac.uh.edu/cogsci/spp/spphp.html

Information on the Society's history, membership, meetings, and constitution can be found on this page. Enquiries about the Society should be directed to John Bickle pybickle@ecuvm.cis.ecu.edu.

Technical Reports: Rutgers Center for Cognitive Science

ftp://ruccs.rutgers.edu/pub/papers

This ftp site provides access to a range of papers on topics in cognitive science of relevance to philosophers. The files are in a variety of formats including MS Word, WordPerfect and PostScript. See the README file for details on papers and formats available.

Politics, Human Rights, & Economics

APSA: Foundations of Political Theory Section

http://www.apsanet.org/~theory/

This is the homepage of the Political Theory Section of the American Political Science Association, which exists to advance the linkage of political theory and philosophy with political science as a discipline. Information on the activities of the organization, its newsletter, recent publications in political theory, and links to relevant online information are provided.

Anarchist Archive

http://www.pitzer.edu/~dward/Anarchist_Archives/archivehome.html

This site, maintained by Dana Ward dward@pitzer.edu, provides information on key anarchist thinkers including Chomsky, Godwin, Stirner, Bakunin, and others, as well as on anarchist movements and history.

Anarchists & Left Libertarians

http://www.tigerden.com/~berios/libertarians.html

This page provides information on left libertarian and anarchist thinkers, "all individuals who have distinguished themselves in the past and present by opposing various forms of coercion, authority and injustice, political and economic, in true libertarian tradition." It is maintained by Jamal Hannah jah@iww.org.

Communitarianism Open Site

http://venus.unive.it/~joyce/cos/

This site, maintained by joyce@unive.it, provides a range of communitarian resources, including an overview and introduction to communitarian movements, books and articles, links to related resources, and a diary of events. A mirror of the site is available at: *http://www.gmt.it/pages/communitarianism/*.

DIANA: International Human Rights Database

http://www.law-lib.utoronto.ca/diana/

This site houses extensive human rights information including links to sites for legal research, links to documents, conventions, reports, bibliographies, and more. It is maintained by Anne Johnstone annej@istar.ca.

John Elster Page

http://home.sol.no/hansom/elster.htm

This page, maintained by Hans O. Melberg hansom@online.no, is intended as a resource for people who are interested in the social sciences in general and the works of Jon Elster in particular. Elster has written extensively on rationality, social choice, Marxism, constitutionalism and democracy, and other areas in social science. The site contains a large database which contains a list of Elster's books (including table of contents, cover texts and prefaces), a list of his articles, a list of reviews, and a general index of terms mentioned in his works. A database containing the full text of the articles mentioned is also being created.

Engaged Buddhist ~ Dharma: Human Rights

http://www.engagedpage.com/

This page, from Lesslie engaged@maui.net, brings together an enormous range of human rights-related resources, including links to human rights news, human rights organizations, and more.

Freemarket.com

http://www.free-market.com/

A website with a magazine approach, freemarket.com pronounces itself to be the "starting point for liberty on the Internet." It lists a host of libertarian links, provides access to libertarian electronic texts, has a directory of libertarian organizations, provides regular reviews of websites, and more. The site is maintained by Chris Whitten chris@free-market.com.

History of Economic Thought

http://socserv2.socsci.mcmaster.ca:80/~econ/ugcm/3ll3/index.html

This site provides an overview of thinkers in the history of economic thought, including: Marx, Mill, Godwin, Locke, Rousseau, and more. It is maintained by Rod Hay hay@sscl.uwo.ca, and mirrored at: *http://melbecon.unimelb.edu.au/het/* and also at: *http://www.ecn.bris.ac.uk/het/index.htm*.

History of Economics Internet Resources

http://cfec.vub.ac.be/cfec/hope.htm

This site, from Bert Mosselmans bmosselm@vnet3.vub.ac.be, includes an extensive range of links to resources relating to the history of economics, political economy, and related fields. Resources are grouped into the following areas: general references, classical political economy, Marxism, neoclassical economics, Keynesianism, specific topics, organizations, forthcoming conferences, and interdisciplinary issues.

Human Rights Internet

http://www.hri.ca/

HRI is an international NGO, publishing house and documentation center. Its website aims to become an online resource, information and documentation center for human rights actors and organizations, as well as interested individuals, around the world, and is maintained by Tanja M. Kisslinger tmkiss@cognita.com.

Human Rights Resources on the Internet

http://shr.aaas.org/dhr.htm

This site is a project of the AAAS Science & Human Rights Program. It features a range of human rights-related materials in a searchable database, and has recently expanded to include electronic texts, a human rights bulletin board, and tools for using the net. The site is maintained by Stephen Hanson shansen@aaas.org.

Human Rights Web

http://www.hrweb.org

This site provides information about human rights, groups which promote human rights, and related issues. It provides a forms-based searchable database of human rights news and press release articles; a searchable database of human rights publications; and a searchable database of human rights organizations addresses, phone numbers, fax numbers, and email addresses. The site is maintained by Catherine Hampton ariel@best.com.

HungerWeb

http://www.hunger.brown.edu/hungerweb

From this site you can access extensive resources relating to hunger, famine, and poverty, including: United Nations documents; United States government documents, speeches, and quotations; basic definitions of hunger and related terms; the economics of hunger and poverty; facts on hunger and poverty; information on the crisis in Rwanda. The site is maintained by Peter Uvin peter_uvin@brown.edu.

Institute for First Amendment Studies

http://apocalypse.berkshire.net/~ifas/

The Institute for First Amendment Studies is a non-profit educational and research organization focusing on the activities of the Religious Right. Whether your interest is in reproductive rights, gay rights, censorship, education, law, politics, religion, televangelists, or church/state issues, you'll find information on the topic here. IFAS can be contacted at ifas@berkshire.net.

International Affairs Resources (IANWeb)

http://www.pitt.edu/~ian/ianres.html

This is a comprehensive guide to the worldwide network-accessible resources available to scholars in the study of international affairs. IANWeb provides scholars, students, and professionals in international affairs with one-stop access to all resources, contacts, and other information relevant to international affairs and available on the Internet. IANWeb maintains subject-specific resource pages containing links pertaining to: international political economy, foreign policy, international security, peace and conflict resolution, economic development, international law, teaching and curriculum development, career resources, grant opportunities, and much more. The site is maintained by Wolfgang Schlör ianadmn+@pitt.edu.

International Economics and Philosophy Society

http://www.qut.edu.au/arts/human/ethics/ieps/index.htm

This site, maintained by Paul Murray pmurray@lingua.cltr.uq.oz.au, provides information on the IEPS and links to philosophy and economics resources.

Left Wing Lingo, Ideologies and History

http://www.dsausa.org/rl/Docs/Lingo.html

This page, by J. Hughes jhughes@changesurfer.com, provides information on a range of left wing political ideologies, including Communitarian Socialism, Anarchism, Communism, Marxism, Social Democracy, Fabianism, Marxist-Leninism, Trotskyism, Maoism, Schactmanism, Euro-Communism, the New Left, Contemporary American Democratic Left, Radical Democracy, Democratic Marxism, Socialist Feminism, Feminism, Black Socialism, Eco-Socialism, and other kinds of green politics. Each entry gives an overview of the theory and praxis associated with the particular ideology, as well as providing links to further information.

A Liberty Library

http://www.well.com/conf/liberty/home.html

This site, maintained by Bob Bickford rab@well.com, is a collection of information relevant to and about libertarians and libertarianism.

Lycos: Political Philosophy

http://a2z.lycos.com/Government/Politics/Political_Philosophy/index-random.html

This is the Lycos search engine's page of resources in political philosophy.

Marx/Engels Archive

http://csf.colorado.edu/psn/marx/

This site, maintained by Ken Campbell kcampbel@colorado.edu, provides links to electronic texts as well as a photo gallery and biographical information on Marx and Engels.

The Marxism Leninism Project

http://www.idbsu.edu/surveyrc/Staff/jaynes/marxism/marxism.htm

This website is maintained by Jonathan D. Jaynes jonathan@netmachine.com and represents a project to set out the theories of Marxism in the most authoritative form possible—in the words of the founders of Marxism and of the greatest of their followers.

Online Discussion Board for Social and Political Thought

http://thor.prohosting.com/~duyuan/cgi-bin/mac_bbs/bbs_top.htm

This is a web-based discussion forum for social and political thought, hosted by Du Yuan duyuan@geocities.com, whose field of interest is normative political theory, but other philosophical topics are also welcome.

PeaceNet

http://www.igc.org/igc/peacenet/

This is a comprehensive site, part of the Institute for Global Communications http://www.igc.apc.org/, providing information for those interested in working for positive social change in the areas of peace, social and economic justice, human rights, and the struggle against racism. The site is maintained by webweaver@igc.org.

Philosophy: A History of Ideas

http://www.saltdal.vgs.no/filoeng.htm

This page, intended for upper secondary level students of political philosophy, provides links to a range of resources in political philosophy. It is maintained by nilslg@saltdal.vgs.no.

Philosophy and Civil Society

http://www.civsoc.com

Liberal democratic civil societies require the support of a special form of culture—civic culture. This site is devoted to the philosophical examination of the nature of civil society and civic culture in general and addresses specifically the contemporary crisis of liberal democratic civic culture in the postmodern era. Maintained by Tom Bridges bridges@civsoc.com, the site provides essays and information on several topics including "civic culture—what it is," "civic culture and modern philosophy," the postmodern reconstruction of civic culture," "the postmodern reconstruction of philosophy." It provides book reviews, articles, and links to web sites relevant to these topics.

Political Economy Web

http://members.tripod.com/~political_economy/index.html

This page, maintained by Peter Bohmer bohmerp@elwha.evergreen.edu, provides access to a range of links leading to information relevant to the interdisciplinary study of political economy.

Political Participation Project

http://www.ai.mit.edu/people/msb/ppp/home.html

The Political Participation Project is a research effort at the MIT Artificial Intelligence Lab exploring how interactive media can be used to facilitate political participation. The PPP directs an electronic mailing list for those interested in exploring the role of interactive media as a catalyst for political participation. The Project is a research element in the doctoral thesis of Mark S. Bonchek bonchek@ai.mit.edu. Some parts of the thesis are accessible online.

Political Philosophy

http://lgxserver.uniba.it/lei/FILPOL/filpolE/homeFPE.htm

This site, created by Maria Chiara Pievatolo pievatolo@dsp.unipi.it, provides a comprehensive index to a range of resources in political philosophy, including journals, events, online papers, and a 'small companion to cyberspace' which groups resources into historical periods and areas of enquiry.

Political Philosophy/Political Theory

http://www.library.ubc.ca/poli/theory.html

From I. Laponce ilaponce@unixg.ubc.ca for the University of British Columbia's online library service, this site provides links to a wide range of materials in political philosophy and political theory.

Political Science Links

http://www.smpcollege.com/smp_govt/ps_links.htm

From St. Martin's Press, this site hosts a collection of links to political science resources, including a page of political theory links.

Political Science Manuscripts

http://www.trenton.edu/~psm

PSM is a project to distribute political science scholarship online. The page, created by William Ball ball@trenton.edu, features a collection of abstracts of manuscripts, with links back to the manuscripts themselves which can be accessed through an online search feature.

PROceedings: Political Research Online

http://PRO.harvard.edu/

Political Research Online (PROceedings) offers selected papers from the 1997 Annual Meeting of the American Political Science Association. These papers will be available online until August, 1998. The PROceedings project is currently in a demonstration of concept phase. A full collection of papers is planned for future conferences. The website is maintained by William J. Ball ball@tcnj.edu.

Prominent Anarchists and Left-Libertarians

http://tigerden.com/~berios/libertarians.html

This page, maintained by jah@iww.org, lists mainly biographical information, but provides some links to further information on a range of anarchist thinkers.

A Select Bibliography of Women's Rights

http://www.law.utoronto.ca/pubs/h_rghts.htm

Compiled by Rebecca Cook and Valerie Oosterveld, this site is part of the DIANA human rights database *http://www.law-lib.utoronto.ca/diana/*, and provides an extensive bibliography on human rights and women's issues. This page is maintained on behalf of the authors by Tracey Pegg tracey.pegg@utoronto.ca.

Systematic Study of Human Rights

http://www.polsci.binghamton.edu/hr.htm

This page is the sister-page to the mailing list HRS-L. It seeks to serve the human rights research community in a variety of ways, mainly by enabling scholars to help themselves. Acting as a depository for data, research papers, conference announcements, and other information, SSHR wishes to broaden the scope and hone the technique of systematic studies of human rights by increasing contact amongst the scholarly community, enabling replication of research, and by helping to provide notice of new research, methodology, etc. The site is maintained by David Richards bd90619@binghamton.edu.

Turn Left: The Home of Liberalism on the Web

http://www.turnleft.com/liberal.html

Turn Left's site includes information of liberal ideas, FAQs, links to other sources, discussion on liberal issues, and much more. It is maintained by Mike Silverman cubsfan@cjnetworks.com.

Ultimate Marxism Links

http://www.hongo.ecc.u-tokyo.ac.jp/~ee77030/marxism-e.html

This site provides a collection of information and links relating to the study of Marx and Marxism. Most of the site is in Japanese, and is maintained by Kosuke OKI kosuke@ grad.e.u-tokyo.ac.jp.

United Nations Human Rights Website

http://www.unhchr.ch/

As part of its continous efforts to keep the world informed of its work and to encourage the active participation of all Governments, non-governmental organizations, groups, and individuals, the Office of the High Commissioner for Human Rights/Center for Human Rights has developed the most complete source of information available on the Internet concerning United Nations action in the field of human rights. Information on all the activities of the United Nations in the field of human rights, including those relating to technical cooperation, field operations, the conventional mechanisms (treaty monitoring bodies), the extra-conventional mechanisms, complaints procedures and voluntary or trust funds can be found on this site. Enquiries about the site can be directed to webadmin. hchr@unog.ch.

Western Michigan University: Political Science Resources Page

http://www.wmich.edu/politics/resources/resource.html

This site, maintained by Neil Pinney neil.pinney@wmich.edu, provides an index to an extensive range of resources relevant to political science and political philosophy, including: electronic texts, journal, organizations, and more.

WWW Virtual Library: Political Science

http://spirit.lib.uconn.edu/PoliSci/polisci.htm

This site provides an index to an extensive range of resources relevant to political science, including libraries, journals, collections of papers, newsgroups and mailing lists, organizations and government agencies, and much more. It is maintained by Thomas Hartley and Chase Harrison psweb@opinion.isi.uconn.edu.

Philosophy of Religion

The 2001 Principle

http://www.jencom.com/2001/

This beautifully designed site re-examines and attempts to re-validate the classical 'Argument from Design' using the concept of Cognitive Dissonance and audience reaction to the film '2001—A Space Odyssey'.

Bible Gateway

http://www.gospelcom.net/bible

This site, part of the Gospel Communications Network, allows you to search for passages in the King James and other versions of the Bible. German, Swedish, Latin, French, and Spanish versions of the site are also available. The maintainer of this page can be contacted at bg@gospelcom.net.

Big Dummies Guide to Theology, Philosophy, and Ethics

http://www.teleport.com/~oro/bdintro.html

By Orrin R. Onken oro@teleport.com, this page serves as a somewhat humorous introduction to philosophy, theology, and ethics.

Buddhist Studies

http://www.ciolek.com/WWWVL-Buddhism.html

This site, part of the WWW Virtual Library series, and edited by T. Matthew Ciolek tmciolek@coombs.anu.edu.au and John C. Powers, provides access to hundreds of Buddhist-related links and resources including: files, graphics, and Buddhist organizations. An extensive list of religious studies resources is also included.

Catholic Encyclopedia

http://www.knight.org/advent/cathen/cathen.htm

This page contains a searchable version of the Catholic Encyclopedia. The editors knight@knight.org of this project are calling for assistance in reproducing articles from the hard copy version for online accessibility.

Christian Classics Ethereal Library

http://ccel.wheaton.edu/

Access to Christian electronic texts including works by St. Alphonsus, St. Athanasius, St. Augustine, St. Bernard, Boehme, Bunyan, Calvin, Donne, Milton, and more is provided at this site, maintained by Harry Plantinga W.H.Plantinga@wheaton.edu.

Christianity Net

http://www.christianity.net/

The ultimate page of Christian resources, including news topics, links to Christian magazines, chat/message boards, and links to over 4,000 Christian sources on the net.

Dunya: CyberMuslim Information Collective

http://www.uoknor.edu:80/cybermuslim/

This multimedia site provides access to the Activist Resource Center, where you can browse resources for Muslim activists; the Whole Dunya Bookstore & NewsStand, where you can access Islamic Books, Magazines, and Newspapers; the HyperQur'aan Project, which allows you to read, see, and hear the Noble Qur'aan!; IslamWare Mart, where you can access Islamic computing services & information and download software; the Madrassa and Jamia, which provides information on schools, universities, and Islamic educational resources; and Masjid of the Ether, basic information on Islamic beliefs, practice, and houses of worship. The site is maintained by Mas'ood Cajee mcajee@aardvark.ucs.uoknor.edu.

The Ecole Initiative

http://www.evansvillle.edu/~ecoleweb/

The Early Church Online Encyclopedia (Ecole) Initiative is a cooperative effort on the part of scholars across the Internet to establish a hypertext encyclopedia of early Church history (to the Reformation) on the World Wide Web. In principle, authors of the various articles that make up the enclyclopedia maintain their own articles at their own locations. Each article is connected to the Ecole Initiatie's Title Index (the URL above). In addition, each article is linked directly to related other articles and other information available on the Web. The Ecole Initiative was created by Anthony F. Beavers tb2@evansville.edu, who serves as the General Editor.

Evangelical Philosophical Society

http://www.chass.utoronto.ca:8080/~davis/evps.htm

EPS is an organization of evangelical Christians who meet annually to discuss philosophical matters of mutual interest. It emphasises philosophy of religion defined broadly to include philosophical theology, ethics, apologetics, as well as other fields as they relate to the faith. EPS was founded in 1974 and has grown to over 200 members. This site, maintained by Richard Davis davis@chass.utoronto.ca, provides information on membership, the Society's journal, and links to related web pages.

Guide to Chabad Literature

http://www.utexas.edu/students/cjso/Chabad/chabad.html

This well-designed and content-rich site, provides a wealth of information on Chabad-Lubavitch culture, literature, and teachings, including online texts, access to electronic journals and mailing lists, as well as video and audio files. It is maintained by Yechezkal-Shimon Gutfreund sgutfreund@gte.com.

Hill Monastic Manuscript Library

http://www.csbsju.edu/hmml/

Since its founding in 1965, the Hill Monastic Manuscript Library (HMML) has sent teams of researchers and technicians to film more than 25 million pages from nearly 90,000 volumes in libraries and archives throughout Europe, the Middle East, and North Africa. Today, HMML represents one of the largest and most comprehensive archives of medieval and Renaissance sources in the world. More than a repository of manuscripts, the Hill Monastic Manuscript Library is one of the best research libraries in medieval studies in the country. Scholars from all over the world visit the Library, for short or extended periods, while others contact the Library by mail to request copies of microfilmed holdings. Efforts are underway to increase accessibility to the HMML collection through CD-ROM and other electronic means. This site provides initial access to HMML for the online community. Enquiries about the site can be made to hmml@csbsju.edu.

Hyper-Weirdness by World Wide Web: Religion Page

http://www.physics.wisc.edu/~shalizi/hyper-weird/wind.html

A hypertext version by shalizi@phenxa.physics.wisc.edu, of Mitchell Porter's High Weirdness by E-Mail. Provides access primarily to electronic texts covering Buddhism, Hinduism, Christianity, Catholicism, Eastern Orthodoxy, C of E, Lutherans, Mormons, Seventh Day Adventists, evangelists and fundamentalists, and more.

Indian Philosophy & Religion

http://www.geocities.com/Athens/Acropolis/1863/index.html

This page provides extensive information and links to resources on the Indian spiritual tradition, plus links to a range of resources on worldwide religions. The page is maintained by sarada@geocities.com

Institute of St. Thomas: Center of High Medieval and Thomistic Research and Studies

http://www.informedia.it/dipiu/st/ist_sth.htm

The Institute of St.Thomas in Rome, advances itself as an international meeting place for all researchers in the field of Scholastic Philosophy and Theology with special reference to the figure of St. Thomas Aquinas. Activities of the Institute include a two year specialisation course in Thomistic Studies, conferences, pubblications, and an International Group of Research, the Consultants of which are world recognised authorities in the fields of Medieval Studies, Philosophy, and Theology.

Links for Thinking Christians

http://coombs.anu.edu.au/~langlois/chlinks.htm

This site is maintained by Anthony J. Langlois anthony.langlois@anu.edu.au, and provides links to a range of electronic Christian journals and magazines which "demonstrate the search for the truth within various traditions of the Christian faith. Each contains full text articles, on everything from straight theology and introductory apologetics to in-depth cultural and academic analysis starting with Christian assumptions and presuppositions." Links to other resource-rich sites are included.

Mysticism in World Religions

http://www.digiserve.com/mystic

This site by Deb Platt mystic@digiserve.com, presents the mystical traditions of Judaism, Christianity, Islam, Buddhism, Hinduism, and Taoism. You can compare and contrast these six religions by going directly to the World Index, or you can look at each religion individually by going to that religion's particular index.

New Advent Catholic Supersite

http://www.knight.org/advent/

This site provides a wide range of links to Catholic resources, including the Summa Theologica, Catholic books, articles on aspects of the Catholic faith, and the Catholic encyclopedia.

Provenzano and Sons: Philosophy and Theology

http://www.smartlink.net/~joepro/

Joe joepro@smartlink.net, Dan, and Gary Provenzano have their say on philosophy and religion. Read their essays, and their points of view based on the work of Teilhard de Chardin.

Religion and Philosophy Gopher, Rice University

gopher://riceinfo.rice.edu:70/11/Subject/RelPhil

A wide range of religion and philosophy resources, including mailing lists, electronic texts, Christian, Jewish and Buddhist resources, electronic and print journals, and more can be accessed from this gopher site.

Scientific Pantheism

http://members.aol.com/heraklit1/index.htm

This site provides extensive information on scientific pantheism by Paul Harrison, author of a range of politico-environmental titles harrison@dircon.co.uk. The discussion of pantheism extends to its historical roots, and links to related resources are provided.

The Temple of the Immortal Spirit: The Western Taoist

http://www.thetemple.com/

Maintained by Steven Ericsson Zenith steven@thetemple.com, this page provides information on Taoism, but is particularly aimed at exploring the meaning of Taoist mystical and spiritual philosophies in the context of Western culture.

Theistic Philosophers on the Web

http://www.chass.utoronto.ca:8080/~davis/phil.htm

This site, maintained by Richard Davis davis@chass.utoronto.ca, provides a list of individuals who classify themselves as both philosophers and theists. They are working in such diverse areas as metaphysics, epistemology, logic, action theory, ethics, aesthetics, philosophy of language, philosophy of logic, philosophy of science, philosophy of religion, philosophical theology, existentialism, phenomenology, political philosophy, and the history of philosophy.

The Virtue of What Is

http://www.marlboro.edu/~nweiner/

This page, the work of Neal Weiner nweiner@marlboro.edu, focuses on "philosophical poetry and fiction about God, growth, truth, and the meeting place of good and evil at the heart of creation."

Unravelling Wittgenstein's Net—Christian Think Tank

http://www.webcom.com/~ctt

This complex of pages represents Glen Miller's gmiller@netcom.com Christian journey through 20th-century Western thought. It contains his reflections on philosophy, on theology, on spirituality, and on apologetics.

The Wall

http://www.faithquest.com

This site focuses on philosophy and theology, and features the works of philosophers such as Platinga, Rescher, Pojman, van Inwagen, Swinburne and others. It also houses a philosophy and theology search engine which is under development, and is maintained by Christoper Fogarty ctf@faithquest.com.

Whereunto Shall I Liken This Generation?

http://www.aaow.com/foliago/

This site houses an online book by Eugene Foliago foliago@aaow.com. The book is "an allegorical interpretation of the Bible. The simplicity of Christianity is disproved, and the views of St. Irenaeus are criticised."

World Union of Deists

http://www.deism.com/

The World Union of Deists site provides an overview of deism, some thoughts on deism vs. atheism and Christianity, and some deist essays by Thomas Paine. The site maintainers can be contacted at info@deism.com.

Yahoo: Society & Culture: Religion

http://www.yahoo.com/Society_and_Culture/Religion/

This is the Yahoo net directory's list of resources in religion, covering a wide range of subtopics including creation/evolution, spiritualism, monasticism, theology, theosophy, world religions, and much more.

Miscellaneous Areas

African Philosophy

http://eagle.cc.ukans.edu/~jmaybee/africanphil.html

This page, from J. Maybee jmaybee@eagle.cc.ukans.edu, provides an extensive range of information and links to African philosophy-related resources including: African philosophers, African philosophy texts, African-American philosophy links, African philosophy in action, course syllabi and conferences on African philosophy.

African Philosophy Resources

http://www.augustana.ab.ca/~janzb/afphilpage.htm

From Bruce Janz janzb@augustana.ab.ca, this page is a collection of links to African Philosophy resources, including introductions, general guides, journals, associations, course materials, and more.

An Alien's Guide to Human Nature

http://www.ftech.net/~devinney/index.htm

This site, from Timothy@devinney.ftech.co.uk, provides an introductory philosophical discussion of human nature directed at undergraduate student level. "It addresses, in ordinary language, many of the philosophical issues that have a direct bearing on our everyday lives as we approach the next millenium. The format is imaginative: it is written as a guide to human nature for alien slave traders. It centers on the question: what would a highly intelligent and rational species make of human beings if they had to deal with us directly?".

Autopoiesis and Enaction: The Observer Web

http://www.informatik.umu.se/~rwhit/AT.html

This impressive page presents extensive materials on autopoiesis, including: a tutorial on autopoiesis and enaction which give a basic taste of Maturana and Varela's work; a Study Plan which is a suggested syllabus for exploring the literature on autopoiesis and enaction; a comprehensive bibliography of the literature on autopoiesis and enaction; an index to *Autopoiesis and Cognition* (Maturana & Varela, 1980); and coming soon, Encyclopaedia Autopoietica, a compendium of the terms and concepts used in auto poietic theory, with emphasis on the core literature of Maturana and Varela. In addition, the site includes links to related resources found elsewhere on the net, plus information on The Observer, an email newsletter which provides a forum for disseminating news and views on autopoietic theory and enactive cognitive science. Maintained by Randall Whitaker rwhitake@alpha. wright.edu, this site is definitely worth a visit by those interested in this area of philosophy.

Bostrom Web

http://www.hedweb.com/nickb/welcome.htm

This page, from Nicholas Bostrom n.bostrom@lse.ac.uk, provides information on transhumanism, neuroscience and futurology, links to other transhumanist sites, and reflects Bostrom's interest in future technology, nanotechnology, and analytic philosophy.

Deborah Charles Publications — Legal Theory Site

http://www.legaltheory.demon.co.uk/

This site, primarily the vehicle for a number of legal journals published by DCP, provides access to bibliographies and course information in areas of law and legal theory, selected articles on legal theory, selected draft articles for comment and review, and book reviews. DCP can be contacted at dcp@legaltheory.demon.co.uk.

Diagrammatic Reasoning

http://morpheus.hartford.edu/cs/faculty/anderson/

The Diagrammatic Reasoning site is dedicated to providing a central repository for information pertaining to the investigation of reasoning with visual representations. Here you will find contributions by researchers, and pointers to research, on diagrammatic, spatial, and other visual representations that will inform you about how natural and artificial agents create, manipulate, reason about, solve problems with, and in general use such representations in a variety of interesting ways. The site is maintained by Michael Anderson anderson@hartford.edu.

Face to Face: Philosophical Counselling

http://www.facetoface.org.uk/

Philosophical counselling is similar, in some ways, to psychotherapy. However, it differs from psychotherapy in that it uses philosophy to help individuals to investigate and explore the most basic ideas underlying their lives. Such an exploration requires a philosophical disposition. Philosophical investigation primarily addresses concepts, assumptions, theories and ideas, rather than attempting to expose concrete events or secret processes hidden inside the individual's head. Find out more about philosophical counselling on this page, maintained by Colin Clayton logos@facetoface.org.uk.

French Philosophy in the Fifties

http://www.france.diplomatie.fr/culture/france/biblio/folio/philo1/index.html

This site provides an overview of French philosophy and philosophers in the 1950s, including a bibliography and glossary of key terms. It is maintained by Michel Deverge deverge@imaginet.fr.

Home Page for Thought Experiments

http://astro.ocis.temple.edu/~souder/thought/index.html

This site brings together a collection of thought experiments used in philosophy and science, and provides links to other sites where thought experiments or discussions about them can be found. This page is maintained by Lawrence Souder souder@astro.ocis.temple.edu.

The Philosophical Counselling Home Page

http://www.geocities.com/Athens/Forum/5914

What is philosophical counselling? This page, maintained by Shlomit C. Schuster msshstar@pluto.mscc.huji.ac.il, provides an introduction, plus links to philosophical counselling organizations, a philosophical practitioner's notebook of quotations, a bibliography, and conference information.

Polish Philosophy Page

http://www.fmag.unict.it/polhome.html

This page presents information on Polish philosophy and philosophers, "and it aims to be an instrument to aid knowledge and diffusion of the philosophical ideas of the main Polish philosophers since 1900." It is maintained by Francesco Coniglione f.coniglione@ mail.fmag.unict.it.

Progressivism

http://www.geocities.com/Athens/8234/

Progressivists believe in improving themselves and society. They base their personal beliefs on the most firm ground available—the sciences. By using the scientific method to arrive at conclusions (not truths, but answers one can act upon) they avoid the corruptions associated with all other methods for interpreting the environment. The Progressivist Bible, available at this site, is a document that attempts systematically arrange these conclusions. This site provides a range of information on progressivism, and is maintained by Roy Speckhardt gomespec@erols.com.

Radical Constructivism

http://www.univie.ac.at/cognition/constructivism/

This site, from the Austrian Society of Cognitive Science *http://www.univie.ac.at/cognition/* and maintained by Alex Riegler riegler@ifi.unizh.ch, brings together a range of resources on radical constructivism, "an unconventional approach to the problem of knowledge and knowing."

Research Sources on Concepts of Person and Self

http://www.canisius.edu/~gallaghr/pi.html

This site, by Shaun Gallagher gallaghr@canisius.edu, provides links to bibliographies, journals, electronic texts, and associations and institutions related to the study of the concepts of person, self, and personal identity.

Semiotics

http://www.cudenver.edu/~mryder/itc_data/semiotics.html

From the University of Colorado at Denver, this page provides extensive information on semiotics: definitions, terms, a brief history, philosophers who have written on semiotics, and links to a range of related resources. Maintained by Martin Ryder mryder@www.cudenver.edu, this page is an excellent source of online information on the subject.

Semiotics for Beginners

http://www.aber.ac.uk/~dgc/semiotic.html

This page from Daniel Chandler dgc@aber.ac.uk, provides an introduction to semiotics, with sections on: signs, paradigms and syntagms, syntagmatic analysis, paradigmatic analysis, denotation and connotation, metaphor and metonymy, codes, intertextuality, strengths of semiotic analysis, criticisms of semiotic analysis, D.I.Y. semiotic analysis, and a suggested reading list.

Sites of Significance for Semiotics

http://www.epas.utoronto.ca:8080/french/as-sa/EngSem1.html

This site provides links to semiotics-related resouces including: periodicals, research groups, resource collections, journals, encyclopedia and dictionaries, semiotics issues, and more. It is maintained by Pascal Michelucci pascal.michelucci@utoronto.ca, and provided by the electronic journal, *Applied Semiotics*.

Synergetics on the Web

http://www.teleport.com/~pdx4d/synhome.html

Synergetics is the "integration of geometry and philosophy in a single conceptual system providing a common language and accounting for both the physical and metaphysical." This website, from 4D Solutions pdx4@teleport.com, provides an intoduction to Synergetics and links to related information.

The Foundations of Transhumanism
http://www.ndirect.co.uk/~transhumanism/welcome.htm

This is a project to lay out the foundations of a transhumanist philosophy. The site features a growing number of academic papers on the science and philosophy of the future of humankind and superhuman artificial intelligence, and is maintained by Nicholas Bostrom n.bostrom@lse.ac.uk.

Wisdom in the Eye of the Frog

http://www.objana.com/frog/

This page is the online version of the book of the same title by Robert Vermeulen robv@ricochet.net. Wisdom in the Eye of the Frog uses the analogy of a frog to explain how free we really are, and why we develop the way we do. It employs first principles, as it answers age-old questions about nature vs. nurture, free will, the possibility of immortality, and how our temperament can be genetically determined at birth.

The Wisdom Page

http://www.cop.com/info/wisdompg.html

The Wisdom Page, maintained by Copthorne Macdonald cop@cop.com, takes a philosophical look at the concept and nature of wisdom. It presents a compilation of wisdom-related resources including various online texts, plus references to books, organizations, activities, and mailing lists.

WWW Virtual Library: Evolution

http://golgi.harvard.edu/biopages/evolution.html

This page from Adam Fagen afaagen@biosun.harvard.edu, provides links to a huge range of resources of interest to philosophers working on evolutionary biology and related issues.

Section 2: Text-Related Resources

Bibliographies

Annotated Bibliography on Teaching Research Ethics

http://www.indiana.edu/~poynter/tre-bib.html

The site provides access to bibliographies on teaching research ethics which were compiled as part of a project called Teaching Research Ethics: A Workshop at Indiana University. The project director was Kenneth D. Pimple <u>Pimple@Indiana.edu</u>.

Annotated Bibliography from *Towards Wisdom*

http://www.cop.com/info/tw-bibli.html

This is the annotated bibliography from Copthorne Macdonald's Book *Towards Wisdom*.

APA: Bibliographies

http://www.apa.udel.edu/apa/asp/bibliographies.asp

This is a collection of links to online bibliographies compiled by the American Philosophical Association.

Autopoiesis Bibliography

http://www.clas.ufl.edu/users/seeker1/noetics/Autopoiesis-bib.html

A listing of materials on the theory of "autopoiesis," developed by the Chilean biologists Humberto Maturana and Francisco Varela. This listing includes both primary and derivative literature, but unfortunately, is incomplete. The site is maintained by Steve Mizrach <u>Seeker1@Anthro.Ufl.Edu</u>.

Berdyaev Bibliography

http://www.maine.com/yfa/philosophy/bibliography.html

This bibliography is in four parts: Part I: Books by Berdyaev; Part II: Berdyaev within Anthologies, Prefaces, etc.; Part III: Journal Articles by Berdyaev; and Part IV: Books about Berdyaev. It was compiled by Fr. S. Janos.

Bibliographia Gramsciana

http://www.soc.qc.edu/cgi-bin/qserve/qserve.perl?DATASET=gramsci&icontravel. bib9.x=go&iconbar=no&return=http:/gramsci/index.html

The most complete scholarly reference bibliography on the life and work of Antonio Gramsci, which combines the Bibliografia Gramsciana, 1922-1988 by John M. Cammett [Rome: Editori Riuniti, 1991] and Bibliografia Gramsciana, Supplement updated to 1993, by John M. Cammett and Maria Luisi Righi [Fondazione Istituto Gramsci, 1995]. The combined works contain 10,357 items in a searchable database.

Bibliography of Bioethics

http://www.ncgr.org/gpi/grn/edures/elsi.tc.html

This page, hosted and maintained by the National Center for Genome Resources ncgr@ncgr.org, provides access to a large and well-organized, searchable bibliography edited by LeRoy Walters and Tamar Joy Kahn of the Kennedy Institute of Ethics, Georgetown University. A list of related journals, and a glossary of genetic terms are also linked to this site.

A Bibliography of Color and Philosophy

http://web.mit.edu/philos/www/color-biblio.html

This site provides access to a bibliography of philosophical works substantially concerned with color, and is compiled by Alex Byrne abyrne@MIT.EDU and David Hilbert.

Bibliography of Media Ethics

http://www.poynter.org/research/biblio/bib_me.htm

This is an extensive bibliography of ethics and media compiled by David Shedden.

A Bibliography of MetaEthics

http://www.gla.ac.uk/Acad/Philosophy/Lenman/bib.html

This extensive bibliography of metaethics, from James Lenman, j.lenman@philosophy. arts.gla.ac.uk, contains references to the work of over 100 authors prominent in this field.

A Bibliography of Non-Conceptual Content

http://www.cogs.susx.ac.uk/users/ronc/ncc-bibliography.html

This is intended to be a complete bibliography of non-conceptual content, which is the content of states which are prior to conceptualization, such as some basic perceptual states or the mental states of infants and animals. It is maintained by Ron Chrisley ronc@cogs. susx.ac.uk.

Bibliography on Buddhism and Human Rights

http://jbe.la.psu.edu/2/rightbib.html

Compiled by Damien Keown d.keown@gold.ac.uk for the *Journal of Buddhist Ethics*, this site also provides links to other philosophy-related bibliographies.

Bibliography on Evolution & Ethics

http://funnelweb.utcc.utk.edu/~asnyder1/bib.htm

Maintained as part of his home page, Allen Snyder asnyder1@utkux.utcc.utk.edu, a doctoral student at the University of Tennessee has compiled this evolving bibliography which relates to his thesis topic.

Bibliography on Feminism and World Politics

gopher://csf.Colorado.EDU:70/00/feminist/bibliography/women.world.politics. bibliography

This extensive bibliography is oriented towards the study of feminism and international relations theory. It is based on a bibliography by V. Spike Peterson's with supplementary materials supplied by Lev Gonick.

Bibliography on Nietzsche

ftp://humanum.arts.cuhk.edu.hk/pub/E-text/Nietzsche/

This bibliography (click on the link nietzsche.bib), compiled by J. F. Humphrey, is divided into two sections. The first covers Nietzsche's works in German and English translations, while the second covers interpretive studies, and is again divided into German and English sections.

Bibliography on Polish Philosophy in Italy

http://www.fmag.unict.it/PolPhil/PolPhilItaly.html

From Frances Coniglione f.coniglione@mail.fmag.unict.it, this bibliography-in-progress focuses on works by and about Polish philosophers and philosophy.

Bibs

http://members.tripod.com/~Lubbe/bibs.html

Bibs is the work of Ludvig Hertzberg ludvig@mail.film.su.se, who has produced a number of bibliographies relating to the philosophy of films.

Buddhism and Medical Ethics: A Bibliographical Introduction

http://jbe.la.psu.edu/2/dkhughes.html

Compiled by James Hughes and Damien Keown d.keown@gold.ac.uk for the *Journal of Buddhist Ethics*, this site provides some introductory comments on Buddhism and medical ethics, including a discussion of abortion and euthanasia, and provides a lengthy bibliography of materials which sourced the discussion.

Cicero Bibliography

http://www.utexas.edu/depts/classics/documents/Cic.html#Bibliography

Compiled largely by Bob Cape and Chris Craig this is a bibliography of works by and about Cicero.

Helene Cixous: A Bibliography

http://sun3.lib.uci.edu/indiv/scctr/Wellek/cixous/index.html

Compiled by Eddie Yeghiayan for the UCI Critical Theory Resource, this site is a searchable bibliography of works by and about Helene Cixous.

Clearinghouse for Social Sciences Subject-Oriented Bibliographies

http://coombs.anu.edu.au/CoombswebPages/BiblioClear.html

This site, maintained by T. Matthew Ciolek tmciolek@coombs.anu.edu.au, provides links to an extensive range of bibliographies including: buddhism, confucianism, feminism, politics and more. The Clearinghouse at the Australian National University will keep track of, and provide access to thematic bibliographies of value/significance to researchers in the field of widely-defined social sciences, Asian-Pacific studies, and humanities.

Cognitive Science and the Arts: A Collaborative Bibliography

http://www.hfac.uh.edu/cogsci/Bibliography.html

This site, maintained by Cynthia Freeland cfreeland@uh.edu, provides an online bibliography with sections including: visual arts, film, literature, linguistics, music, and more.

A Comprehensive Anarchist Bibliography

http://www.pitzer.edu/~dward/Anarchist_Archives/unifiedbiblio.html

This bibliography provides information on books and articles dealing with anarchism and anarchist theorists compiled by Dana Ward dward@pitzer.edu.

Concepts of Self, Person, and Personal Identity—A Bibliography

http://www.canisius.edu/~gallaghr/pi.html#bib

This bibliography, maintained by Shaun Gallagher gallaghr@canisius.edu, lists in alphabetical order, a range of philosophical works related to the concepts of self, person, and personal identity. The site also houses two smaller bibliographies, one on medical issues and the person, and the other on personalism.

Contemporary Philosophy of Mind: An Annotated Bibliography

http://ling.ucsc.edu/~chalmers/biblio.html

Compiled by David Chalmers chalmers@paradox.ucsc.edu, the bibliography provides information on works on consciousness and qualia, mental content, psycho-physical relations and psychological explanations, philosophy of artificial intelligence, and other miscellaneous topics.

Core Lists in Women's Studies

http://www.library.wisc.edu/libraries/WomensStudies/core/coremain.htm

These core lists of books in women's studies are intended to assist women's studies librarians and collection development librarians in building women's studies collections. Because the lists include only books currently in print, they also serve as a guide to teaching faculty in selecting available course readings. The focus of the lists is on women in the United States. Each list consists of twenty to fifty titles, and the most important five to ten titles are starred. The lists are updated each January. Titles no longer in print are dropped, and newly published titles added. The lists' topics include: feminist theory, feminist pedagogy, feminist philosophy, politics, law and legal studies, plus many more. The site is maintained by University of Wisconsin System Women's Studies Librarian wiswsl@doit.wisc.edu.

Derrida Bibliography

http://www.lake.de/home/lake/hydra/lib.html

From Peter Krapp derridabase@hydra.lake.de, this site provides access to a bibliography of works by and about Derrida and deconstruction.

Ecofeminism: An Introductory Bibliography

gopher://silo.adp.wisc.edu:70/00/.uwlibs/.womenstudies/.bibs/.ecofem

A selective and annotated bibliography on sources concerning political activism within womens groups on the environment and surrounding issues. Part of a series of bibliographies published by the University of Wisconsin System Women's Studies Librarian's Office.

Essential Readings on Chinese Philosophy

http://vassun.vassar.edu/~brvannor/bibliography.html

Compiled by Brian Van Norden brvannorden@vassar.edu, this bibliography is extensive in range, covering general histories, Confucianism, Taoism, Mohism, Buddhism, Neo-Confucianism and much more.

Euthanasia: Recommended Reading

http://www.netlink.co.uk/users/vess/booklist.html

This site provides a selected list of some key euthanasia-related books, compiled by the Scottish Voluntary Euthanasia Society. The page is maintained by Chris Docker didmsnj@easynet.co.uk.

Human Rights Bibliographies

http://www.law.uc.edu:81/Diana/bib.html

A selection of human rights bibliographies are collected at this site, part of the DIANA Human Rights Database site at *http://www.law.uc.edu:81/Diana/*

Hyle: Collected Bibliographies of Philosophy of Chemistry

http://rz70.rz.uni-karlsruhe.de/~ed01/Hyle/biblio.htm

This page is provided by the electronic journal, *Hyle*, and currently links to three separate bibliographies in the area of philosophy of chemistry: Chemistry and Humanities (1260 titles); Philosophy of Chemistry in the German Democratic Republic (260 titles); and Collected Bibliographic Section of HYLE Issues (past 1992 literature).

Hypertext Bibliography of Measures of Complexity

http://www.cpm.mmu.ac.uk/~bruce/combib/

This is a bibliography produced by Bruce Edmonds B.Edmonds@mmu.ac.uk covering some of the philosophical and practical references to the concept and measurement of Complexity. It does not attempt to cover all the new sciences that might come under the "Complexity" banner, unless they are relevant to the idea of Complexity per se.

International Society for Environmental Ethics Comprehensive Bibliography

http://www.phil.unt.edu/bib/

This bibliography is an ongoing project of the International Society for Environmental Ethics. It contains all the bibliographic entries from the Newsletter of the Society, as well as articles and abstracts from the journals *Environmental Ethics*, *Environmental Values*, and the *Journal of Agricultural and Environmental Ethics*. The maintainer of the site can be contacted at rolston@lamar.colostate.edu.

JSCOPE Bibliography

http://www.duke.edu/jscope/articles.htm

This is a bibliography of military ethics, compiled by J. H. Toner.

Levinas: English Bibliography

http://pw1.netcom.com/~cyberink/lev/prim.html

This page, which presents a bibliography of works by and on Emmanuel Levinas, is maintained by atterton@rohan.sdsu.edu.

NOEMA: Collaborative Bibliography of Women in Philosophy

http://billyboy.ius.indiana.edu/WomeninPhilosophy/WomeninPhilo.html

This project is an attempt to produce a first rate, comprehensive and continually updated bibliography of works in philosophy published by women. The bibliography, arranged in alphabetical order, represents a database now containing over 11,000 records representing the work of over 3,600 women. The bibliography is edited by Noël Parish Hutchings nhutchin@ius.indiana.edu.

Objectivity Home Page

http://www.artsci.wustl.edu/~pjmandik/objectivity.html

This site is dedicated to philosophical investigations of objectivity, subjectivity, allocentricity, and egocentricity. It contains the Objectivity Bibliography, and is maintained by Pete Mandik pete@twinearth.wustl.edu.

Online Philosophy Bibliographical Resource

http://sun3.lib.uci.edu/~scctr/philosophy/

This site houses a collection of philosophy bibliographies, compiled by Eddie Yeghiayan eyeghiay@uci.edu arising from 2 lecture series in 1996 sponsored by the Philosophy Department at the University of California at Irvine. Eight leading philosophers in the field of Ethics were invited to give 2 public lectures, and these bibliographies are collections of materials relevant to those lectures.

Patrologiae Analiticae Libri C

http://www.wolfson.ox.ac.uk/~floridi/pantana.htm

This site provides access to a short bibliography on analytic philosophy with a list of the top 100 books in the field selected by members of the Internet community and compiled by Luciano.Floridi@philosophy.ox.ac.uk.

Philosophical Counselling Bibliography

http://www.geocities.com/Athens/6553/biblio.htm

This site provides access to a small bibliography on philosophical counselling compiled by Kenneth Cust kencust@sprintmail.com.

Philosophical Debates

http://www.mindspring.com/~mfpatton/debates.htm

This page, compiled by Cheryl and Michael Patton mfpatton@mindspring.com and part of their Patton's Argument Clinic site, provides a growing bibliography on central philosophical questions such as: What is Knowledge? What is the nature of Reality? What is the relationship between the Mind and the Body? Is there a God? How can Science tell us anything? Links to primary texts available online are also included.

Philosophical Writings on Film

http://www.liv.ac.uk/Philosophy/film.html

Compiled by Daniel Frampton d.frampton@philosophy.bbk.ac.uk, this site provides a bibliography of materials relevant to philosophy in films and the philosophy of films.

Philosophy & AI: Annotated Bibliography

http://kent.edu/~brosmait/aibib_gs.html

The annotations for this bibliography were completed by graduate students in the Department of Philosophy at Kent State University. The site is maintained by Brian Rosmaita brosmait@kent.edu.

Philosophy and the Neurosciences Online Resources

http://www.artsci.wustl.edu/~pjmandik/philneur.html

This site is dedicated to neurophilosophy: research at the intersection of philosophy and neuroscience. It contains the Neurophilosophy Bibliography, and is maintained by Pete Mandik pete@twinearth. wustl.edu.

Philosophy: A Selected Bibliography

http://www.library.yale.edu/ref/err/Philosophy.html

This site, maintained by Emily Horning Emily.Horning@yale.edu of Yale University, houses a bibliography relating to holdings within the university's library, and is divided into the following sections: I. Guides and Handbooks, II. Histories and Surveys, III. Current Bibliographies, IV. Retrospective Bibliographies—General, V. Retrospective Bibliographies—Specialized, VI. Encyclopedias, VII. Dictionaries, VIII. Directories and Other Biographical Sources, IX. Selected Sources on Major Philosophers, X. Selected Internet Resources for Philosophy.

Philosophy Bibliographies

http://www.earlham.edu/~peters/philinks.htm#bibliographies

This page, from Peter Suber peters@earlham.edu, provides access to an enormous collection of philosophy-related bibliographies.

Philosophy Documentation Center: Bibliographies

http://www.bgsu.edu/pdc/biblios.html

The Philosophy Documentation Center publishes an ongoing series of Bibliographies of Famous Philosophers. The following titles in this series are currently available from the

Center: *Thomas Aquinas: International Bibliography, 1977-1990; Bradley: A Research Bibliography; R. G. Collingwood: A Bibliographic Checklist; Hegel's Wissenschaft der Logik; Julia Kristeva: A Bibliography of Primary and Secondary Sources in French and English 1966-1996; Charles S. Peirce: A Comprehensive Bibliography; Sartre: Bibliography 1980-1992;* and *Vico: A Bibliography of Works in English from 1884 to 1994* . The Center also publishes a series of Philosophical Bibliographies. Bibliographies currently available include: *Analytic Philosophy of Religion: A Bibliography 1940-1995; The Collaborative Bibliography of Women in Philosophy; 50 Years of Events: An Annotated Bibliography 1947 to 1997; Theodicy: An Annotated Bibliography on the Problem of Evil;* and *Women Philosophers: A Bibliography of Books through 1990*. Ordering information is provided online. The site is maintained by Jennifer Karches karches@bgnet.bgsu.edu.

Philosophy of Artificial Life Bibliography

http://artsci.wustl.edu/~bkeeley/work/alife_bib.html

This site contains a bibliography of AI compiled by Brian Keeley keeley@ twinearth.wustl.edu. Brian's aim is to gather together citations and minimal annotations of all work concerning philosophical issues in the pursuit of Artificial Life. This is to include work of "professional" philosophers, scientific work with important discussions of foundational issues, as well as seminal and landmark work in the field itself.

Philosophy of Psychiatry Bibliography

http://www.uky.edu/~cperring/PhiPsybib.html

Christian Perring cperring@UKCC.UKY.EDU has compiled this bibliography on the ethical, social, political, legal, historical, and philosophical issues in mental health and psychiatry.

St. Thomas Aquinas and Medieval Philosophy: Bibliography

http://www.knuten.liu.se/~bjoch509/works/aquinas/aq_and_med_phi/staampbi.htm

This is a small bibliography on Aquinas and Medieval Philosophy.

A Select Bibliography of the Historical Orientation of the Philosophy of Science

http://socrates.ida.org/vtsts/biblios/phil_hist_bib.html

Originally published as an occasional paper by the Center for the Study of Science in Society, this bibliography is compiled by Peter Barker & Xiang Chen. The page is maintained by Richard White rwhite@ida.org.

A Select Bibliography of Women's Rights

http://www.law.utoronto.ca/pubs/h_rghts.htm

Compiled by Rebecca Cook and Valerie Oosterveld, this site is part of the DIANA human rights database *http://www.law-lib.utoronto.ca/diana/*, and provides an extensive bibliography on human rights and women's issues. This page is maintained on behalf of the authors, by Tracey Pegg tracey.pegg@utoronto.ca.

A Selected Bibliography of Works on Philosophical Counselling

http://www.geocities.com/Athens/Forum/5914/pc-bibl.html

This site provides a short collection of work in philosophical counselling.

Selection Theory Bibliography

http://www.ed.uiuc.edu/facstaff/g-cziko/stb/

This bibliography is a revised, hypertext version of the bibliography which was originally published as Cziko, Gary A., and Campbell, Donald T. (1990), "Comprehensive Evolutionary Epistemology Bibliography," *The Journal of Social and Biological Sciences*, 13(1), 41-81. It is maintained by Gary Cziko g-cziko@uiuc.edu.

The Tavani Bibliography of Computing, Ethics, and Social Responsibility

http://www.siu.edu/departments/coba/mgmt/iswnet/isethics/biblio/

Organized into five main parts with fourteen sections and forty-eight subsections, the bibliography includes more than 2,000 entries. In addition to books and journal articles, works cited include reports, conference proceedings, doctoral dissertations, professional papers presented at seminars and workshops, newsletter articles, and video programs. The site is maintained by David Vance dvance@siu.edu.

UC Irvine Critical Theory Resource

http://sun3.lib.uci.edu/~scctr/online.html

This resource features a large number of the scholarly bibliographies prepared by UC Irvine Library's Special Collections Bibliographer Eddie Yeghiayan eyeghiay@uci.edu. At present, this resource is divided into two subsections, both of which can be browsed and searched.

Bookstores Online

Academic Press—APNet

http://www.apnet.com/

This well-designed site provides links to online journals, product catalogues, textbooks, and an online journal delivery service. The maintainer of the site can be contacted at lalexander@acad.com.

Amazon.com Books

http://www.amazon.com

According to Amazon.com Books, they have over 1 million titles to select from, including a huge range of philosophy titles. Order online for shipments to anywhere in the world.

Blake's Books

http://www.blakesbooks.com/

Blake's Books is an online used and antiquarian bookstore. They carry a wide array of books for scholars and readers in all subjects, including art, philosophy, religion, math, science, history, literature, and the humanities. You can search for individual titles by author, subject, publisher or keyword, or browse through catalogues in over forty subject areas. Blake's can be contacted at feedback@blakesbooks.com.

Books in Philosophy

http://booksinphilosophy.bgsu.com

This online bookstore and reference service offers discounted prices on more than 16,000 philosophy titles published by 130 publishers. The database contains a growing amount of information on each title, and can be browsed at no charge. The site is operated by the Philosophy Documentation Center, and the project manager, Jennifer Karches may be contacted at booksinphil@mailserver.bgsu.edu.

Book Stacks Unlimited, Inc.

http://www.books.com/

Online since 1992, Book Stacks offers over 425,000 titles – many discounted. Features of the site include author information, new releases, and book discussion forums. Order books from a huge online collection and have them delivered to you anywhere in the world.

CARL UnCover

http://uncweb.carl.org/

CARL is the Colorado Alliance of Research Libraries. Through its database UnCover, CARL provides article level access to the journal collections of selected CARL system libraries. The databases are continually being updated, and there are over 5 million articles currently available. Some databases require a password and licensing fee, but there are a number of library catalogues and free databases available. Once you have searched the databases and identified an article of interest, you may decide to order the article and have it faxed to your personal fax number (payment for such orders is by VISA or MASTERCARD). Copyright royalties are carefully tracked and paid to publishers. Once ordered, articles usually take only 24 hours to be delivered.

Full Circle Books

http://www.bookgrrls.com/fcb/

Full Circle Books carries books of interest to women, their friends, families, and children. They have a large selection of beautiful non-sexist, non-racist books for kids of all ages. They also feature books on women and technology—cybergrrls, women and computing, the interface of technology and women's lives and such. This site is maintained by dorothy @bookgrrls.com.

IBS, Internet Bookshop

http://www.bookshop.co.uk

The Internet Bookshop claims to be the largest online bookshop in the world with over 750,000 books available for purchase online, including access to Blackwell Academic's diverse selection of titles, and McGraw-Hill, Penguin, and Pluto Press (broad left) titles. The site includes a mailing list with over 1000 subjects to keep you informed of new titles in your specific area of interest. Any problems with using the site can be referred to support@bookshop.co.uk.

InteLex Corporation

http://www.nlx.com/

InteLex Corporation provides access to the Past Masters series which is the largest collection of classic, scholarly full-text databases in philosophy in the world. From this site you may view and order from an online catalogue. In the near future InteLex will be adding a bookstore containing books of interest to members of the philosophy and religion academic communities, offering sample, trial, and full access to our databases, as well as providing locations for scholarly research. Enquiries about the website should be directed to webmaster@nlx.com.

Kessinger Publishing

http://montanaweb.com/kessinger/

Kessinger Publishing is a bookstore offering rare esoteric reprints, hundreds of scarce books on freemasonry, alchemy, gnosticism, metaphysics, hermeticism, occultism, theosophy, philosophy, magic, religion, tarot, rosicrucianism, and mysticism. They can be contacted at books@kessingerpub.com.

Rescogitans

http://www.rescogitans.it/sitenew/eng/index.htm

This site offers free access to a library of electronic texts, and a bookshop offering a catalogue of electronic titles. The Services section offers articles and reviews from *Informazione Filosofica* (an electronic philosophy periodical in Italian only). A free copy of LibraryLab, Rescogitans software running on Windows95, can be downloaded to facilitate work on electronic titles.

Electronic Journals: A to Z

Aesthetics Ideas

Subscribe: Not necessary
Current/Back Issues: *http://www.indiana.edu/~asanl/ideas.html*
Contact: Dominic Lopes at: dlopes@indiana.edu

Aethestics Ideas is a collection of brief articles on aesthetics, many reproduced from recent issues of the American Society for Aesthetics Newsletter. You're invited to submit your own work, especially if it addresses teaching aesthetics. Copyright is held in all cases by the authors, therefore the author's permission must be obtained before copying, distributing or otherwise using their work.

Animus

Subscribe: Send 'subscribe animus' followed by your name to: listserv@morgan.ucs.mun.ca
Current/Back issues: *http://www.mun.ca/animus/*
Contact: fdoull@morgan.ucs.mun.ca

Animus aims at an understanding of the works of Western civilization and contemporary views of these works. It seeks to promote a standpoint which is critical of dogmatic positions both within contemporary views and within the Western tradition itself.

AntePodium

Subscribe: Not necessary
Current/Back Issues: *http://www.vuw.ac.nz/atp/*
Contact: Editors at: AntePodium@vuw.ac.nz

AntePodium (AtP) is an electronic journal dedicated to scholarly research on the politico-strategic, politico-economic, and politico-cultural dimensions of world affairs. Interdisciplinary and eclectic, it is published by the politics department at Victoria University, Wellington, New Zealand.

Applied Semiotics

Subscribe: Not necessary
Current/Back Issues: *http://www.epas.utoronto.ca:8080/french/as-sa/index.html* Contact: Editors at: pmartein@chass.utoronto.ca

Applied Semiotics is an academic journal devoted to literary semiotic research. Published at the Department of French of the University of Toronto, the review appears exclusively on the World Wide Web. Scholarly contributions are invited.

Arob@se

Subscribe: Not necessary
Current/Back Issues: *http://www.liane.net/arobase/*
Contact: Editors at: pbrun@planete.net or Philippe.Romanski@univ-rouen.fr

Arob@se is published twice a year as an interdisciplinary bilingual forum (English-French) for researchers in literature and human sciences wishing to promote their work through electronic publishing.

Bryn Mawr Reviews

Subscribe: Send "*subscribe BMCR*" and/or "*subscribe BMMR*" to: listserv@cc.brynmawr.edu
Current/Back Issues: *gopher://gopher.lib.virginia.edu:70/11/alpha/bmcr* and *gopher:// gopher.lib.virginia.edu:70/11/alpha/bmmr*

The *Bryn Mawr Classical Review (BMCR)* and the *Bryn Mawr Medieval Review (BMMR)* publish reviews of current work in all areas of classical and medieval studies. There is also opportunity for authors' replies, discussion of earlier reviews, and well-conceived columns of opinion on the current classical and medieval scholarly scene.

Carleton University Student Journal of Philosophy

Subscribe: Not necessary
Current/Back Issues: *http://www.carleton.ca/philosophy/cusjp/*
Contact: Diane Dubrule at ddubrule@ccs.carleton.ca

The *Carleton University Student Journal of Philosophy* is a free journal containing articles written on a wide variety of philosophical topics by graduate and undergraduate students studying at any university. Papers are refereed by faculty members in the Philosophy Department at Carleton University in Ottawa, Canada. The journal, available only on the web, is edited by fourth year honors and graduate students at Carleton University.

Cathesis

Subscribe: Not required
Current Issue: *http://www.abdn.ac.uk/~src068/cathexis.html*
Contact: Editors at: src068.@abdn.ac.uk

Cathesis is an electronic journal for those interested in philosophy. It is published by the student-run Aberdeen University Philosophy Society.

Colibri

Subscribe: Send *"subscribe yourname"* to: colibri-request@let.ruu.nl
Back Issues: *http://colibri.let.ruu.nl*
Information: *http://colibri.let.ruu.nl/HELP*
Contact: Koen Versmissen/Renee Pohlsmann at: colibri@let.ruu.nl

Colibri is an electronic newsletter for those interested in language, speech, logic, or related issues.

Complexity International

Subscribe: Not necessary
Back Issues: *http://www.csu.edu.au/ci/*
Contact: Herbert Jelinek at: hjelinek@csu.edu.au

Complexity International is a refereed journal for papers dealing with any area of complex systems research. Relevant topics include: artificial intelligence, cellular automata, chaos theory, control theory, fractals, neural networks.

Connexions

Subscribe: See information below
Current/Back Issues: *http://www.shef.ac.uk/~phil/connex*

Connexions is a web-based journal of cognitive science. Unlike traditional journals, it is not a showcase for finished work but a forum for the discussion of work-in-progress. Readers can comment on journal articles by way of a mailing list, which can be subscribed to by mailing listproc@sheffield.ac.uk and including *"subscribe connex-l your name"* in the body of the message.

Ctheory

Subscribe: ctheory-request@concordia.ca
Current/Back Issues: *http://www.ctheory.com/ctheory.html*
Contact: Editors at: ctheory@vax2.concordia.ca

Ctheory is a refereed electronic journal: multidisciplinary, multiplatform, and multimedia with an internationally-oriented review focusing on theory, technology, and culture from a critical and feminist perspective.

Disputation

Subscribe: Not necessary
Current/Back Issues: *http://bruxelas.inesc.pt/~jlb/disputatio/web/home.htm*
Contact: Editors at: disputatio@mail.telepac.pt

This is the online version of the print journal of the same name. Articles which appear online are those which the author permits to be published in electronic format. *Disputatio* is the first Portuguese philosophy journal in the analytic tradition. Its aims are to provide an international forum for high standard work in the field, to open up the Portuguese philosophy community to the outside, and to stimulate the local study of analytic philosophy.

Electronic Journal of Analytic Philosophy

Subscribe: Send *"subscribe ejap yourname"* to: listserv@iubvm.usc.indiana.edu
Back Issues: *http://www.phil.indiana.edu/ejap/*
Contact: Editor at: ejap@phil.indiana.edu

The *Electronic Journal of Analytic Philosophy* is a blind peer-reviewed electronic journal for the publication of articles and reviews (in English) relevant to analytic philosophy both as a historical movement and as a current program.

E-Logos

Subscribe: Send *"subscribe yourname"* to: listserv@pub.vse.cz
Back Issues: *ftp://ftp.vse.cz/pub/VSE/logos/* or *http://nb.vse.cz/kfil/win/welcome.htm*
Contact: Karel Pstruzina at: pstruzin@vse.cz

E-Logos covers the fields of epistemology, history of philosophy, logic, philosophy of language, philosophy of mind, and philosophy of science. Papers from the field of ethics, and philosophical essays are also accepted.

Feminist Studies in Aoteoroa Electronic Journal

Subscribe: Send *"subscribe FMST your email address"* to: uotago@stonebow.otago.ac.nz
Contact: Lynne Alice at: l.c.alice@massey.ac.nz

FMST provides a venue for substantive discussions exploring a wide variety of topics, social and textual issues and controversies within feminism and its applications. From time to time book and film reviews are offered, and debates on issues with a Pacific-rim modality are featured.

Host

Subscribe: Contact the Editor, Julian Smith at: jsmith@epas.utoronto.ca

An electronic bulletin for the history and philosophy of science and technology, which contains articles, works in progress, research notes, communications, book reviews, information on electronic resources, and news of interest to the profession. The *HOST* bulletin is distributed in several formats.

HYLE: An International Journal for the Philosophy of Chemistry

Subscribe: Send *"subscribe HYLE"* to: Joachim.Schummer@geist-soz.uni-karlsruhe.de
Current/Back Issues: *http://www.uni-karlsruhe.de/~philosophie/hyle.html*
Contact: Joachim Schummer at: Joachim.Schummer@geist-soz.uni-karlsruhe.de

HYLE is an international journal for the philosophy of chemistry dedicated to all philosophical aspects of chemistry. These include: epistemological, methodological, foundational, and ontological problems of chemistry and its subfields; peculiarities of chemistry and relationships to other scientific and non-scientific fields; aesthetical, ethical, and ecological aspects of chemistry; and those facets of the history, sociology, linguistics, and education of chemistry which are of philosophical relevance.

Injustice Studies

Subscribe: Not necessary
Current Issue: *http://wolf.its.ilstu.edu/injustice/*
Contact: Thomas Simon at: twsimon@ilstu.edu

Injustice Studies (IS) is a refereed international electronic journal that helps focus academic attention on the study of injustices around the world. The editors welcome essays devoted to understanding the nature of injustice, types of injustice, and the history, politics, and moral psychology of particular injustices, ranging from global to local events. Disagreements over which injustices warrant attention also are part of the problematique of *IS*. Since *IS* has an interdisciplinary orientation, its articles should aim to be accessible to the general reader.

Journal of Artificial Intelligence Research

Subscribe: Send *"subscribe yourname"* to: jair@p.gp.cs.cmu.edu
Back Issues: *http://www.cs.washington.edu/research/jair/home.html*
Contact: Steven Minton at: minton@ptolemy.arc.nasa.gov

JAIR is a refereed journal for scientific papers covering all areas of artificial intelligence.

Journal of Buddhist Ethics

Subscribe: Send "subscribe jbe" to: listserv@lists.psu.edu
Back Issues: *http://jbe.la.psu.edu/ and http://www.gold.ac.uk/jbe/jbe.html*
Contact: Damien Keown at: hsa01dk@scorpio.goldsmiths.ac.uk or Charles S. Prebish at: csp1@psuvm.psu.edu.

The *Journal of Buddhist Ethics* has been established to promote the study of Buddhist ethics through the publication of research articles, discussions and critical notes, bulletins, and reviews.

Journal of Transhumanism

Current/Back Issues: *http://www.transhumanist.com/*

The *Journal of Transhumanism* is a peer-reviewed electronic journal publishing contemporary research into the science and philosophy of the future. Submissions should be sent to n.bostrom@lse.ac.uk.

Logic Journal of the IGPL

Subscribe: Contact www-admin@oup.co.uk
Current/Back Issues: *http://www.oup.co.uk/mind/* or *http://theory.doc.ic.ac.uk/Journals/iglpl*

Logic Journal of the IGPL publishes papers in all areas of pure and applied logic, including pure logical systems, proof theory, model theory, recursion theory, type theory, nonclassical logics, nonmonotonic logic, numerical and uncertainty reasoning, logic and AI, foundations of logic programming logic and computation, logic and language, and logic engineering. The journal is published in both hard copy and in electronic form.

Journal of Memetics

Subscribe: Not necessary
Current/Back Issues: *http://www.cpm.mmu.ac.uk/jom-emit/*
Contact: Bruce Edmonds, publisher, at: B.Edmonds@mmu.ac.uk

The *Journal of Memetics* is a new peer-reviewed academic journal. The editors feel that a journal on memetics can be an important place for scientists and professionals to discuss their views and research in memetics. The journal, which seeks to develop the memetic perspective, with space devoted to relevant evolutionary issues and other related topics, is published on the Internet without subscription fee.

Journal of World-Systems Research

Subscribe: Send *"subscribe wsn your name"* to: listproc@csf.colorado.edu
Back Issues: *http://csf.colorado.edu/wsystems/jwsr.html*
Contact: Editor at: chriscd@jhu.edu

The *Journal of World-Systems Research* is an electronic journal dedicated to scholarly research on the modern world-system and earlier, smaller intersocietal networks. It is intentionally interdisciplinary in focus. *JWSR* is published under the sponsorship of the Program in Comparative International Development in the Sociology Department of Johns Hopkins University. The current Editor is Christopher Chase-Dunn.

Ko'aga Rone'eta

Subscribe: Not necessary
Current/Back Issues: *http://www.derechos.org/koaga/main.htm*
Contact: Editors at: koaga@derechos.org

Ko'aga Rone'eta is an online journal of human rights and humanitarian affairs. It is designed to encourage thinking about human rights issues and to encourage actions that promote human rights all over the world. The journal is available in English and Spanish versions.

Law & Politics Book Review

Subscribe: Send *"subscribe LPBR-L your name"* to: listserv@listserv.acns.nwu.edu
Back Issues: *gopher://nuinfo.nwu.edu/11/library/journal*
Contact: Editor at: mzltov@nwu.edu

The *Law & Politics Book Review* is a free publication of the Law and Courts Section of the American Political Science Association. All reviews are solicited and edited by the editor.

Mathesis Universalis

Subscribe: Not necessary
Current/Back Issues: *http://www.pip.com.pl/MathUniversalis/index.html*
Contact: Editors at: aleph@saxon.pip.com.pl

This is an electronic journal in which mechanised deduction is seen as a key to the research in logic and intelligence, intended as a contribution to science-oriented philosophy, developed in a Leibnizian perspective, this set of issues being fittingly covered by the 17th century catchword Mathesis Universalis.

Metaphysical Review—Essays on the Foundation of Physics

Subscribe: Send name/email address to: metaphysical.review@unh.edu
Back Issues: *http://www.meta.unh.edu*
Contact: metaphysical.review@unh.edu

Metaphysical Review: Essays on the Foundations of Physics is an electronic journal comprising of essays, comments, letters, and book reviews related to conceptually difficult problem in physics and science in general.

Minerva: Internet Journal of Philosophy

Current/Back Issues: *http://www.ul.ie/~philos/index.html*
Contact: Editor, Dr. Stephen Thornton, at: stephen.thornton@mic.ul.ie

Published annually and freely available on the Internet, the journal publishes articles relating to philosophy construed in a broad but scholarly sense, without preference for any particular school or intellectual tradition.

Monitors: A Journal of Human Rights and Technology

Subscribe: No direct subscription
Current/Back Issues:*http://www.cwrl.utexas.edu/~monitors/*
Contact: Editors at: monitors@lists.cwrl.utexax.edu

An electronic journal encouraging both activist and academic approaches to the broad concerns of human rights by focusing specifically on the impact of technological advance. Intended to fill a gap in contemporary human rights scholarship by using new information technologies to analyse the various forms of oppression/repression and human rights violations that have always accompanied the advancement of technology. The scope of the journal includes: prisons, political prisoners, torture and disappearance, transnational/multinational corporate expansion, labor rights and exploitation, transfer of technology, population control, states and NGOs, military research and development, and much more.

Moral Musings

Subscribe: Send *"subscribe announce"* to: maiser@integral.on.ca
Current/Back Issues: *http://www.integral.on.ca/musings/*
Contact: Editors at: musings@integral.on.ca

A quarterly electronic journal for writings on moral, social, and political topics. The journal's aim is to provide a forum for people interested in reading and writing about moral and political philosophy in a way that is accessible to a broader readership than is the case with traditional academic journals. The subscription address listed above is for notification of forthcoming issues and tables of contents.

Noetica

Subscribe: Not necessary
Current/Back Issues: *http://psy.uq.edu.au/CogPsych/Noetica/toc.html*
Contact: Editors at: noetica@psy.uq.edu.au

Noetica is an electronic journal of the Australasian Cognitive Science Society. It is sponsored by the Department of Psychology, University of Queensland and mirrored by the Department of Computer Science, Indiana University. The aim of Noetica is to promote the interests of the multi-disciplinary field of Cognitive Science. The participation of scholars from all areas of Cognitive Science is invited, including: Computer Science, Linguistics, Mathematics, Neuroscience, Philosophy, and Psychology. Additionally, the journal will aim to promote applications of Cognitive Science.

Non Serviam

Subscribe: Send *"subscribe your name"* to: listserv@math.uio.no
Back Issues: *http://www.math.uio.no/~solan/non_serviam/*
Contact: Editors at: solan@math.uio.no

Non Serviam is an electronic newsletter that provides a forum for discussion of the theory of egoism, especially as outlined by Max Stirner, author of Der Einzige und Sein Eigentum (*The Ego and its Own*). The aim is to encourage more elaborate and soundly reasoned articles than are often found in mailing lists and newsgroups.

Nordic Journal of Philosophical Logic

Subscribe: *http://www.scup.no/forms/njpl_reg.html*
Current/Back Issues: *http://www.hf.uio.no/filosofi/njpl/*
Contact: Johan Kluwer at J.W.Kluwer@filosofi.uio.no

This journal, covering all aspects of philosophical logic, appears in hard copy as well as online. All articles can be accessed online after a free online registration procedure has been completed.

Online Journal of Ethics

Subscribe: Not required
Current Issue: *http://condor.depaul.edu/ethics/ethg1.html*
Contact: Editors at: lpincus@wppost.depaul.edu

An online journal of cutting edge research in the field of business & professional ethics.

Other Voices

Subscribe: Not required
Current Issue: *http://dept.english.upenn.edu/~ov/*
Contact: Vance Bell, Editor-in-Chief at: vbell@dept.english.upenn.edu

Other Voices is an interdisciplinary journal featuring critical essays, interviews/lectures, hypertext/multimedia projects and reviews in the arts and humanities.

Philosophia

Subscribe: Not necessary
Current/Back Issues: *http://usuarios.isid.es/users/eurema/phi.htm*
Contact: eurema@isid.es

Philosophia is an electronic journal of philosophy in Spanish. Articles can be downloaded from this web site in Word or Word Perfect format, or a Word Viewer can be downloaded if you do not have access to either of these programs.

POIESIS: Philosophy Online Serials

Current/Back Issues: *http://www.nlx.com/posp/*
Contact: poiesis@mailserver.bgsu.edu

This project, a joint venture of the Philosophy Documentation Center and InteLex Corporation, offers searchable online access to a single database containing the full-text of current, recent, and back issues of a growing number of philosophy journals.

Postmodern Culture

Subscribe: Not necessary
Current/Back Issues: *http://jefferson.village.Virginia.EDU:80/pmc/*
Contact: Editors at: pmc@jefferson.village.virginia.edu

Postmodern Culture is an electronic journal published by North Carolina State University and the University of Virginia's Institute for Advanced Technology in the Humanities.

The Proceedings of the Fresian School

Subscribe: Not required
Current/Back Issues: *http://www.friesian.com/*
Contact: Kelley L. Ross at: kross@friesian.com

This is a non-peer-reviewed electronic journal of philosophy that takes up the tradition of the Friesian School and seeks to promote the further development of the critical philosophy of Immanuel Kant.

Psyche Journal of Research on Consciousness

Subscribe: Send *"subscribe psyc firstname lastname"* to: listserv@iris.rfmh.org
Back Issues: *http://psyche.cs.monash.edu.au*
Contact: Patrick Wilken at: patrickw@cs.monash.edu.au

A refereed electronic journal dedicated to supporting the interdisciplinary exploration of the nature of consciousness and its relation to the brain. Psyche publishes material relevant to that exploration from the perspectives afforded by the disciplines of cognitive science, philosophy, psychology, neuroscience, artificial intelligence, and anthropology.

Psycoloquy

Subscribe: Send *"subscribe psyc firstname lastname"* to: listserv@pucc.princeton.edu
Back Issues: *http://cogsci.ecs.soton.ac.uk/psycoloquy/*
Contact: Editor at: psyc@pucc.princeton.edu

Psycoloquy is a refereed electronic journal sponsored on an experimental basis by the American Psychological Association and currently estimated to reach a readership of 20,000. *Psycoloquy* publishes brief reports of new ideas and findings on which the author wishes to solicit rapid peer feedback, international and interdisciplinary, in all areas of psychology and its related fields (bio-behavioral, cognitive, neural, social, etc.) All contributions are refereed by members of Psycoloquy's Editorial Board.

(Re)Soundings

Subscribe: Not necessary
Current/Back Issues: *http://www.millersv.edu/~resound/*
Contact: resound@marauder.millersv.edu

(Re)Soundings, a world wide web publication, is a collaborative effort among an international group of scholars publishing in hypermedia format on the Internet. The journal is innovative in comprising music, visual art, and verbal texts while allowing readers to engage these texts with their own multimedia commentary "hotbuttons" which would become part of the journal. This is an environment in which scholars and artists can create and discuss texts, sharing and building commentary in a variety of media, integrating sound and graphics as well as written materials. The format encourages interaction among traditional disciplines including; English, Foreign Languages, art, history, literature, and music as well as newer disciplines such as Women's Studies, Ethnic Studies, Folklore, Multimedia, and Computer Science so long as the materials have a humanities focus.

Sic et Non: Online Forum for Philosophy and Culture

Subscribe: Not required
Current/Back Issues: *http://www.cogito.de/sicetnon/*
Contact: Editors at: sicetnon@cogito.de

A journal currently published in German, but planning an English version. Open to all philosophers on all philosophical topics and themes.

Society for Philosophy and Technology: Quarterly Electronic Journal

Subscribe: Not required
Current/Back Issues: *http://scholar.lib.vt.edu/ejournals/SPT/spt.html*
Contact: General Editor at: 18512@udel.edu

SPT has no party line or narrow focus; papers, from the beginning, have been welcomed from any and all philosophical perspectives; the only unifying factor is a focus on technology, particular technologies, modern or traditional, or social problems associated with technology in any era—though most of our authors concentrate on the modern world. Some papers criticise our contemporary technological culture in global terms; others critique particular technologies; but just as many analyse technological phenomena with no a priori critical or negative bias. All that the editorial board insists upon is rigorous philosophical analysis, from whatever philosophical perspective the author chooses. In addition, contributions are welcome from authors who are not identified as academic philosophers—from social scientists, engineers, managers of scientific or technological organizations or institutions, for example—as long as their work meets the standards of some philosophical perspective.

Sorites

Subscribe: Send request to: sorites@pinar2.csic.es
Current/Back Issues: *http://sowi.iwp.uni-linz.ac.at/Sorites/Home.html*
Contact: Prof. Lorenzo Penya at: laurentius@pinar1.csic.es

Sorites is a refereed all-English electronic international quarterly of analytical philosophy. It is indexed and abstracted by *The Philosopher's Index.*

Tabula Rasa

Subscribe: Not necessary
Current/Back Issues: *http://www.uni-jena.de/~xnx/tabula_rasa.html*
Contact: Editors at: xnx@rz.uni-jena.de

Tabula Rasa has two main concerns: (a) to offer an informal forum where first (second, third, ...) steps into science can be brought to a wider public with the hope to raise comments and criticism, and (b) to publish scientific papers at a stage, where the patterns of argument and the main statements are not yet fully established. The journal is published online in German.

Textual Reasoning

Subscribe: Send *"subscribe tr-list your.email.address"* to: majordomo@bu.edu
Back Issues: *http://forest.drew.edu/~pmjp/*
Contact: Peter Ochs at: pochs@forest.drew.edu

Textual Reasoning is the name of the electronic journal and e-mail discussions of the Postmodern Jewish Philosophy Network. It is dedicated both to a philosophic review of the postmodern Jewish discourses and postmodern reflections on the variety of Jewish philosophies and Jewish philosophic theologies. Further information about the journal and its mailing list can be found at *http://web.bu.edu/mzank/Textual_Reasoning/.*

Theory and Event

Subscribe: Not necessary
Contact: lora@chaos.press.jhu.edu (Note: an annual fee applies)
Current/Back Issues: *http://muse.jhu.edu/journals/tae/*
Contact: Thomas Dumm at: tldumm@amherst.edu,
   or Anne Norton at: anorton@sas. upenn.edu

Theory & Event chronicles creative political thought in the humanities and the social sciences. It features Essays and other forms of writing and representation, including poetry, photos, montage, hypertext links, and as the medium matures, video and sound, that address the power of sovereignty, territory, and government; old, new, and emerging forms of identity; and the politics of representation as it appears in elections, protest, commodities, and high and popular cultures. It encourages contributions that are both rigorous and lively, and that are attentive to scholarship without sacrificing creativity or timeliness.

Undercurrent

Subscribe: Send *"subscribe undercurrent your.email.address"* to:
   mailserv@oregon.uoregon.edu
Back Issues: *http://darkwing.uoregon.edu/~heroux/home.html*
Contact: Erick Heroux at: heroux@darkwing.uoregon.edu

Undercurrent is an interdisciplinary journal publishing articles in applied theory, accessible to those without knowledge of any specialised vocabulary, and demonstrating "an awareness of who we are now"—highlighting a force, trend, limit, idea, custom, event or structure which exerts some contemporary influence.

Volga Journal of Philosophy and Social Sciences

Current/Back Issues: *http://www.ssu.samara.ru/research/philosophy/vjpss.htm*
Contact: Editor-in-Chief, Prof. Dr. A.A.Shestakov (Samara State University) at:shest@ssu. samara.ru, or Co-editor, Prof. Dr. Valentin Bazhanov (Ulyanovsk State University) at: bazhan@bazh.univ.simbirsk.su

This monthly journal is being produced in both electronic and print formats. The main goal is to present Russian (and overseas) philosophical thought on the Internet. The journal presents hot information related to all types of philosophical activity in Russia, especially the mid-Volga region. Papers are accepted in Russian, English, and German.

Electronic Journals: Directories

E-Journals in Philosophy and Related Subjects

http://www.phil.indiana.edu/ejournals.html

The philosophy department at Indiana University maintains this short but useful list of philosophy-related electronic journals. The site's maintainer can be contacted at webmaster @phil.indiana.edu.

HyperJournal: Directories of Electronic Journals

http://www.ukoln.ac.uk/isg/hyperjournal/contents.htm

This is the Hyperjournal discussion list web site which provides access to a range of databases and directories, as well as reviews of electronic journals, newsletters, and zines. This excellent site was created by Dr. Damien Keown dkeown@gold.ac.uk. Queries about the site should be directed to hyperadmin@ukoln.ac.uk.

Journals: Electronic and Paper

http://users.ox.ac.uk/~worc0337/phil_journals.html

Peter King's peter.king@philosophy.ox.ac.uk site provides a small, up-to-date list of philosophy journals in print and electronic formats.

National Library of Australia: Australian Journals

http://www.nla.gov.au/oz/ausejour.html

This is a current listing of over 1,200 Australian electronic journals, magazines, webzines, e-mail fanzines, etc.—including overseas works with Australian content, authorship, and/ or emphasis. Compiled by the NLA, queries about the site can be directed to www@ nla.gov.au.

NewJour

http://gort.ucsd.edu:80/newjour/

This page facilitates access to a database of new online journals and newsletters, searchable in alphabetical or reverse chronological order. It is maintained by Paul Schaffner pfs@umich.edu.

Philosophy Journals and Newsletters

http://www.earlham.edu/~peters/philinks.htm#journals

From Peter Suber peters@earlham.edu, this page provides another large listing of philosophy journals, both print and electronic.

POIESIS: Philosophy Online Serials

http://www.nlx.com/posp/

This project, a joint venture of the Philosophy Documentation Center and InteLex Corporation, offers searchable online access to a single database containing the full-text of current, recent, and back issues of a growing number of philosophy journals.

Scholarly Journals distributed via WWW

http://info.lib.uh.edu/wj/webjour.html

This site, maintained by Robert Spragg RSpragg@UH.EDU of the University of Houston, provides a searchable, alphabetic listing of a wide range of scholarly journals available online.

World Wide Web Virtual Library: Electronic Journals

http://www.edoc.com/ejournal/

This well-designed page, from e.doc ejournal@edoc.com, provides a searchable database of electronic journals in the following categories: Academic and Reviewed Journals, College or University, Email Newsletters, Magazines & Newspapers, Political, Print Magazines, Publishing Topics, Business/Finance, and Other Resources.

Electronic Texts

Akamac Etexts

http://www.cpm.ll.ehime-u.ac.jp/AkamacHomePage/Akamac_E-text_Links/Akamac_E-text_Links.html

With a focus on texts relevant to the history of economics and social thought, this site provides links arranged in alphabetical order by author. It is maintained by Akama Michio akamac@ll.ehime-u.ac.jp.

Alex Catalogue of Electronic Texts

http://www.lib.ncsu.edu/stacks/alex-index.html

Alex helps users to find and retrieve the full text of documents on the Internet. It currently indexes over 2000 books and shorter texts by author and title, incorporating texts from Project Gutenberg, Wiretap, the Online Book Initiative, the Eris system at Virginia Tech, the English Server at Carnegie Mellon University, Project Bartlesby, CCAT, the online portion of the Oxford Text Archive, and many others. It is maintained by Eric Morgan eric_morgan@ncsu.edu.

Chinese Classics

http://www.cnd.org:8010/Classics/

This site provides access to Chinese classics texts, in Chinese and English translations. The maintainers of the site cnd-ib@cnd.org aim at collecting as much Chinese classic literature as possible for the benefit of the Internet community.

Christian Classics Ethereal Library

http://ccel.wheaton.edu/

Access to Christian electronic texts including works by St. Alphonsus, St. Athanasius, St. Augustine, St. Bernard, Boehme, Bunyan, Calvin, Donne, Milton, and more is provided at this site, maintained by Harry Plantinga W.H.Plantinga@wheaton.edu.

Digital Text Project

http://www.ilt.columbia.edu/academic/digitexts/index.html

This site, maintained by the Institute for Learning Technologies webmaster@ilt.columbia.edu, provides access to a range of philosophical texts online in an easy-to-read format. Includes works by Aristotle, Bentham, Berkeley, Dante, Descartes, Dewey, Emerson, Hegel, Hobbes, Hume, Kant, Leibniz, Locke, Machiavelli, Mill, Plato, Rousseau, Socrates, Spinoza, and Virgil, with promises of more to come.

Electronic Texts

http://www.epistemelinks.com/Main/MainText.htm

From Tom Stone trstone@rpa.net, this page provides links to electronic philosophy texts, arranged alphabetically by author.

English Server Philosophy Page

http://english-www.hss.cmu.edu/philosophy/

This site is the philosophy section of the English Server's webmaster@eng.hss.cmu.edu pages. Access to a range of philosophical texts, including Aristotle, Bacon, Berkeley, Descartes, Hegel, Hume, Kant, Marx, Mill, Nietzsche, and Plato is provided.

Greek Philosophy Archive

http://iris.dissvcs.uga.edu/~archive/Greek.html

This site provides access to a range of Greek philosophy electronic texts, and is maintained by David Knox dknox@uga.cc.uga.edu.

Hyper-Weirdness by World Wide Web: Philosophy Page

http://www.physics.wisc.edu/~shalizi/hyper-weird/philosophy.html

A hypertext version by shalizi@phenxa.physics.wisc.edu, of Mitchell Porter's High Weirdness by E-Mail. Provides links primarily to electronic texts covering a vast range of philosophers including Aristotle, Plato and the Ancients, Descartes, Hobbes, Locke, Marx, Mill, and more contemporary philosophers.

Hyper-Weirdness by World Wide Web: Religion Page

http://www.physics.wisc.edu/~shalizi/hyper-weird/wind.html

A hypertext version by shalizi@phenxa.physics.wisc.edu, of Mitchell Porter's High Weirdness by E-Mail. Provides access primarily to electronic texts covering Buddhism, Hinduism, Christianity, Catholicism, Eastern Orthodoxy, C of E, Lutherans, Mormons, Seventh Day Adventists, evangelists and fundamentalists, and more.

The Internet Classics Archive

http://webatomics.com/Classics/

A beautifully-presented, searchable collection of almost 400 classical Greek and Roman texts (in English translation) with user-provided commentary is provided at this site. The maintainer can be contacted at classics@webatomics.com.

Malaspina Great Books

http://www.mala.bc.ca/~mcneil/template.htx

This site provides access to an enormous collection of online texts, organised by historical period, discipline, and searchable alphabetically.

Minerva Text Archive

http://www.sozialwiss.uni-hamburg.de/phil/ag/minerva/

MINERVA is an archive for philosophical texts on the Internet. Anyone can access the archive via a simple web interface, carry out researches in the available texts and add philosophical texts to the archive. This site allows for searching on keywords, titles, authors, or full text abstracts. The texts will be available for (free) download. *MINERVA* is a project of the German Philosophy Knot. Conception and technical realisation is with PhilNet ph6a002@server2.rrz.uni-hamburg.de in Hamburg; programming is done by Jan Boddin.

OmniMedia: Electronic Books & Texts

http://www.awa.com/library/omnimedia/links.html

This site aims to provide the most comprehensive listing of sites which provide online access to electronic texts.

Online Book Initiative

ftp://ftp.std.com/obi

The Online Book Initiative collects electronic texts which are available for download. Directories are arranged in alphabetical order by authors' names. Enquiries can be directed to Barry Shein bzs@world.std.com.

The Online Books Page

http://www.cs.cmu.edu/Web/books.html

This site allows users to search electronic texts by author or title, or browse by subject listing. It also provides links to other electronic text repositories. The maintainer can be contacted at spok+books@cs.cmu.edu.

Oxford Text Archive

http://users.ox.ac.uk/~archive/ota.html

The Oxford Text Archive contains electronic versions of literary works by many major authors, in Greek, Latin, English, and over a dozen other languages. Over 1500 titles can be accessed. The maintainer of this site can be contacted at archive@vax.ox.ac.uk.

The PastMasters Series

http://www.nlx.com/pstm/index.htm

This is the world's largest collection of electronic texts in philosophy. Titles include editions of Anselm, Aquinas, Aristotle, Berkeley, Dewey, Hobbes, Hume, Kierkegaard, Locke, Nietzsche, Peirce, Poinsot, Santayana, Sidgwick, and Wittgenstein. Also available are collections of British Philosophy, Economic Philosophy, Political Philosophy, The Rationalists, and The Utilitarians. For more information contact Brad Lamb at lamb@nlx.com.

Philosophy Etexts

http://www.earlham.edu/~peters/philinks.htm#etexts

From Peter Suber peters@earlham.edu, this page provides links to a range of sites which house electronic texts in philosophy.

Philosophy & Theology

http://www.georgetown.edu/labyrinth/subjects/philosophy/phil.html

This site, part of the Labyrinth Medieval Studies site at *http://www.georgetown.edu/labyrinth*, provides access to electronic philosophy and theology texts from ancient and medieval thinkers.

Project Gutenberg

http://promo.net/pg/

Project Gutenberg began in 1971 and has been converting texts to electronic format on an ongoing basis ever since. At this site you will find an enormous collection of electronic texts, with new texts being added regularly.

Project Libellus

ftp://ftp.u.washington.edu/public/libellus/

Project Libellus is an ftp site providing access to a range of texts in Latin, plus learning aides and commentaries on the primary texts.

The Romanitas Reference Series

http://www.paratext.com

This CD-ROM series includes Latin and English versions of the complete works of Vergil, Ovid, and Catullus. The series is edited by Sally Davis, and is published by PARATEXT: Electronic Reference Publishing.

Texts and Contexts

http://paul.spu.edu/~hawk/t&c.html

This well-designed site, maintained by Haakon Sorensen hawk@spu.edu, provides links to a variety of electronic texts and short biographical details on each of the text's authors. Access works by Aquinas, Aristotle, Augustine, Bacon, Dante, Descartes, Dostoevsky, Freud, Homer, Kierkegaard, Machiavelli, Marx, Mill, More, Nietzsche, Plato, and others.

Wesleyan Chinese Philosophical Etext Archive

http://www.wesleyan.edu/~sangle/etext/

Maintained by Stephen C. Angle sangle@wesleyan.edu, this site provides online access to a range of Chinese philosophical texts.

Encyclopedias & Glossaries

A Buddhist Glossary

http://easyweb.easynet.co.uk/~pt/buddhism/books/glossary.htm

This small glossary of Buddhist terms is from Paul Trafford pt@easynet.co.uk.

Catholic Encyclopedia

http://www.knight.org/advent/cathen/cathen.htm

This page contains a searchable version of the *Catholic Encyclopedia*. The editors knight@knight.org of this project are calling for assistance in reproducing articles from the hard copy version for online accessibility.

ChurchRodent

http://www.dialnet.net/users/rtatum/glossary/

This is R. A. Tatum's rtatum@mail.orion.org *Glossary of Christian History*, based in-part on Bruce Shelley's *Christian History in Plain Language*.

Critical Thinking Glossary

http://www.sonoma.edu/cthink/University/univlibrary/Gloss/intro.nclk

This glossary is produced with teachers of critical thinking in mind, and is maintained at the Center for Critical Thinking CCT@sonoma.edu.

Dictionary of Philosophy of Mind

http://wwwartsci.wustl.edu/~philos/MindDict/

The page provides access to a dictionary of terms used in philosophy of mind. It is compiled by Chris Eliasmith chris@twinearth.wustl.edu, who welcomes suggestions for additions to help expand the usefulness of the site.

A Dictionary of Philosophical Terms & Names

http://people.delphi.com/gkemerling/dy/

This site presents a concise guide to technical terms and personal names often encountered in the study of philosophy. Although its entries are extremely brief, many of them include links to more detailed discussions located elsewhere on this site and in other on-line resources, including especially the Internet Encyclopedia of Philosophy, the Stanford Encyclopedia of Philosophy, Peter Saint-Andre's The Ism Book, and Stephen Downes's Guide to the Logical Fallacies. It is maintained by Garth Kemerling gkemerling@delphi.com.

Encephi: L'encyclopedie Electronique de la philosophie

http://www.cvm.qc.ca/carrefo/encephi/encephi.htm

This beautifully-designed site houses a small French-language encyclopedia of philosophy.

Ethics Update Glossary

http://ethics.acusd.edu/Glossary.html

This site, from Lawrence Hinman hinman@acusd.edu provides a small glossary of philosophical terms.

Glossary of Kant's Technical Terms

http://www.hkbu.edu.hk/~ppp/ksp1/KSPglos.html

From Stephen Palmquist StevePq@hkbu.edu.hk, this site lists Kant's most important technical terms, together with a simple definition of each, originally written as a study aid to help make the intricate web of Kant's terminology comprehensible to students who had little or no familiarity with Kant's writings.

A Glossary of Pali and Buddhist Terms

http://world.std.com/~metta/glossary.html

This glossary, from metta@world.std.com, is adapted (with permission) directly from the glossaries in the books, *Straight from the Heart*, *Things As They Are*, and *The Wings to Awakening*.

Glossary of Philosophical Terms

http://www.blackwellpublishers.co.uk/PHILOS/philglos/htm

This glossary is taken from Nicholas Bunnin's and E. P. Tsui-James's *The Blackwell Companion to Philosophy*, and is intended for an undergraduate audience.

Glossary of Philosophical Terms and Names

http://www.nwmissouri.edu/~0100355/gloss.htm

The glossary was prepared for the courses of Dr. James W. Eiswert 0100355@ acad. nwmissouri.edu, Department of History, Humanities and Philosophy, Northwest Missouri State University.

Glossary of Religious Terms

http://www.religioustolerance.org/glossary.htm

This glossary of religious terms is prepared by the Ontario Consultants on Religious Tolerance.

Glossary: Philosophy of Mind

http://www.cogsci.ed.ac.uk/~ddb/contents/glossary.htm

This is Darren Brierton's ddb@cogsci.ed.ac.uk glossary for philosophy of mind. Other teaching resources can also be located at this site.

GTH: Glossary-Guide for Translating Husserl

http://www.filosoficas.unam.mx/~gth/gthi.htm

This site, created by Antonio Zirion Quijano zirion@servidor.unam.mx in Spanish and English versions, aims to extend the project initiated by Dorion Cairns in his *Guide for*

Translating Husserl. It's ultimate aim is to give the glossary a multilingual character so that it may serve to aid in the translation of the works of Husserl to every language dead or alive.

Internet Encyclopedia of Philosophy

http://www.utm.edu:80/research/iep/

A searchable online encyclopedia edited by James Fieser jfieser@utm.edu. Articles in the Internet Encyclopedia of Philosophy are currently from three sources (1) adaptations from public domain sources, (2) adaptations from student papers, and (3) original contributions by professional philosophers. Over time, the editor seeks to replace all of the first two type of articles with original contributions by professional philosophers.

The Ism Book: A Hypertext Dictionary of Philosophy

http://www.plantagenet.com/~stpeter/ism/ism.html

From Peter Saint-Andre stpeter@plantagenet.com, the Ism Book was written in 1990 at the request of a businessman who wanted a brief guide to philosophy in the form of a dictionary (and who was influenced by Ayn Rand's philosophy of Objectivism). Because of its original audience and the author's own humanistic vision of philosophy, the author included the popular meanings of the isms, brought out the practical consequences of viewpoints in all the branches of philosophy, defined various types of isms, and even tried to make it entertaining. While several of these aspects over the years have been adjusted, the book retains much of its original stamp.

Meta-Encyclopedia of Philosophy

http://www.ditext.com/encyc/frame.html

This site allows users to compare entries in the most important encyclopedias and dictionaries of philosophy on the Internet. The site is maintained by Andrew Chrucky Encyclopedia@ditext.com.

Philosophical Terms and Definitions

http://www.geocities.com/Athens/Delphi/2795/phildef.htm

This site provides an A to Z of common philosophical terms from Ryan Breedon eco@sympatico.ca and part of his larger Philosophy for Everyone site at *http://www.geocities.com/Athens/Delphi/2795/home.htm*.

Philosophy and Logic

http://www1.ch.transnet.de/~wiedem/philweb/

This site provides a glossary of logical terms, a biographical dictionary of key figures in the history of logic, and an overview of the history of philosophy at Leipzig. It is maintained by Uwe Widemann *U.Wiedemann@link-c.cl.sub.de*.

RBJ's Glossary

http://www.rbjones.com/rbjpub/philos/glossary/index.htm

This is R. B. Jones' small but useful philosophy glossary, part of his Factasia site at *http://www.rbjones.com/rbjpub/philos/*.

The Red Feather Dictionary of Critical Social Science

http://www.uvm.edu/~tryoung/dict3rd.html

From T. R. Young tryoung@uvm.edu, this site is "a teaching dictionary of key words for progressive, radical, critical, Marxist, feminist, left-liberal, as well as postmodern scholars and students."

Shaping Genes: Glossary of Bioethics

http://www.biol.tsukuba.ac.jp/~macer/SG18.html

This glossary, which focuses on genetic technology, is by Darryl R. J. Macer, and from his book, *Shaping Genes*.

The Skeptics Dictionary

http://dcn.davis.ca.us/~btcarrol/skeptic/dictcont.html

From Robert T. Carroll btcarrol@wheel.dcn.davis.ca.us, *The Skeptic's Dictionary & Guide for the New Millennium* provides definitions, essays, and references on topics from acupuncture to zombies.

Stanford Encyclopedia of Philosophy

http://plato.stanford.edu/

The *Stanford Encyclopedia of Philosophy* is the first dynamic encyclopedia. Each entry is maintained and kept up-to-date by an expert or group of experts in the field. Unlike static reference works which are fixed on the printed page or on CD-ROM, which often become outdated soon after they are published, this document constantly changes with the addition of new entries and the modification of existing entries. Consequently, you can expect the entries in this encyclopedia to be responsive to new research. Moreover, the entries are evaluated by an Editorial Board. Whenever an entry is added or significantly modified, the Board member in charge of that entry is automatically notified and it is then his or her responsibility to evaluate the new material. The Principal Editor is Edward N. Zalta. Correspondence should be directed to editors@plato.stanford.edu. This site is mirrored at *http://setis.library.usyd.edu.au/stanford/*.

Library Catalogues

Australian National University—Elisa

http://elisa.anu.edu.au/elisa/elibrary/libcat.html

From this site you can search for Australian library catalogues. Access is also provided to international library catalogues. Some Australian University Libraries worth searching include:

Monash University Library
http://www.lib.monash.edu.au/wwwlib/

Melbourne University Library (log in as library)
telnet://opac.unimelb.edu.au

University of New South Wales Library
http://www.library.unsw.edu.au/

ANU Library
http://info.anu.edu.au/elisa.html

Canadian Libraries and Library Catalogues

http://www.nlc-bnc.ca/canlib/eindex.htm

In English and French, this National Library of Canada site provides access to libraries all over Canada, sorted by region, and soon to be sorted alphabetically and by type.

Einet Galaxy's European Library List

http://galaxy.einet.net/hytelnet/SITES1B.html

From this site you can access a directory of online libraries throughout Europe (including Eastern Europe and the Baltic States), with multiple listings for each country.

New Zealand Library Catalogues

http://www.auckland.ac.nz/lbr/libcats.htm

This site provides access to New Zealand University and public library catalogues.

Online Catalogues with 'Webbed' Interfaces

http://www.lib.ncsu.edu/staff/morgan/alcuin/wwwed-catalogs.html

This is an extensive list of worldwide library and related catalogues which use a web interface. The list is maintained by Eric Morgan <u>ericmorgan@ncsu.edu</u> and is an excellent resource.

United Kingdom: Higher Education and Research Catalogues

http://www.niss.ac.uk/reference/opacs.html

From this site you can access online library catalogues at Universities throughout the United Kingdom. This site organises the catalogues into region, and in alphabetical order. An excellent research resource which includes access to:

Cambridge University Library
telnet://ul.cam.ac.uk

Oxford University Library
telnet://129.67.146

Newsletters & Magazines

Bioethics Bulletin

http://wings.buffalo.edu/faculty/research/bioethics/news.html

This is the bulletin of the UB Center for Clinical Ethics and Humanities in Health Care. The bulletin is a monthly publication, and archives of all editions back to 1994 are accessible from the web site. The bulletin is edited by Tim Madigan timmadigan@aol.com.

Community Ethics

http://www.pitt.edu/~caj3/commie.html

Community Ethics is the newsletter of the Consortium Ethics Program. This site contains articles from the current and back issues, and is maintained by Alan Joyce caj3+@pitt.edu.

Computers & Texts

http://info.ox.ac.uk/ctitext/publish/comtxt/

Computers & Texts is the journal/newsletter of the CTI Center for Textual Studies. It is edited by Michael Fraser and published around March, July, and December of each year. The printed edition is available free of charge to academics in the United Kingdom. This site contains full text of current and back issues, plus an online subscription form.

Crossings: The Mariage de Raison Cyberzine

http://mdr.aletheia.be/zine/currentf.htm

Crossings is an initiative of the Society Mariage de Raison. 'Crossings' means first of all to be a space where intellectual, theoretical, philosophical discussion can take place. It offers electrictronic space for articles, interviews, columns, and letters. The editor can be contacted at editor@aletheia.be.

Ends & Means

http://www.abdn.ac.uk/~phl002/techno.htm

Ends and Means is the electronic newsletter of the University of Aberdeen Center for Philosophy Technology and Society. *Ends and Means* is issued, free of charge, twice a year—in October and April. For information contact Ellis Perry at j.e.perry@abdn.ac.uk.

The Ethical Spectacle

http://www.spectacle.org/

The Ethical Spectacle is a net zine or newsletter which accepts articles on any ethical, political, or legal topic. It is edited by Jonathan Wallace jw@bway.net, and the site contains links to other ethics-related resources. A mailing list advising of new issues can be subscribed to at: *http://www.greenspun.com/spam/home.tcl?domain=ethspec.*

E-Zine List

http://www.meer.net/~johnl/e-zine-list/

One of the earliest directories of electronic publications, John Labovitz's johnl@meer.net list focuses on electronic zines fanzines or magazines usually produced for fun, but sometimes of interest to philosophers. John's list is updated monthly, and currently lists well in excess of 1600 zines.

The Philosopher

http://www.rmplc.co.uk/eduweb/sites/cite/staff/philosopher/

The Philosopher is the interactive, electronic journal of the Philosophical Society of England. "It provides a forum for short, original, brilliant and accessible articles (and, it is true, space for a few rather less good ones!)" *The Philosopher* is edited by Martin Cohen 99mismec@mis.marjon.ac.uk.

The Philosophers' Web Magazine

http://www.philosopher.demon.co.uk/

Edited by Jerry Stangroom jerry@ubird.demon.co.uk, *The Philosophers' Web Magazine* includes news, reviews, features, interviews, new philosophy and over 200 philosophy links, and "aims to be the most accessible and entertaining forum for general philosophy on the net."

Philosophy from the Mining Co.

http://philosophy.miningco.com/

Matt Runge philosophy.guide@miningco.com puts together this weekly page on philosophy which includes news, articles, and new finds on the net.

Philosophy Now

http://www.kcl.ac.uk/kis/schools/hums/philosophy/PhilNowHome.html

"*Philosophy Now* is a news-stand magazine for everyone interested in ideas. It aims to corrupt innocent citizens by convincing them that philosophy can be exciting, worthwhile and comprehensible, and also to provide some light and enjoyable reading matter for those already ensnared by the muse, such as philosophy students and academics." This site provides a sneak preview of the magazine, and is maintained by Rick Lewis rick.lewis@ kcl.ac.uk.

Social Justice Ezine

http://members.tripod.com/~goforth/socialjustice.html

Social Justice electronic magazine includes such topics as Amnesty International, gay rights, human rights, sexual harassment, and so on. For information, contact goforth@ igc. apc.org.

Pre-Prints & Reviews

AMS Preprint Server

http://www.ams.org/preprints/

This is a preprint service covering a variety of topics in mathematics including set theory, mathematical logic and foundations, number theory, category theory, functional analysis, and more. The maintainer of the site can be contacted at webmaster@ams.org.

BEARS: Brown Electronic Article Review Service

http://www.brown.edu/Departments/Philosophy/bears/homepage.html

BEARS provides brief reviews of current journal articles in moral and political philosophy. It also provides links to a number of other useful philosophy resources. BEARS is maintained by James Dreier james_dreier@brown.edu and David Estlund david_estlund@ brown.edu.

Behavioural and Brain Sciences Target Article Preprints

http://www.princeton.edu/~harnad/bbs.html

Behavioural & Brain Sciences (BBS) is an international, interdisciplinary journal of "open peer commentary," published by Cambridge University Press, with its editorial offices in Southampton, UK and New York, NY. *BBS* publishes important and controversial interdisciplinary "target articles" in psychology, neuroscience, behavioural biology, cognitive science, artificial intelligence, linguistics and, philosophy. Articles are rigorously refereed and, if accepted, are circulated to a large number of potential commentators around the world in the various specialties on which the article impinges. Their 1000-word commentaries are then co-published with the target article as well as the author's response to each. The commentaries consist of analyses, elaborations, complementary and supplementary data and theory, criticisms and cross-specialty syntheses. This site includes an archive of articles, as well as instructions for authors. The maintainer of the site can be contacted at harnad@princeton.edu.

Brock's Philosophy Page: Metaphysics

http://www.magibox.net/~brock/philosophy/

This page, maintained by Carl Brock Sides cbks@magibox.net, provides a range of papers written on metaphysics-related topics.

CogPrints: Cognitive Sciences EPrint Archive

http://cogprints.soton.ac.uk/cogprints.html

This is an electronic preprint archive for works in cognitive science. The project is overseen by Prof. Stevan Harnad harnad@cogsci.soton.ac.uk.

Danny Yee's Book Reviews

http://www.anatomy.su.oz.au/danny/book-reviews/subjects.html

Danny Yee danny@cs.su.oz.au is obviously an avid reader! His book reviews look informative and interesting, and he covers an enormous range of topics, but of particular interest here are his book reviews in philosophy, feminism, history and philosophy of science, linguistics, mathematics, and politics. Updated regularly, this site is worth a visit.

Essays on the Philosophy of Technology

http://wwwfaculty.mccneb.edu/commhum/PHILOS/techessay.htm

From Frank Edler fedler@metropo.mccneb.edu, this site provides links to a collection of over 40 papers on the philosophy of technology.

Individuals with Online Papers in Philosophy

http://ling.ucsc.edu/~chalmers/online.html

Compiled by David Chalmers chalmers@paradox.ucsc.edu, this site provides a list of individuals who have made available online papers in philosophy and related areas. The list concentrates mostly on academic philosophers, particularly in philosophy of mind, although a few scientists and others are included.

The International Directory of Online Philosophy Papers

http://www.hku.hk/philodep/directory

The aim of this directory is to provide a place for gathering and disseminating online papers in philosophy, and to encourage others to put their work online. Authors can announce their new papers on this page and interested parties can check here to see where such papers are, without having to look through other philosophers' websites to see if there is anything new. Primarily a page of links that points to papers available at other sites, this site is maintained by Joe Lau jyflau@hkuxa.hku.hk at the University of Hong Kong.

International Philosophical Preprint Exchange (IPPE)

http://phil-preprints.l.chiba-u.ac.jp/IPPE.html

IPPE is a service on the Internet intended to make it easy for philosophers with Internet access of any kind to exchange working papers in all areas of philosophy, and to comment publicly on each other's work. IPPE, which is located at Chiba University in Japan, provides storage for working papers, abstracts, and comments, and provides a variety of means by which papers and abstracts may be browsed and downloaded. The service is provided free of charge to any interested parties. IPPE welcomes submissions from all areas of philosophy. IPPE can be contacted at phil-preprints-admin@phil-preprints.l.chiba-u.ac.jp.

Logic Eprints

http://www.math.ufl.edu/~logic/

Logic Eprints is a system for the electronic distribution of announcements of recent results in logic, as well as an electronic preprint service to make available the electronic source for currently unpublished papers or notes. The site is maintained by William Mitchell mitchell@math.ufl.edu.

Logic Group Preprint Series

http://www.phil.ruu.nl:80/home/marco/preprints.html

This page, maintained at the University of Utrecht Philosophy Department by Marco Hollenberg hollenb@phil.ruu.nl, provides access to a collection of preprints in logic.

Metapsychology

http://www.cmhc.com/perspectives/metapsychology/

Metapsychology is a column in an online magazine, *Perspectives*, at *http://www.cmhc.com/ perspectives/*. The column focuses on reviews of books on philosophical, ethical, and historical issues in mental health, and is written by Christian Perring cperring@ukcc.uky.edu.

Online Archive

http://www.shef.ac.uk/uni/academic/N-Q/psysc/staff/rmyoung/papers/index.html

On this site you will find a huge collection of the work of Prof Robert Young robert@ RMY1.DEMON.CO.UK from the Centre for Psychotherapeutic Studies (UK) on a range of topics focusing on evolutionary biology.

Online Papers on Consciousness

http://ling.ucsc.edu/~chalmers/mind.html

Compiled by David Chalmers chalmers@paradox.ucsc.edu, this site is a directory of about 170 online papers on consciousness and closely-related topics. Most papers are by academic philosophers or scientists, and suggestions for new papers are welcome.

Papers by Hans O. Melberg

http://home.sol.no/hansom/papers/papers.htm

This page contains a selection of articles by Hans Melberg hansom@online.no. There are papers in Russian history, decision theory and social science theory, and also in political philosophy and economics. Hans promises that a new paper will appear online every Monday.

Philosophy of Science Papers

http://easyweb.easynet.co.uk/~thonemann/index.html

This is Philip Thonemann's thonemann@easynet.co.uk page comprising a number of his papers in the area of philosophy of science.

Political Science Manuscripts

http://www.trenton.edu/~psm/

PSM is a project to distribute political science scholarship online. The page, created by William Ball ball@trenton.edu, features a collection of abstracts of manuscripts, with links back to the manuscripts themselves which can be accessed through an online search feature.

Print Journals: A to Z

American Journal of Philology

http://ww.press.jhu.edu/press/journals/titles/ajp.html

AJP has acheived worldwide recognition as a forum for international exchange amoung classicists and philologists by publishing original research in Greek and Roman literature; classic linguists; and Greek and Roman history, society, religion, and philosophy. In-depth coverage and a substantial book review section are featured in every issue. *AJP* is open to a wide variety of contemporary approaches including literary interpretation and history, textual criticism, historical investigation, and epigraphy.

American Philosophical Quarterly

http://www.bgsu.edu/pdc/apq.html

American Philosophical Quarterly is one of the principal English vehicles for the publication of scholarly work in philosophy. The scope of the journal encompasses the entire range of philosophical inquiry. Each issue is given entirely to self-sufficient articles of high quality, regardless of the school of thought from which they derive. This page provides subscription information, a table of contents of current issue, and information on ordering the journal.

Analysis

http://www.shef.ac.uk/uni/academic/N-Q/phil/analysis/homepage.html

Analysis was established in 1933 to provide a forum for the rapid publication of shorter papers in analytical philosophy, and has maintained this role ever since. This page lists recent and current contents, provides information on how to subscribe, how to get an inspection copy by e-mail, and information for contributors.

Anarchist Studies

http://www.erica.demon.co.uk/AS.html

Anarchist Studies is a refereed journal concerned with all aspects of anarchist theory, history and culture.

Annals of Pure and Applied Logic

http://www.elsevier.nl/inca/publications/store/5/0/5/6/0/3/505603.pub.shtml

The *Annals of Pure and Applied Logic* publishes papers and short monographs on topics of current interest in pure and applied logic, the foundations of mathematics, and those areas of theoretical computer science and other disciplines which are of direct interest to mathematical logic. The *Annals* serves primarily but not exclusively as a vehicle for the publication of papers too long to be published promptly by other journals, but too short to form a separate book.

Annals of Science

http://www.tandf.co.uk/jnls/asc.htm

Annals of Science was launched in 1936 as an independent review dealing with the development of science since the Renaissance. Now firmly established as the leading scholarly journal in the field, its scope has widened to cover developments since the thirteenth century and to include articles in French and German. Contributions from Australia, Canada, China, France, Germany, Greece, Hungary, Italy, Japan, USA, and Russia bear testimony to its international appeal. Each issue includes a comprehensive book reviews section and essay reviews on a group of books on a broader level. The editor is supported by an active international board. The original index has been extended to cover the period 1970 to 1986, and is available from the publisher. A unique feature of the journal is the reproduction of selected illustrations in colour.

Aporia

http://humanities.byu.edu/Phil/aporia.htm

Aporia is published once a year by the Department of Philosophy at Brigham Young University and is dedicated to recognising exemplary philosophical work at the undergradute level. Each year, the winning essays of the annual David H. Yarn Philosophical Essay Competition are published along with other outstanding undergraduate philosophical essays. The winners of the Yarn Competition are selected by a faculty committee independent of the student editors and staff. While the Yarn Competition is open only to BYU students, *Aporia* welcomes submissions from all undergraduate students.

Arabic Sciences and Philosophy

http://www.cup.cam.ac.uk/Journals/JNLSCAT/asp/asp.html

This international journal is devoted to the history of the Arabic sciences, mathematics, and philosophy in the world of Islam between the eighth and the eighteenth centuries in a cross-cultural context. It publishes original studies of the highest standard on the history of these disciplines as well as studies of the inter-relations between Arabic sciences and philosophy and Greek, Indian, Chinese, Latin, Byzantine, Syriac, and Hebrew sciences and philosophy. *Arabic Sciences and Philosophy* casts new light on the growth of these disciplines as well as on the social and ideological context in which this growth took place. Articles are published in English, French, or German with abstracts in French and English. A special issue, "Arabic into Latin," is also included.

Arcana: Inner Dimensions of Spirituality

http://www.evpro.com/arcana/

The journal *Arcana* is devoted to bringing the teachings revealed in Swedenborg's works to all those who are deeply concerned with their spiritual condition, who are seeking answers to personal and universal issues of vital spiritual importance, and who want to achieve spiritual renewal. It is a quarterly publication of the Swedenborg Association.

Archiv für Begriffsgeschichte

http://www.ruhr-uni-bochum.de/philosophy/series/archiv.htm

This is a German journal for research in history and definition of concepts and history of ideas.

Argumentation

http://kapis.www.wkap.nl/kapis/CGI-BIN/WORLD/journalhome.htm?0920-427X

Argumentation is an international and interdisciplinary journal. Its aim is to gather academic contributions from a wide range of scholarly backgrounds and approaches to reasoning, natural inference and persuasion: communication, rhetoric (classical and modern), linguistics, discourse analysis, pragmatics, psychology, philosophy, logic (formal and informal), critical thinking, history, and law. Its scope includes a diversity of interests, varying from philosophical, theoretical, and analytical to empirical and practical topics. *Argumentation* publishes papers, book reviews, a yearly bibliography, and announcements of conferences and seminars.

Artificial Intelligence

http://www.elsevier.nl/inca/publications/store/5/0/5/6/0/1/505601.pub.shtml

Artificial Intelligence, which commenced publication in 1970, is now the generally accepted international forum for the publication of results of current research in this field. The journal welcomes basic and applied papers describing mature work involving computational accounts of aspects of intelligence. Specifically, it welcomes papers on: automated reasoning, computational theories of learning, heuristic search, knowledge representation, qualitative physics, signal, image and speech understanding, robotics, natural language understanding, and software and hardware architectures for AI.

Artificial Intelligence Review

http://kapis.www.wkap.nl/kapis/CGI-BIN/WORLD/journalhome.htm?0269-2821

Artificial Intelligence Review serves as a forum for the work of researchers and application developers from Artificial Intelligence, Cognitive Science and related disciplines. The *Review* publishes state-of-the-art research reports and critical evaluations of applications, techniques, and algorithms from these fields. *Artificial Intelligence Review* also presents refereed survey and tutorial articles, as well as reviews and commentary on significant developments from these disciplines.

Augustinian Studies

http://www.bgsu.edu/pdc/august.html

Augustinian Studies is devoted to the scholarly study of the life, teachings, and influence of Augustine. The journal publishes articles from a variety of disciplines and perspectives including philosophy, theology, and history, article-length reviews of appropriate publications, and the annual Saint Augustine Lecture given each Fall at Villanova University.

Australasian Journal of Philosophy

http://www.qut.edu.au/arts/human/ethics/ajp.htm

This site provides subscription and editorial information, information for authors, tables of contents of current and back issues.

Behavioural and Brain Sciences

http://www.cup.cam.ac.uk/Journals/JNLSCAT/bbs/bbs.html

Behavioral and Brain Sciences is the internationally renowned journal with the innovative format, known as Open Peer Commentary. Particularly significant and controversial pieces of work are published from researchers in any area of psychology, neuroscience, behavioural biology, or cognitive science, together with 20-30 commentaries on each article from specialists within and across these disciplines, plus the author's response to them. The result is a fascinating and unique forum that contributes to the communication, criticism, stimulation, and particularly the unification of research in behavioural and brain sciences—from molecular neurobiology to artificial intelligence and the philosophy of the mind.

Between the Species: A Journal of Ethics

http://www.cep.unt.edu/between.html

Between the Species is a quarterly publication of the Schweitzer Center of the San Francisco Bay Institute/Congress of Cultures. This site is rather light on for information, containing only a mailing address for the journal and subscription rates.

Bioethics

http://www.blackwellpublishers.co.uk/scripts/webjrn1.idc?issn=02699702

As medical technology continues to develop, the subject of bioethics has an ever increasing practical relevance for all those working in philosophy, medicine, law, sociology, public policy, education, and related fields. *Bioethics* provides a forum for well-argued articles on the ethical questions raised by current issues such as: abortion, euthanasia, AIDS, in vitro fertilisation, genetic engineering, and experimentation on embryos. These questions are considered on the basis of concrete ethical, legal, and policy problems, or in terms of the fundamental concepts, principles, and theories used in discussions of such problems.

Biology and Philosophy

http://kapis.www.wkap.nl/kapis/CGI-BIN/WORLD/journalhome.htm?0169-3867

Biology and Philosophy is a vehicle for serious exchange on the philosophical foundations of biology and the philosophical and conceptual implications of biological work. It is likely to become fairly important in fostering interdisciplinary interaction. It offers both biologists and philosophers a useful vehicle for publication and a reasonable centralised locus for following the interactions between their disparate disciplines.

Brain and Language

http://www.apnet.com/www/journal/bl.htm

An interdisciplinary journal, *Brain and Language* publishes original research articles, theoretical papers, critical reviews, case histories, historical studies, and scholarly notes. Contributions are relevant to human language or communication in relation to any aspect of the brain or brain function. Articles have theoretical import, either formulating new hypotheses, or supporting or refuting new or previously established hypotheses.

British Journal for the History of Philosophy

http://www.leeds.ac.uk/philosophy/bshp/bjhp/bjhp.htm

The *BJHP* is the official journal of the British Society for the History of Philosophy. It publishes Articles, Discussions, Notes and Queries, Review Articles, Reviews and other items.

British Journal for the Philosophy of Science

http://www.oup.co.uk/jnls/list/phisci/

The *British Journal for the Philosophy of Science* encourages the application of philosophical techniques to issues raised by the natural and human sciences. These include general questions of scientific knowledge and objectivity, as well as more particular problems arising within specific disciplines. This page provides subscription information, guidelines for authors, lists the aims and scope of the journal, and details the contents and abstracts of current issues.

British Journal of Aesthetics

http://www.oup.co.uk/jnls/list/aesthj/

The *British Journal of Aesthetics* is published to promote study, research, and discussion of the fine arts and related types of experience from a philosophical, psychological, sociological, scientific, historical, critical, and educational standpoint. Founded in 1960, *The British Journal of Aesthetics* is highly regarded as an international forum for debate in aesthetics and the philosophy of art. Appearing quarterly—in January, April, July, and October—it publishes lively and thoughtful articles on a broad range of topics from the nature of aesthetic judgement and the principles of art criticism to foundational issues concerning the visual arts, literature, music, dance, film, and architecture. A substantial reviews section offers searching analyses of major new work in the field.

Bulletin of Symbolic Logic

http://www.math.ucla.edu/~asl/bslcontents.html

This is the journal of the Association for Symbolic Logic. Articles (in postcript format) may be downloaded from this site for personal and educational uses only.

Business Ethics: A European Review

http://www.blackwellpublishers.co.uk/scripts/webjrn1.idc?issn=09628770

Business Ethics aims to provide a forum for business people and academics to exchange experience and informed insights on the various moral and ethical challenges and opportunities which increasingly face modern business in Britain, Continental Europe, and throughout the world.

Business Ethics Quarterly

http://www.bgsu.edu/pdc/beq.html

Business Ethics Quarterly publishes scholarly articles from a wide variety of disciplines that focus on the general subject of the application of ethics to the international business community. This journal addresses theoretical, methodological, and issue-based questions that can advance ethical inquiry or improve the ethical performance of business organizations. *BEQ* is the journal of the Society for Business Ethics, and a subscription includes membership in the Society. This page provides information on ordering the journal, its subscription rates, and a table of contents of the current issue.

Cambridge Quarterly of Healthcare Ethics

http://www.cup.cam.ac.uk/journals/JNLSCAT/cqh/cqh.html

The *Cambridge Quarterly of Healthcare Ethics* is designed to address the challenges of biology, medicine, and healthcare and to meet the needs of professionals serving on healthcare ethics committees in hospitals, nursing homes, hospices, and rehabilitation centers. The aim of the journal is to serve as the international forum for the wide range of serious and urgent issues faced by members of healthcare ethics committees, physicians, nurses, social workers, clergy, lawyers and community representatives.

Canadian Journal of Philosophy

http://www.ucalgary.ca/UofC/departments/UP/UCP/CJP.html

The purpose of the *Canadian Journal of Philosophy* is the publication in Canada of philosophical work of high quality, in English or French, and in any field of philosophy. All submissions are given blind editorial review; those of departmental colleagues are externally refereed.

Canadian Journal of Political Science

http://www.wlu.ca/~wwwpress/jrls/cjps/cjps.html

The first objective of *CJPS* is the publication of outstanding scholarly manuscripts on all areas of political science, including manuscripts on the history of political thought, contemporary political theory, international relations and foreign policy, governmental institutions and processes, political behaviour, public administration, and public policy. Published work reflects the main methodological approaches used in the discipline: normative arguments; quantitative methods; interpretative analysis; historical and institutional studies; pluralist, statist and class analyses. In evaluating manuscripts for publication, the primary considerations are, first, whether they make a contribution to political research in general and, second, whether they will be of interest to a broad cross-section of readers than simply a narrow group of specialists in a particular subfield. This aim to publish excellent manuscripts in all major subfields of political science is accomplished mainly by the publication of scholarly articles. Research notes are another form of publication for original scholarship in all subfields. The quality and significance of all manuscripts submitted for consideration as articles or research notes are assessed through anonymous peer review.

The Classical Quarterly

http://www.oup.co.uk/clquaj/

The Classical Quarterly is one of the major journals devoted to Greco-Roman antiquity in the English-speaking world. It publishes research papers and short notes in the fields of language, literature, history, and philosophy, and appears in May and December every year.

The Classical Review

http://www.oup.co.uk/clrevj/

The Classical Review publishes reviews of a new work dealing with the literatures and civiliazations of ancient Greece and Rome. Over three hundred books are reviewed each year, the full-length reviews being followed by shorter notices of less important works.

Cogito

http://www.bris.ac.uk/Depts/Philosophy/cogito.html

Cogito is the journal of the COGITO Society. It aims to publish articles from all areas of philosophy and philosophical traditions. The journal, in keeping with the basic aims of the COGITO Society, seeks to promote an interest in philosophy both in the general public and among young people in particular. Contributors should have these audiences in mind.

Cognition

http://www.elsevier.nl/inca/publications/store/5/0/5/6/2/6/505626.pub.shtml

Cognition is an international journal publishing theoretical and experimental papers on the study of the mind. Contributions include research papers in the fields of psychology, linguistics, computer science, neuroscience, mathematics, ethology, and philosophy.

Common Knowledge

http://www.utdallas.edu/research/common_knowledge/index.html

Common Knowledge, a multidisciplinary journal of Oxford University Press, is dedicated to undermining all foundational structures that impede agreement. The Editorial Board consists in large part of intellectuals who made their reputations arguing that "commensurability" of alien languages or viewpoints or cultures is out of the question, but now find themselves bored with or anxious about the consequences and are therefore patiently building bridges between individuals, between "schools" or ideologies, between academics and the educated public, between theory and practice, fiction and nonfiction, Left and Right, East and West.

Conference: A Journal of Philosophy & Theory

http://www.columbia.edu/cu/conference/

Conference is an interdisciplinary journal of philosophy and theory produced by graduate students at the City University of New York Graduate Center, Columbia University, Fordham University, the New School for Social Research, and New York University. The journal's editors hold no particular theoretical position and accept submissions from any school of thought. They encourage submissions exploring issues in all scholarly and theoretical areas, especially those on exploratory or unconventional topics.

Consciousnss and Cognition

http://www.apnet.com/www/journal/cc.htm

Consciousness and Cognition provides a forum for a natural-science approach to the issues of consciousness, voluntary control, and self. The journal features two types of articles: empirical research (in the form of regular articles and short reports) and theoretical articles.

Book reviews, integrative theoretical and critical literature reviews, and tutorial reviews are also published. The journal aims to be both scientifically rigorous and open to novel contributions.

Constellations: An International Journal of Critical and Democratic Theory

http://www.blackwellpublishers.co.uk/scripts/webjrn1.idc?issn=13510487

The astonishing transformations in Central and Eastern Europe and the Soviet Union since 1989 have undermined and deeply challenged the relevance of Marxism for any future critique of society. Although many Western theorists anticipated the "post-Marxian moment," no one foresaw the events themselves or the new forms of politics that would emerge in their wake. *Constellations* examines the creative ferment of critical social and political thought with the goal of setting the international agenda for radical philosophy and social criticism for the future. In addition to substantive full-length articles, *Constellations* features "Political Chronicle"—regular analyses and commentaries on contemporary political situations of urgent concern to engaged thinkers, plus book reviews and special symposia.

Continental Philosophy Review

http://kapis.www.wkap.nl/kapis/CGI-BIN/WORLD/journalhome.htm?0025-1534

The central purpose of *Continental Philosophy Review* is to foster a living dialogue within the international community on philosophical issues of mutual interest. The journal seeks to elicit, within this international dialogue space, discussions of fundamental philosophical problems and original approaches to them. Encompassing in its focus and gender-inclusive by editorial policy despite its now problematic title, the journal invites essays on both expressly theoretical topics and topics dealing with practical problems that extend to the wider domain of sociopolitical life. It encourages explorations in the domains of art, morality, science, and religion as they relate to specific philosophical concerns. Although not an advocate of any one trend or school in philosophy, the journal is committed to keeping abreast of developments within phenomenology and contemporary continental philosophy and is interested in investigations that probe possible points of intersection between the continental and the Anglo-American traditions.

Critical Inquiry

http://www.journals.uchicago.edu/CI/home.html

Founded in 1974, *Critical Inquiry* is an interdisciplinary journal devoted to publishing the best critical thought in the arts and humanities. Combining a commitment to rigorous scholarship with a vital concern for dialogue and debate, the journal presents articles by eminent critics, scholars, and artists on a wide variety of issues central to contemporary criticism and culture.

Critical Review

http://www.sevenbridgespress.com/cr/crindex.html

Critical Review seeks to draw on all of the social sciences in examining the effects on human well-being—not just on material prosperity—of not only laissez-faire captialism and the alternatives to it, but of all other conceivable forms of social life. The journal is interested not only in publishing research on the politics and economics of the interventionist and redistributive state, and on the economic effects of capitalism, but arthropoligical research on the effects of modernity on human happiness; studies of the influence of capitalism on art; historical work on the origins of the modern state and its nationalist-liberal development; historical and political-economy studies of whether that state is a necessary concomitant of modernity, or is instead the product of popular or intellectual misapprehensions about the failings of capitalism; political science research on public opinion formation, public ignorance, and the real-world nature of mass democaracy and state bureaucracy; cultural studies of the dynamics of human desires under capitalism and deomcracy; and sociological work informed by (or critical of) state theory as well as classic sociological theory.

Cultural Critique

http://www.oup.co.uk/jnls/list/cultur/

Since its first issue, *Cultural Critique* has brought together some of the most important work in the field of cultural analysis. Perhaps no other journal investigates cultural interpretation from such a broad perspective and from such an international point of view. The journal takes an interdisciplinary approach to cultural criticism, covering literary, philosophical, anthropological, and sociological studies and using Marxist, feminist, psychoanalytic, and post-structural methods. It draws on a large group of international corresponding editors to gather articles that examine intellectual controversies, trends, and movements in various parts of the world.

Cultural Values

http://www.blackwellpublishers.co.uk/scripts/webjrn1.idc?issn=13625179

The journal provides a unique forum for transdisciplinary discussion of cultural values. Contributions, incorporating ethnographic, theorteical, deconstructvive and evaluative approaches explore the following key questions: What significance to values possess, and what consequences do they have? Are values disintegrating? Do values merely serve to mask strategies of preference and power? Why and how do values change? What is the value of the critical evaluation of value? Is the discourse of value flawed from its inception?

Dialogue: Canadian Philosophical Review

http://www.uwindsor.ca/cpa/dialogue/index.html

Dialogue publishes, in English and French, articles in all branches of philosophy and is open to contributions from any philosophical perspective. The articles and reviews in *Dialogue* are peer reviewed.

Deutsche Zeitchrift für Philosophie

http://www.vchgroup.de/akademie-verlag/office/dzphil

A German-language philosophy journal, this page, in German only, lists tables of contents, provides information on the editorial board, abstracts of select articles, and enables visitors to order a free sample copy of the journal.

Didascalia

http://www.sal.tohoku.ac.jp/phil/DIDASCALIA/

Didascalia is a journal for philosophy and philology from late Antiquity to the Renaissance. This site provides information on the editorial board, a table of contents and subscription details.

Differences: Journal of Feminist Cultural Studies

http://www.indiana.edu/~iupress/journals/dif.html

Differences focuses on how concepts and categories of difference—notably but not exclusively gender—operate within culture. Situated at the point of intersection of cultural studies and feminism, the two most exciting fields of critical inquiry to have opened up in recent years, *Differences* is affiliated with the Pembroke Center for Teaching and Research on Women at Brown University. It is published three times a year.

Discourse

http://www.usfca.edu/usf/discourse/Discourse.html

The mission of this journal is to afford people from a diverse educational and ethnic backgrounds the opportunity to express their philosophical points of view. The journal editors and staff realise that philosophy is not a subject restricted only to the corridors of philosophy departments. The philosophical questions concerning ethics, knowledge, beauty and being are tacitly acknowledged in the hearts and minds of people of various educational levels and backgrounds. This site provides information on the journal, tables of contents, and calls for papers.

The Dualist

http://www-leland.stanford.edu/group/dualist/

The *Dualist* is Stanford University's undergraduate journal of philosophy. It accepts papers on all topics of philosophical interest. Essays written for classes, as well as honours papers, are welcome. This page provides archives of the journal, calls for papers, and information on the journal's staff.

Earth Ethics

http://www.center1.com/ethics.html

Earth Ethics publishes the best thinking in emerging earth ethics. Articles focus on sustainable practices in education, religion, the arts, business, agriculture, and other fields. Writers provide updates on international forums which are challenging current economic and development practices. The journal promotes alternative models for sustainable communities and lifestyles, based in ecospiritual practice and principles. Book reviews, event calendars, and feature articles bring fresh resources for those wishing to accelerate our transition to a just and sustainable future.

Economics and Philosophy

http://www.cup.cam.ac.uk/Journals/JNLSCAT/eap/eap.html

The disciplines of economics and philosophy each possess their own special analytical methods, whose combination is powerful and fruitful. Each discipline can be enriched by the other. *Economics and Philosophy* aims to promote their mutual enrichment by publishing articles and book reviews in all areas linking these subjects. Topics include the methodology and epistemology of economics, the foundations of decision theory and game theory, the nature of rational choice in general, historical work on economics with a philosophical purpose, ethical issues in economics, the use of economic techniques in ethical theory, and many other subjects. It has published articles by Wlodek Rabinowica and Jan Österberg, David Wasserman, Pierluigi Barrotta, Hans Jorgen Jacobsen, Robert Stalmaker, Jonathan Baron, Frank Hahn, David Miller, and Dan Hausman.

Eidos

http://watarts.uwaterloo.ca/PHIL/cpshelle/eidos.html

Eidos has been published by students at the University of Waterloo since July, 1978. From its inception it has been devoted to providing a forum for academic discussion on philosophical themes to graduate students in Canada and abroad. This page provides information on submissions, subscriptions, calls for papers, and topics of recent and forthcoming editions.

Environmental Ethics

http://www.cep.unt.edu/enethics.html

Environmental Ethics is an interdisciplinary journal dedicated to the philosophical aspects of environmental problems. It is a product of the Center for Environmental Philosophy *http://www.cep.unt.edu/centerfo.html*. This page provides subscription information, guidelines for authors, bibliographical indexing and abstracting services, a cumulative index, and information on ordering back issues.

Environmental Values

http://www.cep.unt.edu/values.html

Environmental Values is concerned with the basis and justification of environmental policy. It aims to bring together contributions from philosophy, law, economics, and other disciplines, which relate to the present and future environment of humans and other species; and to clarify the relationship between practical policy issues and more fundamental underlying principles or assumptions. An alternative site for this journal is *http://www.erica.demon.co.uk/EV.html*.

Environment and History

http://www.erica.demon.co.uk/EH.html

Environment and History is an interdisciplinary journal which aims to bring scholars in the humanities and biological sciences closer together, with the deliberate intention of constructing long and well-founded perspectives on present day environmental problems.

Erkenntnis

http://kapis.www.wkap.nl/kapis/CGI-BIN/WORLD/journalhome.htm?0165-0106

Erkenntnis is a philosophical journal publishing papers which are committed in one way or another to the philosophical attitude which is signified by the label 'analytic philosophy'.

It concentrates on those philosophical fields which are particularly inspired by this attitude, though other topics are welcome as well. These fields are: epistemology, philosophy of science, foundations and methodology of science in general, and natural and human sciences such as physics, biology, psychology, economics, social sciences, etc. in particular philosophy of mathematics, logic, philosophy of logic, and all kinds of philosophical logics, philosophy of language, ontology, metaphysics, theory of truth, theory of modality, philosophical psychology, philosophy of mind, practical philosophy, i.e. ethics, philosophy of action, philosophy of law, etc.

Ethics

http://www.journals.uchicago.edu/Ethics/home.html

Founded in 1890, *Ethics* is an interdisciplinary journal devoted to the study of the ideas and principles that form the basis for individual and collective action. It publishes work arising from a variety of disciplines and intellectual perspectives, including philosophy, social and political theory, theories of individual and collective choice, jurisprudence, international relations, and social and economic policy analysis. Subscription information, table of contents of current issue, and ordering information are available from this site.

Ethics and Behaviour

http://www.erlbaum.com/992.htm

Ethics and Behaviour publishes articles on an array of topics pertaining to various moral issues and conduct. These matters may include but are not restricted to: the exercise of social and ethical responsibility in human behaviors; ethical dilemmas or professional misconduct in health and human service delivery; the conduct of research involving human and animal participants; fraudulence in the management or reporting of scientific research; and public policy issues involving ethical problems. Data-based, theoretical, and particularly instructive case analyses as well as brief summaries of problem cases are also published. An editorial board consisting of specialists in ethics with backgrounds in law, medicine, pediatrics, psychiatry, psychology, public health, sociology, and theology allows for a wide spectrum of perspectives toward ethical issues.

Ethics and the Environment

http://www.phil.uga.edu/eande/

Ethics and the Environment is an interdisciplinary forum for theoretical and practical articles, discussions, reviews, comments, and book reviews in the broad area encompassed by environmental ethics. Supported by the Humanities Center, the Philosophy Department, and the Environmental Ethics Certificate Program at the University of Georgia, and edited by Victoria Davion, Associate Professor in the Department of Philosophy, the journal focuses on conceptual approaches in ethical theory and ecological philosophy, including deep ecology and ecological feminism as they pertain to environmental issues such as environmental education and management, ecological economics, and ecosystem health.

European Journal of Philosophy

http://www.essex.ac.uk/ejp/

The *European Journal of Philosophy* constitutes a platform to which philosophers, both inside and outside Europe, can turn to rediscover the diversity and variety of the European tradition. The forum is open to all philosophers with an interest in this tradition, regardless of their geographical location. While enhancing the scope for fruitful exchanges across national and intellectual boundaries, the *European Journal of Philosophy* maintains a healthy respect for the existing variety of concerns within the European tradition.

Existentia

http://www.kfki.hu/~ferenczi/Societas_html/Existentia.html

Existentia is an international journal of philosophy and related subjects, focusing on classical European thought. Priority is given to texts of purely philosophical content. The journal is published in Hungary, its first edition appearing in 1991.

Feminist Collections: A Quarterly of Women's Studies Resources

http://www.library.wisc.edu/libraries/WomensStudies/fcmain.htm

Feminist Collections contains news of the latest print and audiovisual resources for research and teaching in women's studies. Recent book reviews have treated such subjects as African American women writers, lesbians in popular culture, and women in the international marketplace. There are guides to new bibliographies and reference works, film and video critiques, computer updates, and news of out-of-the-way materials—pamphlets, reports, rare book dealers' catalogs, microforms, and more. Thoughtful articles by experts explore women's publishing, Internet resources, library organization, archives, and other tools for feminist scholarship. New periodicals and special issues of journals in other disciplines are announced in each issue.

Feminist Legal Studies

http://www.legaltheory.demon.co.uk/fls.html

Feminist Legal Studies is a leading European journal of feminist legal studies, with special interests in both the application of law to women's issues, and contemporary debates in feminist legal theory.

Film and Philosophy

http://www.hanover.edu/philos/film/home.htm

Film and Philosophy is published annually by the Society for the Philosophic Study of the contemporary Visual Arts (SPSCVA). All issues of the journal are available at this website in either WordPerfect 5.1 or html format.

Foundations of Chemistry

http://www.cco.caltech.edu/~scerri/

This journal features special issues devoted to particular themes, and also contains book reviews and discussion notes. The major aim is to foster discourse between chemists, biochemists, philosophers, historians, sociologists, and educators with an interest in foundational issues relating to the chemical sciences. The journal is published by Kluwer, and the Editor-in-Chief is Eric Scerri scerri@bradley.edu.

Foundations of Science

http://kapis.www.wkap.nl/kapis/CGI-BIN/WORLD/journalhome.htm?1233-1821

Foundations of Science focuses on methodological and philosophical topics of foundational significance concerning the structure and the growth of science. It serves as a forum for exchange of views and ideas among working scientists and theorists of science and it seeks to promote interdisciplinary cooperation.

Gender and History

http://www.blackwellpublishers.co.uk/scripts/webjrn1.idc?issn=09535233

Gender and History is now established as the major international journal for research and writing on the history of femininity and masculinity and of gender relations.

Greece and Rome

http://www.up.co.uk/gromej

Designed to meet the needs of a wide audience, *Greece and Rome* publishes scholarly (not technical) articles on ancient history, art, archeology, religion, philosophy, and the classical tradition. A special feature of the journal is the Subject Reviews section. More than 90 books are covered in each issue, and the speed with which they are reviewed after publication is a particular strength of the journal.

Halcyon: Journal of the Humanities

http://www.press.uchicago.edu/cgi-bin/hfs.cgi/66/nevada/halcyon.ctl

Halcyon emphasises scholarship in the traditions of the core disciplines in the humanities—history, philosophy, and literature—as well as perspectives from a very new humanistic field, film studies. Information on the editorial policy of the journal, and subcription and ordering details are available from this site.

Helios

http://www.press.uchicago.edu/cgi-bin/hfs.cgi/66/texas_tech/h.ctl

Helios publishes articles that explore innovative approaches to the study of classical culture, literature and society. Of special interest are articles that embrace contemporary critical methodologies, such as anthropological, deconstructive, feminist, reader response, social history, and text theory.

The Heythrop Journal

http://www.blackwellpublishers.co.uk/scripts/webjrn1.idc?issn=00181196

Founded on the conviction that the disciplines of theology and philosophy have much to gain from their mutual interaction, *The Heythrop Journal* provides a medium of publication for scholars in each of these fields, and encourages interdisciplinary comment and debate. *The Heythrop Journal* embraces all the disciplines which contribute to theological and philosophical research, notably hermeneutics, exegesis, linguistics, history, religious studies, philosophy of religion, sociology, psychology, ethics, and past oral theology.

History and Philosophy of Logic

http://www.tandf.co.uk/jnls/hpl.htm

History and Philosophy of Logic is devoted to the study of the historical development of logic and its broader philosophical concerns. The journal also deals with general philosophical questions in logic—existential and ontological aspects, the relationship between classical and non-classical logics—including their historical development. In addition, it treats the relationships between logic and other fields of knowledge, such as mathematics, physics, philosophy of science, epistemology, linguistics, ontology, psychology, and computing. *History and Philosophy of Logic* also contains special features on manuscript collections and projects in progress, translations of important or neglected historical texts, and a substantial book review section (including essay reviews).

History and Philosophy of the Life Sciences

http://www.tandf.co.uk/jnls/hps.htm

History and Philosophy of the Life Sciences is an international journal devoted to the historical development of the life sciences and of their social and epistemological implications. The journal also covers the broader philosophical concerns of biology and medicine. The main interest of the journal is modern western scientific thought, although it also includes any period in the history of the life sciences, (e.g., classical antiquity, the Middle Ages) and any cultural area, (e.g., Chinese and Indian medicine).

History and Theory: Studies in the Philosophy of History

http://www.wesleyan.edu/histjrnl/hthome.htm

History and Theory publishes articles, review essays, and summaries of books principally in these areas: critical philosophy of history, speculative philosophy of history, historiography, historical methodology, critical theory, time and culture, and related disciplines.

History of European Ideas

http://www.elsevier.nl/inca/publications/store/6/0/5/605.pub.shtml

History of European Ideas is devoted to the intellectual history of Europe from the Enlightenment onwards. It is interdisciplinary in that it aims to publish papers on the history of ideas in a number of different fields: political, philosophical, historiographical, theological, sociological, literary, and cultural. Treatments of the history of ideas which cut accross these categories or which trace connections between them in different European countries are particularly welcome. Proposals for special issues devoted to particular themes or to proceedings of conferences are also encouraged.

History of Philosophy Quarterly

http://www.bgsu.edu/pdc/hpq.html

A leader in the publication of articles concerning the history of philosophy, *HPQ* specialises in papers that cultivate philosophical history with a strong interaction between contemporary and historical concerns. Historical material is exploited to deal with matters on the agenda of current discussion, or present-day concepts, methods, distinctions, and arguments are used to illuminate historical questions. The journal regards historical studies as a way of dealing with problems of continued interest and importance. This page provides subscription information, a table of contents of the current issue, and details on ordering the journal.

History of Political Thought

http://www.zynet.co.uk/imprint/hpt.html

History of Political Thought (HPT) is a quarterly journal which was launched in 1980 to fill a genuine academic need for a forum for work in this multi-disciplinary area. Although a subject central to the study of politics and history, researchers in this field previously had to compete for publication space in journals whose intellectual centers of gravity were located in other disciplines. The journal is devoted exclusively to the historical study of political ideas and associated methodological problems. The primary focus is on research papers, with extensive book reviews and bibliographic surveys also included. All articles are refereed.

Humanitas

http://www.access.digex.net/~nhi/hum.htm

Humanitas is an interdisciplinary journal dedicated to the invigoration of the humanities, including the social sciences properly understood. The journal seeks to foster among its readers and contributors a spirit of open inquiry, a willingness to subject cherished doctrines to challenge and look beyond conventional categories of thought. *Humanitas* explores issues of moral and social philosophy, epistemology, and aesthetics, and the relations among them, such as the moral and cultural conditions of knowledge. This site provides subscription information, as well as selected articles, poems, and reviews.

Human Rights Quarterly

http://www.press.jhu.edu/press/journals/titles/hrq.html

HRQ provides up-to-date information on the important developments within the United Nations and regional human rights organizations, both governmental and non-governmental. It presents current work in human rights research and policy analysis, reviews of related books, and philosophical essays probing the fundamental nature of human rights as defined by the Universal Declaration of Human Rights.

Human Studies: A Journal for Philosophy and the Social Sciences

http://kapis.www.wkap.nl/kapis/CGI-BIN/WORLD/journalhome.htm?0163-8548

Human Studies is devoted primarily to advancing the dialogue between philosophy and the human sciences. In particular, such issues as the logic of inquiry, methodology, epistemology and foundational issues in the human sciences exemplified by original empirical, theoretical, and philosophical investigations are addressed. Phenomenological perspectives, broadly defined, are a primary, though not an exclusive focus. *Human Studies* is attractive to scholars in a variety of fields, since it provides a forum for those who address these issues in attempting to bridge the gap between philosophy and the human sciences. The contributions published have been drawn from sociology, psychology, anthropology, history, geography, linguistics, semiotics, communication studies, ethnomethodology, political science and, of course, philosophy.

Husserl Studies

http://kapis.www.wkap.nl/kapis/CGI-BIN/WORLD/journalhome.htm?0167-9848

Husserl Studies is an international journal which underlines the relevance of Husserl's phenomenology, both for Husserl scholars and for the wider academic field. The journal serves as a forum for Husserlian studies, both systematic and historical. The publication of important texts from Husserl's Nachla makes such a forum even more necessary. Intercultural and interdisciplinary contributions are particularly welcomed by the journal. Occasionally, material by Husserl himself, or connected with the historical background of his thought is published.

Hypatia: Journal of Feminist Philosophy

http://www.indiana.edu/~iupress/journals/hyp.html

Hypatia is the only journal for scholarly research at the intersection of philosophy and women's studies and is a leader in reclaiming the work of women philosophers. This page provides information on the editorial policy of the journal, as well as subscription and ordering details.

Imprints: A Journal of Analytical Socialism

http://www.bris.ac.uk/~plcdib/imprints.html

Imprints aims to promote a critical discussion of socialist ideas, freed from theoretical dogma but committed to the viability of an egalitarian and democratic politics. Tables of contents for the current and previous issues, subscription information, and mailing addresses for the editor are available from this page.

Informal Logic: Reasoning and Argumentation in Theory and Practice

http://www.uwindsor.ca/faculty/arts/philosophy/IL/

Informal Logic publishes articles which advance the dialectic in reasoning and argumentation in theory and practice, including but not restricted to: theory of argument, fallacy analysis and fallacy theory, criteria of good argument, rationality and argument, psychology of argumentation, argument fields, theory of critical thinking, the teaching of argumentation, informal logic and critical thinking, and related topics in cognate fields. Articles, reviews, and critical studies are blind refereed.

Inquiry

http://www.scup.no/journals/en/j-108.html

Inquiry was founded in 1958 and publishes scholarly articles, discussions, and review discussions in all areas of philosophy. It is editorial policy regularly to include "round-tables" on special themes and significant new books. It is a general aim of *Inquiry* to present problems from an integrating perspective to which both specialists from various academic fields and non-specialists may have critical access.

Inquiry: Critical Thinking Across the Disciplines

http://www.bgsu.edu/pdc/inq.html

This journal serves as a forum for the discussion of issues related to critical thinking across the disciplines, with an emphasis on the theory and practice of critical thinking in post-secondary educational contexts. *Inquiry* seeks to engage its readers in reflection about educational practices and to make available to them educational vehicles potentially useful in providing support for students' efforts to think critically.

International Journal for Philosophy of Religion

http://kapis.www.wkap.nl/kapis/CGI-BIN/WORLD/journalhome.htm?0020-7047

The organ of no single institution or sectarian school, philosophical or religious, the *International Journal for Philosophy of Religion* provides a medium for the exposition, development, and criticism of important philosophical insights and theories relevant to religion in any of its varied forms. It also provides a forum for critical, constructive, and interpretative consideration of religion from an objective philosophical point of view. Articles, symposia, discussions, reviews, notes, and news in this journal are intended to serve the interests of a wide range of thoughtful readers, especially teachers and students of philosophy, philosophical theology, and religious thought.

International Journal for the Psychology of Religion

http://www.erlbaum.com/1019.htm

IJPR is devoted to psychological studies of religious processes and phenomena in all religious traditions—the only international publication concerned exclusively with the psychology of religion. This journal provides a means for sustained discussion of psychologically relevant issues that can be examined empiracally and concern religion in the most general sense. It presents articles covering a variety of important subjects such as psychoanalytic interpretations of religion; Pentecostalism, the "charismata" and conversion; and the BAV (behavior, attitude, values) model for predicting religious behavior. Each issue also includes a major essay and commentary, plus an additional article on the psychology of religion in a specific country.

International Journal for the Semiotics of Law

http://www.legaltheory.demon.co.uk/ijsl.html

This journal applies different forms of textual analysis to the discourses of the law. They include the semiotics of Greimas and Peirce, rhetoric, philosophy of language, pragmatics, sociolinguistics and deconstructionism, as well as more traditional legal philosophical approaches to the language of the law. The journal includes occasional articles in French, though most are published in English.

International Journal of Applied Philosophy

http://www.bgsu.edu/pdc/ijap.html

This journal is committed to the view that philosophy can and should be brought to bear upon the practical issues of life. Accordingly, the journal publishes philosophical articles dealing with practical issues in such realms as education, business, law, government, health care, psychology, science, and the environment.

International Studies in the Philosophy of Science

http://www.carfax.co.uk/isp-ad.htm

International Studies in the Philosophy of Science is an interdisciplinary journal that welcomes articles not only from philosophers, but also from historians and sociologists of science. Theoretical articles are drawn from a variety of disciplines including physics, chemistry, biology, psychology, neuroscience, and mathematics. The journal has a particular interest in publishing papers from a wide range of countries around the world, thus fostering cooperation between scholars and students from a variety of backgrounds. This page provides subscription information, submission guidelines, editorial board, list of current contents, and offers a free inspection copy.

Journal for General Philosophy of Science

http://kapis.www.wkap.nl/kapis/CGI-BIN/WORLD/journalhome.htm?0925-4560

The *Journal for General Philosophy of Science* is a forum for the discussion of a variety of attitudes concerning the philosophy of science. It has as its subject matter the philosophical, especially methodological, ontological, epistemological, anthropological, and ethical foundations of the individual sciences. Particular emphasis is laid on bringing both the natural, the cultural, and the technical sciences into a philosophical context, within which the historical presuppositions and conditions of the current problems of the philosophy of science are also included in the discussion.

Journal for the Theory of Social Behaviour

http://www.blackwellpublishers.co.uk/scripts/webjrn1.idc?issn=00218308

Truly interdisciplinary, the *Journal for the Theory of Social Behaviour* publishes original theoretical and methodological articles which aim to further the links between social structures and human agency. It is widely read by philosophers, sociologists and psychologists.

Journal of Aesthetics and Art Criticism

http://www.louisville.edu/groups/philosophy-www/

Established in 1942 by the American Society for Aesthetics, the *Journal of Aesthetics and Art Criticism* publishes current research articles, symposia, special issues, and timely reviews of books in aesthetics and the arts. Guidelines for submission of articles, pre-publication book reviews, forthcoming issues, calls for papers, and tables of contents of back issues are available at this site.

Journal of Applied Philosophy

http://www.blackwellpublishers.co.uk/scripts/webjrn1.idc?issn=02643758

Journal of Applied Philosophy provides a unique forum for philosophical research, linking an audience of both professional and non-professional philosophers. Open to the expression of diverse viewpoints, the journal brings critical analysis to areas of practical concern as well as directly exploring questions of value. The *Journal of Applied Philosophy* covers a broad spectrum of issues in environment and medicine, science policy, law, and education.

The Journal of Artificial Societies and Social Simulation

http://www.soc.surrey.ac.uk/JASSS/

The Journal of Artificial Societies and Social Simulation is an inter-disciplinary journal for the exploration and understanding of social processes by means of computer simulation. It is published quarterly, in January, March, June, and September.

Journal of Business Ethics

http://kapis.www.wkap.nl/kapis/CGI-BIN/WORLD/journalhome.htm?0167-4544

The *Journal of Business Ethics* publishes original articles from a wide variety of methodological and disciplinary perspectives concerning ethical issues related to business. The editors believe that the scope should be as broad as possible: the term 'business' is understood in a wide sense to include all systems involved in the exchange of goods and services, while 'ethics' is circumscribed as all human action aimed at securing a good life. Systems of production, consumption, marketing, advertising, social and economic accounting, labour relations, public relations, and organizational behaviour are analyzed from a moral viewpoint. The style and level of dialogue involves all who are interested in business ethics—the business community, universities, governmental bodies, and consumer groups.

Journal of Ethics

http://kapis.www.wkap.nl/kapis/CGI-BIN/WORLD/journalhome.htm?1382-4554

The *Journal of Ethics: An International Philosophical Review* contains articles, commentaries, and reviews on mainstream topics and work in ethics and public affairs, including work on ethical theory, political liberalism, communitarianism, libertarianism, Marxism, moral responsibility, punishment, rights, ethics and language, ethics and metaphysics, etc. It also contains a significant number of articles and discussions on neglected areas in philosophy, such as African-American philosophy (i.e., political separation versus integration, the nature of ethnicity, the moral status of reparations, racism, the history of African-American philosophy, etc.), international terrorism, secession, etc. Moreover, this journal seeks to include a limited number of studies on neglected areas in business ethics, medical ethics, and legal ethics.

Journal of Experimental and Theoretical Artificial Intelligence

http://turing.pacss.binghamton.edu/jetai/index.html

The aim of *JETAI* is to advance scientific research in Artificial Intelligence by providing a public forum for the presentation, evaluation, and criticism of research results, the discussion of methodological issues, and the communication of positions, preliminary findings, and research directions. This site provides further information on the journal's aims and scope, as well as guidelines for authors, ordering information, order a free sample edition, and links to contents, abstracts, and editorials.

Journal of Indian Philosophy

http://kapis.www.wkap.nl/kapis/CGI-BIN/WORLD/journalhome.htm?0022-1791

The *Journal of Indian Philosophy* encourages creative activities among orientalists and philosophers along with the various combinations that the two classes can form.

Contributions to the journal are bounded by the limits of rational enquiry and avoid questions that lie in the fields of speculative sociology and parapsychology. In a very general sense, the method is analytical and comparative, aiming at a rigorous precision in the translation of terms and statements. Space is devoted to the work of philosophers of the past as well as to the creative researches of contemporary scholars on such philosophic problems as were addressed by past philosophers.

Journal of Islamic Studies

http://www.oup.co.uk/islamj/

The *Journal if Islamic Studies* is a multi-disciplinary publication dedicated to the scholarly study of all aspects of Islam and of the Islamic world. Particular attention is paid to works dealing with history, geography, political sience, economics, anthropology, sociology, law, literature, religion, philosophy, international relations, environmental, and developmental issues, as well as ethical questions related to scientific research.

Journal of Jewish Thought and Philosophy

http://www.gbhap-us.com/journals/382/382-top.htm

This journal provides an international forum for Jewish thought, philosophy, and intellectual history. The historical range is not limited to any given period, nor is there any religious or political orientation determining the acceptance or rejection of articles. The emphasis is on high scholarly standards with an interest in issues of interpretation and the contemporary world. It is to be expected that articles will cover philosophy, biblical studies, mysticism, literary criticism, political theory, sociology, and anthropology.

Journal of Mass Media Ethics

http://www.erlbaum.com/1025.htm

This journal is devoted to stimulating and contributing to reasoned discussions of mass media ethics and morality among academic and professional groups in the various branches and subdisciplines of communication and ethics. By bridging the gap between academics and professionals interested in issues concerning mass media, the journal stimulates mutually beneficial dialogues between these two groups. It publishes original essays exploring the philosophical bases of decisions, reports from empirical studies, and literature searches and reviews dealing with mass media content and the behavior or practitioners in journalism, broadcasting, public relations, advertising, and other mass communication disciplines.

Journal of Medical Ethics

http://www.bmjpg.com/data/jme.htm

The *Journal of Medical Ethics* is a leading international journal in the field of medical ethics. It publishes interdisciplinary articles on ethical aspects of health care. It is now being published bi-monthly. Contributions to the journal originate in many countries and disciplines, and all undergo rigorous assessment. In addition to publishing original articles it provides a forum for reasoned debate on ethical issues. Case conferences, editorials, book reviews, correspondence, and news and notes are also included. Occasional series focus on teaching medical ethics, experiences of medico-moral dilemmas ('At the Coalface'), and medical ethics in literature.

Journal of Medicine and Philosophy

http://kapis.www.wkap.nl/kapis/CGI-BIN/WORLD/journalhome.htm?0360-5310

This bi-monthly publication has been established under the auspices of the Society for Health and Human Values to explore the shared themes and concerns of philosophy and the medical sciences. Central issues in medical research and practice have important philosophical dimensions, for in treating disease and promoting health, medicine involves presuppositions about human goals and values. Conversely, the concerns of philosophy often significantly relate to those of medicine, as philosophers seek to apprehend the nature of knowledge and the human condition in the modern world. In addition, recent developments in medical technology and treatment raise ethical problems that overlap with philosophical interests. The *Journal of Medicine and Philosophy* aims to provide an ongoing forum for the discussion of these themes and issues.

Journal of Mind and Behaviour

http://kramer.ume.maine.edu/~jmb/welcome.html

The *Journal of Mind and Behavior (JMB)* is dedicated to the interdisciplinary approach within psychology and related fields—building upon the assumption of a unified science. Mind and behavior position, interact, and causally relate to each other in multidirectional ways; *JMB* urges the exploration of these interrelationships. The editors are particularly interested in scholarly work in the following areas: the psychology, philosophy, and sociology of experimentation and the scientific method; the relationship between methodology, operationism, and theory construction; the mind/body problem in the social sciences, psychiatry and the medical sciences, and the physical sciences; philosophical impact of a mind/body epistemology upon psychology and its theories of consciousness; phenomenological, teleological, existential, and introspective reports relevant to psychology, psychosocial methodology, and social philosophy; and historical perspectives on the course and nature of psychological science.

Journal of Moral Education

http://www.carfax.co.uk/jme-ad.htm

The *Journal of Moral Education* provides a unique interdisciplinary forum for consideration of all aspects of moral education and development across the lifespan. It contains philosophical analyses, reports of empirical research, and evaluation of educational strategies which address a range of value issues and the process of valuing, not only in theory and practice, but also at the social and individual level. The journal regularly includes country based state-of-the-art papers on moral education and publish es special issues on particular topics.

Journal of Nietzsche Studies

http://www.swan.ac.uk/german/fns/jns.htm

The *Journal of Nietzsche Studies* was founded in Spring 1991 and has made its mark as a forum for innovative work by both new and established scholars. It is available free to Nietzsche Society members. This page lists tables of contents for current and earlier editions, subscription rates, and previous contributors.

Journal of Philosophical Logic

http://kapis.www.wkap.nl/kapis/CGI-BIN/WORLD/journalhome.htm?0022-3611

The *Journal of Philosophical Logic* publishes papers that utilise formal methods or that deal with topics in logical theory, such as: contributions to branches of logical theory directly related to philosophical concerns, such as inductive logic, modal logic, deontic logic, quantum logic, tense logic, free logic, logic of questions, logic of commands, logic of preference, logic of conditionals, many-valued logic, and relevance logics. Contributions to philosophical discussions that utilise the machinery of formal logic, as in recent treatments of abstract entities, non-existent possibles, essentialism, existence, propositional attitudes, meaning and truth. Discussions of philosophical issues relating to logic and the logical structure of language, such as conventionalism in logic, ontic commitment, logical or semantic paradoxes, the logic of hypotheses and of pre-suppositions, constructivism, and extensionality. Philosophical work relating to specific sciences (such as linguistics, history of logic, or physics), with an emphasis on foundational problems, and making use of logical theory. Some instances of recent work of this kind are the treatments of universal grammar, pragmatics, conceptions of possibility, theories and mathematical truth in the history of philosophy, formalisation of scientific theories, or logical structure in quantum mechanics.

Journal of Philosophy of Education

http://www.blackwellpublishers.co.uk/scripts/webjrn1.idc?issn=03098249

The *Journal of Philosophy of Education* publishes articles representing a wide variety of philosophical traditions. They vary from examination of fundamental philosophical issues in their connection with education, to detailed critical engagement with current educational practice or policy from a philosophical point of view. The journal aims to promote rigorous thinking on educational matters and to identify and criticise the ideological forces shaping education. Ethical, political, aesthetic, and epistemological dimensions of educational theory are covered.

Journal of Philosophical Research

http://www.bgsu.edu/pdc/jpr.html

This scholarly journal publishes outstanding papers in any branch of philosophy and from any philosophical orientation. *JPR* provides an outlet for the abundance of excellent philosophical thought and promotes scholarship about various philosophical views and areas of expertise. This page provides information on subscription rates and ordering, and a table of contents of the current issue is also available.

Journal of Political Ideologies

http://www.carfax.co.uk/jpi-ad.htm

The *Journal of Political Ideologies* is dedicated to the analysis of political ideology both in its theoretical and conceptual aspects, and with reference to the nature and roles of concrete ideological manifestations. The journal promotes research into political ideologies which are indispensable to the understanding of political thought within social, temporal, and spatial contexts. It emphasizes both the general phenomenon of ideologies and their particular instances. In parallel, it seeks to underline that political action, processes and institutions are endowed with ideological import and shaped to a considerable extent by political ideologies.

Journal of Political Philosophy

http://www.blackwellpublishers.co.uk/scripts/webjrn1.idc?issn=09638016

The *Journal of Political Philosophy* is an international journal devoted to the study of theoretical issues arising out of moral, legal, and political life. It welcomes, and hopes to foster, work cutting across a variety of disciplinary concerns, among them philosophy, sociology, economics, and political science. The journal encourages new approaches, including (but not limited to): feminism; environmentalism; critical theory, post-modernism and analytical Marxism; social and public choice theory; law and economics, critical legal studies and critical race studies; and game theoretic, socio-biological and anthropological approaches to politics. It also welcomes work in the history of political thought which builds to a larger philosophical point and work in the philosophy of the social sciences and applied ethics with broader political implications.

Journal of Religion

http://www.journals.uchicago.edu/JR/home.html

The *Journal of Religion* promotes critical and systematic inquiry into the meaning and import of religion. Not limited by ideological orientation, the journal embraces all areas of theology (biblical, historical, ethical, constructive) as well as other types of religious studies (literary, social, psychological, philosophical).

Journal of Speculative Philosophy

http://www.press.uchicago.edu/cgi-bin/hfs.cgi/66/penn_state/jsp.ctl

The *Journal of Speculative Philosophy* publishes systematic and interpretive essays about basic philosophical questions. Scholars examine the constructive interaction between Continental and American philosophy, as well as novel developments in the ideas and theories of past philosophers that have relevance for contemporary thinkers. The *Journal of Speculative Philosophy* also features discussions of art, religion, and literature that are not strictly or narrowly philosophical. Book reviews and "News from Abroad" are included in every volume. Information on the editorial policy of the journal, as well as subscription and ordering details can be accessed at this site.

Journal of Symbolic Logic

http://www.press.uchicago.edu/cgi-bin/hfs.cgi/66/illinois/jsl.ctl

Distributed for the Association for Symbolic Logic, *JSL* is the leading academic journal in this expanding field. Aimed at mathematicians, philosophers, computer scientists, and linguists, the journal covers the entire spectrum of work in the field. Information on the editorial policy of the journal, as well as subscription rates and ordering details, can be found at this site.

Journal of the History of Ideas

http://muse.jhu.edu/journals/journal_of_the_history_of_ideas/

The *Journal of the History of Ideas* examines the evolution of ideas and their influence on historical developments. An interdisciplinary publication, *JHI* covers several fields of historical study including the history of philosophy, literature, the natural and social sciences, religion, the arts, and culture in general. This site provides online access to the journal's articles for subscribers. For non-subscribers, access is available to the following information: Publisher's Statement, Editors and Editorial Board information, Subscription Information, Indexing and Abstracting, Advertising Rates and Policies, Bookstore Terms and Policies, Thematic and Special Issues, Links to Related Web Sites, Conferences and Calls for Papers, Guidelines for Contributors, Back Issues Tables of Contents, and an Author/Title Index.

Journal of Value Inquiry

http://kapis.www.wkap.nl/kapis/CGI-BIN/WORLD/journalhome.htm?0022-5363

The *Journal of Value Inquiry* is an international philosophical quarterly, founded in 1967 by James Wilbur, devoted to the stimulation and communication of research in value studies. The essays published in the journal concern the nature, origin, experiences, and scope of value in general, as well as problems of value in such fields as culture, aesthetics, religion, social and legal theory or practice, ethics, education, methodology, technology, and the sciences. The *Journal of Value Inquiry* is a forum for presentation of the rich diversity of approaches available to value inquiry. It is committed to openness, cosmopolitanism, and the sharing of insights about humanity. Besides full-length essays, the journal publishes notes, communications to the editors, book reviews, interviews, dialogues, reports, and a news column.

Kantian Review

http://www.swan.ac.uk/uwp/kant.htm

Since the 1960s Kant's philosophy has become strongly relevant to many current philosophical debates. (Epistemology—intentionality and holism: moral and political philosophy, freedom, status (rationality) of moral principles, structures of moral motivation, etc.) The UK Kant Society, which was founded in 1994 specifically to promote the discussion of Kant's philosophy in relation to those current debates, has channeled that current interest into a journal. Although the journal will concentrate on that current interest, it will not exclude scholarly or historical accounts of Kant's texts or the background to their discussion since the 18th century. Nor will it exclude any school of philosophy. The journal is intended to reflect and provide a focus for that current interest, and contributions will be solicited from all countries and philosophers with such an interest. The purpose of the journal is, therefore, to provide a forum for the discussion of Kant's philosophy in the English language. It is particulary intended to encourage and to reflect present debate on issues arising from Kant's work. Articles are invited from all the main branches of philosophy, not only those connected with the principal areas of philosophy which Kant explored such as the theory of knowledge, practical philosophy and judgement, but also in such areas as the philosophy of history, art, science and religion. The journal also aims to promote the discussion of the reception of Kant's philosophy in British, North American and European philosophy. Kant is a focus for a great deal of debate in philosophy, and, increasingly, historical and social studies. This new journal will reflect this development and seek to extend it further.

Kennedy Institute of Ethics Journal

http://muse.jhu.edu/press/tocs/ken.html

The *Kennedy Institute of Ethics Journal* offers a scholarly forum for diverse views on major issues in bioethics, such as active euthanasia, fetal tissue research, human embryo cloning, genetics, health care reform, and organ transplantation. Each issue includes "Scope Notes," an overview and extensive annotated bibliography on a specific topic in bioethics, and "Bioethics Inside the Beltway," a report written by a Washington insider updating bioethics activities on the federal level.

Law and Critique

http://www.legaltheory.demon.co.uk/l&c.html

Law and Critique is the leading journal of critical legal studies in Europe, with special interests in the application to law of deconstructionist, psychoanalytical and literary approaches, as well as the radical politics of law.

Law and Philosophy

http://kapis.www.wkap.nl/kapis/CGI-BIN/WORLD/journalhome.htm?0167-5249

Law and Philosophy is a forum for the publication of work in law and philosophy which is of common interest to members of the two disciplines of jurisprudence and legal philosophy. It is open to all approaches in both fields and to work in any of the major legal traditions— common law, civil law, or the socialist tradition. The editors of *Law and Philosophy* encourage papers which exhibit philosophical reflection on the law informed by a knowledge of the law, and legal analysis informed by philosophical methods and principles.

Law and Social Inquiry

http://www.journals.uchicago.edu/LSI/home.html

This multidisciplinary quarterly features both empirical and theoretical studies that make original contributions to the understanding of sociolegal processes. *Law and Social Inquiry* is an indispensable source for research and critical commentary spanning law and sociology, economics, history, philosophy, and other social sciences. *LSI* readers find a remarkable range of empirical and theoretical works on specific topics in law and society, including legal institutions, the legal profession, and legal history.

Legal Theory

http://www.cup.cam.ac.uk/Journals/JNLSCAT/leg/leg.html

Legal Theory draws contributions not only from academic law, but from a wide range of related disciplines in the humanities and social sciences, including philosophy, political science, economics, history, and sociology. Topics covered fall mainly into the broad categories of analytical and normative jurisprudence, doctrinal theory, policy analyses of legal doctrines, and critical theories of law. Recent articles include: "Speech, Truth and the Free Market for Ideas"; "The Legal Regulation of Religious Groups"; and "Why When She Says No, She Doesn't Mean Maybe and Doesn't Mean Yes: A Critical Reconstruction of Consent, Sex and the Law."

Linguistics and Philosophy: A Journal of Natural Language Syntax, Semantics, Logic, Pragmatics, and Processing

http://kapis.www.wkap.nl/kapis/CGI-BIN/WORLD/journalhome.htm?0165-0157

Linguistics and Philosophy is a journal for studies focused on natural language, and is of interest to practitioners in the disciplines covered in the title. Although the field thus described is so extensive that a complete listing of relevant topics is precluded, at least the following specifically fall within it: traditional areas in the philosophy of language such as meaning, truth; reference, description, entailment, speech acts; traditional areas of linguistics such as syntax, semantics, and pragmatics (when the studies are of sufficient explicitness, and generality to be also of philosophical interest); aspects of artificial intelligence concerned with language such as computational linguistics and natural language processing; systems of logic with strong connections to natural language: modal logic, tense logic, epistemic logic, intensional logic; philosophical questions raised by linguistics as a science: linguistics methodology, the status of linguistics theories, the nature of linguistic universals; and philosophically interesting problems at the intersection of linguistics and other disciplines: language acquisition, language and perception, language as a social convention.

The Liverpool Law Review

http://www.legaltheory.demon.co.uk/llr.html

The Liverpool Law Review deals with a wide range of practical and theoretical legal issues of contemporary relevance—including public law, private law, criminal justice, international law, legal systems, ethics, and legal theory.

Logical Analysis and History of Philosophy

http://www.uni-bonn.de/PLA/

This journal, published annually, intends to provide a forum for articles in which classical philosophical texts are interpreted by drawing on the resources of modern formal logic.

Medieval Philosophy and Theology

http://www.cup.cam.ac.uk/Journals/JNLSCAT/mpt/mpt.html

Medieval Philosophy and Theology is devoted to the publication of original articles in all areas of medieval philosophy, including logic and natural science, and in medieval theology, including Christian, Jewish, and Islamic. Its coverage extends from the Patristic period through the neoscholasticism of the seventeenth century. *Medieval Philosophy and Theology* will occasionally publish review articles and article-length critical discussions of important books in the field. It does not publish editions and translations except when they are integral parts of articles.

Medioevo Rivista per la Storia della Filosofia Medievale

http://www.maldura.unipd.it/~storf/index.html

This is the Italian-language version of the *Journal for the History of Medieval Philosophy*. This page provides indexes arranged in topics, as well as chronological order by issue. Enquiries about the journal can be made to Francesco Bottin bottin@ux1.unipd.it.

Metaphilosophy

http://www.blackwellpublishers.co.uk/scripts/webjrn1.idc?issn=00261068

Metaphilosophy publishes articles and reviews books stressing considerations about philosophy or some particular school, method, or field of philosophy. The intended scope is very broad: no method, field nor school need be excluded. Some areas of interest might be: the foundation, scope, function, and direction of philosophy; justification of philosophical methods and arguments; the interrelations among schools or fields of philosophy (for example, the relation of logic to problems in ethics or epistemology); aspects of philosophical systems; pre-suppositions of philosophical schools; the relation of philosophy to other disciplines (for example, artificial intelligence, linguistics, or literature); sociology of philosophy; the relevance of philosophy to social and political action.

Metaphor and Symbol

http://www.erlbaum.com/1055.htm

This innovative journal is dedicated to the study of figurative language and the cognitive processes behind it. By applying a variety of perspectives to their investigations, contributors provide a broad spectrum of unique and thought-provoking articles—theoretical essays, original empirical research, and literature and book reviews. Its international editorial board is composed of scholars and experts in linguistics, education, artificial intelligence, sociology, anthropology, philosophy, and psychology.

Metascience

http://www.sct.gu.edu.au/~sctforge/index.html

Metascience is a review journal which covers the fields that comprise the disciplines of History and Philosophy of Science, Technology and Science, and Technology and Society. This page provides information for prospective reviewers, sample reviews, subscription information, tables of contents, and notices of forthcoming conferences.

Method: Journal of Lonergan Studies

http://www.concentric.net/~mmorelli/#MJLS

MJLS was founded in 1983. It aims, first, at furthering interpretive, historical, and critical study of the philosophical, theological, economic, and methodological writings of Bernard Lonergan. Secondly, it aims at promoting original research into the methodological foundations of the sciences and disciplines. *MJLS* is published twice yearly, in April and October, by the Lonergan Institute at Boston College.

Mind

http://www.oup.co.uk/mind/

Mind has long been a leading journal in philosophy. For well over 100 years it has presented the best of cutting-edge thought in most areas of analytical philosophy. On this site you can access the full text version of *Mind* via a subscription service. Free acess to information on the editorial policy of the journal, as well as subscription and ordering details is also available.

Mind and Language

http://www.blackwellpublishers.co.uk/scripts/webjrn1.idc?issn=02681064

The phenomena of mind and language are currently studied by researchers in linguistics, philosophy, psychology, artificial intelligence, and cognitive anthropology. *Mind and Language* brings this work together in a genuinely interdisciplinary way. Along with original articles, the journal publishes forums, survey articles, and reviews, enabling researchers to keep up-to-date with developments in related disciplines as well as their own. It is an important forum for sharing the results of investigation and for creating the conditions for a fusion of effort, thus making real progress towards a deeper and more far-reaching understanding of the phenomena of mind and language.

Minds and Machines

http://kapis.www.wkap.nl/kapis/CGI-BIN/WORLD/journalhome.htm?0924-6495

Minds and Machines affords an international forum for the discussion and debate of important and controversial issues concerning significant developments within its areas of editorial focus. Well-reasoned contributions from diverse theoretical perspectives are welcome and every effort will be made to ensure their prompt publication. Among the features that make this journal distinctive within the field are these: Strong stands on controversial issues are especially encouraged; Important articles exceeding normal journal length may appear; Special issues devoted to specific topics are a regular feature; Critical responses to previously published pieces are invited; Review essays discussing current problem situations will appear. This journal fosters a tradition of criticism within the AI and philosophical communities on problems and issues of common concern. Its scope explicitly encompasses philosophical aspects of computer science. All submissions will be subject to review.

Modernism/Modernity

http://muse.jhu.edu/journals/mod/

Concentrating on the period extending roughly from 1860 to the present, *Modernism/Modernity* focuses systematically on the methodological, archival, and theoretical exigencies particular to modernist studies. It encourages an interdisciplinary approach linking music, architecture, the visual arts, literature, and social and intellectual history. The journal's broad scope fosters dialogue between social scientists and humanists about the history of modernism and its relations to modernization. Each issue features a section of thematic essays, as well as book reviews and books received. *Modernism/Modernity* is published three times a year in January, May, and September.

The Modern Law Review

http://www.blackwellpublishers.co.uk/scripts/webjrn1.idc?issn=00267961

Authoritative and accessible, for over fifty years *The Modern Law Review* has been providing a unique forum for the critical examination of contemporary legal issues and the law as it functions in society. One of the leading journals in its field, *The Modern Law Review* is noted for its progressive, reformist approach, and its commitment to placing the study of law within a wider intellectual tradition. Each issue contains: articles focusing on key areas of legal scholarship, critiques of recent legislation and reports, case notes discussing matters of current concern and wide ranging, and review articles.

Modern Logic

http://www.ed.ac.uk/~pmilne/ml/home.html

Modern Logic: International Journal for the History of Mathematical Logic, Set Theory, and Foundations of Mathematics serves as a vehicle for rapid publication of high-quality historical studies and expository surveys of nineteenth- and twentieth-century mathematical logic, set theory, and foundations of mathematics. The journal strives to represent every major area of mathematical logic, including model theory, recursion theory, algebraic logic and Boolean algebras, general set theory and point set theory, proof theory, and constructive mathematics. Topics are defined broadly to include the connections of logic and set theory with such related areas as universal algebra, lattice theory and ordered sets, combinatorics, category theory, foundations of analysis, topology, philosophy, and computer science. This web site provides information on subscriptions, guidelines for contributors, an author index, and tables of contents with abstracts.

The Modern Schoolman

http://www.slu.edu/colleges/AS/philos/ms.html

The Modern Schoolman is a quarterly journal that promotes historical research and analysis of all the periods of philosophy: ancient, medieval, Renaissance, modern, and contemporary.

The Monist

http://wings.buffalo.edu/philosophy/Publications/Monet/

The Monist is an international journal of general philosophical enquiry. Each journal has a particular theme or topic, and topics are wide-ranging. This site provides all the necessary information about the journal: its editorial board and policy, submission guidelines, calls for papers, etc.

Natural Language Semantics

http://kapis.www.wkap.nl/kapis/CGI-BIN/WORLD/journalhome.htm?0925-854X

Natural Language Semantics is devoted to semantics and its interfaces in grammar, especially syntax. The journal seeks to encourage the convergence of approaches employing the concepts of logic and philosophy with perspectives of generative grammar on the relations between meaning and structure. *Natural Language Semantics* publishes studies focused on linguistic phenomena as opposed to those dealing primarily with the field's methodological and formal foundations. Representative topics include, but are not limited to: quantification, negation, modality, genericity, tense, aspect, aktionsarten, focus, presuppositions, anaphora, definiteness, plurals, mass nouns, adjectives, adverbial modification, nominalization, ellipsis, and interrogatives. The journal features mainly research articles, but also short squibs as well as remarks on and replies to pertinent books and articles.

Notre Dame Journal of Formal Logic

http://www.nd.edu/~ndjfl/index.html

The journal aims to provide a common ground where both philosophers and mathematicians can read and publish original and significant work in all areas of philosophical and mathematical logic, as well as the philosophy of language and the philosophy, history, and foundations of mathematics.

Noûs

http://www.blackwellpublishers.co.uk/scripts/webjrn1.idc?issn=00294624

Noûs, the ancient Greek term for intellect, or mind, is one of the premier philosophy journals today. In its commitment to a broad, pluralist, non-doctrinal approach, *Noûs* publishes high-quality critical essays, brief discussions, and important results of philosophic research. *Noûs* has developed a high reputation for the stature of its book reviews and the range of its contributors.

NTM: International Journal of History and Ethics of Natural Sciences, Technology, and Medicine

http://www.birkhauser.ch/fields/journals/4800/4800_tit.htm

NTM is an international journal for history and ethics of natural sciences, technology, and medicine that publishes original research papers, book reviews, and news. In addition, every issue features a survey article of topical interest on current questions in the history of science. The journal welcomes articles dealing with ethics, history of civilizaiton, and theory of science.

Objectivity

http://www.bomis.com/objectivity/

Objectivity is a journal of metaphysics, epistemology, and theory of value—informed by modern science. Published since 1990, *Objectivity* has established itself as one of the finest philosophical journals on the market today. A haven for non-political, non-social articles, *Objectivity's* high editorial standards have attracted academics and amateurs alike. The journal is published by Stephen C. Boydstun, at a rate of about three issues every two years. This site provides information on subscription, ordering, tables of contents, and summaries of selected articles.

October

http://mitpress.mit.edu/jrnls-catalog/october.html

At the forefront of contemporary arts criticism and theory, *October* focuses critical attention on the contemporary arts and their various contexts of interpretation: film; painting; music; photography; performance; sculpture; literature. Examining relationships between the arts and their critical and social contexts, *October* addresses a broad range of readers. Original, innovative, and provocative, each issue presents the best, most current texts by and about today's artistic, intellectual, and critical vanguard.

Osiris

http://www.journals.uchicago.edu/Osiris/home.html

Founded in 1936 by George Sarton as a companion to the journal *Isis*, this annual thematic publication deals with important emerging research in the history of science and its cultural influences. Selected volumes of *Osiris* cover such topics as Historical Writing on American Science, Science in Germany, Science after '40, Research Schools, Instruments, and Constructing Knowledge in the History of Science.

The Owl of Minerva

http://www.bgsu.edu/pdc/owl.html

The *Owl of Minerva* is a biannual journal that features articles, discussions, translations, reviews, and bibliographical information that pertains to Hegel, his predecessors, contemporaries, successors, and influences today, as well as those who use a Hegelian approach to philosophical issues or enter into debate with this approach. The journal welcomes work which falls into various disciplines: philosophy, religion, history, law, economics, literature, the empirical sciences, and any others that deal with Hegel's thought in a rigorous, systematic way. This page provides subscription and ordering information as well as a table of contents of the current issue.

Pacific Philosophical Quarterly

http://www.blackwellpublishers.co.uk/scripts/webjrn1.idc?issn=00315621

Pacific Philosophical Quarterly is a journal of general philosophy, publishing original articles from all areas of epistemology, philosophy of language, philosophy of mind, ethics, and aesthetics.

Parol—Quaderni d'Arte e di Epistomologia

http://www.unibo.it/parol/

Parol is an Italian journal of art and epistomology. Articles engage with the arts in general, with a particular emphasis on the relation between aesthetics, epistemology, and the arts: music, poetry, visual art, narrative, theatre, cinema, etc. The journal was conceived by Professor Luciano Nanni in 1985, initially as part of his course of aesthetics at the Department of Philosophy of the University of Bologna. At present it is also a web-zine, with the full text of selected articles online.

The Personalist Forum

http://www.canisius.edu/~gallaghr/pf.html

The Personalist Forum seeks to provide a forum for thinkers interested in exploring two personalist hypotheses: it is the personal dimension of our being and living that is definitive of our humanity, and the personal dimension of being human offers a clue to the ordering of reality. Having no ready-made answers to offer nor a creed to demand, we take personal categories seriously and speak in language that strives for maximum comphrehensibility. This web site provides tables of contents for current and earlier editions of the journal, subscription information, and guidelines for prospective authors.

Perspectives on Science

http://www.journals.uchicago.edu/POS/home.html

This journal is devoted to studies of the sciences that integrate historical, philosophical, and sociological perspectives. Its interdisciplinary approach is intended to foster a more comprehensive understanding of the sciences and the contexts in which they develop. Includes theoretical essays, case studies, review essays, and book reviews.

Philosophia Mathematica

http://www.amath.umanitoba.ca/PM/

Philosophia Mathematica is the only journal in the world devoted specifically to philosophy of mathematics. The aim of the journal is scholarly interchange. To that end it will publish peer-reviewed new work in philosophy of mathematics, including what can be learned from the study of mathematics, whether under instruction or by research, and including the application of mathematics.

Philosophical Books

http://www.blackwellpublishers.co.uk/scripts/webjrn1.idc?issn=00318051

Philosophical Books publishes prompt, scholarly reviews to assist both librarians and individuals in the choice of professional works of philosophy. It carries extensive reviews of major new publications in all areas of philosophy ranging from full-blown critical notices to short, one-page reviews. The journal also publishes regular 'Recent Work' pieces. Recent reviews include Gerald Dworkin on Rawls and Crispin Wright on Michael Dummett.

Philosophical Explorations

http://www.phil.ruu.nl/~brink/announcement.html

Philosophical Explorations aims to provide a forum for analytically minded philosophers interested in a genuine dialogue with continental philosophy and the (social) sciences. The editors believe that a comprehensive understanding of mind and action requires insights of philosophers working in both traditions, and of scientists working in the field.

Philosophical Investigations

http://www.blackwellpublishers.co.uk/scripts/webjrn1.idc?issn=01900536

Philosophical Investigations features articles in every branch of philosophy. Whether focusing on traditional or on new aspects of the subject, it offers thought-provoking articles and maintains a lively readership with an acclaimed discussion section and wide-ranging book reviews. Special issues are published on topics of current philosophical interest.

Philosophical Papers

http://sunsite.wits.ac.za/wits/fac/arts/philosophy/phl_papers/philp.htm

Philosophical Papers is an international journal published in South Africa three times a year. Since 1986, *Philosophical Papers* has been publishing articles of the highest standard by philosophers from all around the English-speaking world on issues in every branch of philosophy within the broad analytic tradition. *Philosophical Papers* is committed to opening and maintaining channels of communication between the philosophy communities in South

Africa and abroad, to encouraging high standards of excellence in philosophical research, to promoting the values of intellectual rigour and clarity, and to providing a forum for open, free, constructive, critical thought.

Philosophical Psychology

http://www.artsci.wustl.edu/~wbechtel/pp.html

Philosophical Psychology is an international journal devoted to developing and strengthening the links between philosophy and the psychological sciences, both as basic sciences and as employed in applied settings, by publishing original, peer referred contributions to this expanding field of study and research. The editorial board is especially keen to encourage publication of articles which deal with issues that arise in the cognitive and brain sciences, and to areas of applied psychology, with emphasis on articles concerned with cognitive and perceptual processes, models of psychological processing, including neural network and dynamical systems models, and relations between psychological theories and accounts of neural underpinnings or environmental context. The journal also publishes theoretical articles concerned with the nature and history of psychology, the philosophy of science as applied to psychology, and explorations of the underlying issues—theoretical and ethical—in educational, clinical, occupational, and health psychology.

The Philosophical Quarterly

http://www.blackwellpublishers.co.uk/scripts/webjrn1.idc?issn=00318094

The Philosophical Quarterly has become a core journal by publishing high quality articles and discussions, lively and comprehensive reviews, prize essays, and special issues. Accessibility of contents to all philosophers, including students, is an editorial priority. By representing exciting developments in the subject—for example, in reflecting on cognitive psychology, the visual arts, and quantum physics—the journal hopes to carry the subject forward for a wider readership.

Philosophical Studies

http://kapis.www.wkap.nl/kapis/CGI-BIN/WORLD/journalhome.htm?0031-8116

This is a periodical dedicated to work in analytic philosophy. The journal is devoted to the rapid publication of analytical contributions, particularly (but not exclusively) in epistemology, philosophical logic, the philosophy of language, and ethics. Papers applying formal techniques to philosophical problems are particularly welcome. The papers published are models of clarity and precision, dealing with some significant philosophical issues; they are intelligible to philosophers whose expertise lies outside the subject matter of the article. A diligent reader of the journal will be kept informed of the major problems and contributions of contemporary analytic philosophy.

Philosophical Writings

http://users.ox.ac.uk/~shil0124/phil-writ.html

Philosophical Writings is an international journal for postgraduates, with articles covering a wide range of philosophical issues. The journal also features poetry, letters, abstracts, competitions, and reviews.

Philosophy and Geography

http://www.cep.unt.edu/geog.html

Philosophy and Geography is a peer reviewed annual, sponsored by the Society for Philosophy and Geography. Each volume of the annual focuses on a specific theme. The heart of the Society for Philosophy and Geography is the interaction between philosophers and geographers on issues of mutual interest. A mirror of this site can be found at: *http://www.umt.edu/phil/PhilGeo.html.*

Philosophy and Literature

http://muse.jhu.edu/journals/philosophy_and_literature/

Philosophy and Literature explores the dialogue between literary and theoretical studies and philosophy. This site provides online access to the journal's articles for subscribers. For non-subscribers, access is available to the following information: Publisher's Statement, Editors and Editorial Board information, Subscription Information, Indexing and Abstracting, Advertising Rates and Policies, Bookstore Terms and Policies, Thematic and Special Issues, Links to Related Web Sites, Conferences and Calls for Papers, Guidelines for Contributors, Back Issues Tables of Contents, and an Author/Title Index.

Philosophy and Phenomenological Research

http://www.brown.edu/Departments/Philosophy/ppr.html

From its founding in 1940, this journal has been open to a variety of methodologies and traditions. This may be seen in the list of outstanding contributors through the years, which includes: Edmund Husserl, Ernest Nagel, C. I. Lewis, Alfred Tarski, Martin Buber, Rudolf Carnap, Arthur Lovejoy, Gustav Bergmann, Nelson Goodman, Arthur Pap, Roy Wood Sellars, Wilfrid Sellars, C. J. Ducasse, Roderick M. Chisholm, Lewis White Beck, Brand Blanshard, John Findlay, Morton White, and J. J. C. Smart. This tradition of openness continues, as reflected by a statement appearing in every issue: *"PPR* publishes articles in a wide range of areas including philosophy of mind, epistemology, ethics, metaphysics, and philosophical history of philosophy. No specific methodology or philosophical orientation is required in submissions."

Philosophy and Public Affairs

http://aaup.pupress.princeton.edu:70/CGI/cgi-bin/hfs.cgi/66/ princeton/papa.ctl

Philosophy and Public Affairs is founded in the belief that a philosophical examination of public issues can contribute to their clarification. It contains philosophical discussion of substantive legal, social, and political problems, as well as discussions of the more abstract questions to which these discussions give rise. *Philosophy and Public Affairs* is designed to fill the need for a periodical in which philosophers with different viewpoints and philosophically inclined writers from various disciplines—including law, political science, economics, and sociology—can bring their distinctive methods to bear on problems that concern everyone. Information on the editorial policy of the journal, as well as subscription and ordering details can be found on this page.

Philosophy and Rhetoric

http://aaup.pupress.princeton.edu:70/CGI/cgi-bin/hfs.cgi/66/ penn_state/pr.ctl

Founded in 1968, *Philosophy and Rhetoric* has published some of the most influential articles on the relations between philosophy and rhetoric. Topics include the connections between logic and rhetoric, the philosophical aspects of argumentation (including argumentation in philosophy itself), philosophical views on the nature of rhetoric among historical figures and during historical periods, philosophical analyses of the relation to rhetoric of other areas of human culture and thought, and psychological and sociological studies of rhetoric with a strong philosophical emphasis. This page provides information on the editorial policy of the journal, as well as subscription and ordering details.

Philosophy & Theology

http://www.bgsu.edu/offices/phildoc/pt.html

Philosophy & Theology addresses all areas of interest to both philosophy and theology. While not a journal of the philosophy of religion, *Philosophy & Theology* promotes fruitful dialogue. One issue each year is devoted to critical contact with Karl Rahner's thought and influence. *Philosophy & Theology* is published both in printed form and on computer disks. This site provides information on ordering and subscription rates, as well as a table of contents of the current issue.

Philosophy East and West

http://www2.hawaii.edu/uhpress/Journals/PW/PWHome.html

Philosophy East and West focuses on Asian and comparative thought. Its specialised articles and essays have an intercultural basis and relate philosophy to the arts, literature, science, and social practices of Asian civilizations.

Philosophy Now

http://www.kcl.ac.uk/kis/schools/hums/philosophy/PhilNowHome.html

Philosophy Now, launched in Britain in 1991, is the only philosophy magazine sold in the U.S. to be aimed both at specialists and at the general public, and covers all aspects of Western philosophy. Occasional special issues cover topics such as ethics, ancient philosophy, and philosophy of mind. Each issue also contains book reviews, letters, and the occasional touch of humor. It is ideal for students and teachers. Subscription rates and ordering information, as well as a table of contents of the current issue are accessible from this page. This site provides a sneak preview of the magazine, and is mantained by Rick Lewis rick.lewis@kcl.ac.uk. It is mirrored at *http://www.bgsu.edu/pdc/pn.html*.

Philosophy of Science

http://www.journals.uchicago.edu/PHILSCI/home.html

Since its inception in 1934, *Philosophy of Science*, along with its sponsoring society, The Philosophy of Science Association, has been dedicated to the furthering of studies and free discussion from diverse standpoints in the philosophy of science. The journal contains essays, discussion articles, and book reviews.

Philosophy, Psychiatry, & Psychology

http://muse.jhu.edu/journals/philosophy_psychiatry_and_psychology/

Philosophy, Psychiatry, & Psychology focuses on the area of overlap among philosophy, psychiatry, and abnormal psychology. The journal advances philosophical inquiry in psychiatry and abnormal psychology while making clinical material and theory more accessible to philosophers. This site provides online access to the journal's articles for subscribers. For non-subscribers, access is available to the following information: Publisher's Statement, Editors and Editorial Board Information, Subscription Information, Indexing and Abstracting, Advertising Rates and Policies, Bookstore Terms and Policies, Thematic and Special Issues, Links to Related Web Sites, Conferences and Calls for Papers, Guidelines for Contributors, Back Issues Tables of Contents, and an Author/Title Index.

Political Analysis

http://aaup.pupress.princeton.edu:70/CGI/cgi-bin/hfs.cgi/66/ michigan/pa.ctl

Political Analysis publishes new research in all areas of political science methodology including statistical models, modeling, measurement, and research design. This site provides information on the editorial policy of the journal, as well as subscription and ordering details.

Principia: An International Journal of Epistemology

http://www.cfh.ufsc.br/~wfil/principia/index.html

Principia, the journal of the Epistemology and Logic Research Group (NEL) of the Federal University of Santa Catarina (UFSC), Brazil, is a philosophical journal that publishes papers on contemporary epistemology. It accepts papers in Portuguese, Spanish, English, and French, and appears twice a year, in June and December. This page provides information on the editorial board and guidelines for contributors.

Proceedings of the Aristotelian Society

http://www.blackwellpublishers.co.uk/scripts/webjrn1.idc?issn=00667373

The Aristotelian Society was founded in 1880 as a discussion group which printed and circulated to members the papers read at its meetings. The *Proceedings of the Aristotelian Society* contains the papers read at the Society's fortnightly meetings in London throughout the academic year. It also contains short discussion notes on these papers. Papers are drawn from an international base of contributors and discuss issues across a broad range of philosophical traditions, including those which are of greatest current interest.

Process Studies

http://supernova.uwindsor.ca/~whitney/blw.process.html

Process Studies explores Whiteheadian-Hartshornean process thought at an advanced level and as it appears in related philosophies and theologies, and applies the Whiteheadian-Hartshornean conceptuality to a wide range of other fields: aesthetics, biology, cosmology, economics, ethics, history of religions, literary criticism, mathematics, political thought, psychology, physics and other natural sciences, the social sciences, sociology, theology (Christian theology and world religions), parapsychology, etc.

Public Affairs Quarterly

http://www.bgsu.edu/pdc/paq.html

Public Affairs Quarterly provides an impartial forum for the philosophical study of public policy issues. The journal features articles that bring philosophical depth and sophistication to current topics in social and political philosophy and that focus on the ethical and justificatory aspects of public policy issues. Some topics addressed include social, economic, and distributive justice; environmental problems; the social and political status of women, senior citizens, and minorities; abortion and euthanasia; patriotism; criminal justice; and ethical issues in medicine, business, and the professions. This site provides information on subscription rates and ordering, as well as a table of contents of the current issue.

Qui Parle

http://socrates.berkeley.edu/~quiparle/

Qui Parle is an interdisciplinary journal published by the University of California at Berkeley and focusing on literature, philosophy, visual arts, and history. This site provides information on ordering and subscription rates, tables of contents and article indexes, and links to other sites of interest.

Radical Philosophy

http://www.ukc.ac.uk/cprs/phil/rp/

Radical Philosophy is a journal of socialist and feminist philosophy. It was founded in 1972 in response to the widely felt discontent with the sterility of academic philosophy at the time (in Britain completely dominated by the narrowest sort of "ordinary language" philosophy), with the purpose of providing a forum for the theoretical work which was emerging in the wake of the radical movements of the 1960s in philosophy and other fields. *Radical Philosophy* is not committed to any particular philosophy, ideology, or political program. The purpose of the journal is to provide a forum for debate and discussion of theoretical issues on the left. It encourages the serious and informed discussion of such issues in clear and non-technical language, aimed to reach a wide audience. As well as major academic articles, it has a large and diverse book reviews section (covering 25-30 books per issue), as well as news and commentary sections. This page provides access to subscription information, instructions for authors, editorial procedures, and links to other philosophy resources.

Ratio

http://www.blackwellpublishers.co.uk/scripts/webjrn1.idc?issn=00340006

Ratio publishes work of a high quality on a wide variety of topics. It encourages articles which meet the highest standards of philosophical expertise, while at the same time remaining accessible to readers from a broad range of philosophical disciplines. The journal has encouraged links between philosophers writing in English, and those who work primarily in German. Its main emphasis is on analytic philosophy.

Ratio Juris

http://www.blackwellpublishers.co.uk/scripts/webjrn1.idc?issn=09521917

Ratio Juris is a leading international journal of philosophy of law and general jurisprudence.

It provides a truly international and trans-cultural forum for the communication of philosophical ideas about law and legal questions. *Ratio Juris* is open to scholars from all backgrounds and traditions, including philosophical, political, cultural, and linguistic.

Res Publica: A Journal of Legal and Social Philosophy

http://www.legaltheory.demon.co.uk/RP.html

Res Publica is a new journal of legal and social philosophy, providing a much-needed forum for those seeking to engage traditional legal, moral, and political philosophy with radical contemporary approaches.

Rhetorica

http://www.press.uchicago.edu/cgi-bin/hfs.cgi/66/california/rhet.ctl

Rhetorica's articles, book reviews, and bibliographies examine the theory and practice of rhetoric in all periods and languages and their relationship with poetics, philosophy, religion, and law. This page provides information on the editorial policy of the journal, as well as subscription rates and ordering details.

Russell: The Journal of the Bertrand Russell Archives

http://www.mcmaster.ca/russdocs/journal.htm

Russell has been in continuous existence since 1971. In 1997, the publishing of the journal was taken over by McMaster University Press. This is the press's first journal. The editor remains Russell's founding editor and the Hon. Russell Archivist, Dr. Kenneth Blackwell. There are two issues a year, published in the summer and the winter.

Semiotica

http://www.deGruyter.de/journals/semiotica/index.html

Semiotica, the journal of the International Association for Semiotic Studies, founded in 1969, appears in five volumes of two double issues per year, in two languages (English and French), and occasionally in German. *Semiotica* features articles reporting results of research in all branches of semiotic studies, in-depth review of selected current literature in this field, and occasional guest editorials and reports. From time to time, special issues, devoted to topics of particular interest, are assembled by guest editors. The publishers of *Semiotica* offer an annual prize, the Mouton d'Or, to the author of the best article each year. The article is selected by an independent international jury.

Signs: Journal of Women in Culture and Society

http://www.journals.uchicago.edu/Signs/home.html

Founded in 1975, *Signs* is recognized as the leading international journal in women's studies. The essays appearing in *Signs* cut across disciplines, across various feminist perspectives, and across the divisions between academic thought and daily life—all in an ongoing effort to illuminate and improve the culture to which we all belong.

Social Epistemology

http://www.tandf.co.uk/jnls/sep.htm

Social Epistemology provides a forum for philosophical and social scientific enquiry that incorporates the work of scholars from a variety of disciplines who share a concern with the production, assessment, and validation of knowledge. The journal covers both empirical research into the origination and transmission of knowledge and normative considerations which arise as such research is implemented, serving as a guide for directing contemporary knowledge enterprises. *Social Epistemology* publishes exchanges which are the collective product of several contributors and take the form of critical syntheses, open peer commentaries interviews, applications, provocations, reviews, and responses.

Social Philosophy and Policy

http://www.cup.cam.ac.uk/Journals/JNLSCAT/soy/soy.html

Social Philosophy and Policy is an interdisciplinary journal with an emphasis on the philosophical underpinnings of enduring social policy debates. The issues are thematic in format, examining a specific area of concern with contributions from scholars in philosophy, economics, political science, and law. While not primarily a journal of policy prescriptions, articles typically connect theory with practice.

Society and Animals

http://www.erica.demon.co.uk/SA.html

Society and Animals publishes studies which describe and analyse our experience of nonhuman animals. The goal of the journal is to stimulate and support an emerging content area within the social sciences. 'Animal studies' consists of investigations of the ways in which nonhuman animals feature in our lives. Findings regarding nonhuman animal experience and behaviour are included only secondarily to that end.

Stanford Humanities Review

http://shr.stanford.edu:80/shreview/

The *SHR* is dedicated to providing a wide, open forum for diverse voices from all over the intellectual landscape. This site provides information on the editorial board and journal contributors, and hopes to enrich the dialogue of the journal by reaching a wider, electronic audience.

Studia Logica

http://kapis.www.wkap.nl/kapis/CGI-BIN/WORLD/journalhome.htm?0039-3215

Studia Logica publishes original papers on various logical systems, which utilise methods of contemporary formal logic (those of algebra, model theory, proof theory, etc.). More specifically, *Studia Logica* invites articles on topics in general logic (as defined in 1991 Mathematical Subject Classification) and on applications of logic to other branches of knowledge such as philosophy, the methodology of science, or linguistics. The distinctive feature of *Studia Logica* is its series of monothematic issues edit ed by outstanding scholars and devoted to important topics of contemporary logic or covering significant conferences.

Substance

http://humanitas.ucsb.edu/depts/french/substance/sub.html

Substance has established itself as a major interdisciplinary journal with an appeal to a general audience. It promotes new thoughts by leading American and European authors which alter the perception of contemporary culture—be it artistic, humanistic, or scientific—and represents disciplines as diverse as literary theory, philosophy, psychoanalysis, art criticism, film studies, photography, physics, biology, mathematics, social science, architecture, and choreography. This site provides information on the editorial policy of the journal, as well as subscription rates and details on ordering the journal.

Synthese

http://kapis.www.wkap.nl/kapis/CGI-BIN/WORLD/journalhome.htm?0039-7857

Synthese publishes articles in the theory of knowledge, the general methodological problems of science, such as the problems of scientific discovery and scientific interest, of induction and probability, of causation and of the role of mathematics, statistics and logic in science, the methodological and foundational problems of the different departmental sciences, insofar as they have philosophical interest, those aspects of symbolic logic and of the foundations of mathematics which are relevant to the philosophy and methodology of science, and those facets of the history and sociology of science which are important for contemporary topical pursuits.

Teaching Business Ethics

http://kapis.www.wkap.nl/kapis/CGI-BIN/WORLD/journalhome.htm?1382-6891

Teaching Business Ethics is an interdisciplinary quarterly journal designed to provide a public forum for teachers and academic researchers in the field of business ethics to exchange views about substantive and methodological issues related to teaching business ethics. Unlike all other scholarly journals devoted to the study of business ethics, the focus of *Teaching Business Ethics* is on the practice of teaching the subject.

Teaching Philosophy

http://www.bgsu.edu/pdc/teachph.html

Teaching Philosophy provides an open forum for the exchange and evaluation of ideas, information, and materials concerning the teaching of philosophy. Published quarterly, each issue contains articles, discussions, reports, and case studies on practical and theoretical issues, including the relationship between philosophy and its teaching, the nature of philosophy curricula, courses and methods, and the unique problems that exist for philosophy teachers. The journal explores experimental and interdisciplinary courses with philosophical content as well as those that develop the philosophical aspects of other fields. Readers will learn about innovative teaching methods, successful classroom stratagems, and the use of new materials. An extensive review section includes reviews of new books, computer software, and instructional videos. This page provides details of subscription rates, information on how to order, and a table of contents of the current issue.

Tekhnema

http://scorpio.gold.ac.uk/tekhnema/

Tekhnema is a philosophical journal which addresses the most crucial question facing humankind in the twentieth century: the explicit dissolution of the limit between the human and the nonhuman. In order to take up this challenge critically, *Tekhnema* proposes an interdisciplinary forum in which philosophy, the sciences, and the arts can meet, reflect and invent upon relations between the human and the technical, thus opening up an urgently needed space for political imagination. The website provides information on subscriptions, the editorial board and policy, and tables of contents for the current and previous issues.

Teorema

http://www.um.es/~logica/english.htm

The philosophy journal *Teorema*, founded in 1971 and published without interruption until 1986, represented a landmark in the development of contemporary philosophical thought in Spain. During its period of publication, *Teorema* featured several articles by such outstanding philosophers as Chomsky, Davidson, Dummett, Habermas, Pears, Popper, Quine, Searle, Strawson, and others. It also organised a significant number of conferences and symposia, on a wide variety of topics including Wittgenstein's Tractatus, knowledge and belief, Quine's philosophy, philosophical and linguistic aspects of Chomsky's works, philosophy of mind, and contemporary German thought. In November 1996 *Teorema* resumed publication. Although papers in any philosophical discipline will be considered, the main aim of the journal is to publish original articles either in Spanish or in English in the following areas: Logic, Philosophy of Language, Philosophical Logic, Philosophy of Mind, Philosophy and History of Science, Epistemology, and related areas. Special attention will be given to the study of Spanish Thought from any period or discipline. This page provides information on publication schedules, editorial board, guidelines for authors, subscription rates, and contents of the current issue.

Theoria

http://www.und.ac.za/und/publications/theoria/

Based in South Africa, *Theoria* is an engaged, multidisciplinary journal of social and political theory. Its purpose is to address, through scholarly debate, the many challenges posed to intellectual life by the major social, political and economic forces that shape the contemporary world. This website provides information for prospective authors, tables of contents, and links to related information.

Theory and Decision

http://kapis.www.wkap.nl/kapis/CGI-BIN/WORLD/journalhome.htm?0040-5833

The field of decision in the social sciences has been investigated from many perspectives. All too often, however, different research approaches have been followed separately by management science, economics, psychology, operations research, praxeology, cybernetics and computer-aided decision making. They need mutual enrichment. *Theory and Decision* addresses the cross-fertilisation of the methods of these disciplines. The purpose of the journal is to let the engineering of decision making (i.e., of intelligence, choice, sorting out, ranking, uncertainty, and conflict resolution) gradually emerge. Special attention is paid to complex or ill-structured situations. Mathematical or other formalised treatments are favoured, if they provide a correct model of the situation under study.

Theory and Society

http://kapis.www.wkap.nl/kapis/CGI-BIN/WORLD/journalhome. htm?0304-2421

Theory and Society is a forum for the international community of scholars that publishes theoretically-informed analyses of social processes. It opens its pages to authors working at the frontiers of social analysis, regardless of discipline. Its subject matter ranges from prehistory to contemporary affairs, from treatments of single individuals and national societies to world culture, from discussions of theory to methodological critique, from First World to Third World—but always in the effort to bring together theory, criticism, and concrete observation.

Thesis Eleven

http://mitpress.mit.edu/journal-home.tcl?issn=07255136

This site provides editorial, subscription and ordering information on the MIT Press journal, *Thesis Eleven*.

Thinking: The Journal of Philosophy for Children

http://www.bgsu.edu/pdc/thinking.html

Thinking is a highly respected academic periodical, published quarterly by the Institute for the Advancement of Philosophy for Children. Since 1979, *Thinking* has been prime reading material for those professionals in education wanting to know more about the latest developments around the world in the theory of Philosophy for Children and its experimental foundations.

Topoi: An International Review of Philosophy

http://kapis.www.wkap.nl/kapis/CGI-BIN/WORLD/journalhome.htm?0167-7411

Topoi publishes articles, reviews, and discussions on philosophy and the history of philosophy. The journal examines the most important topics that have emerged in recent years, indicates the growth of discussion on these topics, and points out the principal tendencies that have developed in the discussions. *Topoi* does not adhere to expression of any one philosophical school or tradition, but rather promotes the exchange between philosophers from a variety of linguistic and cultural backgrounds. Each issue of *Topoi* is organised around a particular theme (topos), but this does not prevent the editor from accepting and publishing stimulating contributions on other themes, which are indicated as Extra-Topos.

Traditio: Studies in Ancient and Medieval History, Thought, and Religion

http://aaup.pupress.princeton.edu/cgi-bin/hfs.cgi/66/fordham/tradit.ctl

Traditio is best known for monographic essays, textual editions, and research tools, as annotated bibliographies of unpublished manuscripts. It publishes articles in French, Italian, and English in a number of disciplines, principally: literature, philosophy, history, art history, philology, patristics, and theology. The period covered is from the first to the fifteenth century.

Ultimate Reality and Meaning: Interdisciplinary Studies in the Philosophy of Understanding

http://www.utpress.utoronto.ca/journal/jour5/uram.htm

This journal publishes studies dealing with axiomatic presuppositions operating in various sciences, philosophies, religions, and value systems as well as in individuals' personal life. Dedicated to high scholarly standards, it offers an opportunity to participate in an ongoing dialogue in which scholars and interested readers from all parts of the world, explore past and present human effort to conceptualise reality, and to find meaning in our world. It is a well-focused, interdisciplinary, international, academic journal.

Utilitas

http://www.ucl.ac.uk/Bentham-Project/utilitas.htm

Utilitas is a pioneering interdisciplinary journal of moral and political philosophy, economic theory, jurisprudence, and intellectual history. It welcomes articles, discussions, debates, and reviews on contemporary themes in these disciplines where utilitarianism has made a particular contribution and on all aspects of the development of utilitarian thought (including that of its opponents). The journal is supported by the International Society for Utilitarian Studies (ISUS), which sponsors major conferences, seminars and other meetings, and makes special offers on books at advantageous rates to members. Individual subscribers to the journal automatically become members of the Society. Other features of the journal include the ongoing Bentham and Mill bibliographies and a number of special issues or parts of issues on particular themes and individuals.

Volga Journal of Philosophy and Social Sciences

http://www.ssu.samara.ru/research/philosophy/vjpss.htm

This monthly journal is being produced in both print and electronic formats. The main goal is to present Russian (and overseas) philosophical thought on the Internet. The journal will present hot information related to all types of philosophical activity in Russia and especially the mid-Volga region. Papers are accepted in Russian, English, and German. The Editor-in-Chief is Prof. Dr. A. A. Shestakov (Samara State University) shest@ssu.samara.ru, and the Co-editor is Prof. Dr. Valentin Bazhanov (Ulyanovsk State University) bazhan@bazh.univ.simbirsk.su, or bazhan@sv.uven.ru.

Word & Image

http://www.tandf.co.uk/jnls/wim.htm

Word & Image concerns itself with the study of the encounters, dialogues, and mutual collaboration (or hostility) between verbal and visual languages, one of the prime new areas of humanistic criticism. *Word & Image* provides a forum for articles that focus exclusively on this special study of the relations between words and images. Themed issues, guest-edited by internationally acknowledged scholars, are a regular feature of the journal. Recent examples include: reading ancient and medieval art, the picture and the text, and artists in two media.

Worldviews: Environment, Culture, Religion

http://www.erica.demon.co.uk/WV.html

Worldviews: Environment, Culture, Religion is an international academic journal that addresses how environmental issues are influencing the world's major religions and giving rise to new forms of religious expression—and how in turn religious belief and cultural background can influence people's attitudes to their environment and its problems.

Zygon: Journal of Religion and Science

http://www.blackwellpublishers.co.uk/scripts/webjrn1.idc?issn=05912385

Zygon works on a broad range of issues relating to religion and science. The journal continues, sometimes against the stream, in the belief that the coupling of long-evolved religious wisdom with recent scientific discoveries is significant for enhancing human life. Each volume contains intriguing articles, enlightening book reviews, and spirited dialogues and is supported by a distinguished, interdisciplinary board of editorial advisors.

Print Journals: Directories

AAUP Journals Catalogue

http://www.press.uchicago.edu/journals/

This link provides access to information on hundreds of print journals published by U.S. university presses—listed in alphabetical order.

Journals: Electronic and Paper

http://users.ox.ac.uk/~worc0337/phil_journals.html

Peter King's peter.king@philosophy.ox.ac.uk site provides a smaller, but up to date list of philosophy journals in print and electronic formats.

Online Information about Journals in Philosophy and Related Fields

http://www.ed.ac.uk/~pmilne/links_html/journals.html#top

This page provides links to a vast range of print journals and is updated regularly. It is maintained by Peter Milne Peter.Milne@ed.ac.uk at the University of Edinburgh.

Philosophy Journals and Newsletters

http://www.earlham.edu/~peters/philinks.htm#journals

From Peter Suber peters@earlham.edu, this page provides another large listing of philosophy journals, both print and electronic.

POIESIS: Philosophy Online Serials

http://www.nlx.com/posp/

A joint venture between the Philosophy Documentation Center and Intelex Corporation, *POIESIS: Philosophy Online Serials* offers searchable online access to a single database containing the full-text of current, recent, and back issues of a growing number of philosophy journals. The service is available on a subscription basis.

Publishers: A to Z

Blackwell Publishers

http://www.blackwellpub.com/

Blackwell Publishers publish an enormous range of philosophy journals and specialise in the supply of books and bibliographic support products to academic, research, and leading public libraries throughout the world. This site provides online versions of Blackwell's reference materials, and links to customer services.

Cambridge University Press

http://www.cup.org/

CUP is the printing and publishing arm of the University of Cambridge. Since its foundation in 1534, CUP has extended the research and teaching activities of the University by making available worldwide, a remarkable range of academic and educational books, journals, Bibles, and English language teaching materials. This site is CUP's online catalogue, providing journal information, new and recent publication listings, news, and reviews of featured titles. CUP can be contacted at <u>information@cup.org</u>.

CSLI Publications

http://csli-www.stanford.edu/publications/

CSLI Publications publishes books, lecture notes, monographs, technical reports, working papers, and conference proceedings relevant to the fields of logic, language, information, and computation. The page is maintained by <u>pubs@roslin.stanford.edu</u>.

Walter de Gruyter

http://www.degruyter.de/

Walter de Gruyter publishes a range of academic journals including *Archiv fuer Geschichte der Philosophie, Kant-Studien, Method & Theory in the Study of Religion*, and *Semiotica*. Enquiries about the site can be made to <u>wdg-info@deGruyter.de</u>.

Edinburgh University Press

http://www.ed.ac.uk/~eup/

Edinburgh has a extensive, well-established philosophy list, covering all aspects of the field, from popular philosophy to high-level research work. This site is maintained by <u>Katy.Lockwood@ed.ac.uk</u>.

Elsevier Science

http://www.elsevier.nl/

Elsevier are publishers of a range of philosophy and cognitive science journals, including *Annals of Pure and Applied Logic, Artificial Intelligence, Cognition, History of European*

Ideas, International Journal of Approximate Reasoning, Journal of Pragmatics, Language & Communication, and more.

Greenwood Publishing Group

http://www.greenwood.com/

Greenwood is leading publisher of academic, reference, trade, general interest, and professional books. In the area of philosophy, Greenwood publishes three series: *Bibliographies and Indexes in Philosophy*, *Contributions in Philosophy*, and *Resources in Asian Philosophy and Religion*. Enquiries about the site can be made to webmaster@greenwood.com.

Indiana University Press

http://www.indiana.edu/~iupress/

From IUP's site you can access online catalogues of books and journals, ordering information, press releases and newsletters, and selections from new books. IUP can be contacted at iupress@indiana.edu.

InteLex Corporation

http://www.nlx.com/

Publisher of the PastMasters series, InteLex has been producing highly-accurate full-text databases in the humanities since 1989 to facilitate scholarly research. Databases are available from InteLex on custom-made CD-ROM, via web subscription, and in SGML format for mounting on university full-text servers. For more information contact Brad Lamb at lamb@nlx.com.

International Thomson Publishing

http://www.thomson.com/

ITP is among the world's largest publishers. Their publishing ranges from elementary to post-graduate levels in science, technology, business, medicine, the humanities, social science, and defense. The thousands of products produced by ITP serve the needs of professionals, teachers, scholars, and librarians throughout the world. They have 10 head offices and 30 regional offices located across the globe and publish in English, German, French, Spanish, Korean, Mandarian Chinese, and Japanese. From this site you can access ITP's online catalogue of books and journals, sales and customer service information, software and multimedia, and links to other publishers. ITP's web site maintainer can be contacted at webmaster@list.thomson.com.

Kluwer Academic Publishers

http://kapis.www.wkap.nl/

Kluwer publishes of an extensive range of philosophy journals. From this site you can search the Kluwer catalogue and connect to the individual pages for each journal. Enquiries can be made to kluwer@wkap.com.

Library of Living Philosophers

http://www.siu.edu/~philos/llp/index.html

The Library of Living Philosophers is a series of works devoted to critical analysis and discussion of some of the world's greatest living philosophers. From this site you can access the list of volumes published, including contents and brief introduction. Catalogue and ordering information is also provided. The editor of the library is Lewis E. Hahn ge2361@siu.edu.

McGraw Hill

http://www.books.mcgraw-hill.com/

McGraw Hill publishes a range of academic titles, including works in philosophy. Link to regional McGraw Hill sites, or search the online catalogue.

MIT Press

http://www-mitpress.mit.edu/

MIT Press's online service allows you to search the online catalogue of books and journals, provides news and information about MIT Press, and online ordering facilities. Its website maintainer can be contacted at webmistress@mitpress.mit.edu.

Oxford University Press—UK

http://www1.oup.co.uk/

OUP is an international publisher of books, journals, and multimedia products with offices in over 20 countries. Here you can find information about OUP publications and online services available worldwide, search and order from online catalogue, access OED online, link to Oxford Physics online, and more. The website is maintained by wwwadmin@oup.co.uk.

Oxford University Press—USA

http://www.oup-usa.org/

This is the U.S. site of OUP where you can search and order from online catalogue, access customer service information, OUP mailing lists, and so forth. This website is maintained by webmaster@oup-usa.org.

PARATEXT: Electronic Reference Publishing

http://www.paratext.com

Paratext publishes a small collection of classics on CD-ROM. *The Romanitas Reference Series* includes collected editions in Latin and English of Vergil, Ovid, and Catullus. Eric Calaluca emc@paratext.com is the president of the company.

Peter Lang Publishing

http://www.peterlang.com/home.htm

Peter Lang is an intenational scholarly publisher of textbooks and monographs in the humanitites and social sciences. The website contains information on the publisher, as well as an electronic catalogue of its publications, including publications in philosophy.

Philosophy Documentation Center

http://www.bgsu.edu/pdc

The PDC is a non-profit organization with a reputation for excellence in the production and distribution of specialized products for philosophers, including directories, bibliographies, scholarly journals, and instructional software. This site provides access to information about the Center's products and services, a link to *Books in Philosophy* (the Center's online bookstore), and a link to *POIESIS: Philosophy Online Serials* (an electronic journals project being developed with InteLex Corporation).

Prentice Hall

http://www.prenhall.com/

Prentice Hall's beautifully-designed site enables users to search the online catalog by author or keyword. It also provides access to mailing lists for notification of new publications. The site maintainer can be contacted at webmaster@prenhall.com.

Princeton University Press

http://pup.princeton.edu/

PUP's charter is to publish books "for the promotion of education and scholarship." At their online site you can search PUP's database for information on philosophy and other titles, read sample chapters, and order online. The site is maintained by Leslie@pupress.princeton.edu.

Routledge

http://www.thomson.com/routledge/philosophy/rprcrout.html

One of the largest philosophy publishers in the world, Routledge publishes over 70 philosophy books every year and has over 500 philosophy titles in print. They are also developing such ambitious new projects as a multi-volume encyclopedia and a journals programme. From this site you can search Routledge titles, read excerpts from new and forthcoming titles, subscribe to Routledge mailing lists which advise of new publications in various areas of philosophy, and access a collection of links to online philosophy resources. Routledge can be contacted at philosophy@routledge.com.

Seven Bridges Press

http://www.sevenbridgespress.com/

Seven Bridges Press is an academic publisher of textbooks and scholarly works in comparative religion, philosophy, political science, and Asian Studies. This site provides links to a host of online resources. The maintainer of the site can be contacted at webmaster@sevenbridgespress.com.

University of Chicago Press

http://www.press.uchicago.edu/

UCP's website allows online searching of their complete catalogue or subject catalogues. It provides links to a style manual and to journals published by this press, as well as excerpts of new titles, featured titles, and information on new and forthcoming titles. The page is maintained by www-team@press.uchicago.edu.

Verlag Karl Alber

http://www.alber.freinet.de/

This is the site of the German language publisher of science, philosophy, and technical books. Verlag Karl Alber can be contacted at alber_verlag@t-online.de.

The White Horse Press

http://www.erica.demon.co.uk/

The White Horse Press publishes books and journals specialising in environmental issues. This site contains details of WHP journals, with complete contents and abstracts from past issues, information on WHP books, and an order form that can be used for all titles.

Publishers: Directories

Academic Publishers

http://www.bookshop.co.uk/ibspub.htm#ACADEMIC

This is the Internet Bookshop's listing of academic publishers with sites on the net. The listing is maintained by Gary Newbrook gary.newbrook@bookshop.co.uk.

Association of American University Presses

http://aaup.princeton.edu/

Access and search the combined online catalog for a host of U.S. university publishers, plus information and links to individual presses from this site, maintained by creesy@ pupress.princeton.edu.

On-line Information on Publishers in Philosophy and Related Disciplines

http://www.ed.ac.uk/~pmilne/links_html/pubs.html

The list on this site aims to be complete with respect to online information on major publishers. It is maintained by Peter Milne Peter.Milne@ed.ac.uk at the University of Edinburgh.

Publishers' Catalogues

http://www.lights.com/publisher/

This site, maintained by Peter Scott scott@lights.com, provides links to an extensive range of publishers' catalogues available online. The list is categorised by geographic location.

WWW Virtual Library: Publishers

http://www.comlab.ox.ac.uk/archive/publishers.html

This is site gathers information and links to a range of publishing sites on the net. It is maintained by J.P.Bowen@reading.ac.uk.

Section 3: Organizations

Organizations & Associations: A to Z

Aberdeen University Philosophy Society

http://www.abdn.ac.uk/~src068/society.html

The AUPS page should be an inspiration for students of philosophy everywhere. This society not only runs its own weekly meetings, but has its own electronic journal, *Cathesis*. This page, maintained by Christian Rhein u03cr@abdn.ac.uk, includes links to philosophy resources as well as society information.

African Americans for Humanism

http://www.SecularHumanism.org/aah/index.html

"The need for critical thinking skills and a humanistic outlook in our world is great. This is no less true in the Black community than in others. Many African Americans have been engulfed by religious irrationality, conned by self-serving 'faith healers', and swayed by dogmatic revisionist historians. Many others, however, have escaped the oppression of such delusions, and live happy and upstanding lives free of superstition. African Americans for Humanism (AAH) exists to bring these secular humanists together, to provide a forum for communication, and to facilitate coordinated action. In an irrational world, those who stand for reason must stand together." This site provides information on the goals and activities of AAH, and is maintained by David Noelle admin@SecularHumanism.org.

Akademie für Ethik in der Medizin

http://www.gwdg.de/~ukee/

The AEM was founded in Göttingen in 1986 by a group of experts in the subject of medical ethics. The form of an academy was chosen to ensure a sophisticated and balanced exchange and collaboration between the disciplines involved, e.g., clinical and theoretical medicine, philosophy, theology, law, psychology, natural and social sciences, health care, and administration. This site, with some information in English, is maintained by simon@ethik.med.uni-goettingen.de.

Alexandria Society

http://www.cosmopolis.com/society/index.html

This is a society for those interested in ancient and modern cosmological speculation and what the humanities have to contribute to contemporary life. The society publishes a journal, *Alexandria*, and an occasional newsletter, *Kosmos*.

Alliance of Secular Humanist Societies

http://www.secularhumanism.org/ashs/

The Alliance of Secular Humanist Societies is a network created for mutual support among local and/or regional societies of secular humanists. This web site provides information on the activities of ASHS and is maintained by David Noelle admin@SecularHumanism.org.

American Association of Philosophy Teachers

http://www.mnsfld.edu/depts/philosop/aapt.html

The AAPT is dedicated to the advancement of the art of teaching philosophy. The page lists information on the Society and its meetings and activities, as well as providing some links to teaching resources. It is maintained by rtimko@mnsfld.edu.

American Atheists

http://www.atheists.org/

American Atheists is a nationwide movement founded by Dr. Madalyn Murray O'Hair for the advancement of Atheism, and the total, absolute separation of government and religion. The web site provides information on the history of the organization, its aims, and various discussions of atheism vs. theism. The association can be contacted at info@atheists.org.

American Catholic Philosophical Association

http://www.acpa-mail.org/

"Since 1926, scholars and thinkers, mostly based in Canada and the United States, have forged a unique tradition and community known as the 'American Catholic Philosophical Association'. Steeped in classical sources and cultivating the Catholic Philosophical heritage, this traditioin is known for creative engagement with major philosophers of every era and bold responses to the themes and issues of contemporary philosophy." This site provides information on the aims and activities of the Association and links to its publications.

American Humanist Association

http://www.infidels.org/org/aha/

This site provides a diverse collection of articles, essays, commentaries, lists, and bulletins about current and future events concerning humanism in general and the American Humanist Association in particular. It is maintained by Steven D. Schafersman schafesd@muohio.edu.

American Nihilism Association

http://www.access.digex.net/~kknisely/nihilism.html

This site provides brief information and a contact address for the American Nihilism Association.

American Philosophical Association

http://www.udel.edu/apa

This site provides information on the APA: membership, publications, activities, etc. The APA online site provides links to a comprehensive range of resources for philosophers. It is maintained by Burt Wilson burt@udel.edu.

American Political Science Association: Foundations of Political Theory Section

http://www.apsanet.org/~theory/

This is the homepage of the Political Theory Section of the APSA, which exists to advance the linkage of political theory and philosophy with political science as a discipline. Information on the activities of the organization, its newsletter, recent publications in political theory, and links to relevant online information are provided.

American Society for Aesthetics

http://www.indiana.edu/~asanl/asa/asa-info.html

The ASA website provides information on the purpose of the Society, forthcoming meetings, conference papers, and the ASA newsletter. The national office of the ASA can be contacted at asastcar@vms.csd.mu.edu. The site is maintained by Dominic Lopes dlopes@indiana.edu.

American Society of Law, Medicine & Ethics

http://lawlib.slu.edu/aslme/

The mission of the American Society of Law, Medicine & Ethics (ASLME) is to provide high-quality scholarship, debate, and critical thought to the community of professionals at the intersection of law, health care, policy, and ethics. This web page provides information on the activities of the Society and is maintained by webmaster@lawlib.slu.edu.

American Society for Philosophy, Counselling, and Psychotherapy

http://www.cmsu.edu/englphil/aspcp.htm

Founded in 1992 as an affiliate of the American Philosophical Association (APA), the American Society for Philosophy, Counselling, and Psychotherapy (ASPCP) promotes the philosophical examination of the theory and practice of counseling and psychotherapy and of philosophy as a private practice profession. It hosts annual program sessions at each of the divisional meetings of the American Philosophical Association, holding its national business meeting with the APA Eastern Division. This society can be contacted via kencust@sprintmail.com.

Anthroposophical Society

http://www.io.com/~lefty/Anthroposophical_Society.html

The Anthroposophical Society in America is the national organ of the General Anthroposophical Society, founded by Rudolf Steiner in 1923 as "an association of people who would foster the life of the soul, both in the individual and in human society, on the basis of a true knowledge of the spiritual world." This website, maintained by lefty@apple.com, provides contact information for the U.S. and Canadian societies, and information on the activities of the Society.

Applied Research Ethics National Association (ARENA)

http://www.anes.hmc.psu.edu/ArenaFolder/ArenaHome.html

ARENA is a membership organization for those involved in the day-to-day application of ethical principles, governmental regulations, and other policies regarding research and clinical practice. The web site provides information on the aims, services, and activities of the Association, and is maintained by PRIMR@Delphi.com.

Association des professeurs de philosophie de l'Académie de Poitiers

http://wwwperso.hol.fr/~felie/appap/

This site, in French, provides information on the activities of the APPAP, as well as links to a variety of philosophy resources.

Association for the Scientific Study of Consciousness

http://www.phil.vt.edu/ASSC/

ASSC promotes rigorous analytic research on consciousness. The official purpose of the organization is to encourage research within cognitive science, neuroscience, philosophy, and other relevant disciplines in the sciences and humanities, directed toward understanding the nature, function, and underlying mechanisms of consciousness. This site, maintained by Valerie Gray Hardcastle valerie@vt.edu, provides information on the Society's by-laws, membership, and links to relevant research materials.

Association for the Study of Persons

http://www.canisius.edu/~gallaghr/asp.html

The Association for the Study of Persons aims at responding to the growing feeling of unease about the depersonalising and dehumanising conditions under which persons have to live. The Association hopes to raise, encourage, and promote national and international awareness of personalism, and issues associated with an understanding of the significance and importance of persons. The site, maintained by Shaun Gallagher gallaghr@canisius.edu, provides information on the activities of the association, plus links to research and other related resources.

Association for Symbolic Logic

http://www.math.uiuc.edu/~asl/

This site provides information on the association, as well as meetings, conferences, announcements, and a link to the *Bulletin of Symbolic Logic*. The site is maintained by adam@math.uiuc.edu.

Association for the Foundations of Science, Language, and Cognition

http://pespmc1.vub.ac.be/AFOS/

AFOS afos@plearn.edu.pl is an international professional association of working scientists, theorists of science, linguists, and logicians that was founded in 1993. This site provides detailed information on AFOS and links to its mailing list.

Association Internationale des Professeurs de Philosophie

http://members.aol.com/Aipph/welcome.htm

In English, French, and German, this site provides information on the aims and activities of the association which promotes the teaching of philosophy in the schools and universities of the member countries. It is maintained by Peter Heinsch pheinsch@rz-online.de.

Atheist Society of Australia

http://www.ozemail.com.au/~ksolway/asa.html

The Atheist Society is a socially concerned organization. It consists of individuals from various academic and social backgrounds, each having a knowledge of the nonexistence of God and an uncompromising rejection of all concepts of God, be they metaphysical or socio-political in nature. Members of this society do not adopt a non-committal, agnostic viewpoint and are therefore openly anti-religious. The site, maintained by Kevin Solway ksolway@ozemail.com.au, provides information on the activities of the Society plus links to atheist resources.

Australasian Association for the History, Philosophy, and Social Studies of Science

http://www.asap.unimelb.edu.au/aahpsss/aahpsss.htm

This website provides information on the activities of the Association, links to its newsletters, membership details and contact information.

Australian Association for Process Thought

http://www.ozemail.com.au/~farleigh/aapthome.html

The Australasian Association for Process Thought is a fairly new organization formed by process philosopher and theologian, Dr. Greg Moses and computer scientist, Peter Farleigh with support from biologist and writer, Professor Charles Birch and humanities professor, Wayne Hudson from Griffith University. The aim of the association is to promote the study of the process-relational thought of Alfred North Whitehead and Charles Hartshorne in southern Pacific region. Membership consists of academics, clergy, students, and other interested people from all over Australia, New Zealand, and Papua New Guinea. This site, maintained by Peter Farleigh farleigh@ozemail.com.au, provides lecture and conference details, discussion papers, and links to process-related resources.

Australian Association of Professional and Applied Ethics

http://www.arts.unsw.edu.au/aapae/

This site provides information on the Association's aims, activities, newsletters, etc. It is maintained by Bill Tarrant b.tarrant@unsw.edu.au.

Australian Philosophy Postgraduates

http://student.uq.edu.au/~s063999/app.htm

This web page is intended to supplement the Australian Postgraduate Philosophy mailing list (app-list—see details in the General and Miscellaneous Mailing List Section) and the annual conference held by the postgraduate philosophy students of New Zealand and Australia. The APP as an organization doesn't actually exist. The idea behind having the list and web page is to give postgrads some of the benefits of an organization like the AAP without the work that a formal organization would entail. The page is maintained by Anthony Cupitt s063999@student.uq.edu.au, and provides information on the mailing list and conference, as well as links to philosophy-related resources.

Austrian Ludwig Wittgenstein Society

http://www.sbg.ac.at/phs/alws/alws.htm

As implied by the name "Wittgenstein Society," its first goal is the analysis, tradition, and dissemination of Wittgenstein's philosophy. Confronted with the mass of present-day Wittgenstein research in the English-speaking countries, this might look like carrying coals to Newcastle. But it should be kept in mind that in many European countries Wittgenstein's philosophy, and Analytic Philosophy in general, were—and up to a point still are—in a minority position. This situation is the reason for the society's second main goal: to continue a philosophy which had strong roots in Austria (as well as in other countries): Analytic Philosophy (Wittgenstein) and philosophy of science (Vienna Circle). Information on the activities of the Society can be found at this site, maintained by Georg Dorn and Alexander Hieke.

Ayn Rand Society: College of New Jersey

http://www.tcnj.edu/~aynrand/

Although this is a small college Society, the information on its page makes it worth the listing. Maintained by Gonzalo E. Mon aynrand@tcnj.edu, it provides links to an extensive range of resources and information on Ayn Rand and Objectivism.

The Bertrand Russell Society

http://daniel.drew.edu/~jlenz/brs.html

Founded in 1974, the Society seeks to foster a better understanding of the life, work, and writings of Bertrand Russell (1872-1970) and how his contributions relate to today's world. This page, maintained by John Lenz jlenz@drew.edu, provides information on membership and the activities of the BRS, plus links to Russell images, writing by and about Russell, and links to other related sites.

Brisbane Philosophy Society

http://www.uq.oz.au/~pdgdunn/bphilsoc.htm

This site, maintained by Julian Lamont J.Lamont@qut.edu.au, provides information on the activities of the Society for philosophers located in Brisbane, Queensland, Australia.

British Logic Colloquim

http://www-theory.dcs.st-and.ac.uk/~rd/blc/

The BLC aims to advance the education of the public within Great Britain and Northern Ireland in the study of formal or mathematical logic and other subjects in so far as they relate to such logic. This web site provides information on the activities of the BLC, links to logic-related resources, and is maintained by Roy Dyckhoff rd@dcs.st-and.ac.uk.

British Society for Aesthetics

http://www.indiana.edu/~asanl/asa/bsa-info.html

This site provides information on the Society, plus contact details and membership application information. The Society can be contacted via Richard Woodfield woodfra@innotts.co.uk.

British Society for Ethical Theory

http://www.gla.ac.uk/Acad/Philosophy/Lenman/bset.html

Information on the Society, and links to its mailing list and ethics-related resources can be found at this site which is maintained my Jimmy Lenman j.lenman@philosophy. arts.gla.ac.uk. A mirror of the site is located at: *http://www.keele.ac.uk/depts/pi/ethics/ index.htm* and maintained by David McNaughton pia02@keele.ac.uk.

British Society for the History of Philosophy

http://www.leeds.ac.uk/philosophy/bshp/bshp.htm

The British Society for the History of Philosophy (BSHP), launched in 1984, exists to promote and foster all aspects of the study and teaching of the history of philosophy. This website provides information on the aims and activities of the Society, its newsletter, and conference information. The site is maintained by Mike Beaney m.a.beaney@leeds.ac.uk.

British Society for Philosophy of Science

http://www.dur.ac.uk/~df10www/bsps/BSPSHome.html

This site provides information on the activities of the BSPS which publishes *The British Journal for Philosophy of Science*. This page is maintained by Ginny Watkins.

Canadian Philosophical Association

http://www.uwindsor.ca/cpa/

This site is devoted to professional philosophical activity in Canada. Membership information is available, as well as details of the activities of the association, links to journals, conference information, and more. An alternative page in French is also available. The site is maintained by Robert Pinto pinto@uwindsor.ca.

Canadian Society for Aesthetics

http://tornade.ere.umontreal.ca/~guedon/AE/ae.html

In French and English, this page provides information on the Society's conference program, its journal, and links to other aesthetics organizations on the web. It is maintained by allegre@ere.umontreal.ca.

Canadian Society for Hermeneutics and Postmodern Thought

http://www.ucalgary.ca/~jking/csh/CSH_Bulletin.html

This site centers on the electronic bulletin of the Society, but also provides membership application information and information on meetings of other learned societies.

Canadian Society for the History and Philosophy of Mathematics

http://www.kingsu.ab.ca/~glen/cshpm/home.htm

This site provides information on the activities of the Society, membership information, links to pages of society members, an email directory, and a comprehensive list of links to resources related to the history and philosophy of mathematics. The page is maintained by Glen Van Brummelen gvanbrum@kingsu.ab.ca.

Canadian Society for Women in Philosophy (C-SWIP)

http://sbrennan.philosophy.arts.uwo.ca/cswip/

The Canadian Society for Women in Philosophy aims to foster philosophical scholarship and teaching in the area of feminist studies as a legitimate area of interest within philosophic inquiry; to provide support and encouragement for the professional work of women philosophers; and to work toward eliminating discrimination against women in philosophy. This site provides information on the activities of the Society, access to its newsletter, conference information, and notification of job vacancies in philosophy. The site is maintained by Samantha Brennan sbrennan@julian.uwo.ca.

Center for Advanced Research in Phenomenology

http://www.fau.edu/divdept/schmidt/carp/

This new website offers an historical overview and a methodological characterisation of phenomenology. It also provides information on the activities of the Center, located at Florida Atlantic University. It includes an international registry of phenomenologists, a bibliography of the phenomenological movement, graduate programs, and links of interest to phenomenologists. Comments about the site can be directed to Embree@acc.fau.edu.

Cognitive Science Society

http://www1.pitt.edu/~cogsci95/

News and information for society members, and details of the Society's conferences can be obtained from this site maintained by Alan Lesgold al@pop.pitt.edu.

Computer Ethics Institute

http://www.brook.edu/recycled/sscc/cei/cei_hp.htm

The Computer Ethics Institute is a non-profit, education and policy study organization interested in ethical issues arising from the development of information technology. It has a broad constituency including business, education, religious, philosophical, computer profession and public policy communities, and welcomes participation from anyone interested. The site is maintained by Patrick Sullivan psullivan@brook.edu.

Council for Secular Humanism

http://www.SecularHumanism.org/home.html

This page provides information on the activities of the Council and also acts as a general educational resource on secular humanism. It includes links to press releases, conferences and events, articles, the humanist manifesto, and a range of secular humanist resources. The site is maintained by David Noelle admin@SecularHumanism.org.

DialogNet

http://dialog.net:85/homepage/dialognet.html

Information on DialogNet, a worldwide consortium of people interested in discussing philosophy through computer-mediated communications, can be found at this site. DialogNet is also responsible for co-ordinating the running of a variety of Thinknet mailing lists. DialogNet is the brainchild of Kent Palmer palmer@think.net.

Drew University Philosophical Society

http://daniel.drew.edu/~dups/

DUPS is a student society, and its web page provides information on its activities, plus links to philosophy-related resources and its own journal. The page is maintained by Paul Bond pbond@drew.edu.

Dutch Association of Aesthetics

http://www.phil.ruu.nl/esthetica/

This page gives information on the activities of the Association.

European Society for the Cognitive Sciences of Music

http://www.mus.cam.ac.uk/ESCOM/

This site, in French and English, provides information on events and activities of the Society. The Society's newsletters are available online, and links are provided to sites related to the cognitive science of music. The Society's secretariat can be contacted at i.deliege@ulg.ac.be.

Evangelical Philosophical Society

http://www.chass.utoronto.ca:8080/~davis/evps.htm

EPS is an organization of evangelical Christians who meet annually to discuss philosophical matters of mutual interest. It emphasises philosophy of religion defined broadly to include philosophical theology, ethics, apologetics, as well as other fields as they relate to the faith. EPS was founded in 1974 and has grown to over 200 members. This site, maintained by Richard Davis davis@chass.utoronto.ca, provides information on membership, the Society's journal, and links to related web pages.

FoLLI: the European Association for Logic, Language and Information

http://www.wins.uva.nl/research/folli/

FoLLI was founded in 1991 to advance the practising of research and education on the interfaces between Logic, Linguistics, Computer Science, Cognitive Science, and related disciplines in Europe. The website provides information on the activities of the Association, including its newsletter, journal, summer schools, and conferences.

Freelance Academy

http://www.freelance.com/

The Freelance Academy website, maintained by Lance Fletcher lance.fletcher@freelance.com provides information on Freelance mailing lists, archives of lists, and assists with subscribing and unsubscribing from the lists. Eventually, the site will serve as a distribution point for essays and monographs relevant to the mailing lists.

Friedrich Nietzsche Society

http://www.swan.ac.uk/german/fns/fns.htm

This site by Duncan Large d.a.g.large@swan.ac.uk, provides information on conferences and other activities of the Friedrich Nietzsche Society, access to the *Journal of Nietzsche Studies*, and links to other Nietzsche resources.

Gruppe Phänomenologie

http://hhobel.phl.univie.ac.at/gph/

This is the site of the Society for the Advancement of the Reception and the Critical Development of Phenomenology and of Its Impulses. This page provides information on the activities of the Society, links to related resources including the Society's journal, and general information on phenomenology. It is maintained by János Békési Janos.Bekesi@univie.ac.at.

Kurt Goedel Society

http://www.logic.tuwien.ac.at/kgs/home.html

An international organization for the promotion and research in all areas of logic, in philosophy, and in history of mathematics. Access information about the activities of the Society, and information on membership. The Society can be contacted through its Secretary, Karin Horwein karin@logic.tuwien.ac.at.

Hegel Society of America

http://www.hegel.org/

The Hegel Society of America is a learned society, founded in 1968, whose goal is to promote the study of the philosophy of Hegel and Hegelianism, its place within the history of thought, and its relation to social, political, and cultural movements since his time. This website provides information on the activities of the Society, conferences, and links to Hegel resources on the net. It is maintained by Andrew Hill 02hill@cua.edu.

History of Science Society

http://weber.u.washington.edu/~hssexec/index.html

This site provides information on the Society's activities, meetings, and membership, and provides links to research tools, information on employment and research opportunities, and various competitions. The Executive of HSS can be contacted at hssexec@u.washington.edu.

Human Behavior and Evolution Society

http://psych.lmu.edu/hbes.htm

HBES is a highly eclectic group, consisting of scholars from a great number of fields, most of whom are professional academics, while approximately 20% are students. This page provides information on the activities of HBES, plus links to resources in modern evolutionary theory. The site is maintained by Michael E. Mills memills@aol.com.

Humanist Association of Canada

http://magi.com/~hac/hac.html

This site, maintained by Galen Thurber godfree2@atheist.com, provides information on the activities of the Association, and links to humanist resources.

Hume Society

http://www.hi.is/~mike/hume.html

Founded in 1974, the Society has over 400 members worldwide. This site, maintained by Mikael M. Karlsson mike@rhi.hi.is, provides information on how to join the Hume Society, access to the Bulletin of the Hume Society (including archives), conference information, and liks to Hume-related resources.

Hungarian Philosophical Association

http://hps.elte.hu:8080/

This page, in Hungarian and English, provides information on the Society as well as links to sites providing philosophy information and resources. The site is maintained by webmaster@hps.elte.hu.

Institute for Global Ethics

http://www.globalethics.org/

The Institute for Global Ethics wethics@globalethics.org is an independent, non-sectarian, and non-political organization dedicated to elevating public awareness and promoting the discussion of ethics in a global context. This non-profit think tank is an international, membership-based organization focusing on ethical activities for corporations, educators, professionals, and communities. This site provides information on the Institute's mission, activities, and products. It also presents a monthly dilemma and calls for participation in solving it. Results are then published the following month.

Institute Vienna Circle

http://hhobel.phl.univie.ac.at/wk/

The international Institute Vienna Circle, a non-profit society founded in Vienna in October 1991, sets as its goals, firstly, the documentation and furtherance of the contributions and development of the 'Vienna Circle' in the areas of science and adult education; and secondly, the cultivation and application of logical empiricism, critical rationalism and linguistic analysis in the sense of a scientific philosophy and coordinated with general socio-cultural developments. This site, maintained by János Békési Janos.Bekesi@univie.ac.at, provides information on membership and activities of the Institute, as well as its history and present aims.

International Academy of Humanism

http://www.SecularHumanism.org/academy.html

The International Academy of Humanism was established to recognise distinguished humanists and to disseminate humanistic ideals and beliefs. This web site provides information on the aims and activities of the Academy, and is maintained by David Noelle admin@SecularHumanism.org.

International Association of Empirical Aesthetics

http://www.ume.maine.edu/~iaea/

This site, maintained by Colin Martindale rpy383@maine.maine.edu, provides information about the activities of the Association, and links to other aesthetics-related resources on the net.

International Association for Greek Philosophy

http://www.hri.org/iagp/

This site, part of the Hellenic Resources Network *http://www.hri.org/* provides information on the activities of the Association, including forthcoming conferences and books published. It also links to the International Center for Greek Philosophy and Culture *http://www.hri.org/iagp/icgpc.html.*

International Economics and Philosophy Society

http://www.qut.edu.au/arts/human/ethics/ieps/index.htm

This site, maintained by Paul Murray pmurray@lingua.cltr.uq.oz.au, provides information on the IEPS and links to philosophy and economics resources.

International Humanist and Ethical Union

http://www.secularhumanism.org/iheu/

This site provides information on the IHEU and its activities, as well as on humanism and the humanist movement generally. It is maintained by David Noelle admin@SecularHumanism.org.

International Quantum Structures Association

http://www.math.latech.edu/iqsa/home.html

IQSA is a non-profit scientific association for the advancement and dissemination of quantum logics and structures based on their mathematical, philosophical, physical, and interdiciplinary aspects. The website provides information on the operation and activities of the Association, and is maintained by G. Yao gya001@math.latech.edu.

International Society for the Empirical Study of Literature

http://www.ualberta.ca/ARTS/RICL/riclseal.html

This site provides information on the aims and activities of the Society, and access to a downloadable bibliography.

International Society for Environmental Ethics

http://www.cep.unt.edu/ISEE.html

This page provides information on the Society and membership. It also provides links to a bibliography and books of relevance to environmental ethics. Part of the Center for Environmental Ethics, the site is maintained by Eugene Hargrove hargrove@unt.edu.

International Society for Utilitarian Studies

http://www.ucl.ac.uk/Bentham-Project/isus.htm

The International Society for Utilitarian Studies reflects the world-wide interest in the Bentham Project, the expansion of Bentham studies, and the growing interest in utilitarianism. The aims of this body are to further the work of the Bentham Project in making available all of Bentham's writings in modern scholarly editions; to organize seminars and conferences on topics relevant to lawyers, philosophers, political scientists and historians; to provide a forum for debate and research on utilitarianism and its present-day relevance in the fields of legal, political, and social reform. This site provides minimal information on the Society.

Internationale Vereinigung für Rechts und Sozialphilosophie (IVR)

http://www_ivr.cirfid.unibo.it/ivr/

This site, maintained by Giovanni Ziccardi ziccardi@cirfid.unibo.it, provides information on the activities of IVR—the International Assoc. for Philosophy of Law and Social Philosophy.

Japan Popper Society

http://www.law.mita.keio.ac.jp/popper

The Japan Popper Society page is maintained by Yoshihisa Hagiwara hagiwara@law.mita.keio.ac.jp. The Society's page is currently in Japanese, but an English version is under construction.

Kierkegaard Societies & Institutions Worldwide

http://www.utas.edu.au/docs/humsoc/kierkegaard/institutions.html

This site, maintained by Julia Watkin julia.watkin@human.utas.edu.au, provides links to Kierkegaard resources, teaching centers and societies all over the world.

Lonergan Philosophical Society

http://www.concentric.net/~Mmorelli/#LPS

The objectives of the Lonergan Philosophical Society are to foster and encourage open exploration of the philosophic significance of Bernard Lonergan's thought both as a primary focus of investigation and in relation to other currents of thought; to promote scholarly fellowship through activities such as meetings, conferences, colloquia, publications, and other exchanges; and to cooperate with the work of the Lonergan Research Institute in Toronto, the West Coast Methods Institute in California, the Los Angeles Lonergan Center, the Boston Lonergan Workshop, and other philosophic and academic societies. This site, from Mark Morelli MMorelli@lmumail.lmu.edu, provides membership information and details the activities of the Society.

National Women's Studies Association

http://www.feminist.com/nwsa.htm

The National Women's Studies Association (NWSA) is a professional organization designed "to further the social, political and professional development of women's studies throughout the country and the world, at every educational level and in every educational setting." NWSA membership includes scholars, educators, students, women's centers, and activists interested in pursuing these common goals. This site provides information on the activities of the Association, as well as links to feminist and women's studies resources.

New Philosophy Society

http://www.ed.ac.uk/~aed/nps.html

A student organization at Edinburgh University, the Society provides this web page which details its activities, including a lecture series, discussion groups, and social activities. The page is maintained by Alice Drewery Alice.Drewery@ed.ac.uk.

North American Kant Society

http://funnelweb.utcc.utk.edu/~philosop/naks.html

The purpose of the North American Kant Society is to further study of the works of Immanuel Kant. The website provides information on conferences, journals, study groups, newsletters, and links to Kant-related resources. This page is maintained by Richard Aquilla raquila@utk.edu.

North American Nietzsche Society

http://www.usc.edu/dept/annenberg/thomas/nans.html

This is a basic page with information about membership and fees. It is maintained by douglast@cwis.usc.edu.

North Carolina Philosophical Society

http://www.davidson.edu/academic/philosophy/NCPS/NCPS.html

This page provides information on the activities of the Society, and is mantained by John Heil joheil@davidson.edu.

Norwegian Soren Kierkegaard Society

http://www.uio.no/~holt/SKS-eng.html

This page, maintained by Anders Holt holt@filosofi.uio.no, provides information on membership and the activities of the Society, and links to several Kierkegaard-related pages on the net.

Philosophy of Science Association

http://scistud.umkc.edu/psa/

This site, maintained by George Gale ggale@cctr.umkc.edu and Elam O'Renick eorenick@umkc.edu, provides links to the Association's mailing list, journal, and newsletter.

Philosophy of Science Society: Japan

http://cogsci.l.chiba-u.ac.jp/PSSJ/pssj.html

This site provides access to the Society's mailing list and journal (in Japanese), as well as links to philosophy of science resources.

Philosophy Society

http://www.gla.ac.uk/Clubs/Philosophy/

This is the home page for the University of Glasgow's student philosophy society, providing information on the aims and activities of the Society, plus links to philosophy-related sites.

Plato's Cave

http://www.philosophy.ilstu.edu/philosophy/phiclub.htm

Plato's Cave is the student philosophy association at Illinios State University.

Radical Philosophy Association

http://www.phil.indiana.edu/~jmusselm/RPA.html

The RPA is an international, non-sectarian forum for philosophical discussion of fundamental change. This site, maintained by Jack Green Musselman jmusselm@phil.indiana.edu, provides information on the goals and activities of the Association.

Scottish Postgraduate Philosophy Association

http://www.st-and.ac.uk/~www_sppa/index.html

This site provides information on the activities of the SPPA, a Scottish graduate student organization. The Association can be contacted at sppa@st-and.ac.uk.

Society for Ancient Greek Philosophy

http://philosophy.adm.binghamton.edu/ssips/sagpnews.html

The SAGP web page provides information on the aims and activities of the Society, and is maintained by Tony Preus apreus@bingvmb.cc.binghamton.edu.

Society for Bioethics & Classical Philosophy

http://www.pitt.edu/~caj3/sbcp/

The Society is interested in facilitating and promoting the study of bioethics informed by classical philosophy, and the cross-fertilisation of ideas that results from the interchange of these two areas. This site provides information on the aims and activities of the Society, and is maintained by Mark Kuczewski mak7+@pitt.edu.

Society of Christian Philosophers

http://www.siu.edu/departments/cola/philos/SCP

This page, maintained by K. Clark kclark@calvin.edu, provides information, announcements, newsletters, and a mailing list relating to the Society, as well as links to related resources.

Society of Christian Philosophers: Canada

http://juliet.stfx.ca/people/fac/wsweet/scp.html

This site provides information on the aims and activities of the Society and is maintained by its Secretary, Will Sweet wsweet@juliet.stfx.ca.

Society for Ethics

http://www-rohan.sdsu.edu/faculty/corlett/se.html

Established in 1995, The Society for Ethics (SE) serves the purpose of promoting philosophical research in ethics, broadly construed, including areas such as (but not limited to) ethical theory, moral, social and political philosophy, as well as areas of applied ethics such as (but not limited to) legal, business, and medical ethics. The Society's page is maintained by J. Angelo Corlett corlett@rohan.sdsu.edu.

Society for Exact Philosophy

http://www.clas.ufl.edu/CLAS/Departments/Philosophy/SEP/index.html

The SEP provides an avenue for sustained discussion among researchers who believe that rigorous methods have a place in philosophical investigations. This website, maintained by Greg Ray gray@phil.ufl.edu, provides information on the activities of the Society.

Society of Humanist Philosophers

http://www.SecularHumanism.org/philosophers.html

This site, maintained by David Noelle admin@SecularHumanism.org, provides information on the aims and activities of the Society.

Society for Judgment and Decision-Making

http://www.sjdm.org/

The Society for Judgment and Decision Making is an interdisciplinary organisation dedicated to the study of normative, descriptive, and prescriptive theories of decision. The website provides information on the aims and activities of the Society, and links to relevant online information.

Society for Philosophy and Geography

http://www.cep.unt.edu/geosoc.html

SPG was formed as a new professional organization dedicated to bringing together in a more systematic fashion discussions between philosophers and geographers. This was in acknowledgement of the increase in the interests of philosophers and geographers in each others' work. In its first year, the Society grew to almost two hundred members in North America and Europe, drawing interest from scholars in sociology, anthropology, political science, public policy, urban and regional planning, architecture, English and comparative literature, and other disciplines in addition to the two core groups. This page provides information on the activities of the Society and is maintained by Johnathan M. Smith J0S7507@ tamvm1.tamu.edu. A mirror of this site can be found at: *http://www.umt.edu/phil/GeoSoc.html*.

Society for Philosophy and Psychology

http://www.hfac.uh.edu/cogsci/spp/spphp.html

Information on the Society's history, membership, meetings, and constitution can be found on this page. Enquiries about the Society should be directed to John Bickle pybickle@ecuvm.cis.ecu.edu.

Society for Philosophy in the Contemporary World

http://www.phil.stmarytx.edu/SPCWhm/

This page provides information on the aims and activities of the Society, and is maintained by James Sauer philjim@stmarytx.edu.

Society for the Study of Islamic Philosophy and Science

http://philosophy.adm.binghamton.edu/ssips/

This site provides information on the aims and activities of the Society, and is maintained by Tony Preus apreus@bingvmb.cc.binghamton.edu.

The Society for Women in Philosophy (SWIP)

http://www.uh.edu/~cfreelan/SWIP/

The Society for Women in Philosophy aims to promote and support women in philosophy. SWIP holds divisional meetings, meetings in conjunction with the meetings of the American Philosophical Association, and it publishes newsletters. This site provides information on the activities of the Society, as well as links to feminist and philosophy resources.

South African Society for Greek Philosophy and the Humanities

http://www.up.ac.za/academic/libarts/philosophy/phil6.html

This website provides general information about the aims and activities of the Society and is maintained by Prof. J. D. Gericke gericke@libarts.up.ac.za.

Southern Society for Philosophy & Psychology

http://funnelweb.utcc.utk.edu/~sspp/

Maintained by L. B. Cebik cebik@utk.edu, this page provides information on the aims and activities of the Society.

Spoon Collective

http://jefferson.village.virginia.edu/~spoons/

The Spoon Collective Spoons@jefferson.village.virginia.edu is a group of net citizens devoted to free and open discussion of philosophical issues. This well-designed website provides access to Spoon Collective mailing lists and archives. It is maintained by Daniel Kern dank@mail.utexas.edu.

Stanford Humanists

http://www-leland.stanford.edu/group/Humanists/

This page, maintained by Carolyn Fairman cfairman@leland.stanford.edu, provides information on the aims and activities of Stanford Humanists, as well as links to humanist resources.

Student Philosophy Association

http://www.uq.edu.au/~pdvparki/

This website for the Student Philosophy Association at the University of Queensland, provides information on the activities of the Association.

Swedish Humanist Foundation

http://www.unicom.se/humanetik.html

This page provides information on the Swedish Humanist Foundation—in Swedish only.

Swiss Society for Logic & Philosophy of Sciences

http://www-ssp.unil.ch/Soc_suisse_de_logique/indexe.html

The Swiss Society promotes the study of logic and philosophy of sciences. To that end, it organises an annual conference, occasional lectures, and an international exchange program. Access to information about the activities of the Society and its newsletter, are available on this site.

Sydney Society of Literature and Aesthetics

http://centrum.arts.su.edu.au/Arts/departs/philos/ssla/

This site, maintained by Paul Redding paul.redding@philosophy.su.edu.au, provides information on the activities of the Society, and links to related resources.

Taiwan Philosophy Association

http://www.sinica.edu.tw/asct/tpa/

Mostly in Chinese, this site provides information on the activities of the Taiwan Philosophy Association, and is maintained by tpawww@gate.sinica.edu.tw.

Tennessee Philosophical Association

http://www.utm.edu/research/tpa/tpa.htm

This site provides information on the aims and activities of the Association, and is maintained by Jim Fieser jfieser@utm.edu.

University of Kent Philosophy Society

http://alethea.ukc.ac.uk/SU/Societies/Philos/

This is the web site of the student philosophy society at the University of Kent.

Vancouver Island Society for Practical Philosophy

http://www.mala.bc.ca/www/ipp/vispp.htm

This page provides information on the aims and activities of the Society.

Voltaire Foundation

http://www.voltaire.ox.ac.uk/aa.index.html

This site provides links to images, texts, publications, and resources related to the work and thought of Voltaire. Enquiries about the site can be made to email@voltaire.ox.ac.uk.

World Federation of Right to Die Societies

http://www.efn.org/~ergo/world.fed.html

This site provides information on the activities of the federation and links to its member organizations. The federation can be contacted at ergo@efn.org.

World Union of Deists

http://www.deism.com/

The World Union of Deists site provides an overview of deism, some thoughts on deism vs. atheism and Christianity, and some deist essays by Thomas Paine. The site maintainers can be contacted at info@deism.com.

Organizations & Associations: Directories

Artificial Intelligence Organizations Directory

http://sigart.acm.org/societies/

This page contains a directory of AI organizations and associations around the world. It is maintained by Amruth N. Kumar amruth@ramapo.edu.

Associations and Societies

http://users.ox.ac.uk/~worc0337/phil_institutions.html#asssoc

From Peter King peter.king@philosophy.ox.ac.uk, this page presents a wide range of philosophical organizations, including student societies.

Associations and Societies: APA Listing

http://www.udel.edu/apa/resources/groups/assoc_soc.html

This is the American Philosophical Society's directory of philosophical associations and societies.

Philosophical Societies

http://www.liv.ac.uk/Philosophy/societies.html

Maintained by Stephen Clark srlclark@liverpool.ac.uk as part of his larger guide to online philosophy resources, this page provides an alphabetical listing of philosophical societies.

Philosophy Associations

http://www.rpi.edu/~cearls/pa.htm

This site provides another listing of philosophical associations, maintained by Sean Cearley.

Philosophy Associations & Societies

http://www.earlham.edu/~peters/philinks.htm#associations

An extensive list of philosophical associations and societies, updated regularly, can be found at this site. It is maintained by Peter Suber peters@earlham.edu.

Resources of Scholarly Societies: Philosophy

http://www.lib.uwaterloo.ca/society/philos_soc.html

This site provides links to a wide range of philosophy societies and organizations. It is one of a set of subject pages created by compilers at the University of Waterloo Library to facilitate access to webpages and gophers maintained by or for scholarly societies across the world.

Yahoo: Philosophy Organizations

http://www.yahoo.com/Arts/Humanities/Philosophy/Organizations/

This is the Yahoo net directory's index to philosophy organizations.

Philosophy Projects & Centers

Automated Reasoning Project, ANU

http://arp.anu.edu.au/home.html

This page provides information on research staff and students, as well as access to software developed by the project team, including: FINDER (Finite Domain Enumerator), MaGIC (Matrix Generator for Implication Connectives), Kripke (A theorem prover for the relevant logic LR). Enquiries about the site can be directed to its head, John Slaney John.Slaney @anu.edu.au.

The Bakhtin Center: University of Sheffield

http://www.shef.ac.uk/uni/academic/A-C/bakh/bakhtin.html

The Center's purpose is to promote multi-and inter-disciplinary research on the work of the Russian philosopher and theorist Mikhail Bakhtin and the Bakhtin Circle, and on related areas of cultural, critical, linguistic, and literary theory. The Center's website provides an analytical database of work by and about the Bakhtin Circle. Visitors are able to search or make contributions to the database. Information is provided on seminars, conferences, and other activities of the Center, and on Bakhtin studies elsewhere. The site is maintained by Carol Adlam c.a.adlam@shef.ac.uk.

The Bentham Project

http://www.ucl.ac.uk/Bentham-Project/index.htm

The Bentham Project aims to produce a new edition of the works of influential utilitarian thinker, Jeremy Bentham. Information about the project, and about Bentham, is available on this page, maintained by Johnathan Harris j.harris@ucl.ac.uk.

Cambridge Center for Hermeneutic and Analytic Philosophy

http://www.anglia.ac.uk/hae/phil/CHRAP.Htm

The Center is a joint activity of the Philosophy Division of Anglia Polytechnic University, and the Department of History and Philosophy of Science of Cambridge University. Its aim is to encourage contacts between the various continental traditions of philosophy and mainstream Anglo-Americal approaches. This page provides information on the activities of the Center. Further information can be obtained from Neil Gascoigne ngascoigne @bridge.anglia.ac.uk.

Center for Advanced Feminist Studies

http://rhetoric.agoff.umn.edu/~cafs//

Located at the University of Minnesota, CAFS' mission is to create and coordinate a coherent, integrated curriculum for graduate students specialising in feminist studies, and to foster intellectual community and collaborative research among feminist scholars within and outside the University of Minnesota.

Center for Advancement of Applied Ethics: Carnegie Mellon University

http://www.lcl.cmu.edu/CAAE/Home/CAAE.html

CAAE is a research and development environment that focuses on teaching people practical methods for analysing and responding to real ethical problems. The Center's members combine knowledge and experience from different areas: interactive multimedia, business and professional ethics, and conflict resolution. This site, maintained by Robert Cavalier rc2z@andrew.cmu.edu, includes links to Project Theoria, discussion on firearms policy, conflict resolution, and more.

Center for Applied Ethics: University of British Columbia

http://www.ethics.ubc.ca/

This site, maintained by Chris MacDonald chrismac@ethics.ubc.ca, provides general information on the workings of the center, plus links to a range of applied ethics resources, and information on the research projects of the center.

Center for Bioethics: University of Pennsylvania

http://www.med.upenn.edu/~bioethic/

This site, overseen by Glenn McGee mcgee@mail.med.upenn.edu, provides information on the Center, plus links to a bioethics library and other related materials.

Center for Cognitive Issues in the Arts

http://www.bris.ac.uk/Depts/Philosophy/confad.html

Located at the University of Bristol, the Center's page advises of forthcoming conferences and other events relevant to aesthetics. The site is maintained by Andrew Harrison Andrew.Harrison@bris.ac.uk.

Center for the Cognitive Science of Metaphor

http://metaphor.uoregon.edu/metaphor.html

This site, maintained by Tim Rohrer rohrer@darkwing.uoregon.edu, provides access to a range of resources including an annotated bibliography of work on metaphor, master metaphor list, and links to other metaphor resources.

Center for Computing & Social Responsibility

http://www.ccsr.cms.dmu.ac.uk/

The Center is located at De Montfort University, and undertakes research and provides teaching, consultancy, and advice to individuals, communities, organizations and governments at local, national, and international levels on the impact of computing and related technologies on society and its citizens. Information on the activities of the Center, and links to related resources can be found at this site, maintained by Steve Dixon c95sd@dmu.ac.uk.

Center for Dewey Studies

http://www.siu.edu/~deweyctr/

The Center for Dewey Studies at Southern Illinois University at Carbondale was established in 1961 as the "Dewey Project." In the course of collecting and editing Dewey's works, the Center amassed a wealth of source materials for the study of America's quintessential philosopher-educator, John Dewey. By virtue of its publications and research, the Center has become the international focal point for research on Dewey's life and work, and its location at the University makes it possible for visitors to take advantage of the resources and professional expertise of the faculty and staff of the Department of Philosophy, the College of Education, Special Collections in Morris Library, and the Southern Illinois University Press. The site is maintained by Dr. Larry Hickman lhickman@siu.edu.

Center for Environmental Philosophy

http://www.cep.unt.edu/centerfo.html

The homepage for the Center for Environmental Philosophy includes links to the Center's journal *Environmental Ethics*, information on workshops and conferences, and the operation of the Center.

Center for Meaning and Metaphysical Studies

http://www.herts.ac.uk/humanities/Res-hum-philcenter.html

The Center for Meaning and Metaphysical Studies, located at the University of Hertfordshire, promotes and encourages quality research into the philosophical study of any aspect of meaning, metaphysics or the relation (or lack thereof) between the two. Although the Center's concerns are philosophical, it encourages collaborative and interdisciplinary discussion. This site, maintained by T. Welling t.d.welling@herts.ac.uk, provides information on the activities of the Center.

Center for the Mind

http://www.anu.edu.au/mind/

The Center for the Mind is a think-tank at the Australian National University that acts as a catalyst for interdisciplinary scientific research into the mind. Its goals are to foster a culture of ideas and inquiry into the sciences of the mind and to bring hard science to bear on questions of central importance to the community as a whole. It crosses academic boundaries and considers questions about the mind not normally dealt with by the traditional disciplines. This site, maintained by Ian Gold ian.gold@mind.anu.edu.au, provides information on the activities of the Center, and on conferences, workshops, and other events relevant to this field of enquiry.

Center for Philosophical Studies: Kings College, London

http://www.kcl.ac.uk/humanities/cch/hrc/centres.htm#CPS

Operating from within the Department of Philosophy is the Center for Philosophical Studies. The purpose of the Center is to provide a platform for philosophy beyond the confines of the academic department and to present to as wide a public as possible, philosophical issues that are of public interest and concern. This site is maintained by Tony Dale a.dale@kcl.ac.uk.

Center for Philosophy of Science

http://www.pitt.edu/~pittcntr/

The Center for Philosophy of Science, located at the University of Pittsburgh, exists to promote scholarship and research, to encourage scholarly exchanges, and to foster publications in the philosophy of science as well as in philosophically informed history of science and related fields. It is dedicated to bridging the gulf between the sciences and the humanities, and to helping to develop and disseminate a philosophical understanding and appreciation of the sciences. The Center pursues its mission not only locally and regionally, but also nationally and internationally. This site, maintained by Jennifer Bushee jmbst24@pitt.edu, provides extensive information on the Center's activities.

Center for Process Studies

http://www.ctr4process.org/

Founded in 1973, the Center for Process Studies facilitates development and application of a holistic-relational worldview. Through seminars, conferences, publications, library, and membership programs, the Center encourages research on that form of process thought which received its primary impetus from philosophers Alfred North Whitehead (1861-1947) and Charles Hartshorne (b. 1897). This site provides comprehensive information on the activities of the Center, plus links to publications and a library of process-related information. Enquires about the Center can be directed to process@ctr4process.org.

Center for Research Ethics: Göteborg, Sweden

http://www.cre.gu.se/

Information on the activities of the Center, its current research projects, and links to related material can be found at this site, maintained by cmunthe@cre.gu.se.

Center for Research on Concepts and Cognition: Indiana University

http://www.cogsci.indiana.edu/

This interdisciplinary center for research in cognitive science, directed by Douglas Hofstadter, provides links to cognitive science resources, information on researchers at CRCC, access to cognitive science papers, and access to Copycat, a computer program modelling the interplay between concepts and perception in the course of analogy-making. Papers produced at the Center can accessed via its ftp archive at *ftp://ftp.cogsci.indiana. edu/pub*. The site is maintained by gem@cogsci.indiana.edu.

Center for Research in Philosophy and Literature

http://www.warwick.ac.uk/fac/soc/Philosophy/CRPL/CRPL.html

The University of Warwick's Center for Research in Philosophy and Literature exists to promote a wide variety of interdisciplinary research activity—lectures, colloquia, and major international conferences. The annual programme of events is supplemented by the contributions of distinguished Visiting Scholars, among whom have been John Sallis, Paul Ricouer, Jean-Francois Lyotard, Julia Kristeva, Gianni Vattimo, Frank Kermode, Christopher Norris, David Krell, Manfred Frank, Stanley Cavell, Geoffrey Hartman, Jaques Derrida, and Edward Saôd. This site provides information on the activities of the Center, its staff, and participating departments. The maintainer of the site can be contacted at PYRBL@ snow.csv.warwick.ac.uk.

Center for the Study of Ethics in the Professions

http://www.iit.edu/~csep/

The Center for the Study of Ethics in the Profession csep@charlie.cns.iit.edu at the Illinois Institute of Technology was established in 1976 for the purpose of promoting education and scholarship relating to the professions. The Center is currently developing a code of ethics database, accessible online. Links to the Center's newsletters and library are also available.

Center for the Study of Language and Information

http://www-csli.stanford.edu/csli/

CSLI was founded in 1983 by researchers from Stanford University, SRI International, and Xerox PARC to further research and development of integrated theories of language, information, and computation. This site, maintained by Emma Pease webmaster@ csli.stanford.edu, provides information on forthcoming events at the Center, details of its research projects and publications, and more.

Center of Technology, Philosophy, and Society

http://www.abdn.ac.uk/~phl002/cpts.htm

Located at the University of Aberdeen, this site maintained by Christian Rhein u03cr@ abdn.ac.uk, provides information on the Cenere's activities, public lectures, postgraduate study, and newsletter.

Center for Thomistic Studies

http://www.magna.com.au/~francis/cts/welcome.htm

The Center for Thomistic Studies Inc. offers year-round courses on Catholic Church teachings, based on the philosophy and theology of the "Angelic Doctor," Saint Thomas Aquinas. Details of courses can be obtained from francis@magna.com.au.

Center for Utopian Studies

http://oak.cats.ohiou.edu/~aw148888/

This is a collection of literature, artwork, and other resources which involve utopian, eutopian, and/or dystopian themes. In this virtual space, you will confront a postmodern "nowhere" ranging from bliss to dispair. Within each section, you will find pieces of commentary, criticism, and even poetry. The site is maintained by Andrew Wood wooda@ ouvaxa. cats.ohiou.edu.

Cognitive Science Initiative

http://www.hfac.uh.edu/cogsci/

This site provides information on the CGI, an interdisciplinary project at the University of Houston. The site includes links to a range of cognitive science-related information, and is maintained by Cynthia Freeland cfreeland@uh.edu.

Computational Epistemology Lab

http://cogsci.uwaterloo.ca/

Located at the Philosophy Department, University of Waterloo, this site provides information on research in the field of cognitive science, including coherence, analogy, visual mental imagery, and scientific hypothesis-generation. The site is maintained by Cameron Shelley cpshelle@watarts.uwaterloo.ca.

Computational Logic: St. Andrews

http://www-theory.dcs.st-and.ac.uk/Groups/logic.html

This research project, headed by Roy Dyckhoff rd@dcs.st-and.ac.uk, comprises the development of proof assistants and theorem-provers for various logics. The site lists recent publications of the project staff, and provides access to logic software, the Logic Work Bench Project at Bern, the AI repository as CMU, and the Computational Logic Network.

The Consciousness in the Natural World Project

http://www.stir.ac.uk/philosophy/cnw/webpage1.htm

The Consciousness in the Natural World Project is based in the Philosophy Department at the University of Stirling. It aims to bring together philosophers from the Scottish Universities and beyond to allow concerted and collective progress to be made on one of the central problems in the philosophy of mind—the problem of explaining the place of conscious psychological life within the natural world. This page is maintained by Fiona Macpherson feml@stir.ac.uk.

Consortium Ethics Program

http://www.pitt.edu/~caj3/CEP.html

The Consortium Ethics Program is co-sponsored by the University of Pittsburgh's Center for Medical Ethics and the Hospital Council of Western Pennsylvania. This site, maintained by Alan Joyce caj3+@pitt.edu, provides links to the Community Ethics Electronic Newsletter, guide to membership, and links to online ethics resources.

The Descartes Project

http://www.utoronto.ca/Dev/InsT/Descartes/home.html

This project is designed to show the use of hypertext and its application on the net, using the works of Descartes as an example of what can be achieved by mixing text and graphics and links to information branching out from a primary text. The page is designed by Brian Baigrie, André Gombay and Calvin Normore.

Ethics Center for Engineering and Science

http://web.mit.edu/ethics/www/

Located at MIT, the Center aims to provide engineers, scientists, and science and engineering students with resources useful for understanding and addressing ethically significant problems that arise in their work life. The Center is also intended to serve teachers of engineering and science students who want to include discussion of ethical problems closely related to technical subject as a part of science and engineering courses, or in free-standing subjects in professional ethics or in research ethics for such students. This site provides access to a range of resources including essays, ethical codes and guidelines, instructional resources, links to research-related materials, and much more. It is maintained by students at MIT, and is also available in a Spanish version.

Ethics & Genetics: A Global Conversation

http://www.med.upenn.edu/~bioethic/genetics.html

What do you think about genetic testing, genetic enhancement, gene therapy, genetic engineering? This "electric conversation" lets you post your comments instantly and engage in live conversation with any of the hundreds who visit the site every week. Ten researchers in the field serve as discussants, posting remarks, papers, and comments upon which visitors can comment. The site is maintained by Glenn McGee mcgee@mail. med.upenn.edu.

Ferrater Mora Chair of Contemporary Thought

http://www.udg.edu/cfm/

The Ferrater Mora Chair of Contemporary Thought was founded in 1989. It organises two sessions of lessons each year (November and June) on contemporary thought conducted by eminent thinkers of international renown. The Chair, whilst devoted to thought, is not however strictly confined to the discipline of Philosophy, welcoming as it does the contribution of interdisciplinary seminars from across the board of Sciences and the Arts. The Chair's Guest Lecturers expose the main lines and questions to which they have devoted their intellectual life. In addition, the Chair publishes these lectures, and organises symposia. It also plans to implement interdisciplinary-meetings in order to bring together researchers, thinkers, technicians, artists, business people, and social workers, around issues and subjects of common interest. Enquiries can be made to its Director, Josep-Maria Terricabras terricabras@skywalker.udg.es.

Institute for Business and Professional Ethics

http://condor.depaul.edu/ethics/

The Institute for Business and Professional Ethics was established in 1985 by a joint effort of the Colleges of Liberal Arts and Sciences and Commerce at DePaul University. The Institute is one of the first ethics-related resources to pioneer a hypertext linked ethics network throughout the Internet. The Mission of the Institute is to foster ethical behavior. The main focus of the Institute is on teaching and training individuals to think before they act. Its aim is not to design or impose rules, regulations and controls. Instead, it concentrates on stirring an individual's conscience by stimulating moral imagination; by encouraging ongoing ethical debate; and by insisting upon individual responsibility. This site provides information about the activities and programs of the Institute, as well as links to a range of ethics-related resources. The site is maintained by S. Walton swalton@wppost.depaul.edu.

Institute for Logic, Language, and Computation

http://www.fwi.uva.nl/research/illc/

The Institute illc@fwi.uva.nl is located at the University of Amsterdam and its web page provides information on courses and syllabi, research conducted at the Institute, newsletters and publications, and information on forthcoming events relevant to the work of the Institute.

Institute for Research on Women and Gender

http://www-leland.stanford.edu/group/IRWG/

The Institute is located at Stanford University. Its primary mission is to support research on women and gender and to organise programs that will make such work accessible to a broader public. By providing thoughtful and in-depth analyses, these programs have contributed to policy making on issues with enormous importance for women and their families. This site provides information on the activities of the institute and its programs and publications. It also provides links to related resources.

Institute for the Study of Applied and Professional Ethics

http://www.dartmouth.edu/artsci/ethics-inst/

This site, maintained by Barbara J. Hillinger ethics.institute@dartmouth.edu, provides information on the activities of the Institute at Dartmouth College.

Institute of St. Thomas: Center of High Medieval and Thomistic Research and Studies

http://www.informedia.it/dipiu/st/ist_sth.htm

The Institute of St. Thomas in Rome advances itself as an international meeting place for all researchers in the field of Scholastic Philosophy and Theology with special reference to the figure of St. Thomas Aquinas. The activities of the Institute consist of a two year specialisation course in Thomistic Studies, conferences, publications, and an International Group of Research, whose Consultants are world recognised authorities in the fields of Medieval Studies, Philosophy, and Theology.

International Centre for Interdisciplinary Psychiatric Research

http://www.cybernet.dk/users/arcirip/

This site provides information on the activities of the Centre, located in Denmark. Besides psychiatry and medicine, researchers at the Centre are concerned with philosophical subjects such as mind-brain and mind-matter problems (related to psychopharmacology), materialism versus idealism, evolutionary epistemology, information theory, second-order cybernetics, spirituality, science, and systems theory. The site is maintained by Axel Randrup arcirip@web4you.dk.

Japan Internet Center for Process Studies

http://www.asahi-net.or.jp/~sn2y-tnk/

This site provides access to the Whitehead Database which consists of a collection of papers by JICPS members and the "Process and Reality" selected bibliography. The page is also accessible in Japanese, and is maintained by Yutaka Tanaka sn2y-tnk@asahi-net.or.jp.

Laboratory for Applied Logic

http://lal.cs.byu.edu/

The Laboratory for Applied Logic is a research unit of the Department of Computer Science at Brigham Young University. The laboratory specialises in applying mathematical methods to problems in computer dependability. This page includes section on formal methods, research projects (modeling abstract hardware components, verified computer systems, and WWW technologies), papers, and technical reports. The site is maintained by Paul Black black@cs.byu.edu.

Lawrence Berkeley National Laboratory's ELSI Project

http://www.lbl.gov/Education/ELSI/ELSI.html

Lawrence Berkeley National Laboratory's Ethical, Legal, and Social Issues in Science program is a pilot project designed to stimulate discussions on the implications of selected areas of scientific research. Aimed at high school students, the project makes materials available to assist educators in designing programs for students to explore social, legal, and ethical issues in science.

Los Angeles Lonergan Center

http://www.concentric.net/~Mmorelli/

The Los Angeles Lonergan Center makes available in a single location a range of research materials for use by visiting scholars. Its web page, maintained by Mark Morelli MMorelli@lmumail.lmu.edu, provides access to numerous Lonergan resources, including: Primary Sources—the Center's collection of published philosophical and theological works, Latin works and English translations, economics manuscripts, course outlines, course transcriptions, transcriptions of lectures, tape recordings, and much more; Secondary Materials—lists the Center's holdings including journals, theses and dissertations, books, and other reference materials; a link to the Lonergan Philosophical Society, and Method: Journal of Lonergan Studies. An excellent site of great value to Lonergan scholars.

Maclean Center for Clinical Medical Ethics

http://ccme-mac4.bsd.uchicago.edu/CCMEHomePage.html

The MacLean Center for Clinical Medical Ethics at the University of Chicago consists of an interdisciplinary group of professionals who study and teach about practical ethical concerns confronting patients and health professionals. The Center's core faculty of physicians, nurses, legal scholars, philosophers, and social scientists direct medical ethics education at the University of Chicago, and provide ethics consultation to the University of Chicago Hospitals, area hospitals, and the media. This site provides information on the activities of the Center, as well as links to a vast range of online bioethics-related resources. The site is maintained by kerielam@midway.uchicago.edu.

The Marxism Leninism Project

http://www.idbsu.edu/surveyrc/Staff/jaynes/marxism/marxism.htm

This website is maintained by Jonathan D. Jaynes jonathan@netmachine.com and represents a project to set out the theories of Marxism in the most authoritative form possible—in the words of the founders of Marxism and of the greatest of their followers.

Medieval Studies Institute: University of Fribourg, Switzerland

http://www.unifr.ch/iem/welcome.html

The Medieval Studies Institute of the University of Fribourg is part of the Arts Faculty. It endeavours to promote and coordinate research and teaching in all fields related to the study of medieval civilization. This site provides information on the research projects currently undertaken at the Institute, as well as providing links to other medieval resources. The page is available in French and German language versions, and is maintained by Alain Nadeau alain.nadeau@unifr.ch.

Metaphysics Research Lab at CSLI

http://mally.stanford.edu/

The Metaphysics Research Lab is located in the Center for the Study of language and Information at Stanford University. The Web server provides information about the research conducted in the lab, and in particular, about the axiomatic theory of abstract objects being developed there. The site is maintained by Edward N. Zalta zalta@mally.stanford.edu.

Minnesota Center for Philosophy of Science

http://www.umn.edu/mcps/center/mcps.html

The University of Minnesota houses the Minnesota Center for Philosophy of Science (MCPS)—the oldest center for philosophy of science in the world. Founded by Herbert Feigl in 1953, the Center is a research unit whose members include faculty from a variety of units on the Twin Cities campus. It is the source of the series, *Minnesota Studies in the Philosophy of Science*, published by the University of Minnesota Press. Overall, the Minnesota Center for Philosophy of Science represents one the world's largest concentrations of resources for the study of philosophy of science. This site, maintained by Steve Lelchuk mcps@maroon.tc. umn.edu, provides information on the activities of the Center and links to resources in philosophy of science.

OSCAR Project: John L. Pollock

http://www.u.arizona.edu/~pollock/

John Pollock mcps@maroon.tc.umn.edu directs the OSCAR Project, funded in part by the National Science Foundation. The goal of the OSCAR Project is the formulation of a general theory of rationality and its implementation in an artificial rational agent. The project is predicated on the view that philosophy has an essential role to play in artificial intelligence. The site details the areas of interest covered by the project and provides online access to its research papers.

The Pascal Center

http://www.redeemer.on.ca/pascal/

This is the home site for the Pascal Center for Advanced Studies in Faith and Science. The Center promotes constructive relations between Christian faith and the natural sciences by means of education, outreach and research in the light of Scripture. This site provides information on the aims and activities of the Center, which can be contacted at pascalcenter@ redeemer.on.ca.

The Philosophical Institute

http://www.machtec.com/philoinst/

The Philosophical Institute provides online teaching of a range of philosophy courses. The Philsophical Institute is not a University. The students must register and gain credit for the courses through their own university or college. The site is maintained by Karen Olesch-Williams g13693@email.mot.com.

Philosophy Documentation Center

http://www.bgsu.edu/pdc

The PDC is a non-profit organization with a reputation for excellence in the production and distribution of specialized products for philosophers, including directories, bibliographies, scholarly journals, and instructional software. This site provides access to information about the Center's products and services, a link to *Books in Philosophy* (the Center's online bookstore), and a link to *POIESIS: Philosophy Online Serials* (an electronic journals project under construction with InteLex Corporation).

Philosophy Neuroscience Psychology Program

http://www.artsci.wustl.edu/~philos/pnp/

This site provides information about the PNP Program at Washington University in St. Louis. The site also provides links to relevant Internet resources, and to an archive of papers and technical reports produced by participants in the program.

POIESIS: Philosophy Online Serials

http://www.nlx.com/posp/

This project, a joint venture of the Philosophy Documentation Center and InteLex Corporation, offers searchable online access to a single database containing the full-text of current, recent, and back issues of a growing number of philosophy journals. For more information contact *poiesis@mailserver.bgsu.edu.*

Political Participation Project: MIT

http://www.ai.mit.edu/people/msb/ppp/home.html

The Political Participation Project is a research effort at the MIT Artificial Intelligence Lab exploring how interactive media can be used to facilitate political participation. The PPP directs an electronic mailing list for those interested in exploring the role of interactive media as a catalyst for political participation. The Project is a research element in the doctoral thesis of Mark S. Bonchek bonchek@ai.mit.edu, some of which is accessible online.

The Poynter Center

http://www.indiana.edu/~poynter/index.html

The Poynter Center for the Study of Ethics and American Institutions is an endowed center at Indiana University, charged with fostering the examination and discussion of ethical issues in American society. This site, maintained by Kenneth D. Pimple pimple@indiana.edu, provides information on the activities of the Center.

Principia Cybernetica Project (PCP)

http://pespmc1.vub.ac.be

The project's aim is the computer-supported collaborative development of an evolutionary-systemic philosophy. PCP tries to tackle age-old philosophical questions with the help of the most recent cybernetic theories and technologies. The site was authored by F. Heylighen fheyligh@vnet3.vub.ac.be, C. Joslyn joslyn@lanl.gov, and V. Turchin turcc@cunyvm.cuny.edu.

The Bertrand Russell Editorial Project

http://www.humanities.mcmaster.ca/~russell/brhome.htm

The focal point of the offices for the Bertrand Russell Editorial Project is a set of blue, hard-bound volumes lined up atop a cabinet in the middle of the room on the seventh floor of Togo Salmon Hall on McMaster's campus. These 14 volumes, one more that is at press and five others at various stages of completion, reflect many years of researchers' time and sweat, about $3 million worth of research funds—and over one-half of the planned set of volumes that will eventually make up The Collected Papers of Bertrand Russell. This site provides information on the project, and is maintained by Arlene Duncan <u>duncana@ mcmaster.ca</u>.

Thomas Instituut te Utrecht

http://www.ktu.ruu.nl/thomas/

This site provides information about the research programs and projects conducted within the Institute, as well as providing access to discussion forums, translations of Aquinas' work, links to Aquinas-related sites, plus news and other information about the activities of the Institute.

University of Chicago Philosophy Project

http://csmaclab-www.uchicago.edu/philosophyProject/philos.html

This project seeks to provide a forum for electronically mediated scholarly discussion of philosophical works. The discussions accessible from this site include: critical discussion of Nelson Goodman's theory of metaphor, discussion of theories of pictorial representation, discussion of the Language of Thought Hypothesis, a reading group on Kripke's Naming and Necessity, and a discussion of counterfactuals. The site is maintained by Jonathan Cohen <u>joncohen@ruccs.rutgers.edu</u>.

Philosophy Departments: Africa

Rand Afrikaans University

http://www.rau.ac.za/faculties/arts/philosophy/

Rhodes University

http://www.ru.ac.za/academic/departments/philosophy/

University of Cape Town

http://www.uct.ac.za/depts/philosophy/

University of Durban-Westville

http://pixie.udw.ac.za/UDW/homepages/phil.html

University of Natal, Durban

http://www.und.ac.za/und/phil/und-phil.htm

University of Orange Free State

http://www.uovs.ac.za/arts/phil/plain.htm

University of Pretoria

http://www.up.ac.za/academic/libarts/philosophy/home.html

University of Stellenbosch

http://www.sun.ac.za/local/academic/arts/philosophy/index.html

University of the Western Cape

http://WWW.UWC.AC.ZA/a_phil/

University of Witwatersrand, Johannesburg

http://www.wits.ac.za/wits/fac/arts/philosophy/philintro.htm

Philosophy Departments: Asia

China

Nanjing University

http://www.nju.edu.cn/njue/yx/yx13.htm

Peking University

http://www.pku.edu.cn/docs/depsy.html#Dept. of Philosophy

Tsinghua University

http://www.tsinghua.edu.cn/docse/yxsz/thdps.html

University of Hong Kong

http://www.hku.hk/philodep/

Zhejiang University

http://www.ent.ohiou.edu/~guting/zuphil.html

Japan

Akita University

http://www.akita-u.ac.jp/~tachiba/index.html

Hiroshima University

http://www.ipc.hiroshima-u.ac.jp/~logos/home1e.html

Hiroshima University: Ethics Department

http://www.ipc.hiroshima-u.ac.jp/~ethica/indexe.html

Hokkaido University

http://www.hps.hokudai.ac.jp

Kansai University

http://www.kansai-u.ac.jp/Guide/htm/fc_let.htm#Department of Philosophy

Keio University

http://phil.flet.mita.keio.ac.jp/person/pub/index.html

Kyoto Univesity

> *http://www.bun.kyoto-u.ac.jp/~phisci/*

Kyushu University

> *http://www.lit.kyushu-u.ac.jp/index_e.htm*

Tohoku University

> *http://www.sal.tohoku.ac.jp/phil/index.html*

Korea

Chung Ang University

> *http://blue.nowcom.co.kr/~hans77/*

Kangnung National University

> *http://www.kangnung.ac.kr/college/humanities/phi/dep_phi.html*

Seoul National University

> *http://phil.snu.ac.kr/*

Middle East

Yerevan State University, Armenia

> *http://www.aua.am/ysu/html/fac/soci.htm*

American University in Cairo, Egypt

> *http://auc-acs.eun.eg/www/f_philosophy.html*

Tel Aviv University, Israel

> *http://spinoza.tau.ac.il/hci/dep/philos/index.htm*

University of Haifa, Israel

> *http://research.haifa.ac.il/~philo/index.htm*

Kuwait University, Kuwait

> *http://www.kuniv.edu.kw/arts_philosophy.html*

Bogazici University, Turkey

> *http://www.boun.edu.tr/academics/faculties/arts_sci/phil.html*

Rest of Asia

Universiti Brunei Darussalam, Brunei

> *http://202.160.0.89/hmcritth.htm*

University of Pune, India

http://www.unipune.ernet.in/dept/cass/san home.htm

Indian Institute of Technology, Kanpur, India

http://www.iitk.ernet.in/hs.html

Ateneo de Manila University, Philippines

http://www.admu.edu.ph/Arts&Sciences/Philosophy/default.htm

De La Salle University, Philippines

http://www.dlsu.edu.ph/colleges/cla/dept/philo.htm

National University of Singapore, Singapore

http://www.nus.sg/NUSinfo/FASS/webarts/phi/homepage.htm

National Chung Cheng University, Taiwan

http://www.ccunix.ccu.edu.tw/~deptphi/

Assumption University, Thailand

http://www.au.ac.th/Newabac/studies/psrs.html

Philosophy Departments: Australia

Australia

Australian National University

http://www.anu.edu.au/philosophy/

Australian National University, (RSSS)

http://coombs.anu.edu.au/Depts/RSSS/Philosophy/PhilosophyHome.html

Charles Sturt University

http://www.csu.edu.au/faculty/arts/humss/philos.htm

Deakin University

http://www2.deakin.edu.au/handbooks/Arts/Artsmajorsug1.htm#PhilosStudies

Flinders University

http://wwwsol.hum.flinders.edu.au/philosophy.html

Latrobe University

http://www.latrobe.edu.au/www/philosophy/

Macquarie University

http://www.mq.edu.au/~phildept/

Monash University

> *http://www.arts.monash.edu.au/phil/*

Murdoch University

> *http://wwwhum.murdoch.edu.au/humanities/progs/phil/philbk.html*

Queensland University of Technology

> *http://www.qut.edu.au/arts/human/ethics/centrehm.htm*

Swinburne University of Technology

> *http://www.swin.edu.au/ssb/pci/pcihome.html*

University of Adelaide

> *http://chomsky.arts.adelaide.edu.au/Philosophy/philhome*

University of Ballarat

> *http://www.ballarat.edu.au/bssh/philo.htm*

University of Melbourne

> *http://www.arts.unimelb.edu.au/Dept/Philosophy/welcome.html*

University of Melbourne: History & Philosophy of Science

> *http://www.arts.unimelb.edu.au/Dept/HPS/*

University of Newcastle

> *http://www.newcastle.edu.au/department/pl/*

University of New England

> *http://www.une.edu.au/~arts/Philosop/philosop.htm*

University of New South Wales

> *http://www.arts.unsw.edu.au/philosophy/index.htm*

University of Queensland

> *http://www.uq.oz.au/philosophy/home.html*

University of Sydney

> *http://www.arts.su.edu.au/Arts/departs/philos/philosophy.home.html*

University of Tasmania

> *http://www.utas.edu.au/docs/humsoc/philosophy/index.html*

University of Western Australia

> *http://www.arts.uwa.edu.au/PhilosWWW/philosophy.html*

University of Wollongong

> *http://www.uow.edu.au/arts/philosophy/*

New Zealand

Lincoln University, Canterbury

> *http://www.lincoln.ac.nz/hals/philhome.htm*

Victoria University of Wellington

> *http://www.vuw.ac.nz/phil/*

University of Auckland

> *http://www.auckland.ac.nz/phi/index.html*

University of Canterbury, Christchurch

> *http://www.phil.canterbury.ac.nz/*

University of Otago, Dunedin

> *http://www.otago.ac.nz/Philosophy/philhome.html*

University of Waikato, Hamilton

> *http://www2.waikato.ac.nz/socsci/philosophy/index.html*

Philosophy Departments: Europe

Austria

University of Graz

> *http://gewi.kfunigraz.ac.at/institute/philosophie/institut.html*

University of Klagenfurt

> *http://www.uni-klu.ac.at/groups/ipg/*

University of Linz

> *http://sowi.iwp.uni-linz.ac.at/iwp/home.html*

University of Salzburg

> *http://www.sbg.ac.at/phs/home.htm*

University of Vienna

> *http://homehobel.phl.univie.ac.at/default.htm*

Belgium

Catholic University of Louvain

> *http://www.isp.ucl.ac.be/*

Université Libre de Bruxelles

    http://www.ulb.ac.be/ulb/fac_inst_ec/philo.html

University of Liege

    http://www.ulg.ac.be/facphl/

University of Louvain

    http://www.kuleuven.ac.be/facdep/hiw/homeeng.htm

France

Université de Bordeaux (Michel de Montaigne)

    http://sunserv0.montaigne.u-bordeaux.fr/UFR/phi.html

Université de Bretagne Occidentale

    http://www.univ-brest.fr/UFR/LETTRE-SOCIAL/iaLettres.html#anchor1662984

Université de Lille (Chaarles De Gaulle)

    http://13av01.univ-lille3.fr/www/UFR_Philosophie.HTML

Université de Marne la Vallée

    http://www.univ-mlv.fr/formations/2cycle/maitrise_philo.htm

Université de Montpellier (Paul Valéry)

    http://www.univ-montp2.fr/newufr.html#UFR 1

Université de Nice Sophia-Antipolis

    http://mili.unice.fr/DOCTORAL/dea/philo/acceuil.htm

Université de Paris (Panthéon-Sorbonne)

    http://panoramix.univ-paris1.fr/UFR10/

Universitè de Paris (Vincennes-StDenis)

    http://www.univ-paris8.fr/up8/ufr.AARTS.shtml

Université Pierre Mendès

    http://melpomene.upmf-grenoble.fr/upmf/RECHERCHE/philolang/

L'Université de Pau et des Pays de l'Andour

    http://www.univ-pau.fr/ser/UFR_LE/sec_philosophie.html

Université de Picardie (Jules Verne)

    http://www.u-picardie.fr/UPIC/UPJV/Amiens/Facs/philo.html

Université des Sciences Humaines de Strasbourg

    http://ushs.u-strasbg.fr/plis_s.htm

Université de Toulouse, Le Mirail

> *http://www.univ-tlse2.fr/univ-UFR.html#e-philo*

Germany

Bildungswissenschaftliche Hochschule, Flensburg

> *http://www.uni-flensburg.de/institut/philosophie/phil.htm*

Bremen University

> *http://www1.uni-bremen.de/~phil/*

Carl von Ossietzky Universität Oldenburg

> *http://www.uni-oldenburg.de/~philo/*

Christian Albrechts University, Kiel

> *http://ikarus.pclab-phil.uni-kiel.de*

Ernst-Moritz-Arndt-Universität Greifswald (Philosophische Fakultät)

> *http://www.uni-greifswald.de/fakul/phil.html*

Fern University, Hagen

> *http://www.fernuni-hagen.de/PHILOSOPHIE/welcome.html*

Heinrich-Heine University of Dusseldorf

> *http://www.phil-fak.uni-duesseldorf.de/philo/*

Hochschule Für Philosophie, München

> *http://www.hfph.mwn.de/index.html*

Humboldt University, Berlin

> *http://www2.rz.hu-berlin.de/inside/phil/*

Ludwig-Maximilians-Universität, München

> *http://www.stat.uni-muenchen.de/f10.html*

Johann Wolfgang Goethe University, Frankfurt

> *http://www.rz.uni-frankfurt.de/presse/brosch/fb07.htm*

Martin Luther University, Halle-Wittenberg

> *http://www.phil.uni-halle.de/frames/start/willkommen.asp*

Otto von Guericke University, Magdeburg

> *http://www.uni-magdeburg.de/~iphi/iphi.html*

Ruhr-Universitaet Bochum

> *http://www.ruhr-uni-bochum.de/philosophy/*

Technical University of Berlin

>   *http://www.kgw.tu-berlin.de/*

Technical University of Darmstadt

>   *http://www.ifs.th-darmstadt.de/philosophie.html*

Technical University of Dresden

>   *http://www.tu-dresden.de/phf/philfak.htm*

Technische Universität Chemnitz

>   *http://www.tu-chemnitz.de/~graupe/FakPhil.html*

Technischen Universitaet, Braunschweig

>   *http://www.tu-bs.de/institute/sem-philos/*

Universitaet Erlangen, Nürnberg

>   *http://www.phil.uni-erlangen.de/~p1phil/lstii.html*

University of Augsberg

>   *http://www.Phil.Uni-Augsberg.DE/phil1/faecher/philos.htm*

University of Bamburg (1)

>   *http://www.uni-bamberg.de/~ba2pl1/home.html*

University of Bamburg (2)

>   *http://www.uni-bamberg.de/~ba2ph2/home.html*

University of Bayreuth

>   *http://www.uni-bayreuth.de/departments/philosophie/INHALT.HTM*

University of Bielefeld

>   *http://www.philosophie.uni-bielefeld.de/main.htm*

University of Bonn

>   *http://ibm.rhrz.uni-bonn.de:80/philosop/*

University of Dortmund

>   *http://www.fb14.uni-dortmund.de/~philosophie/*

University of Erlangen

>   *http://www.phil.uni-erlangen.de/~p1phil/home.html*

University of Essen

>   *http://www.uni-essen.de/fbze.html#Fachbereiche*

University of Freiburg

>   *http://www.uni-freiburg.de/univ/3w/fakults/phil/philo1.htm*

University of Gesamthochschule, Siegen

http://www.fb1.uni-siegen.de/

Universität Greifswald (Institut Für Philosophie)

http://www.uni-greifswald.de/~philoso/index.htm

University of Hamburg

http://www.sozialwiss.uni-hamburg.de/phil/philmain.html

University of Hannover

http://sun1.rrzn.uni-hannover.de/nhridicd/fb/phi/philhome.htm

University of Heidelberg

http://www.urz.uni-heidelberg.de/institute/d/14/

University of Jena

http://www.uni-jena.de/fsu/phil.html

University of Kaiserslautern

http://www.uni-kl.de/FB-SoWi/FG-Philosophie/

University of Karlsruhe

http://www.uni-karlsruhe.de/~philosophie/

University of Kassel

http://www.uni-kassel.de/fb1/Philo.html

University of Koblenz

http://www.uni-koblenz.de/veranstaltungen/fb1ss98.html#philo

University of Koeln

http://www.uni-koeln.de/phil-fak/phil/index.html

University of Konstanz

http://www.uni-konstanz.de/FuF/Philo/Philosophie/

University of Leipzig

http://www.uni-leipzig.de/~philos/

University of Mainz

http://www.Uni-Mainz.DE/UniInfo/Fachbereiche/philosophie_paedagogik.html

University of Mannheim

http://www.uni-mannheim.de/fakul/phil/phil.html

University of Paderborn

http://www.uni-paderborn.de/extern/fb/1/index.html

University of Passau

http://www.phil.uni-passau.de/philosophie/

University of Potsdam

http://www.uni-potsdam.de/u/philosophie/index.htm

University of Regensburg

http://www.uni-regensburg.de/Fakultaeten/phil_Fak_I/Philosophie/

University of Rostock

http://www.uni-rostock.de/fakult/philfak/fakt.htm

University of Saarlandes

http://www.uni-sb.de/philfak/

University of Stuttgart

http://www.uni-stuttgart.de/Cis/Fakultaeten/Philosophie/fak.html

University of Tübingen

http://www.uni-tuebingen.de/uni/f07/

University of Wuerzburg

http://www.uni-wuerzburg.de/personal/phi3ins.html#2

Westfälische Wilhelms-Universität, Münster

http://www.uni-muenster.de/GeschichtePhilosophie/Welcome-d.html

Ireland

All Hallows College, Dublin

http://homepages.iol.ie/~ahallows/co1.htm

St. Patrick's College, Maynooth

http://www.may.ie/pontifical/philosophy.html

University College, Cork

http://www.ucc.ie/ucc/depts/phil/

University College, Dublin

http://www.ucd.ie/~philosop/index.html

Italy

CIRFID, Bologna

http://www.unibo.it/STSE/orgamm/ammi/annu/files/c2p5sp3.htm

University of Bologna

> *http://sofia.philo.unibo.it/*

University of Chieti

> *http://www.unich.it/filosofia/*

University of Firenze

> *http://www.unifi.it/universita/dipartimenti/umanisti/i_filoso.htm*

University of Genova

> *http://www.lettere.unige.it/sif/strutture/9/index.htm*

University of Gregoriana

> *http://www.unigre.urbe.it/tizuni/filosofia.html*

University of Lecce

> *http://silos.unile.it/struttuni_f/dipist_F/Filosofia.html*

University of Messina

> *http://www.unime.it/facolta/lettere/filosofi/filosofi.htm*

University of Milan

> *gopher://gopher.csi.unimi.it/00/ateneo-info/guida*

University of Naples

> *http://www.unina.it/difil/index.html*

University of Padua

> *http://www.maldura.unipd.it/~filos/philos.htm*

University of Parma

> *http://www.unipr.it/Dipartimenti/Filos/*

University of Pavia

> *http://www.unipv.it/annuario-91-92/filoso/FilosoIndex.html*

University of Pisa

> *http://www.cisiau.unipi.it/filosofia/*

University of Rome - 'Tor Vergata'

> *http://www.utovrm.it/dipartim/linlettc/linlettc.htm*

University of Rome 3

> *http://www.uniroma3.it/letterefilosofia.html*

University of Siena

> *http://www.unisi.it/ateneo/facolta/lettere/fac_lettere.html*

University of Venice - 'Ca' Foscari'

http://www.unive.it/unive/guida/Dipartimenti/FI.html

University of Verona

http://www.univr.it/lettere/filosofi.htm

Netherlands

Dutch Graduate School in Logic

http://www.cs.rug.nl/OZSL/

Erasmus University, Rotterdam

http://www.eur.nl/fw/

Netherlands School for Research in Practical Philosophy

http://www.xs4all.nl/~ozse/

Rijksuniversiteit Groningen

http://www.philos.rug.nl:80/

University of Leiden

http://www.leidenuniv.nl/wijs/

University of Tilberg

http://cwis.kub.nl/~fsw_2/fww/index.htm

Utrecht University

http://www.phil.ruu.nl/

Russia

Moscow State University

http://log.philos.msu.su/MSUFPserv/main_eng.html

Novgorod State University

http://www.novsu.ac.ru/novsu/fac_09.html

Novosibirsk State University

http://iceman.cnit.nsk.su/cgi-bin/engnsu?302+7

Russian Academy of Sciences

http://www.ras.ru/RAS/ofcpp.html

Scandinavia

Odense University, Denmark

http://www.ou.dk/hum/da/ansatte/FI_personal.html

University of Aalborg, Denmark

http://www.hum.auc.dk/cfv/cfvindex.htm

University of Åarhus, Denmark

http://www.aau.dk/uk/hum/filosofi/index.html

University of Copenhagen, Denmark

http://www.ihi.ku.dk/fpr/philosophy/deptphi.html

Åbo Akademi University, Finland

http://www.abo.fi/fak/hf/filosofi/

University of Helsinki, Finland

http://www.helsinki.fi/valttdk/kfil/

University of Jyväskylä, Finland

http://www.jyu.fi/~yhtfil/

University of Tampere, Finland

http://www.uta.fi/laitokset/mattiet/filosofia/

University of Turku, Finland

http://www.utu.fi/yht/filosofia/

University of Iceland, Iceland

http://www.hi.is/~mhs/skor/ensskor/hsp.ens.html

University of Bergen, Norway

http://www.hf-fak.uib.no/i/Filosofisk/

University of Oslo, Norway

http://www.hf.uio.no/

University of Trondheim, Norway

http://www.hf.unit.no/fil/filosofi.htm

Lund University, Sweden

http://lucat.lu.se:8080/cgi-bin/lucat/orgbild.sh?0:015001000

Umeå University, Sweden

http://www.umu.se/philos/

University of Göteborg, Sweden

http://www.phil.gu.se/Philosophy.html

University of Uppsala, Sweden

http://strix.udac.uu.se/kat/deps/HH7.html

Spain

Universidad Autònoma, Madrid

http://www.uam.es:80/estructura/departamentos/FiloyLetras/filosofia/paginas/hgh

Universidad Complutense, Madrid

http://fs-morente.filol.ucm.es/

Universidad Pontificia Comillas, Madrid

http://www.upco.es/pag/fi.htm

Universitat Autònoma, Barcelona

http://www.uab.es/filosof.htm

University of Barcelona

http://www.ub.es/div-fac/div1/facultat/fis/fis.htm

University of Oviedo

http://www3.uniovi.es/Vicest/Estudios/Centros/filosofia.html

Switzerland

University of Bern

http://sauron.unibe.ch/philo/index.html

University of Geneva

http://www.unige.ch/lettres/philo/philo.html

University of Geneva (History & Phil of Science)

http://www.unige.ch/hps/welcome.html

University of Zurich

http://www.unizh.ch/philosophie/

United Kingdom

Anglia Polytechnic University

http://www.anglia.ac.uk/hae/phil/home.htm

Birbeck College, University of London

http://www.bbk.ac.uk/Departments/Philosophy/

Cambridge University

http://www.phil.cam.ac.uk/index.html

City University

http://www.city.ac.uk/sociology/

John Moores University, Liverpool

http://www.livjm.ac.uk/courses/philos.htm

Keele University

http://www.keele.ac.uk/depts/pi/pihome.htm

Kings College, London

http://www.kcl.ac.uk/kis/schools/hums/philosophy/top.html

Lancaster University

http://www.lancs.ac.uk/users/philosophy/

London School of Economics

http://www.lse.ac.uk/depts/cpnss/

Manchester Metropolitan University

http://darion.mmu.ac.uk/h&ss/p&p/home.html

Middlesex University

http://www.mdx.ac.uk/www/philosophy/

Open University

http://www.open.ac.uk/OU/Academic/Arts/philos/philos.htm

Oxford University

http://units.ox.ac.uk/departments/philosophy/

Queens University, Belfast

http://www.qub.ac.uk/pas/phil/

Staffordshire University

http://www.staffs.ac.uk/schools/humanities_and_soc_sciences/philosophy/philo.html

University of Aberdeen

http://www.abdn.ac.uk/cpts/phildept.htm

University of Birmingham

http://www.bham.ac.uk/philosophy/

University of Bristol

http://www.bris.ac.uk/Depts/Philosophy/

University of Dundee

http://www.dundee.ac.uk/Philosophy/

University of Durham

http://www.dur.ac.uk/~dfl0www/home.html

University of Edinburgh

http://www.ed.ac.uk/~pmilne/philinfo.html

University of Essex

http://www.essex.ac.uk/philosophy/

University of Glasgow

http://www.gla.ac.uk/Acad/Philosophy/

University of Hertfordshire

http://www.herts.ac.uk/humanities/hum-phil.html

University of Hull

http://www.hull.ac.uk/prospectus/phil-c.html

University of Kent, Canterbury

http://www.ukc.ac.uk/cprs/phil/

University of Leeds University of Leeds

http://www.leeds.ac.uk/philosophy/philosophy.html

University of Liverpool

http://www.liv.ac.uk/Philosophy/handbook.html

University College London

http://www.ucl.ac.uk/philosophy/

University of London: School of Advanced Studies

http://www.sas.ac.uk/Philosophy/

University of North London

http://www.unl.ac.uk/humanIT/hpcs.htm

University of Nottingham

http://www.ccc.nottingham.ac.uk/~apzwww/apzwww.html

University of Reading

> *http://www.rdg.ac.uk/AcaDepts/ld/*

University of St. Andrews

> *http://www.st-and.ac.uk/~www_spa/home.html*

University of Sheffield

> *http://www.shef.ac.uk/uni/academic/N-Q/phil/department/homepage.html*

University of Stirling

> *http://www.stir.ac.uk/philosophy/*

University of Sunderland

> *http://www.sunderland.ac.uk/~os0dwe/phi1.html*

University of Sussex

> *http://www.cogs.susx.ac.uk/lab/phil/index.html*

University of Ulster

> *http://www2.ulst.ac.uk/faculty/humanities/default.html*

University of Wales, Cardiff

> *http://www.cf.ac.uk/uwcc/secap/philosophy/index.html*

University of Wales, Lampeter

> *http://www.lamp.ac.uk/philosophy/*

University of Wales, Swansea

> *http://www.swan.ac.uk/philosophy/home.html*

University of Warwick

> *http://www.warwick.ac.uk/fac/soc/Philosophy/*

University of Wolverhampton

> *http://www.wlv.ac.uk/shass/div6.html*

University of York

> *http://www.york.ac.uk/depts/phil/*

Rest of Europe

University of Zagreb, Croatia

> *http://grgur.ffzg.hr/*

University of Cyprus, Cyprus

> *http://www.ucy.ac.cy/depart/philos.html*

University of Ostrava, Czech Republic

http://www.osu.cz/ff.html

Vysoka School of Economics, Prague, Czech Republic

http://nb.vse.cz/kfil/win/welcome2.htm

Estonian Humanities Institute, Estonia

http://www.ehi.ee/ehi/oppetool/oppekavad/filosoofia/filosoofia.html

University of Tartu, Estonia

http://www.ut.ee/teaduskond/Filosoofia/english/

University of Crete, Greece

http://www.cc.uch.gr/Tmhmata/RETHYMNO/PHILOSOFY.html

Eötvös Loránd University, Budapest, Hungary

http://hps.elte.hu/

Jate University, Szeged, Hungary

http://www.arts.u-szeged.hu/dep/philosophy/philosophy.html

University of Latvia, Latvia

http://www.lanet.lv/members/LU/f_hist.html

International Academy of Philosophy, Lichtenstein

http://www.iap.li/

Vilnius University, Lithuania

http://tauras.vu.lt/university/depart/philosophy.html

Jagiellonian University, Krakow, Poland

http://www.uj.edu.pl/cgi-bin/lang-en-std-none/uj-guide/inst_phi.html

The Marie Curie-Sklodowska University, Lublin, Poland

http://www.umcs.lublin.pl/umcs/fil/filp.html

Philosophy Departments: North America

Canada

Acadia University

http://ace.acadiau.ca/arts/phil/HOME.HTM

Algoma University

http://thunderbird.auc.laurentian.ca/academic/phildpt/phil1.html

Augustana University College

http://www.augustana.ab.ca/prospective/info-pages/philosophy.html

Brandon University

http://www.brandonu.ca/Departments/Arts/Philosophy/welcome.html

Brock University

http://www.BrockU.CA/philosophy/

Carleton University

http://www.carleton.ca/philosophy/

Concordia University

http://artsci-ccwin.concordia.ca/philosophy/philosophy.html

Dalhousie University

http://www.dal.ca/~philwww/hmpage/phpage2.htm

Kwantlen University College

http://www.kwantlen.bc.ca/calendar/phil.htm

Lakehead University

http://www.lakeheadu.ca/~regwww/philosop.html

Malaspina University College

http://www.mala.bc.ca/www/ipp/cpr.htm

McGill University

http://www.arts.mcgill.ca/programs/philo

McMaster University

http://www.humanities.mcmaster.ca/~philos/philhome.htm

Memorial University of Newfoundland

http://www.mun.ca/phil/

Mount Allison University

http://www.mta.ca/faculty/humanities/philosophy/

Mount St. Vincent University

http://www.msvu.ca/calendar/phil.htm

Okanagan University College

http://www.arts.ouc.bc.ca/phil/home.html

St. Francis Xavier University

http://cwaves.stfx.ca/academic/philosophy/

St. Mary's University

> *http://www.stmarys.ca/administration/registrar/calendar/phi.html*

St. Thomas University

> *http://www.stthomasu.ca/courses/courphil.htm*

Simon Fraser University

> *http://www.sfu.ca/philosophy/*

Trent University

> *http://ivory.trentu.ca/www/phil/*

University of Alberta

> *http://www.ualberta.ca/~philosop/phil-home.html*

University of British Columbia

> *http://www.arts.ubc.ca/philos/philos.html*

University of British Columbia: Center for Applied Ethics

> *http://www.ethics.ubc.ca/*

University of Calgary

> *http://www.ucalgary.ca/philosophy/*

University College of Cape Breton

> *http://faculty.uccb.ns.ca/~rkeshen/frontpage.htm*

University College of the Cariboo

> *http://www.cariboo.bc.ca/ae/php/home.htm*

University College of the Fraser Valley

> *http://cheam.ucfv.bc.ca/calendar/PHILOSOPHY/*

University of Guelph

> *http://www.uoguelph.ca/philosophy/philohome.html*

Université Laval

> *http://www.ulaval.ca/sg/annuaires/philosophie/index.html*

University of Lethbridge

> *http://home.uleth.ca/phl/*

University of Manitoba

> *http://www.umanitoba.ca/faculties/arts/philosophy/*

University of Montreal

> *http://brise.ere.umontreal.ca/~lepagef/*

University of New Brunswick

http://www.unb.ca/arts/Phil/index.html

Université du Quebec

http://www.philo.uqam.ca/

University of Regina

http://www.uregina.ca/~arts/phil/

University of Saskatchewan

http://www.usask.ca/philosophy/

University of Toronto

http://www.chass.utoronto.ca:8080/philosophy/

University of Victoria

http://web.uvic.ca/philosophy/

University of Waterloo

http://watarts.uwaterloo.ca/PHIL/cpshelle/philosophy.html

University of Western Ontario

http://www.uwo.ca/philosophy/

University of Windsor

http://www.uwindsor.ca/faculty/arts/philosophy/index.html

University of Winnipeg

http://www.uwinnipeg.ca/academic/as/philosophy/index.htm

Wilfred Laurier University

http://www.wlu.ca/~wwwphil/

York University

http://www.yorku.ca/dept/philo/philhome.htm

Mexico

Universidad Autonoma de Baja California

http://sunrec1.rec.uabc.mx/uabc/uniacad/tijuana/eschums.html

Universidad Autonoma de Nuevo Leon

http://www.uanl.mx/UANL/Escuelas/Facultades/ffyl/

Universidad de Guadalajara

http://fuentes.csh.udg.mx/CUCSH/Carreras/licfilosofia.html

Universidad Michoacana de San Nicolas de Hidalgo

http://www.ccu.umich.mx/univ/lic/filos.html

Universidad Panamericana Sede

http://www.mixcoac.upmx.mx/UPpags/Filosofia.html

Universidad Veracruzana

http://www.coacade.uv.mx/uv/lic-filosofia.html

USA

Adelphi University

http://www.adelphi.edu/acad_depts/artsci/phi/

Agnes Scott College

http://www.agnesscott.edu/academic/phil/deptpage.htm

Albertson College

http://www.acofi.edu/~philo/index.html

Albertus Magnus College

http://www.albertus.edu/cc_de-ph.htm

Albion College

http://www.albion.edu/fac/phil/

Allegheny College

http://www.alleg.edu/Academic/Philosophy/

Allentown College

http://www4.allencol.edu/~philtheo/

American University

http://www.american.edu/academic.depts/cas/philorel/

Amherst College

http://www.amherst.edu/amherst/academ/philosophy/menu.html

Appalachian State University

http://www.acs.appstate.edu/dept/phil-rel/

Arizona State University

http://www.asu.edu/clas/philosophy/

Arkansas State University

http://csm.astate.edu/~engphil/engphil.html

Assumption College

> *http://www.assumption.edu/HTML/Academic/Philosophy/philmain.html*

Auburn University

> *gopher://gopher.duc.auburn.edu:70/11/Academic/LibArts/Philosophy*

Augsberg College

> *http://www.augsburg.edu/philosophy/*

Augustana College, Illinois

> *http://www.augustana.edu/acadept/pl.html*

Augustana College, South Dakota

> *http://www.augie.edu/dept/courses/phil.html*

Austin College

> *http://www.austinc.edu/Academics/RelPhil/index.html*

Austin Peay State University

> *http://www.apsu.edu/www/colleges/philosophy/index/htmlx*

Azusa Pacific University

> *http://www.apu.edu/academics/theology/index_ug.html*

Baker University

> *http://www.main.bakeru.edu/html/d-phil.htm*

Baldwin-Wallace College

> *http://www.baldwinw.edu/academics/phl.html*

Bard College

> *http://www.bard.edu/divisions/socstud/default.nclk#philosophy*

Barry University

> *http://www.barry.edu/artsci/theology/philo.html*

Baruch College

> *http://www.baruch.cuny.edu/slas/departments/philosophy/philosophy.html*

Bates College

> *http://www.bates.edu/Faculty/Philosophy%20and%20Religion/index.html*

Baylor University

> *http://www.baylor.edu/~Philosophy/*

Belmont University

> *http://www.belmont.edu/humanities/philosophy/homepage.html*

Beloit College

http://www.beloit.edu/~philorel/

Berea College

http://www.berea.edu/PHI/PHI.home.html

Bethany College

http://www.bethany.wvnet.edu/Academics/Departments/Philosophy/*index.html

Bethel College

http://www.bethel.edu/college/acad/dept/phil.htm

Birmingham-Southern College

http://www.bsc.edu/cgi-bin/counter.pl/catalog/philo.htm

Bloomsburg University

http://www.bloomu.edu/academic/undergrad/pages/phil.html

Boston College

http://fmwww.bc.edu:80/pl/

Bowdoin College

http://www.bowdoin.edu/cwis/acad/dept/phil.html

Bowie State University

http://www.bowiestate.edu/academic/phi/philhom.htm

Bowling Green State University

http://www.bgsu.edu/departments/phil/

Brandeis University

http://www.brandeis.edu/departments/philosophy/philosophy.html

Bridgewater College

http://www.bridgewater.edu:80/departments/phrel/phrel.html

Brigham Young University

http://humanities.byu.edu/phil/phil.htm

Brooklyn College

http://www.brooklyn.cuny.edu/bc/depts/ug/phil.html

Brown University

http://www.brown.edu/Departments/Philosophy/homepage.html

Bryn Mawr University

http://www.brynmawr.edu/Adm/academic/phil.html

Bucknell University

> *http://www.bucknell.edu/departments/philosophy/*

Buena Vista University

> *http://www.bvu.edu/depts/philosophy_religion/*

California Institute of Integral Studies

> *http://www.ciis.edu/SharedFiles/Candice/ACADEMICFILES.html/AcadPAR.html/
> AcadPar.html*

California Lutheran University

> *http://robles.callutheran.edu/Philo.html*

California Polytechnic State University

> *http://www.calpoly.edu/~phil/*

California State Polytechnic University, Pomona

> *http://www.class.csupomona.edu/phl/welcome.html*

California State University, Chico

> *http://www.csuchico.edu/phil/index.html*

California State University, Dominguez Hills

> *http://www.csudh.edu/philosophy/default.htm*

California State University, Longbeach

> *http://www.csulb.edu/~philos/*

California State University, Northridge

> *http://www.csun.edu/~vfeed00a/*

California State University, Sacramento

> *http://www.csus.edu/phil/index.html*

California University of Pennsylvania

> *http://www.cup.edu/dephmpgs/libarts/philo/philhp.htm*

Calvin College

> *http://www.calvin.edu/academic/philosophy/*

Canisius College

> *http://www.canisius.edu/canhp/departments/philosophy/*

Carleton College

> *http://www.carleton.edu/curricular/PHIL/index.html*

Carnegie Mellon University

> *http://hss.cmu.edu/HTML/departments/philosophy/philosophy.html*

Case Western Reserve University

http://www.cwru.edu/artsci/phil/phil.html

Catholic University of America

http://www.cua.edu/www/phlu/

Central Michigan University

http://www.cmich.edu/UG-PHL.HTML

Christopher Newport University

http://www.cnu.edu/academics/phil/

City University of New York

http://www.gc.cuny.edu/ACADEMICPROGRAMS/DISCIPLINES/philo.htm

Claremont Graduate School

http://www.cgs.edu/hum/phi/homepage.html

Clark University

http://www.clarku.edu/departments/philosophy/

Clarke College

http://www.clarke.edu/academic/departments/philosophy/index.htm

Clemson University

http://hubcap.clemson.edu/aah/phil/index.html

Colby College

http://www.colby.edu/philosophy/

College of the Holy Cross

http://sterling.holycross.edu/departments/philosophy/website/index.html

College of Misericordia

http://www.miseri.edu/academic/departs/phil/phil1.htm

College of Mount St. Joseph

http://www.msj.edu/academics/Philosophy/Philoso.htm

College of New Jersey

http://www.tcnj.edu/~phaedrus/

College of Saint Benedict & Saint John's University

http://www.csbsju.edu/School-info/ucatalog/depts/phil.html

College of William and Mary

http://www.wm.edu/CAS/PHIL/philhome.htm

College of Wooster

http://www.wooster.edu/Philosophy/index.html

Colorado College

http://www.cc.colorado.edu/Dept/PH/

Colorado State University

http://www.ColoState.EDU/Depts/Philosophy/

Columbia University

http://www.columbia.edu/cu/philosophy/

Concordia College

http://www.cord.edu/dept/philosophy/

Cornell University

http://www.arts.cornell.edu/phil/

Creighton University

http://puffin.creighton.edu/phil/phil.htm

Daemen College

http://www.daemen.edu/departments/phy/default.html

Dana College

http://www.dana.edu/text_catalog/html/phyphil_polcor.html

Davidson College

http://www.davidson.edu/academic/philosophy/philosophy.html

Denison University

http://www.denison.edu/philosophy/

DePauw University

http://www.depauw.edu/phil/philhome.htm

Dickinson College

http://www.dickinson.edu/academics/philoso.html

Drew University

http://forest.drew.edu/~courses/dept/phil.html

Duke University

http://www.duke.edu/philosophy/

Duquesne University

http://www.duq.edu/liberalarts/underphilo/philosophy.html

Earlham College

    http://www.earlham.edu/departments/philosophy/philhome.htm

East Carolina University

    http://ecuvax.cis.ecu.edu/academics/schdept/phil/ecuphil.html

East Tennessee State University

    http://www.etsu-tn.edu/philos/

Eastern Kentucky University

    http://www.philosophy.eku.edu/

Eastern Michigan University

    http://www.emich.edu/public/philosophy/phihome.htm

Eckerd College

    http://www.eckerd.edu/academics/ltr/pll/

Emory University

    http://www.emory.edu/PHILOSOPHY/

Fairfield University

    http://www.fairfield.edu/academic/artssci/majors/philosop/ugphhome.htm

Florida State University

    http://www.fsu.edu/~philo/

Fontbonne College

    http://www.fontbonne.edu/replss.html

Fort Hays State University

    http://www.fhsu.edu/htmlpages/fhsu/dept_of_philo.html

Fort Lewis College

    http://www.fortlewis.edu/acad-aff/arts-sci/philos/phidegr.html

Franciscan University

    http://Gabriel.franuniv.edu/phil.html

Franklin & Marshall College

    http://www.fandm.edu/Departments/Philosophy/Philosophy.html

Frostburg State University

    http://www.fsu.umd.edu/dept/phil/philhome.htm

Furman University

    http://www.furman.edu/academics/dept/philo.htm

George Mason University

http://web.gmu.edu/departments/philosophy/

Georgetown University

http://www.georgetown.edu/departments/philosophy/

Georgia Southern University

http://www.gsu.edu//~wwwphl/philosophy.html

Georgia State University

http://www.gsu.edu/~wwwphl/philosophy.html

Gonzaga University

http://www.gonzaga.edu/academic/philosophy/index.html

Grand Valley State University

http://www.gvsu.edu/acad/flyers/phil.html

Grinnell College

http://www.grin.edu/~philoweb/

Guilford College

http://www.guilford.edu/Academic/philo.htm

Gustavus Adolphus College

http://www.gac.edu/Academics/philosophy/philosophy.html

Hamilton College

http://www.hamilton.edu/html/academic/Philosophy/default.html

Hamline University

http://www.hamline.edu/depts/philosophy/index.html

Hampden-Sydney College

http://lion.hsc.edu/acad/phil/index.html

Hanover College

http://www.hanover.edu/philos/home.html

Hardin Simmons University

http://www.hsutx.edu/main/phil.htm

Hartwick College

http://www.hartwick.edu/academic/phil.html

Harvard University

http://www.fas.harvard.edu/~phildept/

Hendrix College

> *http://www.hendrix.edu/dept/Philosophy.html*

Highpoint University

> *http://acme.highpoint.edu/academic/religion/index.html*

Hillsborough Community College

> *http://www.hcc.cc.fl.us/services/departmt/philo/philo.htm*

Hillsdale College

> *http://www.hillsdale.edu/dept/Phil&Rel/Phil&RelHomePage.html*

Hofstra University

> *http://www.hofstra.edu/Communities/frame.html?bounce=/web/docs/HCLAS/philosophy/index.html*

Hollins College

> *http://www.hollins.edu/html/undergraduate/philosophy/philhome.htm*

Hope College

> *http://www.hope.edu/academic/philosophy/*

Humboldt State University

> *http://www.humboldt.edu/~phil/*

Huntingdon College

> *http://local.huntingdon.edu/local/Academics/Religion/*

Huntington College

> *http://www.huntcol.edu/academics/philosophy/philo.html*

Idaho State University

> *http://www.isu.edu/departments/english/*

Illinois College

> *http://squirrel.ic.edu/phil/*

Illinois State University

> *http://www.cas.ilstu.edu/philosophy/webpage.htm*

Indiana University

> *http://www.phil.indiana.edu/*

Indiana University: Cognitive Science

> *http://www.psych.indiana.edu/home.html*

Indiana University: History & Philosophy of Science

> *http://www.indiana.edu/~hpscdept/index.html*

Indiana University, South Bend

http://www.iusb.edu/~phil/

Indiana University Southeast

http://macserver.ius.indiana.edu/humanities/philosophy/philosophy.html

Iowa State University

http://www.public.iastate.edu:80/~phil_info/

Ithaca College

http://www.ithaca.edu/hs/philrel/philrel1/

Jacksonville State University

gopher://jsucc.jsu.edu/0/acadinfo/catalog/philosophy.txt

Jacksonville University

http://junix.ju.edu/HomePages/Philosophy/index.html

James Maddison University

http://www.jmu.edu/philrel/dept.htm

Jersey City State College

http://www.jcstate.edu/philos.html

Johns Hopkins University

http://www.jhu.edu/~phil/philfold/deptinfo.html

Juniata College

http://www.juniata.edu/hum/philosophy/

Kalamazoo College

http://www.kzoo.edu:80/~phil/

Kansas State University

http://www.ksu.edu/philos/

Kansas Wesleyan University

http://www.kwu.edu/religion/rephbro.htm

Kent State University

http://www.kent.edu/philo/index.htm

Kenyon College

http://www.kenyon.edu/acad/c_of_s/philos.htm

King's College

http://www.kings.edu/philosophy.html

Knox College

> *http://www.knox.edu/knoxweb/academic/philosophy/philosophy.html*

Kutztown University of Pennsylvania

> *http://www.kutztown.edu/acad/phil/*

Lafayette College

> *http://www.lafayette.edu/slaghtrl/home.htm*

LaGrange College

> *http://www.lgc.peachnet.edu/academic/religion/phi_home.htm*

Lake Forest College

> *http://www.lfc.edu/philosophy/*

Lake Michigan College

> *http://raptor.lmc.cc.mi.us/liberal/philo/philos.html*

Lawrence University

> *http:/www.lawrence.edu/~boardmaw/deptphil.html*

Le Moyne College

> *http://www.lemoyne.edu/academic_affairs/departments/philosophy/index.html*

Lebanon Valley College

> *http://www.lvc.edu/www/religion/index.html*

Lehigh University

> *http://www.lehigh.edu/~inphil/inphil.html*

Lenior Rhyne College

> *http://www.lrc.edu/www/departments/phi_department.html*

Lewis & Clark College

> *http://www.lclark.edu/COLLEGE/DEPAR/PHIL/index.html*

Lock Haven University of Pennsylvania

> *http://www.lhup.edu/academics/departments/jour/phwebdir.htm*

Louisiana College

> *http://www.lacollege.edu/depart/religion/religion.home*

Louisiana State University

> *http://chaos.artsci.lsu.edu/phil/*

Loyola College

> *http://www.loyola.edu/dept/philosophy/philosophy.html*

Loyola University

> *http://www.luc.edu/depts/philosophy/*

Lycoming College

> *http://www.lycoming.edu/depart/philos/philos.htm*

Macalester College

> *http://www.macalstr.edu/updates/philosophy.html*

Mansfield University

> *http://www.mnsfld.edu/depts/philosop/index.html*

Mary Washington College

> *http://www.mwc.edu/~dambuel/*

Marywood College

> *http://ac.marywood.edu/ug_cat/phil.htm*

Massachusetts Institute of Technology

> *http://web.mit.edu/philos/www/index.html*

Mesa Community College

> *http://www.mc.maricopa.edu/academic/philosophy/*

Metropolitan Community College

> *http://wwwfaculty.mccneb.edu/commhum/PHILOS/philosmain.htm*

Metropolitan State College of Denver

> *http://clem.mscd.edu/~sullivad/welcome.html*

Miami University

> *http://www.muohio.edu/~phlcwis/*

Michigan State University

> *http://pilot.msu.edu/unit/phl/*

Middle Tennessee State University

> *http://www.mtsu.edu/~phil/*

Middlebury College

> *http://www.middlebury.edu/~philo/*

Mississippi State University

> *http://www.msstate.edu/Dept/PR/philrel.html*

Monmouth University

> *http://www.monmouth.edu/monmouth/academic/polysci/polysci.html*

Montana State University, Billings

http://www.msubillings.edu/academic/cas/engprog.html

Montana State University, Bozeman

http://www.montana.edu/wwwhi/index.htm

Montclair State University

http://www.shss.montclair.edu/philrelg/homepage.html

Moorhead State University

http://www.moorhead.msus.edu:80/Maps/Bridges/3rd/philosophy.html

Morehouse College

http://www.morehouse.edu/phi.htm

Morgan State University

http://www.morgan.edu/catalog/artscien/phil/phil.htm

Mount Holyoke College

http://www.mtholyoke.edu/acad/phil/

Mount St. Mary's College

http://msmc.la.edu/phlsophy.htm

Murray State University

http://www.mursuky.edu/qacd/chs/phirgs/home.htm

New Mexico Highlands University

http://www.nmhu.edu/Departments/english

New Mexico State University

http://www.nmsu.edu/~artsci/academic.html#Philosophy

New School for Social Research

http://www.newschool.edu/gf/phil/

New York University

http://www.nyu.edu/gsas/dept/philo/

Newberry College

http://www.newberry.edu/acad/phil/

North Carolina State University

http://www2.ncsu.edu/ncsu/chass/philo/

North Carolina Wesleyan College

http://www.ncwc.edu/ncwc/humanities/philosophy.html

Northeastern University

> *http://www.northeastern.edu/registrar/catalog/phl.html*

Northern Arizona University

> *http://www.nau.edu/~philo/*

Northern Illinois University

> *http://sun.soci.niu.edu/~phildept/*

Northern Kentucky University

> *http://www.nku.edu/~philos/*

Northland College

> *http://www.northland.edu/phr/HOME.HTML*

Northwest Missouri University

> *http://www.nwmissouri.edu/~0700304/index.html*

Northwestern University

> *http://www2.mmlc.nwu.edu/philosophy/*

Norwich University

> *http://www.norwich.edu/acad/phio.htm*

Oberlin College

> *http://www.oberlin.edu/~philosop/*

Occidental College

> *http://www.oxy.edu/~traiger/phil-oxy/philos.html*

Oglethorpe University

> *http://www.oglethorpe.edu/academics/d1/philosophy.asp*

Ohio Northern University

> *http://www.onu.edu/Admin-offices/admission/Fact-Sheet/phil-relg.html*

Ohio State University

> *http://www.cohums.ohio-state.edu/philo/*

Ohio Wesleyan University

> *http://www.owu.edu/~acadweb/abs_phil.htm*

Oklahoma City University

> *http://frodo.okcu.edu/www/departments/petree/humanities/philosophy/philosophy.html*

Oklahoma State University

http://www.okstate.edu/artsci/philosophy/

Old Dominion University

http://www.odu.edu/~artsltrs/philosophy/welcome.htm

Oregon State University

http://www.orst.edu/Dept/philosophy/

Our Lady of the Lake University

http://www.ollusa.edu/academic/cas/PHILOSOPhy/phlo.htm

Pacific Lutheran University

http://www.plu.edu/print/deptfact/phil.html

Pennsylvania State University

http://www.la.psu.edu/philo/welcome.html

Pepperdine University

http://www.pepperdine.edu/seaver/hute/phil.html

Plymouth State College

http://oz.plymouth.edu/~phil/

Pomona College

http://www.pomona.edu/academics/dept/HumArt/Phil.html

Ponta Loma Nazarene College

http://www.ptloma.edu/AcademicDepartments/philrel/index.htm

Portland State University

http://www-adm.pdx.edu/user/phil/

Princeton University

http://webware.Princeton.EDU/philosph/

Principia College

http://www.prin.edu/college/majors/phil.htm

Providence College

http://www.providence.edu/admiss/phl.htm

Purdue University

http://www.sla.purdue.edu/academic/phil/

Quincy University

http://www.quincy.edu/divisions/theology/

Randolph Macon College

   http://www.rmc.edu:80/academic/departments/phil/

Reed College

   http://web.reed.edu/academic/deptinfo/philosophy.shtml

Rensselaer Polytechnic Institute

   http://www.rpi.edu/~brings/DEPT/ppcs.htm

Rhodes College

   http://blair.library.rhodes.edu/default1htmls/PHIL.HTML

Rice University

   http://www.ruf.rice.edu/~philos/

Rivier College

   http://www.rivier.edu/departments/philos/

Rockford College

   http://www.rockford.edu/academic/catalog/philosop/philosop.htm

Rockhurst College

   http://www.rockhurst.edu/academic_programs/arts_and_sciences/philtheo.htm

Rutgers University

   http://www.philosophy.rutgers.edu

Saginaw Valley State University

   http://www.svsu.edu/philosophy/philos.html

Saint Andrews College

   http://www.sapc.edu/phil.html

Saint Anselm College

   http://www.anselm.edu/academic/philosophy.html

Saint Bonaventure University

   http://www.sbu.edu/academics/departments/philosophy/phil.index.html

Saint Cloud State University

   http://pooh.stcloud.msus.edu/~ugb/phil/

Saint Edward's University

   http://www.stedwards.edu/hum/phil/index.html

Saint Francis College

   http://www.sfcpa.edu/academic/humaniti/philhome.htm

Saint Joseph's College

http://www.saintjoe.edu/academics/religion/

Saint Joseph's University

http://www.sju.edu/ACADEMIC_PROGRAMS/COL_ART_SCIENCE/
PHILOSOPHY/index.html

Saint Lawrence University

http://www.stlawu.edu/slu:http/acadpro/phil.htm

Saint Louis University

http://www.slu.edu/colleges/AS/philos/

Saint Mary's University

http://www.phil.stmarytx.edu/philhp/Home.htm

Saint Norbert College

http://www.snc.edu/phil/

Saint Olaf College

http://www.stolaf.edu/depts/philosophy/

Salisbury State University

http://www.ssu.edu/Schools/Fulton/PhilDept.html

Salve Regina University

http://www.salve.edu/phl.html

Sam Houston State University

http://www.shsu.edu/~psy_ww2/

San Diego State University

http://www-rohan.sdsu.edu/dept/phil/wwwphil.html

San Francisco State University

http://phil.sfsu.edu/

San Jose State University

http://www.sjsu.edu/depts/philosophy/philosophy.html

Santa Barbara City College

http://www.sbcc.net/academic/Philosophy/

Santa Clara University

http://www.scu.edu/SCU/Departments/zztmp/Philosophy.html

Santa Rosa Junior College

http://www.santarosa.edu/philosophy

Seattle University

> *http://www.seattleu.edu/artsci/departments/philosop.htm*

Seton Hall University

> *http://www.shu.edu/academic/arts_sci/Undergraduate/philoso/ndex.html*

Sewanee University

> *http://www.sewanee.edu/CollegeCatalog/CollegeDepartments/Philosophy.html*

Shippensburg University

> *http://www.ship.edu/~pubinfo/HISTORY97.HTML*

Siena College

> *http://www.siena.edu/academic_programs/ph/*

Simpson College

> *http://storm.simpson.edu/academics/catalog/philosophy.html*

Skidmore College

> *http://don.skidmore.edu/academics/philosophy/departmentpage.htm*

Slippery Rock University

> *http://www.sru.edu/depts/artsci/phil/phlhome.htm*

Sonoma State University

> *http://www.sonoma.edu/Depts/Philo.html*

Southern Illinois University, Carbondale

> *http://www.siu.edu/~philos*

Southern Illinios University, Edwardsville

> *http://www.siue.edu/PHILOSOPHY/*

Southern Methodist University

> *http://www.smu.edu/~dedman/philmenu.html*

Southern Nazarene University

> *http://www.snu.edu/departme/philosop/index.htm*

Southwest Missouri State University

> *http://www.smsu.edu/contrib/phi/phihome.htm*

Southwest State University

> *http://www.southwest.msus.edu/Programs/PHIL/*

Southwest Texas State University

> *http://www.swt.edu/acad_depts/philos_dept.html*

Spring Hill College

http://www.shc.edu/philosop.htm

Stanford University

http://www-philosophy.stanford.edu/philosophy/

State University of New York, Binghamton

http://philosophy.adm.binghamton.edu/

State University of New York, Binghamton (PACCS)

http://turing.pacss.binghamton.edu/index.html

State University of New York, Brockport

http://cc.brockport.edu/~ucatalog/phl.html

State University of New York, Buffalo

http://wings.buffalo.edu/academic/department/philosophy/

State University of New York, Cortland

http://www.cortland.edu/www/philosophy/page.htm

State University of New York, Oneonta

http://www.oneonta.edu/~shradedw/philhome.html

State University of New York, Potsdam

http://www.potsdam.edu/PHIL/PHIL.html

State University of New York, Stony Brook

http://www.sunysb.edu/philosophy/

Stephen F. Austin State University

http://titan.sfasu.edu/~english/index.html

Syracuse University

http://www-hobbes.syr.edu/phil/

Tennessee State University

http://acad.tnstate.edu/~english/

Tennessee Technological University

http://www.tntech.edu/www/acad/soc/index.html

Texas A&M University

http://www-phil.tamu.edu/Philosophy/

Texas Christian University

http://www.phil.tcu.edu/phil/

Texas Tech University

http://www.ttu.edu/Philosophy/

Thomas More College

http://www.thomasmore.edu/dept/deptphi.html

Towson University

http://www.towson.edu/~scales/philhom.html

Transylvania University

http://www.transy.edu/academics/philosophy.htm

Trinity College

http://www.trincoll.edu/academics/departments/phil/

Trinity College, DC

http://www.trinitydc.edu/catalog/philos.html

Trinity International University

http://www.trin.edu/cas/academic/degree/phil.html

Trinity University

http://WWW.Trinity.edu/departments/philosophy/

Tufts University

http://www.tufts.edu/as/cogstud/philgrad.htm

Tulane University

http://www.tulane.edu/~phil/index.html

Union College, NY

http://www.union.edu/union_info/catalog/philos.htmld

University of Akron

http://www.uakron.edu/philosophy/phl.html

University of Alabama at Birmingham

http://www.uab.edu/philosophy/

University of Arizona

http://w3.arizona.edu/~phil/

University of Arkansas

http://www.uark.edu:80/depts/philinfo/

University of California at Berkeley

http://socrates.berkeley.edu/~frege/

University of California at Davis

> *http://www-philosophy.ucdavis.edu/*

University of California at Irvine

> *http://www.hnet.uci.edu/philosophy/*

University of California at Riverside

> *http://www.ucr.edu/philosophy/phil.html*

University of California at San Diego

> *http://orpheus.ucsd.edu/philo/*

University of California at Santa Barbara

> *http://humanitas.ucsb.edu/depts/philosophy/index.html*

University of California at Santa Cruz

> *http://humwww.ucsc.edu/phil/phil.html*

University of Central Arkansas

> *http://www.uca.edu/philo/philpage.htm*

University of Central Florida

> *http://www.cas.ucf.edu/philosophy/*

University of Chicago

> *http://humanities.uchicago.edu/humanities/philosophy/*

University of Cincinatti

> *http://ucaswww.mcm.uc.edu/philosophy/*

University of Colorado, Boulder

> *http://www.colorado.edu/philosophy/*

University of Colorado, Denver

> *http://carbon.cudenver.edu/public/phil/*

University of Connecticut

> *http://www.ucc.uconn.edu/~wwwphil/*

University of Dallas

> *http://www.udallas.edu/phildept/phil_hpg.html*

University of Dayton

> *http://www.as.udayton.edu/www/phlweb/philindex.html*

University of Denver

> *http://www.du.edu/philosophy/*

University of Detroit

http://libarts.udmercy.edu/dep/phl/index.html

University of Evansville

http://www.evansville.edu/~philweb/

University of Florida

http://www.clas.ufl.edu/CLAS/Departments/Philosophy/

University of Georgia

http://www.phil.uga.edu/

University of Hawaii

http://www2.hawaii.edu/catalog/arts-sci-files/phil.html

University of Houston

http://www.uh.edu/phil

University of Idaho

http://www.uidaho.edu/Letters_and_Science/Phil/

University of Illinois, Chicago

http://www.uic.edu/depts/phil/

University of Illinois, Urbana-Champaign

http://www.phil.uiuc.edu/

University of Iowa

http://www.uiowa.edu/~phil/

University of Kansas

http://www.ukans.edu/cwis/units/philos/public_html/

University of Kentucky

http://www.uky.edu/ArtsSciences/Philosophy/

University of La Verne

http://www.ulaverne.edu/academ/dept/relphl/rpp.html

University of Louisville

http://homer.louisville.edu:80/groups/philosophy-www/

University of Maryland

http://www.inform.umd.edu:8080/EdRes/Colleges/ARHU/Depts/Philosophy

University of Massachusetts, Amherst

http://www-unix.oit.umass.edu/~philos/

University of Massachusetts, Boston

http://www.cas.umb.edu/phil.html

University of Massachusetts, Dartmouth

http://www.umassd.edu/1Academic/CArtsandSciences/Philosophy/philosophy homepage.html

University of Memphis

http://www.people.memphis.edu/~philos/phil.html

University of Miami

http://www.miami.edu/phi/

University of Michigan, Ann Arbor

http://www.umich.edu/~philos

University of Michigan, Dearborn

http://www.umd.umich.edu/dept/acad/casl/hum/phil/

University of Minnesota

http://www.umn.edu/mcps/dept/phil.html

University of Mississippi

http://www.olemiss.edu/depts/philosophy/

University of Missouri at Columbia

http://www.missouri.edu/~philwww/

University of Missouri at Kansas City

http://philosophy.umkc.edu/

University of Missouri at Rolla

http://www.umr.edu/~plainfo/pla/phil.html

University of Missouri at St. Louis

http://www.umsl.edu/~philo/

University of Montana

http://www.umt.edu/phil/

University of Montevallo

http://www.mindspring.com/~mfpatton/contents.htm

University of Nebraska-Lincoln

http://www.unl.edu/philosop/

University of New Hampshire

http://www.unh.edu/philosophy/index.html

University of New Haven

http://www.newhaven.edu/UNH/academics/Departments/Philosophy.html

University of New Mexico

http://www.unm.edu/~thinker/

University of New Orleans

http://www.uno.edu/~phil/Welcome.html

University of North Carolina, Chapel Hill

http://www.unc.edu/~unc-phil/

University of North Carolina, Charlotte

http://www.uncc.edu/colleges/arts_and_sciences/philosophy/

University of North Carolina, Wilmington

http://www.uncwil.edu/p&r/

University of North Dakota

http://www.und.nodak.edu/dept/philrel/index.html

University of North Florida

http://www.unf.edu/coas/hpr/

University of North Texas

http://www.phil.unt.edu/

University of Northern Colorado

http://www.univnorthco.edu/philosophy/phil.html

University of Northern Iowa

http://www.uni.edu/philrel/

University of Notre Dame

http://www.nd.edu/~ndphilo/

University of Oklahoma

http://www.ou.edu/cas/ouphil/

University of Oregon

http://metaphor.uoregon.edu/

University of Pennsylvania

http://ccat.sas.upenn.edu/~phil/

University of Pittsburgh

http://www.pitt.edu/~philosop/philosophy.html

University of Portland

http://www.uofport.edu/academicsl/phil.html

University of Puget Sound

http://www.ups.edu/philosophy/index.html

University of Redlands

http://newton.uor.edu/Departments&Programs/PhilosophyDept/Philosophy.html

University of Richmond

http://www.richmond.edu/~philo/

University of Rochester

http://www.cc.rochester.edu:80/College/PHL/

University of Saint Thomas

http://www.stthomas.edu/www/ugacad/phil.html

University of Scranton

http://academic.uofs.edu/department/philosophy/

University of South Alabama

http://www.usouthal.edu/usa/artsandscience/philosop.htm

University of South Carolina

http://www.cla.sc.edu/PHIL/

University of South Florida

http://www.cas.usf.edu/philosophy/index.html

University of Southern California

http://www.usc.edu/dept/LAS/philosophy/

University of Southern Mississippi

http://www-dept.usm.edu/~philrel/phil.html

University of Southwestern Louisiana

http://www.ucs.usl.edu/~isb9112/dept/philosophy.html

University of Tennessee at Chattanooga

http://www.utc.edu/phildept

University of Tennessee at Knoxville

http://funnelweb.utcc.utk.edu/~philosop/

University of Tennessee at Martin

http://www.utm.edu/departments/artsci/ppr/phil/phil.htm.

University of Texas, Arlington

http://www.uta.edu/philosophy/

University of Texas, Austin

http://www.dla.utexas.edu/depts/philosophy/main.html

University of Texas, El Paso

http://www.utep.edu/philos/

University of Texas, San Antonio

http://www.utsa.edu/Academics/COFAH/ECPC/index.htm

University of Toledo

http://www.utoledo.edu/www/philosophy/

University of Tulsa

http://www.utulsa.edu/CollegeofArts&Sciences/philosop/philhome.htm

University of Utah

http://www.hum.utah.edu/philosophy/phil_welcome.html

University of Vermont

http://www.uvm.edu/~phildept/

University of Virginia

http://minerva.acc.Virginia.EDU/~philos/

University of Washington

http://weber.u.washington.edu:80/~dashap/UWPhil/

University of West Florida

http://www.uwf.edu/~logos/

University of Wisconsin, Colleges

http://www.manitowoc.uwc.edu/staff/awhite/uwcphi.htm

University of Wisconsin, Green Bay

http://www.uwgb.edu/www/acad/WWW-DEPT-PHIL.HTML

University of Wisconsin, Madison

http://polyglot.lss.wisc.edu/philosophy/

University of Wisconsin, Milwaukee

http://www.uwm.edu/Dept/Philosophy/

University of Wisconsin, Oshkosh

http://www.uwosh.edu/departments/philosophy/

University of Wisconsin, Parkside

http://www.uwp.edu/academic/philosophy/

University of Wisconsin, Platteville

http://vms.www.uwplatt.edu/~humanities/philosophy.htmlx

University of Wisconsin, Stevens Point

http://www.uwsp.edu/acad/phil/

University of Wisconsin, Stout

http://www.uwstout.edu/english/english.htm

University of Wisconsin, Whitewater

http://www.uww.edu/factsheets/philoso.html

University of Wyoming

http://www.uwyo.edu/A&S/phil/index.htm

Ursinus College

http://www.ursinus.edu/academics/depts/philosophy.html

Utah State University

http://www.usu.edu/~langphil/

Utah Valley State College

http://www.uvsc.edu/depts/academic/hum-phil/

Valdosta State University

http://www.valdosta.peachnet.edu/~rbarnett/phi/

Valparaiso University

http://www.valpo.edu/philosophy/RootPage/OuterSet.html

Vanderbilt University

http://www.vanderbilt.edu/AnS/philosophy/

Vassar College

http://depts.vassar.edu/~philos/philosophy.html

Villanova University

http://www.vill.edu/academic/artsci/arts/philosop/philosoph.htm

Virginia Polytechnic & State University

http://gopher.phil.vt.edu/philpage.html

Virginia Wesleyan College

http://www.vwc.edu/wwwpages/pgoold/philpage.htm

Wake Forest University

http://www.wfu.edu/Academic-departments/Philosophy/

Wartburg College

http://www.wartburg.edu/academics/docs/religion/re11.html

Washburn University

http://www.wuacc.edu/cas/cas_philosophy.shtml

Washington State University

http://134.121.31.99/catalog/academics/phil

Washington University, St. Louis

http://www.artsci.wustl.edu/~philos/index.html

Wayne State University, Detriot

http://www.langlab.wayne.edu/Philosophy/Philosophy.html

Wesleyan University

http://www.wesleyan.edu/phil/home.html

West Chester University

http://www.wcupa.edu/_ACADEMICS/sch_cas.phi/

West Virginia University

http://www.as.wvu.edu/phil

Western Illinois University

http://www.wiu.edu/users/miphil/

Western Kentucky University

http://www2.wku.edu/www/Philosophy/

Western Michigan University

http://www.wmich.edu/philosophy

Westminster College

http://www.westminster.edu/Acad/rhpc/

Westmont College

http://www.westmont.edu/Academics/catalog/Curriculum/Philosophy.html

Wheaton College

http://www.wheaton.edu/PhilosHome.html

William Paterson College

http://www.wilpaterson.edu/wpcpages/sch-hmss/philosophy/default.htp

Williams College

>   *http://www.williams.edu/acad-depts/philosophy/*

Wilson College

>   *http://www.wilson.edu/MAJORS4.HTM#PHR*

Wingate University

>   *http://www.wingate.edu/acad/religionphilo/page1.html*

Wittenberg University

>   *http://www.wittenberg.edu/academics/phil/index.html*

Wofford College

>   *http://truth.wofford.edu/~kaycd/philos.htm*

Worcester State College

>   *http://www.worc.mass.edu/philoso/default.htm*

Wright State University

>   *http://philos.wright.edu/Dept/PHL/PHL.html*

Xavier University of Louisiana

>   *http://www.xula.edu/Academic/as_college/phil_dept/phil.htm*

Yale University

>   *http://www.yale.edu/philos/*

Youngstown State University

>   *http://www.cis.ysu.edu/home/divisions/admin/publication/career_ops/a_s/phil_relstds.html*

Philosophy Departments: South America

Universidad Nacional de La Plata, Argentina

>   *http://www.unlp.edu.ar/pf_filos.htm*

University of Buenos Aires, Argentina

>   *http://www.filo.uba.ar/*

Universidad Catolica, Boliviana, Bolivia

>   *http://www.ucbcba.edu.bo/carreras/filosofia/filosofia.html*

Federal University of Parana, Brazil

>   *http://www.humanas.ufpr.br/defi/default.htm*

Federal University of Rio de Janeiro, Brazil
http://www.cfch.ufrj.br/

Federal University of Santa Catarina, Brazil
http://www.cfh.ufsc.br/~wfil/

Pontificia Universidade Catolica do Parana, Brazil
http://www.pucpr.br/filosofia.html

Pontificia Universidade Catolica do Rio, Brazil
http://www.puc-rio.br/depto/filosof.html

Pontificia Universidade Catolica do Rio Grande do Sul, Brazil
http://music.pucrs.br/~pgfilosofia/http/home.htm

Pontificia Universidade Catolica de Sao Paulo, Brazil
http://www.pucsp.br/areas/cursos/filosof.html

Pontificia Universidad Catolica del Chile, Chile
http://www.puc.cl/facultades/texto/ffilosof.htm

Universidad de Chile, Chile
http://www.uchile.cl/facultades/filosofia/index.html

Universidad de Concepcion, Chile
http://www.udec.cl/postgrado/p2.htm#12

Universidad de La Salle, Santafe de Bogota, Colombia
http://www.lasalle.edu.co/licfillet.html

Universidad Nacional, Costa Rica
http://www.una.ac.cr/filo/

University of Panama, Panama
http://www.up.ac.pa/UnidadesAcademicas/facultad/humanidades/FHLIFI.HTM

El Instituto Superior de Estudios Humanísticos y Filosóficos, Paraguay
http://www.quanta.net/isehf/

Pontificia Universidad Catolica del Peru, Peru
http://www.pucp.edu.pe/www.2.0/acad/acad.human.fil.html

Universidad Católica Andrés Bello, Venezuela
http://www.ucab.edu.ve/UCAB/Facultades/Humanidades/Escuelas/Filosofia/

Philosophy Departments: Directories

Graduate Study

http://www.petersons.com/graduate/select/210005se.html

This is Peterson's guide to graduate studies in philosophy at universities and colleges in the United States.

Philosophy Abroad

http://www.liv.ac.uk/Philosophy/foreign.html

This is Stephen Clark's srlclark@liverpool.ac.uk list of links to philosophy departments outside the UK.

Philosophy Departments Around the World

http://www.sfu.ca/philosophy/otherdpt.htm

From Paul Wong wongas@arp.anu.edu.au, this page provides a comprehensive list of philosophy departments around the world.

Philosophy Departments In...

http://www.rpi.edu/~cearls/phil.departments.html

Sean Cearly cearley@matrix-media.com maintains this list of links to philosophy departments throughout the world.

Philosophy Departments: UK & Ireland

http://www.liv.ac.uk/Philosophy/depts.html

From Stephen Clark srlclark@liverpool.ac.uk, this page provides information and contact details for philosophy departments in the UK and Ireland, including those departments which do not have a presense on the net.

Undergraduate Study in Philosophy

http://www.petersons.com/ugrad/select/u43310se.html

This is Peterson's guide to undergraduate programs in philosophy in the United States, providing information on over 900 four-year college courses.

Universities

http://users.ox.ac.uk/~worc0337/phil_universities.html

This is Peter King's peter.king@philosophy.ox.ac.uk listing of philosophy departments across the world.

Section 4: Discussion Forums

Two types of discussion forums are indexed in this section: mailing lists and newsgroups. While both are public forums, they differ quite markedly in their style and usefulness. See the following information sections for details.

Mailing List Information

Mailing lists are public discussion forums. Unlike newsgroups which can be accessed relatively easily and anonymously, users must first subscribe to a mailing list before they can read any of the messages posted to it (some mailing list software does not prevent unsubscribed users posting messages, but this appears to happen rarely).

Mailing lists are generally set up in order to facilitate discussions of particular topics between interested parties. Mailing lists (sometimes called listservs) use email as the means by which participants take part in discussions, and they are generally managed by software which automates the processing of email messages, ensuring that all those subscribed to the list receive each message sent by other participants.

Mailing lists have two addresses: a subscription address, and a submission address. In order to join a mailing list, one must first send a short email message to the subscription address—more on this in a moment. An automated response is generally sent to subscribers, confirming their subscription and advising of various commands that can be sent to the mailing list software. These commands tell the software to provide information on how to unsubscribe, how to find out who else is subscribed, how to access archives of the list (if any are kept), and so on. All commands (subscribe, unsubscribe, help, etc.) must be sent to the subscription address.

Messages intended for general communication to list participants are sent to the second address, the submission address. It is important to be clear about the distinction between these two addresses, otherwise you could become frustrated in your attempts to unsubcribe from a list, while participants might become annoyed by your sending commands to the submission address.

Where possible, I have provided the name and email address of the owner or moderator of the mailing list. If you are having any difficulties, you should contact them.

There are various types of software that automate mailing list administration. Different software responds to different commands. I have summarised the subscription commands for the most commonly-encountered mailing list software on the following page. Once you have subscribed, your confirmation message from the server will detail the other commands recognised by its particular software. It is a good idea to keep these messages for future reference.

To subscribe to a mailing list whose subscription address indicates majordomo software, the body of your message should read:

> *subscribe listname*
> (e.g., subscribe aesthetics)

Optionally, you can include your email address:

> *subscribe listname your.email.address*
> (e.g., subscribe aethetics <u>dey@silas.cc.monash.edu.au</u>)

To subscribe to a mailing list whose subscription address indicates listserv or listproc software, the body of your message should read:

> *sub listname*
> (e.g., sub activ-l)

Again, you can optionally include your email address, in the same manner as above.

To subscribe to a mailing list whose subscription address indicates mailbase software, the body of your message should read:

> *subscribe listname yourfirstname yourlastname*
> (e.g., subscribe ecotheol dey alexander)

If all else fails, you can always send a help message to the subscription address. In this case the body of your message should simply read:

> *help*

The messages from any mailing list to which you subscribe will arrive in your mailbox like any other email. It is advisable to exercise restraint in subscribing to mailing lists—some have very high levels of activity, and your mailbox can become very full, very quickly!

There are hundreds of mailing lists with a philosophical focus. The following sections of the guide provide details of those currently available, indexed by topic.

Newsgroup Information

Newsgroups on the Internet are public discussion forums referred to collectively as Usenet. There are literally thousands of newsgroups available on the net, covering virtually any topic you could think of. There are numerous philosophy-related newsgroups—listed following the mailing list indexes—but their usefulness varies enormously. One major problem with newsgroups is the phenomenon known as 'crossposting'. Crossposting is the posting of a particular message across a range of newsgroups, most of which have little to do with the topic of the message. This is the electronic version of what we might call 'junk mail'. On the net it is referred to as 'spam'.

Another difficulty with newsgroups is that the discussion is often unmoderated. That is, anyone can post anything to the newsgroup, regardless of whether it bears any relationship to the general topical nature of the group. Some newsgroups are moderated, and posts are diverted electronically to a moderator or moderators who then assess their suitability for forwarding to the newsgroup.

Newsgroups can now be accessed with the current versions of web browsers, though most people tend to prefer to use dedicated newsreader programs, as they are more powerful and versatile (at least at this point in time).

Mailing Lists: Aesthetics

Listname: aesthetics-l
Moderator: Dominic Lopes at dlopes@indiana.edu
Subscribe: majordomo@indiana.edu
Article Submission: aesthetics-l@indiana.edu

A discussion forum on aesthetics. Further information about this list can be obtained at *http://www.indiana.edu/~asanl/net/lists.html*.

Listname: aesthetics
Moderator: Kent Palmer at palmer@think.net
Subscribe: listserv@think.net
Article Submission: aesthetics@think.net

A list for the discussion of aesthetics. A Thinknet BBS and DialogNet philosophy list.

Listname: artcrit
Moderator: Michele Macaluso at macal@nexus.yorku.ca
Subscribe: listserv@yorku.ca
Article Submission: artcrit@yorku.ca

A discussion forum open to anyone interested in the visual arts. Topics will reflect the diversity of art critical discourse, for instance, postmodernism, Marxist and feminist theories, curatorial practices, funding and any issue which affects artists, critics, and art viewers.

Listname: avant-garde
Moderator: Malgosia Askanas at ma@panix.com
Subscribe: majordomo@lists.village.virginia.edu
Article Submission: avant-garde@lists.village.virginia.edu

Avante-garde is an electronic forum for discussing the theory and practice of the avant-garde. It is an open list—all interested parties are invited and encouraged to participate.

Listname: musical-aesthetics
Moderator: Nathan Charlton at seul2@central.sussex.ac.uk
Subscribe: mailbase@mailbase.ac.uk
Article Submission: musical-aesthetics@mailbase.ac.uk

A philosophical discussion of problems in musical aesthetics, and a forum for debating current issues in this field.

Listname: surrealism
Moderator: Kent Palmer at palmer@think.net
Subscribe: listserv@think.net
Article Submission: surrealism@think.net

A list for the discussion of surrealism. A Thinknet BBS and DialogNet philosophy list.

Mailing Lists: Environmental Philosophy

Listname: activ-l
Subscribe: listproc@envirolink.org
Article Submission: activ-1@envirolink.org

This list is concerned with discussion of issues relating to peace, justice, empowerment, and environment.

Listname: austral-ecopolitics-l
Moderator: Dr Kate Crowley at Kate.Crowley@polsci.utas.edu.au
Subscribe: majordomo@coombs.anu.edu.au
Article Submission: austral-ecopolitics-1@coombs.anu.edu.au

This list is for anyone working on, or interested in the study of environmental politics; green movements policies, strategies, origins and history; public opinion and media coverage of environmental issues.

Listname: biosph-l
Subscribe: listserv@listserv.aol.com
Article Submission: biosph-1@listserv.aol.com

A forum for the discussion of anything relating to the biosphere, including pollution, CO_2 effects, ecology, habitat, climate, and so on.

Listname: deep-ecology
Moderator: Kent Palmer at palmer@think.net
Subscribe: listserv@think.net
Article Submission: deep-ecology@think.net

A Dialognet and Thinknet BBS forum for discussing matters pertaining to deep-ecology.

Listname: ecolog-l
Moderator: David W. Inouye at inouye@umail.umd.edu
Subscribe: listserv@umdd.umd.edu
Article Submission: ecolog-l@umdd.umd.edu

This is the discussion list for the Ecological Society of America. Information distributed on this list includes grants, jobs, and news.

Listname: ecology
Moderator: Kent Palmer at palmer@think.net
Subscribe: listserv@think.net
Article Submission: ecology@think.net

A Dialognet and Thinknet BBS forum for discussing the philosophy of ecology.

Listname: ecol-econ
Moderator: Will Toor at toor@csf.colorado.edu
Subscribe: listserv@csf.colorado.edu
Article Submission: ecol-econ@csf.colorado.edu

This list is for the discussion of ecological economics. It is founded on the idea that it is necessary to have major change in the way we think about economics if we intend to make a credible response to the environmental threats to the planet.

Listname: ecotheol
Moderator: Ian Tilsed at i.j.tilsed@.ex.ac.uk
Subscribe: mailbase@mailbase.ac.uk
Article Submission: ecotheol@mailbase.ac.uk

Ecology and Theology is a forum for discussion of ecological theology. The goal of the list is to enable academic discussion of environmental issues from a theological or ethical perspective.

Listname: egt
Subscribe: listproc@csf.colorado.edu
Article Submission: egt@csf.colorado.edu

This list facilitates a discussion of game theory and the environment.

Listname: enviroethics
Moderator: Clare Palmer at c.a.palmer@greenwich.ac.uk
                 Ian Tilsed at i.j.tilsed@exeter.ac.uk
Subscribe: mailbase@mailbase.ac.uk
Article Submission: enviroethics@mailbase.ac.uk

This list is a forum for academic discussion of environmental ethics and philosophy. Topics for discussion range from value theory to applied ethics in an environmental context. The list is open to anyone with an academic interest in environmental ethics and contributions from those in a range of disciplines as well as philosophy are welcome.

Listname: envtecsoc
Subscribe: listproc@csf.colorado.edu
Article Submission: envtecsoc@csf.colorado.edu

This mailing list is for the discussion of environment, technology and society.

Mailing Lists: Ethics & Bioethics

Listname: aaashran
Moderator: emunoz@aaas.org
Subscribe: listserv@gwuvm.gwu.edu
Article Submission: aaashran@gwuvm.gwu.edu

This is the American Association for the Advancement of Science, Human Rights Action Network mailing list. More information on the Network can be found at *http://www.aaas.org/ spp/dspp/shr/shr.htm.*

Listname: activ-l
Subscribe: listproc@envirolink.org
Article Submission: activ-l@envirolink.org

This list is concerned with discussion of issues relating to peace, justice, empowerment, and environment.

Listname: ar-news
Moderator: Allen Schubert at alathome@clark.net
Subscribe: listproc@envirolink.org
Article Submission: ar-news@envirolink.org

The purpose of this list is to provide mechanisms for the exchange of ideas and information pertaining to the issues of animal rights and welfare.

Listname: ar-views
Moderator: Hillary Morris at oceana@ibm.net
Subscribe: listproc@envirolink.org
Article Submission: ar-news@envirolink.org

The purpose of this list is to provide mechanisms for the exchange of ideas and information pertaining to the issues of animal rights and welfare.

Listname: biomed-l
Moderator: Michelle Francl at MFRANCL@brynmawr.edu

Subscribe: listserv@listserv.nodak.edu
Article Submission: biomed-l@listserv.nodak.edu

This list provides for discussion of the broad range of topics relevant to biomedical ethics.

Listname: cei-l
Moderator: Patrick Sullivan at psullivan@brook.edu
Frank Connolly at frank@american.edu
Ramon Barquin at rbarquin@aol.com
Subscribe: listserv@american.edu
Article Submission: cei-l@american.edu

This is the listserv for the Computer Ethics Institute, a non-profit, education and policy study organization interested in ethical issues arising from the development of information technology. Issues of interest include: user-specific concerns, security, privacy and community, general ethics and technology, and so on. The CEI has a broad constituency including business, education, religious, philosophical, computer profession and public policy communities, and welcomes participation from anyone interested. For more information about the list and the Institute, see *http://www.brook.edu/sscc/cei/cei_hp.htm.*

Listname: clone
Subscribe: mailbase@mailbase.ac.uk
Article Submission: clone@mailbase.ac.uk

This list has been established for academics and researchers in the UK and elsewhere to discuss all issues relating to human cloning particularly moral and social aspects. Archives and other list information is available at *http://www.mailbase.ac.uk/lists/clone/.*

Listname: cpae
Moderator: Ron Barnette at rbarnett@grits.valdosta.peachnet.edu
Subscribe: listserv@catfish.valdosta.peachnet.edu
Article Submission: cpae@catfish.valdosta.peachnet.edu

An academic forum for the discussion of issues related to professional and applied ethics, administered by the Center for Professional and Applied Ethics.

Listname: cryonet
Moderator: Kevin Q. Brown at kqb@cryonet.org
Subscribe: majordomo@cryonet.org
Article Submission: cryonet@cryonet.org

The cryonics mailing list (CryoNet) is a forum for topics related to cryonics, which include technical reports of cryopreservations, low temperature biology, mechanisms of freezing injury and progress in avoiding it, legal status of cryonics and cryopreserved people, new research and publications, conferences, mass media coverage of cryonics, local cryonics group meetings, and even the philosophical issues that cryonics raises. More information about the list can be found at: *http://www.c2.org/~kqb/cryonet.html.*

Listname: egoism
Moderator: David G. McDivitt at mcdivitt@iamerica.net
Subscribe: listserv@maelstrom.stjohns.edu
Article Submission: egoism@maelstrom.stjohns.edu

The egoism and morality discussion list is for discussion of the following: egoism as a philosophy; various moral systems; inherent morality; ethics and morality from an egoist perspective; self and identity; control; and current events and topics for people of like mind.

Listname: enviroethics
Moderator: Clare Palmer at c.a.palmer@greenwich.ac.uk
              Ian Tilsed at i.j.tilsed@exeter.ac.uk
Subscribe: mailbase@mailbase.ac.uk
Article Submission: enviroethics@mailbase.ac.uk

This list is a forum for academic discussion of environmental ethics and philosophy. Topics for discussion range from value theory to applied ethics in an environmental context. The list is open to anyone with an academic interest in environmental ethics and contributions from those in a range of disciplines, as well as philosophy, are welcome.

Listname: ethics
Moderator: Kent Palmer at palmer@think.net
Subscribe: listserv@think.net
Article Submission: ethics@think.net

This list is a DialogNet forum for the discussion of ethics.

Listname: fab
Moderator: Corinne Bekker at cbekker@phil.ruu.nl
Subscribe: fab-request@phil.ruu.nl
Article Submission: fab@phil.ruu.nl

This list is for the discussion of Feminist Approaches to Bio-ethics. Its purpose is for the exchange of information and discussion on research related issues. Calls for papers, references, job postings, and the like are welcome. The list was initiated by a few members of the Network for Feminist Approaches to Bio-ethics. Anyone interested in joining the network should contact Anne Donchin at ista100@indycms.bitnet.

Listname: gen-ethics
Moderator: Gilles Frydman at gilles@dorsai.org
Subscribe: listserv@acor.org
Article Submission: gen-ethics@acor.org

This list is for the discussion of the ethical, legal, and policy implications of the Genome Project and its clinical applications.

Listname: g-ethic
Moderator: Dr. Ingrid Schafer at facshaferi@mercur.usao.edu
Subscribe: listserv@vm.temple.edu
Article Submission: g-ethic@vm.temple.edu

This list co-ordinates the work of thinkers, scholars, and activists from around the world working to develop and implement a global ethic.

Listname: ideal
Moderator: Jay Drydyk at jdydyk@alfred.carleton.ca
Subscribe: listprocessor@cunews.carleton.ca
Article Submission: ideal@cunews.carleton.ca

This is the mailing list for the International Development Ethics Association. Ideal provides a medium for worldwide exchange of information, news, views, and work in the field of development ethics, including but not restricted to members of the International Development Ethics Association.

Listname: jscope
Subscribe: majordomo@acpub.duke.edu
Article Submission: jscope@acpub.duke.edu

Jscope is maintained by the Joint Services Conference on Professional Ethics, and is devoted to the discussion of issues in military ethics.

Listname: phil-action-l
Moderator: Christian Perring at cperring@ukcc.uky.edu
Subscribe: listserv@lsv.uky.edu
Article Submission: phil-action-l@lsv.uky.edu

The main topic for discussion on this mailing list is the philosophy of action. Other possible topics include the nature of autonomy and free will, philosophical issues in the explanation of action in psychology or the social sciences, moral psychology and ethical theory. Set up for people familiar with the basic literature in the area, the list will involve announcements, discussion, and substantive reviews of new literature in the field. Ideally, the list will be especially useful for those doing research in this area with little opportunity to engage in discussion with others on these topics.

Listname: soceth-l
Moderator: Aditi Gowri at gowri@scf.usc.edu
David Edward Armstrong at dearms@scf.usc.edu
Subscribe: listproc@usc.edu
Article Submission: soceth-l@usc.edu

Social Ethics is a forum for interdisciplinary approaches to social ethics. Topics of discussion include: major traditions of ethical thought, values and moral and cultural norms, professional ethics and public policy, and so on. Sponsored by the University of Southern California.

Mailing Lists: Feminism & Women's Studies

Listname: abigails-l
Moderator: Jennifer Gagliardi at gagliajn@netcom.com
Subscribe: listserv@netcom.com
Article Submission: abigails-l@netcom.com

Abigails-l is a mailing list named in honour of Abigail Adams, woman of letters, American patriot, businesswoman, wife, and mother who is quoted as saying "We are determined to foment a rebellion, and will not hold ourselves bound by any law in which we have no voice or representation." Abigails-l is an activist list, dedicated to gaining full and equal women's rights through immediate actions.

Listname: araca
Moderator: Mabel Campagnoli at owner-araca@ccc.uba.ar
Subscribe: majordomo@ccc.uba.ar
Article Submission: araca@ccc.uba.ar

Araca is a open, self-moderated mailing list devoted to gender and women studies. The contributions are only in Spanish. The main purpose of this list is the exchange of information and experiences, and the discussion of relevant topics.

Listname: ecofem
Moderator: Priya Kurain and Stefanie Rixecker
Subscribe: listproc@csf.colorado.edu
Article Submission: ecofem@csf.colorado.edu

Ecofem is an unmoderated forum in which a variety of viewpoints concerning women and the environment can be discussed. These include the wide-ranging views of feminism (liberal, radical, socialist, postmodern, and yours) and the multi-hued 'environment'.

Listname: fab
Moderator: Corinne Bekker at cbekker@phil.ruu.nl
Subscribe: fab-request@phil.ruu.nl
Article Submission: fab@phil.ruu.nl

This list is for the discussion of Feminist Approaches to Bio-ethics. Its purpose is for the exchange of information and discussion on research related issues. Calls for papers, references, job postings and the like are welcome. The list was initiated by a few members of the Network for Feminist Approaches to Bio-ethics.

Listname: femisa
Moderator: Welling Hall at wellingh@earlham.edu
Greg Kelson at gkelson@kentlaw.edu
Subscribe: listproc@csf.colorado.edu

Article Submission: femisa@csf.colorado.edu

This list is for the discussion of feminist international issues. More information about the list and its sponsors—the Feminist Theory and Gender Studies Section (FTGSS) of the International Studies Association—is available from: *http://csf.Colorado.EDU/isa/ftgs/.*

Listname: femjur
Moderator: Mark Folmsbee at zzfolm@acc.wuacc.edu
                          Michelle Rabouin at zzrabo@acc.wuacc.edu
Subscribe: listserv@assocdir.wuacc.edu
Article Submission: femjur@assocdir.wuacc.edu

The list provides a forum for discussing theories and issues regarding feminism and women and law. It is also a good place to share research questions, scholarship, calls for papers, job announcements, and provide support for people working in this area of law.

Listname: fmst-talk
Moderator: Lynne Alice at l.c.alice@massey.ac.nz
Subscribe: majordomo@massey.ac.nz
Article Submission: fmst-talk@massey.ac.nz

This is a list for subscribers to FMST (Feminist Studies in Aotearoa Electronic Journal). The list offers the opportunity to give feedback on FMST journal articles, make comments on its topic areas, communicate with other subscribers, and make your views and research known. Because it augments FMST, it is not a general discussion list. It is unmoderated, but its success depends on subscribers confining comments to issues related to materials or view expressed in FMST.

Listname: french-feminism
Moderator: Spoon Collective at spoons@jefferson.village.virginia.edu
Subscribe: majordomo@jefferson.village.virginia.edu
Article Submission: french-feminism@jefferson.village.virginia.edu

This list, sponsored by the Spoon Collective, is for the discussion of French feminism.

Listname: intlwom-1
Moderator: Usha Venkatachallam at usha@chuck.acc-lab.american.edu
Subscribe: listserv@american.edu
Article Submission: intlwom-1@american.edu

This is a gathering place for anyone interested in looking at gender issues from cross-cultural perspectives. Originally started as a support network for the International Women's Group of American University, now the list is open to all audiences, far and wide. The list seeks to raise awareness about specific issues affecting international women, promote cross-cultural understanding, and provide a network of support and friendship for women of all nations.

Listname: libfem
Moderator: Thomas Gramstad at thomasg@ifi.uio.no
Subscribe: majordomo@ifi.uio.no
Article Submission: libfem@ifi.uio.no

Liberty and Feminism is a discussion forum for issues relating to the classical liberty and individual rights perspective as applied to feminist issues. For more information see: *http://www.math.uio.no/~thomas/lists/lists.html.*

Listname: paglia-l
Moderator: Boyd Holmes at bpholmes@ac.dal.ca
Subscribe: mailserv@ac.dal.ca
Article Submission: paglia-l@ac.dal.ca

This list is devoted to the exploration of the writings and ideas of Camille Paglia, Professor of the Humanities at the University of the Arts in Philadelphia. Camille Paglia is the author of the books *Sexual Personae: Art and Decadence from Nefertiti to Emily Dickinson* (1990) and *Sex, Art, and American Culture* (1992). She is currently completing the second volume of *Sexual Personae,* and remains one of the most controversial classroom subjects in the field of women's studies.

Listname: randian-feminism
Moderator: Thomas Gramstad at thomas@math.uio.no
Subscribe: majordomo@ifi.uio.no
Article Submission: randian-feminism@ifi.uio.no

The Randian-Feminism mailing list is a forum for Objectivist Feminists and Randian Feminists—people who share a common interest in Feminist philosophy, issues, and perspectives, and in Ayn Rand's ideas and philosophy. Archives and further information can be obtained at *http://www.math.uio.no/~thomas/lists/randian-feminism.html.*

Listname: swip-l
Moderator: Linda McAllister at dllafaa@cfrvm.cfr.usf.edu
Subscribe: listserv@cfrvm.cfr.usf.edu
Article Submission: swip-l@cfrvm.cfr.usf.edu

The messages on the Society for Women In Philosophy list are mostly informational in nature: calls for papers in feminist philosophy, announcements of SWIP meetings and other conferences, requests for references, or information. A SWIP-L file of course syllabi in feminist philosophy is maintained and is retrievable by the list members. The list is an appropriate place for substantive discussion of issues and controversies within feminist philosophy.

Listname: vs-online-strat
Moderator: Scarlet Pollock & Jo Sutton at vsister@igc.apc.org
Subscribe: majordomo@igc.apc.org

Article Submission: <u>vs-online-strat@igc.apc.org</u>

This mailing list provides a place to link up globally with women (and men) to discuss issues directly related to our struggles and successes in getting women's information, ideas, and perspectives online. This list is supported by Virtual Sisterhood, a global electronic support network dedicated to increasing women's access to and effective use of electronic communications.

Listname: wisp-l
Subscribe: <u>listserv@iubvm.ucs.indiana.edu</u>
Article Submission: <u>wisp-l@iubvm.ucs.indiana.edu</u>

This list provides a discussion forum for women in scholarly publishing.

Listname: wmst-l
Subscribe: <u>listserv@umdd.umd.edu</u>
Article Submission: <u>wmst-l@umdd.umd.edu</u>

This list serves academic and professional needs of people involved in Women's Studies teaching, research, libraries, and programs.

Listname: women
Moderator: Hatice Kubra Bahsisoglu at <u>kubra@hun.tr</u>
            Mujgan San at <u>msan@hun.edu.tr</u>
Subscribe: <u>listproc@bilkent.edu.tr</u>
Article Submission: <u>women@bilkent.edu.tr</u>

Women aims to be a communication medium for people interested in women's issues in Turkey, in developing countries, and all over the world. The list accepts messages in English and Turkish, and is intended primarily to serve the academic and professional needs of people involved in women's issues and gender as researchers, librarians, or program administrators, particularly in developing countries.

Listname: womens-studies
Moderator: Kent Palmer at <u>palmer@think.net</u>
Subscribe: <u>listserv@think.net</u>
Article Submission: <u>womens-studies@think.net</u>

A Thinknet BBS philosophy list facilitating the discussion of issues relevant to women's studies.

Listname: womenz-l
Moderator: <u>womenz8@womenz.net.au</u>
Subscribe: <u>majordomo@womenz.net.au</u>
Article Submission: <u>womenz-l@womenz.net.au</u>

Womenz-l is a moderated feminist/women's list located in Australia. For more information check out the Womenz Website at: *http://www.womenz.net.au/*.

Mailing Lists: General & Miscellaneous

Listname: aapt-l
Moderator: Robert Timko at rtimko@mnsfld.edu
Subscribe: listserv@lsv.uky.edu
Article Submission: aapt-l@lsv.uky.edu

The American Association of Philosophy Teachers maintains AAPT-L whose primary focus is the discussion and exchange of ideas about teaching philosophy at all levels and in all venues.

Listname: abtapl
Subscribe: mailbase@mailbase.ac.uk
Article Submission: abtapl@mailbase.ac.uk

This is the mailing list of the Association of British Theological and Philosophical Libraries. The list will be used as a forum for professional exchange and development in the fields of theological and philosophical librarianship. Archives and more information are available at *http:/www.mailbase.ac.uk/lists/abtapl/*.

Listname: afri-phil
Moderator: Emmanuel Eze at eeze@bucknell.edu
Bruce B. Janz at janzb@augustana.ab.ca
Frank Wilson at fwilson@bucknell.edu
Subscribe: listserv@bucknell.edu
Article Submission: afri-phil@bucknell.edu

AFRI-PHIL is for the discussion of topics related to the philosophy of African society and history, its current issues, and future directions. This list provides a forum for the exchange of views, experiences, techniques, and professional information pertaining to the teaching and study of the philosophical thought of African and African-diaspora cultures. The principal emphasis of the list is upon the philosophical examination of African thought and culture. Further information on the list can be found at: *http://www.idot.aol.com/mld/pro duction/yiaz1184.html*.

Listname: analyst
Moderator: analysis@sheffield.ac.uk
Subscribe: listproc@sheffield.ac.uk
Article Submission: analyst@sheffield.ac.uk

A list for discussion of the journal *Analysis*. For more information see the *Analysis* home page at: *http://www.shef.ac.uk/uni/academic/N-Q/phil/analysis/homepage.html*.

Listname: analyst-lyte
Moderator: analysis@sheffield.ac.uk
Subscribe: listproc@sheffield.ac.uk

Article Submission: analyst-lyte@sheffield.ac.uk

A cut-down version of the list above, posting only news and brief updates concerning the journal *Analysis* and its accompanying website at: *http://www.shef.ac.uk/uni/academic/N-Q/phil/analysis/homepage.html.*

Listname: analytic
Moderator: Rodrigo Vanegas at vanegas@shore.net
Subscribe: analytic-request@shore.net
Article Submission: analytic@shore.net

Analytic is a public and moderated mailing list for the discussion of analytical philosophy, its history, its literature, and other topics of related interest. The criteria for the moderation of the list are little more than a check for common courtesy and the rules of netiquette. The intended audience is anyone who is well acquainted with at least a few of the basic philosophical writings in the analytic tradition. Students and professors, professionals and amateurs, are all welcome.

Listname: analytic-philosophy
Moderator: Kent Palmer at palmer@think.net
Subscribe: listserv@think.net
Article Submission: analytic-philosophy@think.net

A Thinknet BBS philosophy list facilitating the discussion of issues relating to analytic philosophy.

Listname: animus
Subscribe: listserv@morgan.ucs.mun.ca
Article Submission: animus@morgan.ucs.mun.ca

Animus—philosophy in the third millennium.

Listname: apacic-l
Moderator: APALIST@cmsa.Berkeley.edu
Subscribe: listserv@cmsa.berkeley.edu
Article Submission: apacic-l@cmsa.berkeley.edu

Apacic-l is an electronic center of international communication and exchange established by the Committee for International Cooperation (CIC) of the American Philosophical Association (APA). APACIC-L will operate on two different levels: 1) The direct distribution through e-mail of news, information, and notices of interest to the international and transnational philosophical community, and including exchange on ideas, problems, experiences, as well as differences and interrelations of philosophical focus and development at the local and national levels; 2) Establishment of an archive of papers and articles of an analytic and/or descriptive philosophical nature that may be of interest to the philosophical community on these or related issues.

Listname: aphil-l
Subscribe: majordomo@coombs.anu.edu.au
Article Submission: aphil-l@coombs.anu.edu.au

An excellent mailing list maintained by the Philosophy Program, Research School of Social Sciences, Australian National University, for people working in philosophy and related disciplines in the Australasian region. Overseas participants are asked to respect the regional nature of the forum.

Listname: app-list
Subscribe: majordomo@explode.unsw.edu.au
Article Submission: majordomo@explode.unsw.edu.au
app-list@explode.unsw.edu.au

The Australian Philosophy Postgraduates list is a mailing list for philosophy graduate students which was conceived following discussions at the 1994 Australasian Philosophy Postgrad Conference. The idea of the list is to allow the organisers of future conferences an easy means of communication with philosophy postgrads, as well as to facilitate a broader discussion amongst participants.

Listname: autopoiesis
Moderator: Kent Palmer at palmer@think.net
Subscribe: listserv@think.net
Article Submission: autopoiesis@think.net

This list is aimed at providing a discussion of the theory of self-organising systems and autopoiesis (self-production) of Maturana and Varela. A Thinknet BBS and DialogNet philosophy list.

Listname: books
Moderator: Kristoffer Kvello at holger@hedda.uio.no
Subscribe: books-request@math.uio.no
Article Submission: books@math.uio.no

This list is designed for seminars on selected books in philosophy. The first such had as its focus Hegel's *Phenomenology of Spirit*.

Listname: cirla-l
Moderator: Ross Emmett at emmer@augustana.ab.ca
Bruce Janz at janzb@augustana.ab.ca
Subscribe: cirla-l-request@agustana.ab.ca
Article Submission: cirla-l@augustana.ab.ca

This is an electronic mailing list for interdisciplinary dialogue on all matters related to the liberal arts and sciences.

Listname: creativity
Moderator: Kent Palmer at palmer@think.net
Subscribe: listserv@think.net
Article Submission: creativity@think.net

Discussion of philosophical questions related to creativity and creativity within philosophy, science, and the arts. A Thinknet BBS philosophy list which is part of DialogNet.

Listname: critical-theory
Subscribe: listserv@uci.edu
Article Submission: critical-theory@uci.edu

This is a distribution list of the Critical Theory Institute's calendar of activities, general information, and work in progress.

Listname: crtnet
Moderator: Tom Benson at t3b@psuvm.psu.edu
Subscribe: listserv@psuvm.psu.edu
Article Submission: crtnet@psuvm.psu.edu

This list discusses all aspects of human communication.

Listname: cybermind
Subscribe: listserv@listserv.aol.com
Article Submission: cybermind@listserv.aol.com

This list discusses the philosophy and psychology of cyberspace.

Listname: epistemology
Moderator: Kent Palmer at palmer@think.net
Subscribe: listserv@think.net
Article Submission: epistemology@think.net

A Thinknet BBS philosophy list facilitating the discussion of epistemological issues.

Listname: existentialism
Moderator: Kent Palmer at palmer@think.net
Subscribe: listserv@think.net
Article Submission: existentialism@think.net

A Thinknet BBS philosophy list facilitating the discussion of issues relevant to existentialist philosophy and thought.

Listname: film-philosophy
Moderator: List Owner at film-philosophy-request@mailbase.ac.uk

Subscribe: mailbase@mailbase.ac.uk
Article Submission: film-philosophy@mailbase.ac.uk

Film-philosophy is an 'email salon' which anticipates the following areas to be within the range of its discussions: film stories, actions and events that illustrate, rehearse, or advance our understanding of traditional philosophical problems; film as philosophy; film as a continuous present; the meanings of reflexive cinema; the ontology of the moving image; and more. More information about the list can be obtained at: *http://www.mailbase.ac.uk/ lists/film-philosophy/files.*

Listname: fnord-l
Moderator: Patrick G. Salsbury at salsbury@acsu.buffalo.edu
Subscribe: listserv@listserv.acsu.buffalo.edu
Article Submission: fnord-l@listserv.acsu.buffalo.edu

A very generic philosophy-related list with widely varying and ranging subject matter.

Listname: hermeneutics
Moderator: Kent Palmer at palmer@think.net
Subscribe: listserv@think.net
Article Submission: hermeneutics@think.net

A Thinknet BBS philosophy list facilitating the discussion of issues relevant to hermeneutics.

Listname: humgrad
Moderator: Stuart Lee at stuart@vax.ox.ac.uk
             Gavin Burnage at gburnage@natcorp.ox.ac.uk
Subscribe: mailbase@mailbase.ac.uk
Article Submission: humgrad@mailbase.ac.uk

Humgrad is a UK-based electronic mailing list for postgraduates working in the humanities. It's a forum for the exchange of ideas, information, and comment on any humanities subject and the work and problems of postgraduates. Subscribing to it will put you in touch with people across the UK and beyond who have interests and difficulties similar to your own. A big advantage of a list for postgraduates is that it provides the opportunity to ask questions away from the minefield of the academic high ground. As well as being a place for general humanities discussion, Humgrad might be able to help you discover the potential of computers in humanities research, even if your computing skills and interests are currently minimal.

Listname: indian-philosophy
Moderator: Kent Palmer at palmer@think.net
Subscribe: listserv@think.net
Article Submission: indian-philosophy@think.net

A Thinknet BBS philosophy list facilitating the discussion of topics in Indian philosophy.

Listname: klein
Moderator: Lance Fletcher at lance.fletcher@freelance.com
Subscribe: listserv@freelance.com

This list is devoted to a slow reading of Jacob Klein's seminal work "Greek Mathematical Thought and the Origin of Algebra."

Listname: listhink
Moderator: Richard Jones at LisThink-owner@usa.net
Subscribe: *http://www.geocities.com/Heartland/4091/*
Article Submission: *http://www.geocities.com/Heartland/4091/*

LisThink is a philosophy discussion list intended for everyone, including those new to philosophy. Discussions are on a range of philosophical topics.

Listname: literature
Moderator: Kent Palmer at palmer@think.net
 Subscribe: listserv@think.net
Article Submission: literature@think.net

This list focuses on discussion of the philosophy of literature. A Thinknet BBS and DialogNet philosophy list.

Listname: love-wisdom-cmc
Moderator: Lance Fletcher at lance.fletcher@freelance.com
Subscribe: listserv@freelance.com
Article Submission: love-wisdom-cmc@freelance.com

Love, Wisdom, and the Internet was created with the intention "to look at what has been going on in the way of philosophical conversation online for the last few years and see what we can discover about its potential for empowering independent thinking and revitalizing liberal education."

Listname: merton-l
Moderator: Ermel Stepp at estepp@byrd.mu.wvnet.edu
Subscribe: listserv@wvnvm.wvnet.edu
Article Submission: merton-l@wvnvm.wvnet.edu

This discussion forum was formed for substantive discourse on research and scholarly inquiry to create and develop knowledge about the contemplative life.

Listname: metaphysics
Moderator: Kent Palmer at palmer@think.net
Subscribe: listserv@think.net
Article Submission: metaphysics@think.net

A Thinknet BBS philosophy list facilitating the discussion of issues in metaphysics.

Listname: midsouth
Moderator: Jack Purcell at jpurcell@frank.mtsu.edu
Subscribe: listproc@frank.mtsu.edu
Article Submission: midsouth@frank.mtsu.edu

This is a forum for discussion of the annual MidSouth philosophy conference. More information about the conference and this discussion list can be obtained at: *http://frank.mtsu.edu/~jpurcell/MidSouth/midsouth.html.*

Listname: myth
Moderator: Kent Palmer at palmer@think.net
Subscribe: listserv@think.net
Article Submission: myth@think.net

A mailing list for the discussion of the philosophy of myth, and the myth of philosophy. A Thinknet BBS and DialogNet philosophy list.

Listname: new-articles
Moderator: Francoise Boller at prismx@earthlink.net
Subscribe: prismx@earthlink.net
Article Submission: read only list

This is a free weekly listing of new articles appearing in selected major English language periodicals. The selection emphasises articles of interest to a multi-national university educated audience and is arranged in the following categories:

1. Literature and the Arts
2. History, Politics, Economics, Philosophy
3. Culture, Social Issues, Psychology
4. Science and Technology.

At the present time approximately 100 different sources are reviewed, with each weekly issue of the list featuring 5 to 10 major periodicals, and approximately 50 to 100 cited articles. This is therefore not an exhaustive index, but access to it is convenient and immediate.

Listname: nihilism
Moderator: Kent Palmer at palmer@think.net
Subscribe: listserv@think.net
Article Submission: nihilism@think.net

A list providing for a discussion of nihilism. A Thinknet BBS and DialogNet philosophy list.

Listname: objectivism
Moderator: Paul Vixie at paul@vix.com
Subscribe: objectivism-request@vix.com
Article Submission: objectivism@vix.com

This mailing list is open to discussion of any aspect of Objectivism, including its application to current events.

Listname: objectivism
Moderator: Chris Catchcart
Subscribe: listserv@whitman.edu
Article Submission: objectivism@whitman.edu

This list provides unmoderated forum for discussion related to the philosophy of Ayn Rand.

Listname: objectivism-l
Moderator: Kirez Korgan at kirez@cornell.edu
Subscribe: listproc@cornell.edu
Article Submission: objectivism-l@cornell.edu

Objectivism-l is a moderated email discussion forum for the philosophy of Objectivism, which originated in the work of Ayn Rand. A web page providing information and archives from the list can be found at *http://www.people.cornell.edu/pages/kjk6/list.html*.

Listname: ontology
Moderator: Kent Palmer at palmer@think.net
Subscribe: listserv@think.net
Article Submission: ontology@think.net

A Thinknet BBS philosophy list facilitating the discussion of ontology and related issues.

Listname: pd-games
Moderator: Thomas Gramstad at thomas@math.uio.no
Subscribe: pd-games-request@math.uio.no
Article Submission: pd-games@math.uio.no

A mailing list for the discussion of games theory, especially Prisoners' Dilemma type problems. Technical issues and questions, as well as discussion of scientific applications and political and ideological aspects and consequences of game theory are welcome.

Listname: phenomenology
Moderator: Kent Palmer at palmer@think.net
Subscribe: listserv@think.net
Article Submission: phenomenology@think.net

A Thinknet BBS philosophy list facilitating the discussion of issues relevant to phenomenology.

Listname: phil-action-l
Moderator: Christian Perring at cperring@ukcc.uky.edu
Subscribe: listserv@lsv.uky.edu
Article Submission: phil-action-l@lsv.uky.edu

The main topic for discussion on this mailing list is the philosophy of action. Other possible topics include the nature of autonomy and free will, philosophical issues in the explanation of action in psychology or the social sciences, moral psychology and ethical theory. Set up for people familiar with the basic literature in the area, the list will involve announcements, discussion and substantive reviews of new literature in the field. Ideally, the list will be especially useful for those doing research in this area with little opportunity to engage in discussion with others on these topics.

Listname: philclub
Subscribe: philclub-request@umassd.edu
Article Submission: philclub@umassd.edu

This is a philosophy discussion list for undergraduates. Graduate departments of philosophy are invited to post program descriptions and updates, and undergraduate philosophy journals are invited to post calls for papers.

Listname: philcomm
Subscribe: listserv@vm.its.rpi.edu
Article Submission: philcomm@vm.its.rpi.edu

This conference offers a forum for the discussion of the philosophy of communication, communication theory, and epistemology.

Listname: phil-counsel
Moderator: Lance Fletcher at lance.fletcher@freelance.com
Subscribe: listserv@freelance.com
Article Submission: phil-counsel@freelance.com

This list is for the discussion of philosophical counselling, philosophical practice, or applied philosophy, and for communication among persons involved or interested in these approaches to philosophy. Archives of this list are available at: *http://www.freelance.com.*

Listname: phil-lit
Moderator: Andreas Ramos at andreas@andreas.com
Subscribe: listserv@listserv.tamu.eu
Article Submission: phil-lit@listserv.tamu.edu

An electronic symposium on topics in the field surveyed by the interdisciplinary journal *Philosophy and Literature* published by Johns Hopkins University Press. Subscribers receive news, job and book announcements, calls for papers, and conference plans. They post queries, trade information, offer advice, preview drafts of articles and reviews, dispute, praise, congratulate, insult, refute, and defend one another.

Listname: phillitcrit
Moderator: Reg Lilly at rlilly@scott.skidmore.edu
Subscribe: majordomo@lists.village.virginia.edu

Article Submission: phillitcrit@lists.village.virginia.edu

This is an electronic forum where individuals may freely exchange ideas concerning philosophy and literature. No canon, 'anti-canon' or other orthodoxy is presupposed or imposed. It is the hope of the initiators of this list that through open and thoughtful exchange participants may develop and deepen their enjoyment and appreciation of philosophy and literature, broadly-conceived, and particularly of the issues and horizons of inquiry that these share. There will be ample room for the full spectrum of conversational modalities, from light-hearted aside to scholarly exegesis to 'metacritical' discussions.

Listname: philofi-l
Moderator: Maria Loren at mloren@newciv.org
Subscribe: majordomo@newciv.org
Article Submission: philofi-l@newciv.org

This is the philosophy of fiction list where discussions mainly concentrate on the question of how philosophical concepts can be conveyed in the form of stories in general and how the storytelling of past writers, from Aesop and Buddha to Voltaire and Heinlein, has influenced today's cultures and perspectives.

Listname: philos-action
Moderator: Angelo Caiazzo at angelo@shadow.net
Subscribe: send personal and professional information to philosaction@coollist.com
Article Submission: details provided on subscription

Philos-action is a mailing list devoted to approaching contemporary problems philosophically. "Philos-action aims to be a place to collect, organise, and then utilise the reflections of the world's greatest thinkers in application to the problems of the present. The emphasis will be on the 'issues' we all feel relevant, not issues particular to a certain interest group or facet of the population. Hence our topics, which will be debated with a view to follow-up action—in the form of organised movements, joint research programmes, and international cooperations—will come from our waking life, from our newspaper headlines, from the methods and conclusions of our most recent scientific releases."

Listname: philos-l
Moderator: Stephen Clark at srlclark@liverpool.ac.uk
Subscribe: listproc@liverpool.ac.uk
Article Submission: philos-l@liverpool.ac.uk

An email conference for philosophers in the United Kingdom to discuss matters of mutual concern, and to encourage other the participation of other philosophers in electronic communications. Archives of the list can be obtained from *http://listserv.liv.ac.uk/archives/philos-1.html.*

Listname: philosop
Moderator: Istvan Berkeley at istvan@usl.edu

Subscribe: majordomo@usl.edu
Article Submission: philosop@usl.edu

A general list for the discussion of philosophy. Its purpose is to provide an easy, informal, and fast way for people interested in academic philosophy to exchange anything relevant that cab be exchanged via this medium, and, taking that as given, to keep reasonably large the ratio of utility to volume. More information about the list can be found at its new website at: *http://www.usl.edu/Departments/Philosophy/philosop.html.*

Listname: philosophy
Moderator: Kent Palmer at palmer@think.net
Subscribe: listserv@think.net
Article Submission: philosophy@think.net

A general list for the discussion of philosophy at the Thinknet site. This list supports all discussions that do not have specific lists at this site. A Thinknet BBS and DialogNet philosophy list.

Listname: philosophy
Moderator: Lance Fletcher at lance.fletcher@freelance.com
Subscribe: listserv@freelance.com
Article Submission: philosophy@freelance.com

This list is for general discussion about the nature of philosophy, the state of the philosophical profession, and for discussion of philosophical topics for which no topic-related list exists. It is the appropriate place for discussions that are deemed inappropriate for lists like philosop which are primarily for professional announcements.

Listname: philosophy-newbooks
Moderator: philosophy@routledge.com
Subscribe: majordomo@list.thomson.com
Article Submission: no submissions, announcements only

This is a Routledge Current Awareness list for announcements of new philosophy titles published by Routledge. It is anticipated that this list will receive between 70 and 100 announcements each year. Information on this and related lists can be found at *http://www.routledge.com/.* Related lists provide for announcements in more restricted areas of philosophy, however a subscription to philosophy-newbooks will include all announcements in related lists. These sub-lists, which can be subscribed to from the address above, include: ethics-newbooks (ethics:15-20 msgs per year), ancphil-newbooks (ancient and medieval philosophy: 10-15 msgs per year), philart-newbooks (philosophy of art and literature: 3-6 msgs per year), nonwestphil-newbooks (non-western philosophy: 3-6 msgs per year), phillaw-newbooks (philosophy of law and legal theory: 4-7 msgs per year), phil-and-ling-newbooks (philosophy of language and linguistics: 2-4 msgs per year), russell-newbooks (Bertrand Russell: 5-10 msgs per year), popper-newbooks (Karl Popper: 2-4 msgs per year), wittgenstein-newbooks (Ludwig Wittgenstein: 2-4 msgs per year), polphil-newbooks (political and social philosophy: 10-15 msgs per year), genderphil-newbooks (feminist and gender: 30-40 msgs per year), introphil-newbooks (introductory philosophy: 10-15 msgs per year), philsci-newbooks (philosophy of science: 5-10 msgs per year), histphil-newbooks (history of philosophy: 4-8 msgs per year), contphil-newbooks (continental philosophy: 20-30 msgs per year), logic-newbooks (logic, philosophy of mathematics, and critical thinking: 2-4 msgs per year), phil-and-psychoanal-newbooks (philosophy and psychoanalysis: 3-6 msgs per year), mind-and-meta-newbooks (philosophy of mind and metaphysics: 5-10 msgs per year), envphil-newbooks (environmental philosophy: 4-8 msgs per year).

Listname: phil-toc-l
Moderator: Andrew Gleeson at jrnl@coombs.anu.edu.au
Subscribe: majordomo@coombs.anu.edu.au
Article Submission: no submissions

This list provides periodic electronic mailings of tables of contents for journals dealing with philosophy. This is a special service by the Coombs Computing Unit, RSSS, Australian National University, and is restricted to scholars and researchers in Australia and New Zealand who are subscribed to the aphil-l list.

Listname: postcolonial
Moderator: Dan Kern at dank@mail.utexas.edu
Subscribe: majordomo@jefferson.village.virginia.edu
Article Submission: postcolonial@jefferson.village.virginia.edu

Postcolonial is an electronic forum for discussion and experimentation grounded in postcolonial literature, film, or theory. Postcolonial is an open list, and all interested parties are invited and encouraged to participate.

Listname: postmodernism
Moderator: Kent Palmer at palmer@think.net
Subscribe: listserv@think.net
Article Submission: postmodernism@think.net

A Thinknet BBS philosophy list facilitating the discussion of issues relevant to postmodernism and postmodern philosophy and thought.

Listname: process-philosophy
Moderator: Kent Palmer at palmer@think.net
Subscribe: listserv@think.net
Article Submission: process-philosophy@think.net

This list facilitates the discussion of process-philosophy such as that of Whitehead. A Thinknet BBS and DialogNet philosophy list.

Listname: process-philosophy
Subscribe: mailbase@mailbase.ac.uk
Article Submission: process-philosophy@mailbase.ac.uk

Process-philosophy is an open forum for discussing topics pertaining to process thought. Emphasis is on Whitehead's metaphysics and Hartshorne's theology, but remarks on historically influential thinkers like Peirce, Bergson, James, and contemporary contributors are welcome.

Listname: prncyb-l
Moderator: Cliff Josslyn at cjosslyn@binghamton.cc.bingvaxu.edu
Subscribe: listserv@bingvmb.cc.binghamton.edu
Article Submission: prncyb@bingvmb.cc.binghamton.edu

The style of the Principia Cybernetica Project discussion list is for long papers to be posted and then commented on by other participants. Memes, cognition, socio-biological explanations of altruism have been recent topics.

Listname: qualrs-l
Subscribe: listserv@uga.cc.uga.edu
Article Submission: qualrs-l@uga.cc.uga.edu

A discussion list for those interested in qualitative research, especially in education. The list was started as a medium for discussion because of the current "paradigm war" in educational research between those who insist on a positivist, verificationist approach to research and those who either eschew this approach altogether or combine it with a more phenomenological approach. The issues on this list are actually more diverse.

Listname: scot-pg-phil
Moderator: Andrew Aberdein at aja@st-andrews.ac.uk
Subscribe: mailbase@mailbase.ac.uk
Article Submission: scot-pg-phil@mailbase.ac.uk

This is the mailing list of the Scottish Postgraduate Philosophy Association which aims to disseminate details of conferences, seminar programmes, jobs, etc. of interest to its members. Further information on the mailing list can be found at *http://www. mailbase.ac.uk/lists-p-t/scot-pg-phil/*.

Listname: semiotics
Moderator: Andrew Aberdein at aja@st-andrews.ac.uk
Subscribe: mailbase@mailbase.ac.uk
Article Submission: scot-pg-phil@mailbase.ac.uk

This is the mailing list of the Scotish Postgraduate Philosophy Association which aims to disseminate details of conferences, seminar programmes, jobs, etc. of interest to its members. Further informationon the mailing list can be found at *http://www.mailbase.ac.uk/lists-p-t/scot-pg-phil/*.

Listname: semiotics
Moderator: Kent Palmer at palmer@think.net
Subscribe: listserv@think.net
Article Submission: semiotics@think.net

A Thinknet BBS philosophy list facilitating the discussion of issues in semiotics.

Listname: slowread
Moderator: Lance Fletcher at lance.fletcher@freelance.com
Subscribe: listserv@freelance.com
Article Submission: slowread@freelance.com

This list is devoted to the discussion of the nature and practice of slow reading and its relationship to philosophy and teaching. Archives of this list are available at: *http://www.freelance.com.*

Listname: tank-l
Moderator: David Spurrett at spurrett@mtb.und.ac.za
Subscribe: maiser@cc.und.ac.za
Article Submission: tank-l@cc.und.ac.za

The purpose of the list is to facilitate professional communication between the members and graduate students of southern African philosophy departments, and interested academics in other disciplines. The expected content of the list includes calls for papers, news about conferences, information about current issues of journals or new journals, notices about international philosophical visitors to Southern Africa, special seminars, job advertisements, and the like.

Listname: teaching-phil
Moderator: Lance Fletcher at lance.fletcher@freelance.com
Subscribe: listserv@freelance.com
Article Submission: teaching-phil@freelance.com

This list is devoted to the discussion of the teaching of philosophy. Archives of this list are available at: *http://www.freelance.com.*

Listname: technology
Moderator: Spoon Collective at spoons@jefferson.village.virginia.edu
Subscribe: majordomo@jefferson.village.virginia.edu
Article Submission: technology@jefferson.village.virginia.edu

A Spoon Collective sponsored list for the discussion of the philosophical aspects of technology.

Listname: urantial
Moderator: Michael Million at mm24681@uafsysb.uark.edu
Subscribe: listserv@uafsysb.uark.edu
Article Submission: urantial@uafsysb.uark.edu

Contributions to this list are invited from the full scope of scientific and theological perspectives as long as they serve to enhance our understanding of ourselves and pertain constructively to the conceptual framework of the Urantia material. The goal of this conference is to utilise *The Urantia Book* to gain integration of knowledge and consolidation of world-views toward an improved life for all on earth.

Mailing Lists: Great Thinkers

Listname: adler
Moderator: Kent Palmer at palmer@think.net
Subscribe: listserv@think.net
Article Submission: adler@think.net

A Thinknet BBS philosophy list facilitating the discussion and slow reading of the work and thought of Adler.

Listname: adorno
Moderator: Kent Palmer at palmer@think.net
Subscribe: listserv@think.net
Article Submission: adorno@think.net

A Thinknet BBS philosophy list facilitating the discussion and slow reading of the work and thought of Theodor Adorno.

Listname: aquinas
Moderator: Lance Fletcher at lance.fletcher@freelance.com
Subscribe: listserv@freelance.com
Article Submission: aquinas@freelance.com

This list is devoted to slow readings of works by Thomas Aquinas. Archives and information about this list are available at: *http://www.freelance.com.*

Listname: arendt
Moderator: Lance Fletcher at lance.fletcher@freelance.com
Subscribe: listserv@freelance.com
Article Submission: arendt@freelance.com

This is a list devoted to slow readings of the works of Hannah Arendt. Archives of this list are available at: *http://www.freelance.com.*

Listname: aristotle
Moderator: Paul Bullen at BUL1@midway.uchicago.edu
Subscribe: majordomo@listhost.uchicago.edu
Article Submission: aristotle@listhost.uchicago.edu

This discussion list is devoted to the study of Aristotle. Topics on any aspect of Aristotle can be raised at any time.

Listname: aristotle
Moderator: Lance Fletcher at lance.fletcher@freelance.com
Subscribe: listserv@freelance.com
Article Submission: aristotle@freelance.com

This is a list devoted to slow reading of the works of Aristotle. Archives of this list are available at: *http://www.freelance.com.*

Listname: aristotle-ethics
Moderator: Lance Fletcher at lance.fletcher@freelance.com
Subscribe: listserv@freelance.com
Article Submission: aristotle-ethics@freelance.com

This list is devoted to a slow reading of Aristotle's *Nichomachean Ethics.* Archives of the list are available at: *http://www.freelance.com.*

Listname: aristotle-logic
Moderator: Lance Fletcher at lance.fletcher@freelance.com
Subscribe: listserv@freelance.com
Article Submission: aristotle-logic@freelance.com

This list is devoted to a slow reading of Aristotle's *Organon.* Archives of the list are available at: *http://www.freelance.com.*

Listname: aristotle-metaphysics
Moderator: Lance Fletcher at lance.fletcher@freelance.com
Subscribe: listserv@freelance.com
Article Submission: aristotle-metaphysics@freelance.com

This list is devoted to a slow reading of Aristotle's *Metaphysics.* Archives of the list are available at: *http://www.freelance.com.*

Listname: aristotle-politics
Moderator: Lance Fletcher at lance.fletcher@freelance.com
Subscribe: listserv@freelance.com
Article Submission: aristotle-politics@freelance.com

This list is devoted to a slow reading of Aristotle's *Politics.* Archives of the list are available at: *http://www.freelance.com.*

Listname: aristotle-soul
Moderator: Lance Fletcher at <u>lance.fletcher@freelance.com</u>
Subscribe: <u>listserv@freelance.com</u>
Article Submission: <u>aristotle-soul@freelance.com</u>

This list is devoted to a slow reading of Aristotle's *De Anima*. The reading will be lead by Daniel Robinson of Georgetown and Oxford Universities. Archives of the list are available at: *http://www.freelance.com.*

Listname: augustine
Moderator: James O'Donnell at <u>jod@ccat.sas.upenn.edu</u>
Subscribe: <u>listserv@ccat.sas.upenn.edu</u>
Article Submission: <u>augustine@ccat.sas.upenn.edu</u>

This discussion list will be used in conjunction with a course at the University of Pennsylvania targeted at beginning graduate students designed to introduce the thought and works of Augustine of Hippo. Topics in the course will broadly cover the main issues and major works of Augustine.

Listname: bacon
Moderator: Kent Palmer at <u>palmer@think.net</u>
Subscribe: <u>listserv@think.net</u>
Article Submission: <u>bacon@think.net</u>

A Thinknet BBS philosophy list facilitating the discussion and slow reading of the work and thought of Francis Bacon.

Listname: bakhtin
Moderator: Kent Palmer at <u>palmer@think.net</u>
Subscribe: <u>listserv@think.net</u>
Article Submission: <u>bakhtin@think.net</u>

A Thinknet BBS and DialogNet philosophy list for the discussion of the thought, and slow reading of the work of Bakhtin.

Listname: barthes
Moderator: Kent Palmer at <u>palmer@think.net</u>
Subscribe: <u>listserv@think.net</u>
Article Submission: <u>barthes@think.net</u>

A Thinknet BBS and DialogNet philosophy list for the discussion of the thought, and slow reading of the work of Roland Barthes.

Listname: bataille
Moderator: Kent Palmer at <u>palmer@think.net</u>

Subscribe: listserv@think.net
Article Submission: bataille@think.net

A Thinknet BBS and DialogNet philosophy list for the discussion of the thought, and slow reading of the work of Bataille.

Listname: bataille
Moderator: Spoon Collective at spoons@jefferson.village.virginia.edu
Subscribe: majordomo@lists.village.virginia.edu
Article Submission: bataille@lists.village.virginia.edu

This list, owned by the Spoon Collective, is for the discussion of the works of G. Bataille.

Listname: baudrillard
Moderator: Kent Palmer at palmer@think.net
Subscribe: listserv@think.net
Article Submission: baudrillard@think.net

A Thinknet BBS and DialogNet philosophy list for the discussion and slow reading of the work and thought of Jean Baudrillard.

Listname: baudrillard
Moderator: Spoon Collective at spoons@jefferson.village.virginia.edu
Subscribe: majordomo@lists.village.virginia.edu
Article Submission: baudrillard@lists.village.virginia.edu

This list is for the discussion of the works of Jean Baudrillard, and is administered by the Spoon Collective.

Listname: bateson
Moderator: Kent Palmer at palmer@think.net
Subscribe: listserv@think.net
Article Submission: bateson@think.net

A Thinknet BBS and DialogNet philosophy list for the discussion and slow reading of the work and thought of Bateson.

Listname: berdyaev-l
Moderator: Mark Dotson at plotinus@ix.netcom.com
Subscribe: listserv@freelance.com
Article Submission: berdyaev-l@freelance.com

This list provides for discussion of the work of the Russian philosopher, Nicolas Berdyaev, and for related topics. Information on this and other Freelance lists can be found at: *http:// www.freelance.com.*

Listname: berkeley
Moderator: Kent Palmer at palmer@think.net
Subscribe: listserv@think.net
Article Submission: berkeley@think.net

A Thinknet BBS and DialogNet philosophy list for the discussion and slow reading of the work and thought of Bishop Berkeley.

Listname: blanchot
Moderator: Kent Palmer at palmer@think.net
Subscribe: listserv@think.net
Article Submission: blanchot@think.net

A Thinknet BBS and DialogNet philosophy list for the discussion and slow reading of the work and thought of Maurice Blanchot.

Listname: blanchot
Moderator: Spoon Collective at spoons@jefferson.village.virginia.edu
Subscribe: majordomo@lists.village.virginia.edu
Article Submission: blanchot@lists.village.virginia.edu

This is a forum for discussion and experimentation pertaining to the writings of Maurice Blanchot and his intersections with Derrida, Heidegger, Foucault, Levinas, Bataille, Deleuze, Nietzsche, Klossowski, etc. The list is open to all interested persons.

Listname: chomsky
Moderator: Kent Palmer at palmer@think.net
Subscribe: listserv@think.net
Article Submission: chomsky@think.net

A Thinknet BBS and DialogNet philosophy list providing a forum for the slow reading and discussion of the works of Noam Chomsky.

Listname: chomsky
Moderator: J. C. Garelli at lagare@attach.edu.ar
Subscribe: listserv@maelstrom.stjohns.edu
Article Submission: chomsky@maelstrom.stjohns.edu

Chomsky is an unmoderated discussion list intended as a resource for both intellectuals and followers of his political ideas and scholars doing research on Noam Chomsky's contribution to linguistics.

Listname: darwin-and-darwinism
Moderator: R. M. Young at robert@RMY1.DEMON.CO.UK
        Ian Pitchford at Ian.Pitchford@mcmail.com
Subscribe: listproc@sheffield.ac.uk

Darwin and Darwinism is a forum for discussion of any and all matters concerned with evolution. This means Darwin, his life and theories, Darwinian scholarship, including other approaches to evolution in the past and present. It is also intended to include findings, debates, concepts and philosophical discussions about Darwinian ideas in other disciplines, including, for example, Darwinian psychology, social science, epistemology, and the relevance of Darwinism to moral, cultural, social, political, and ideological matters.

Listname: deleuze
Moderator: Kent Palmer at palmer@think.net
Subscribe: listserv@think.net
Article Submission: deleuze@think.net

A Thinknet BBS and DialogNet philosophy list providing a forum for the slow reading and discussion of the works of Deleuze.

Listname: deleuze-guattari
Moderator: Spoon Collective at spoons@jefferson.village.virginia.edu
Subscribe: majordomo@lists.village.virginia.edu
Article Submission: deleuze-guattari@lists.village.virginia.edu

This list is a forum for discussion and experimentation rooted in both the separate and joint works of Gilles Deleuze and Felix Guattari. It is an open list—all interested parties are welcome to participate.

Listname: dennett
Moderator: Kent Palmer at palmer@think.net
Subscribe: listserv@think.net
Article Submission: dennett@think.net

A Thinknet BBS and DialogNet forum for the slow reading and discussion of the works of Dennett.

Listname: derrida
Moderator: Kent Palmer at palmer@think.net
Subscribe: listserv@think.net
Article Submission: derrida@think.net

A Thinknet BBS and DialogNet forum for the slow reading and discussion of the works of Jacques Derrida.

Listname: derrida
Subscribe: listserv@cfrvm.cf.usf.edu
Article Submission: derrida@cfrvm.cf.usf.edu

A mailing list for the discussion of the works and thought of Derrida.

Listname: descartes
Moderator: Lance Fletcher at lance.fletcher@freelance.com
Subscribe: listserv@freelance.com
Article Submission: descartes@freelance.com

This list is devoted to a slow reading of the works of Rene Descartes. Archives of this list are available at: *http://www.freelance.com.*

Listname: dewey
Moderator: Kent Palmer at palmer@think.net
Subscribe: listserv@think.net
Article Submission: dewey@think.net

A Thinknet BBS and DialogNet forum for the slow reading and discussion of the works of John Dewey.

Listname: einstein
Moderator: Kent Palmer at palmer@think.net
Subscribe: listserv@think.net
Article Submission: einstein@think.net

A Thinknet BBS and DialogNet forum for the discussion of the works of Albert Einstein.

Listname: feyerabend
Moderator: Kent Palmer at palmer@think.net
Subscribe: listserv@think.net
Article Submission: feyerabend@think.net

This list is devoted to the discussion of the philosophy of science of Paul Feyerabend. It is a Thinknet BBS and DialogNet philosophy list.

Listname: feyerabend
Moderator: Spoon Collective at spoons@jefferson.village.virginia.edu
Subscribe: majordomo@lists.village.virginia.edu
Article Submission: feyerabend@lists.village.virginia.edu

The Feyerabend forum is intended to support active discussion and debate of issues related to the writings of, and beliefs about, Paul Feyerabend.

Listname: foucault
Moderator: Kent Palmer at palmer@think.net
Subscribe: listserv@think.net
Article Submission: foucault@think.net

A discussion list for those interested in the work of social theorist, Michel Foucault. A Thinknet BBS and DialogNet philosophy list.

Listname: frankl
Moderator: Kent Palmer at palmer@think.net
 Subscribe: listserv@think.net
Article Submission: frankl@think.net

This list is devoted to the discussion of the works of Frankl. It is a Thinknet BBS and DialogNet philosophy list.

Listname: frege
Moderator: Kent Palmer at palmer@think.net
Subscribe: listserv@think.net
Article Submission: frege@think.net

This list is devoted to the discussion of the philosophy of Gottlob Frege. It is a Thinknet BBS and DialogNet philosophy list.

Listname: freud
Moderator: Kent Palmer at palmer@think.net
Subscribe: listserv@think.net
Article Submission: freud@think.net

This list is devoted to the discussion of the thought and work of Sigmund Freud. It is a Thinknet BBS and DialogNet philosophy list.

Listname: freud-l
Moderator: Siegfried Schmitt at Siegfried.Schmitt@rz.uni-karlsruhe.de
Subscribe: listserv@rz.uni-karlsruhe.de
Article Submission: freud-l@rz.uni-karlsruhe.de

Freud-l is an interdisciplinary discussion for German researchers who are interested in depth psychology and psychoanalysis. The language of the list is German.

Listname: gadamer
Moderator: Kent Palmer at palmer@think.net
Subscribe: listserv@think.net
Article Submission: gadamer@think.net

This list is devoted to the discussion of the thought and work of Gadamer. It is a Thinknet BBS and DialogNet philosophy list.

Listname: girard
Moderator: Kent Palmer at palmer@think.net
Subscribe: listserv@think.net
Article Submission: girard@think.net

A Thinknet BBS and DialogNet philosophy list devoted to the discussion and slow reading of the work of Girard.

Listname: habermas
Moderator: Kent Palmer at palmer@think.net
Subscribe: listserv@think.net at palmer@think.net
Article Submission: habermas@think.net

A Thinknet BBS and DialogNet philosophy list devoted to the discussion and slow reading of the work of Jurgen Habermas.

Listname: habermas
Moderator: Spoon Collective at spoons@jefferson.village.virginia.edu
Subscribe: majordomo@lists.village.virginia.edu
Article Submission: habermas@lists.village.virginia.edu

A list for the discussion of the work of Jurgen Habermas.

Listname: hayek-l
Moderator: Greg Ransom at gregransom@aol.com
                    Juan Carlos Garelli at lagare@attach.edu.ar
Subscribe: listserv@maelstrom.stjohns.edu
Article Submission: hayek-l@maelstrom.stjohns.edu

This is an international network for the discussion of the ideas of Friedrich A. Hayek. Hayek-L is intended as a resource for scholars and others doing research connected to the contributions of Friedrich Hayek. The basic purpose of the list is to serve as a forum for scholarly discussions and as a clearing house the distribution of information on academic conferences, publication opportunities, fellowship information, academic grants, and job openings of interest to Hayek scholars. Subscribers are encouraged to post questions, comments, or announcements of interest to individuals working on topics related to Hayek's writings. Appropriate postings might pertain to work currently in progress, the development of course materials, bibliographical material of interest to Hayek scholars, useful Internet resources, etc. Archives of the mailing list can be located at *http://maelstrom. stjohns.edu/archives/hayek-1.html.*

Listname: hegel
Moderator: Kent Palmer at palmer@think.net
Subscribe: listserv@think.net
Article Submission: hegel@think.net

A Thinknet BBS and DialogNet philosophy list devoted to the discussion and slow reading of the work of Hegel.

Listname: heidegger
Moderator: Spoon Collective at spoons@jefferson.village.virginia.edu
Subscribe: majordomo@lists.village.virginia.edu
Article Submission: heidegger@lists.village.virginia.edu

This list provides for a discussion of the work of Martin Heidegger.

Listname: heidegger
Moderator: Kent Palmer at <u>palmer@think.net</u>
Subscribe: <u>listserv@think.net</u>
Article Submission: <u>heidegger@think.net</u>

A Thinknet BBS and DialogNet philosophy list facilitating a discussion of the work and thought of Martin Heidegger.

Listname: hobbes
Moderator: Lance Fletcher at <u>lance.fletcher@freelance.com</u>
Subscribe: <u>listserv@freelance.com</u>
Article Submission: <u>hobbes@freelance.com</u>

This list is devoted to a slow reading of the works of Hobbes. Archives of the list are available at: *http://www.freelance.com.*

Listname: homer
Moderator: Lance Fletcher at <u>lance.fletcher@freelance.com</u>
Subscribe: <u>listserv@freelance.com</u>
Article Submission: <u>homer@freelance.com</u>

This list is devoted to a slow reading of the works of Homer. Archives of the list are available at: *http://www.freelance.com.*

Listname: hume-l
Moderator: Dorothy Coleman at <u>dpcole@mail.wm.edu</u>
Subscribe: <u>listserv@listserv.cc.wm.edu</u>
Article Submission: <u>hume-l@listserv.cc.wm.edu</u>

This list provides a forum for discussion of topics of interest to students and scholars of the philosophy and writings of David Hume.

Listname: husserl
Moderator: Kent Palmer at <u>palmer@think.net</u>
Subscribe: <u>listserv@think.net</u>
Article Submission: <u>husserl@think.net</u>

A Thinknet BBS and DialogNet philosophy list and discussion and slow reading of the work and thought of Edmund Husserl.

Listname: jaspers
Moderator: Lance Fletcher at <u>lance.fletcher@freelance.com</u>
Subscribe: <u>listserv@freelance.com</u>
Article Submission: <u>jaspers@freelance.com</u>

This list is devoted to a slow reading of the works of Karl Jaspers. New subscribers are encouraged to send a message introducing themselves, and indicating if there is a passage whose discussion they are willing to lead. Archives of the list are available at: *http:// www.freelance.com.*

Listname: jdewey-l
Moderator: Tom Burke at burke@sc.edu
Subscribe: listserv@vm.sc.edu
Article Submission: jdewey-l@vm.sc.edu

JDEWEY-L is an international electronic forum devoted to the interpretation and extension of John Dewey's philosophy. The list is open to anyone with an interest in any facet of Dewey's philosophy.

Listname: kant-l
Moderator: Frank Wilson at fwilson@coral.bucknell.edu
            Ted Chappen at chappen@bucknell.edu
Subscribe: listserv@bucknell.edu
Article Submission: kant-l@bucknell.edu

This is an open, largely unmoderated discussion list which is primarily intended to be a forum for scholarly and interdisciplinary discussions of the philosophy of Immanuel Kant; and for sharing information regarding conferences, lectures, recent publications, bibliographies, and other information of potential relevance to those interested in Kant's philosophy. The primary aim of the List is to enable and encourage thoughtful, sustained, and competent discussion of issues involved in the understanding of the thought of Immanuel Kant. The list is open to anyone, from any discipline, having a serious interest in this area of study. The list managers have a particular concern to encourage close critical discussions and "slow readings" of the Kantian texts and of secondary sources (commentaries, biographies, etc.) pertaining to these works, but the activities of the list will not be restricted to such discussions.

Listname: kant
Moderator: Lance Fletcher at lance.fletcher@freelance.com
Subscribe: listserv@freelance.com
Article Submission: kant@freelance.com

This list is devoted to a slow reading of Kant's three Critiques. Archives of this list are available at: *http://www.freelance.com.*

Listname: kant-critique3
Moderator: Lance Fletcher at lance.fletcher@freelance.com
Subscribe: listserv@freelance.com
Article Submission: kant-critique3@freelance.com

This list is for the slow reading of Kant's 3rd Critique, the *Critique of Judgement.* Archives of the list are available at: *http://www.freelance.com.*

Listname: kirkegaard
Moderator: Kent Palmer at <u>palmer@think.net</u>
Subscribe: <u>listserv@think.net</u>
Article Submission: <u>kirkegaard@think.net</u>

A Thinknet BBS and DialogNet philosophy list which provides a forum for the discussion and slow reading of the work of Soren Kierkegaard.

Listname: kristeva
Moderator: Kent Palmer at <u>palmer@think.net</u>
Subscribe: <u>listserv@think.net</u>
Article Submission: <u>kristeva@think.net</u>

A Thinknet BBS and DialogNet philosophy list which provides a forum for the discussion and slow reading of the work of French feminist philosopher, Julia Kristeva.

Listname: kuhn
Moderator: Kent Palmer at <u>palmer@think.net</u>
Subscribe: <u>listserv@think.net</u>
Article Submission: <u>kuhn@think.net</u>

A Thinknet BBS and DialogNet philosophy list which provides a forum for the discussion and slow reading of the work of Thomas Kuhn.

Listname: lacan
Moderator: Kent Palmer at <u>palmer@think.net</u>
Subscribe: <u>listserv@think.net</u>
Article Submission: <u>lacan@think.net</u>

A Thinknet BBS and DialogNet philosophy list for the discussion and slow reading of the work of Lacan.

Listname: leibniz
Subscribe: <u>listcom@scistud.umkc.edu</u>
Article Submission: <u>leibniz@scistud.umkc.edu</u>

A philosophy mailing list for the discussion of the work of Gottfried Leibniz.

Listname: leibniz
Moderator: Kent Palmer at <u>palmer@think.net</u>
Subscribe: <u>listserv@think.net</u>
Article Submission: <u>leibniz@think.net</u>

A Thinknet BBS and DialogNet philosophy list for the discussion and slow reading of the work of Gottfried Leibniz.

Listname: leibniz
Moderator: Lance Fletcher at lance.fletcher@freelance.com
Subscribe: listserv@freelance.com
Article Submission: leibniz@freelance.com

This list is devoted to a slow reading of works by Gottfried Leibniz. Archives of this list are available at: *http://www.freelance.com.*

Listname: leo-strauss
Moderator: Lance Fletcher at lance.fletcher@freelance.com
Subscribe: listserv@freelance.com
Article Submission: leo-strauss@freelance.com

This list is devoted to a slow reading of the works of the political philosopher, Leo Strauss (not Levi Strauss the anthropologist). Archives of this list are available at: *http://www. freelance.com.*

Listname: levinas
Moderator: Lance Fletcher at lance.fletcher@freelance.com
Subscribe: listserv@freelance.com
Article Submission: levinas@freelance.com

This list will be devoted to a slow reading of *Totality and Infinity* by the French philosopher, Emmanuel Levinas. Archives of this list are available at: *http://www.freelance.com.*

Listname: locke
Moderator: Kent Palmer at palmer@think.net
Subscribe: listserv@think.net
Article Submission: locke@think.net

A Thinknet BBS and DialogNet philosophy list for the slow reading and discussion of the work of John Locke.

Listname: lonergan-1
Moderator: James B. Sauer at philjim@STMARYTX.EDU
Subscribe: listserv@stmarytx.edu
Article Submission: longeran-1@listserv@stmarytx.edu

This moderated list links scholars and advanced students interested in the work of Canadian philosopher and theologian Bernard Lonergan.

Listname: lyotard
Moderator: Kent Palmer at palmer@think.net
Subscribe: listserv@think.net
Article Submission: lyotard@think.net

A Thinknet BBS and DialogNet philosophy list for the slow reading and discussion of the work of Jean-Francois Lyotard.

Listname: lyotard
Moderator: Spoon Collective at spoons@jefferson.village.virginia.edu
Subscribe: majordomo@lists.village.virginia.edu
Article Submission: lyotard@lists.village.virginia.edu

This list, sponsored by the Spoon Collective, is for the discussion of the work and thought of Jean-Francois Lyotard.

Listname: machiavelli
Moderator: Kent Palmer at palmer@think.net
Subscribe: listserv@think.net
Article Submission: machiavelli@think.net

A Thinknet BBS and DialogNet philosophy list for the slow reading and discussion of the work of Machiavelli.

Listname: macintyre
Moderator: Helder Buenos at buenos@oraculo.lcc.ufmg.br
Subscribe: listserv@freelance.com
Article Submission: macintyre@freelance.com

This list is devoted to a slow reading of the works of Alasdair MacIntyre. Archives of the list are available at: *http://www.freelance.com*.

Listname: maimonides
Moderator: Scott Michael Alexander at smalexa@ibm.net
Subscribe: listserv@freelance.com
Article Submission: maimonides@freelance.com

This list is for a slow reading and discussion of the works of Maimonides. The discussion should examine the Guide, as well his other philosophical writings, including The Book of Knowledge section of the *Mishneh Torah, The Treatise on Resurrection, The Eight Chapters*, and others.

Listname: marx
Moderator: Kent Palmer at palmer@think.net
Subscribe: listserv@think.net
Article Submission: marx@think.net

A Thinknet BBS and DialogNet philosophy list which facilitates a discussion and slow reading of the works of Karl Marx.

Listname: merleau-ponty
Moderator: Kent Palmer at palmer@think.net
Subscribe: listserv@think.net
Article Submission: merleau-ponty@think.net

This list is a forum for the slow reading and discussion of the work of Merleau-Ponty.

Listname: montaigne
Moderator: Tony Brezovski at tonyb@epix.net
Subscribe: listserv@freelance.com
Article Submission: montaigne@freelance.com

This list is devoted to a slow reading of the works of Michel Montaigne. Archives and information on the list are available at: *http://www.freelance.com.*

Listname: newton
Moderator: Kent Palmer at palmer@think.net
Subscribe: listserv@think.net
Article Submission: newton@think.net

A Thinknet BBS and DialogNet philosophy list for the discussion and slow reading of the work of Isaac Newton.

Listname: nietzsche
Moderator: Kent Palmer at palmer@think.net
Subscribe: listserv@think.net
Article Submission: nietzsche@think.net

A Thinknet BBS and DialogNet philosophy list for the discussion and slow reading of the work of Nietzsche.

Listname: nietzsche
Moderator: Spoon Collective at spoons@jefferson.village.virginia.edu
Subscribe: majordomo@lists.village.virginia.edu
Article Submission: nietzsche@lists.village.virginia.edu

Nietzsche is an electronic forum for discussion and experimentation rooted in both the work of Friedrich Nietzsche and the tradition(s) that this work has inspired. It is an open list—all interested parties are invited and encouraged to participate.

Listname: peirce
Moderator: Lance Fletcher at lance.fletcher@freelance.com
Subscribe: listserv@freelance.com
Article Submission: peirce@freelance.com

This list is devoted to a slow reading of the work of Charles S. Peirce. It is a supplement to the peirce-l list run by Joseph Ransdell. Archives of this list are available at: *http://www.freelance.com.*

Listname: philcamus
Moderator: Frank Wilson at <u>fwilson@bucknell.edu</u>
Subscribe: <u>listserv@bucknell.edu</u>
Article Submission: <u>philcamus@bucknell.edu</u>

Discussions of the philosophical ideas of Albert Camus are the focus of this mailing list.

Listname: plato
Moderator: Lance Fletcher at <u>lance.fletcher@freelance.com</u>
Subscribe: <u>listserv@freelance.com</u>
Article Submission: <u>plato@freelance.com</u>

This list is devoted to general discussions of Plato and the interpretation of Plato, and as a kind of incubation chamber for slow readings of particular dialogues. Some of the topics which the list could consider include: How should one read Plato? Why did Plato write dialogues? Is there any such thing in Plato's work as a "Platonic Theory of Ideas"? The question of the chronology of composition—do we know, and does it matter? Archives of the list are available at: *http://www.freelance.com.*

Listname: plato-parmenides
Moderator: Lance Fletcher at <u>lance.fletcher@freelance.com</u>
Subscribe: <u>listserv@freelance.com</u>
Article Submission: <u>plato-parmenides@freelance.com</u>

This list is devoted to a slow reading of Plato's *Parmenides.* Archives of the list are available at: *http://www.freelance.com.*

Listname: plato-republic
Moderator: Lance Fletcher at <u>lance.fletcher@freelance.com</u>
Subscribe: <u>listserv@freelance.com</u>
Article Submission: <u>plato-republic@freelance.com</u>

This list will be devoted to a slow reading of Plato's *Republic.* No previous reading of Plato is assumed, but the discussion will be rigorous and intellectually demanding, with the intention being to explore everything, and presuppose nothing. Archives of the list are available at: *http://www.freelance.com.*

Listname: plotinus
Moderator: Lance Fletcher at <u>lance.fletcher@freelance.com</u>
Subscribe: <u>listserv@freelance.com</u>
Article Submission: <u>plotinus@freelance.com</u>

This list is devoted to a slow reading of the Enneads of Plotinus. Archives of this list are available at: *http://www.freelance.com.*

Listname: plotnitsky
Moderator: Kent Palmer at palmer@think.net
Subscribe: listserv@think.net
Article Submission: plotnitsky@think.net

A Thinknet BBS and DialogNet philosophy list for the discussion and slow reading of the work of Plotnitsky.

Listname: polanyi
Moderator: John Apczynski at apczynski@sbu.edu
Subscribe: owner-polanyi@sbu.edu
Article Submission: polanyi@sbu.edu

Polanyi aims to facilitate discussion of the thought of Michael Polanyi and its implications for a wide variety of fields, including art, rhetoric, education, medicine, psychiatry, philosophy, and religion. It is a moderated list open to all who wish to explore how Polanyi's "post-critical" thought may have relevance to a wide range of disciplines. The sharing of papers, bibliographies, and other material will be fostered. Information for submitting and obtaining such material will be forwarded to subscribers.

Listname: popper
Moderator: Kent Palmer at palmer@think.net
Subscribe: listserv@think.net
Article Submission: popper@think.net

A Thinknet BBS and DialogNet philosophy list for the discussion of the work of Karl Popper.

Listname: popper
Moderator: J. C. Garelli at garelli@attach.edu.ar
Subscribe: listserv@maelstrom.stjohns.edu
Article Submission: popper@maelstrom.stjohns.edu

Popper is an unmoderated list intended as a resource for scholars and others doing research connected to the contributions of Karl Popper. The basic purpose of the list is to serve as a forum for scholarly discussions and as a clearinghouse for the distribution of information on academic conferences, publication opportunities, fellowship information, academic grants, and job openings of interest to Popper scholars. Subscribers are encouraged to post questions, comments, or announcements of interest to individuals working on topics related to Popper's writings. Appropriate postings might pertain to work currently in progress, the development of course materials, bibliography material of interest to Popper scholars, useful Internet resources, etc.

Listname: putnam
Moderator: Kent Palmer at palmer@think.net

Subscribe: listserv@think.net
Article Submission: putnam@think.net

A Thinknet BBS and DialogNet philosophy list for the discussion of the work of Hilary Putnam.

Listname: quine
Moderator: Kent Palmer at palmer@think.net
Subscribe: listserv@think.net
Article Submission: quine@think.net

A Thinknet BBS and DialogNet philosophy list for the discussion of the work of Quine.

Listname: rousseau
Moderator: Kent Palmer at palmer@think.net
Subscribe: listserv@think.net
Article Submission: rousseau@think.net

A Thinknet BBS and DialogNet philosophy list for the discussion of the work of Jacques Rousseau.

Listname: russell-l
Moderator: Kenneth Blackwell at blackwk@mcmaster.ca
Subscribe: listproc@mcmaster.ca
Article Submission: russell-l@mcmaster.ca

This list is an unmoderated discussion list about the ideas and life of Bertrand Russell (1872-1970), British philosopher, essayist, and peace activist. Postings include news from the Bertrand Russell Archives and the Bertrand Russell Editorial Project at McMaster University.

Listname: sartre
Moderator: Kent Palmer at palmer@think.net
Subscribe: listserv@think.net
Article Submission: sartre@think.net

A Thinknet BBS and DialogNet philosophy list for the slow reading and discussion of the works of Jean-Paul Sartre.

Listname: schopenhauer
Moderator: Lance Fletcher at lance.fletcher@freelance.com
Subscribe: listserv@freelance.com
Article Submission: schopenhauer@freelance.com

This list is devoted to a slow reading of works by Schopenhauer. Archives of this list are available at: *http://www.freelance.com.*

Listname: siris-l
Moderator: Joyce Rappaport at rappapor@nexus.chapman.edu
Subscribe: listserv@psuvm.psu.edu
Article Submission: siris-l@psuvm.psu.edu

This list is devoted to a slow and detailed reading and discussion of Bishop Berkeley's *Siris*. Those interested in 18th-century studies, the history of philosophy, etc. are welcome to join the discussion.

Listname: spinoza
Moderator: Lance Fletcher at lance.fletcher@freelance.com
Subscribe: listserv@freelance.com
Article Submission: spinoza@freelance.com

This list is devoted to a slow reading of works by Spinoza. Archives of this list are available at: *http://www.freelance.com*.

Listname: steiner
Moderator: David "Lefty" Schlesinger at lefty@apple.com or dns@netcom.com
Subscribe: listserv@maelstrom.stjohns.edu
Article Submission: steiner@maelstrom.stjohns.edu

STEINER is an unmoderated mailing list dedicated to the discussion and investigation of the philosophy of the Austrian philosopher Rudolf Steiner (1861-1925).

Listname: thucydides
Moderator: Lance Fletcher at lance.fletcher@freelance.com
Subscribe: listserv@freelance.com
Article Submission: thucydides@freelance.com

This list is devoted to a slow reading of works by Thucydides, led by Abe Shulsky. Archives of this list are available at: *http://www.freelance.com*.

Listname: versterl
Moderator: rousset@altern.com
Subscribe: versterl@mcom.fr
Article Submission: versterl@mcom.fr

This list is to facilitate a discussion of the works of Ulrich Verster, a contemplative monk with both Western and Eastern (Buddhist, Taoist) theological background, and who was trained in philosophy, sociology, psychiatry, and maths.

Listname: virgil
Moderator: Lance Fletcher at lance.fletcher@freelance.com
Subscribe: listserv@freelance.com

Article Submission: virgil@freelance.com

This list is devoted to readings and discussions of works by Virgil. Archives of the list are available at: *http://www.freelance.com.*

Listname: voltaire
Moderator: Kent Palmer at palmer@think.net
Subscribe: listserv@think.net
Article Submission: voltaire@think.net

A Thinknet BBS and DialogNet philosophy list for the discussion of the thought, and slow reading of the work of Voltaire.

Listname: whitehead
Moderator: Lance Fletcher at lance.fletcher@freelance.com
Subscribe: listserv@freelance.com
Article Submission: whitehead@freelance.com

This list is devoted to a slow reading of the work of Alfred N. Whitehead. Archives of the list are available at: *http://www.freelance.com.*

Listname: wittgenstein
Moderator: Kent Palmer at palmer@think.net
Subscribe: listserv@think.net
Article Submission: wittgenstein@think.net

A Thinknet BBS and DialogNet philosophy list for the discussion of the thought, and slow reading of the work of Wittgenstein.

Listname: xenophon
Moderator: Lance Fletcher at lance.fletcher@freelance.com
Subscribe: listserv@freelance.com
Article Submission: xenophon@freelance.com

This list is devoted to a slow reading of the work of Xenophon, with discussion being lead by Elizabeth Janairo of Loyola University Chicago. Archives of the list are available at *http://www.freelance.com.*

Mailing Lists: History of Philosophy

Listname: alexandria
Moderator: David Fideler at phanes@aol.com
Subscribe: majordomo@world.std.com
Article Submission: alexandria@world.std.com

Alexandria is a mailing list for the discussion of the Western cosmological traditions. The focus of this symposium is interdisciplinary and it is hoped that this list will foster discussion in two main areas: historical and philosophical. It welcomes postings and discussions which relate to any of the spiritual, philosophical, and scientific traditions that flourished in Hellenistic Alexandria: Platonism, Neoplatonism, Pythagoreanism, the mystery religions, astronomy, astrology, alchemy, mathematics, harmonics, Gnosis, Hermeticism, Greek religion and mythology, mysteriosophical traditions, and emerging Christianity.

Listname: c18-l
Moderator: Kevin Berland at bcj@psuvm.psu.edu
Subscribe: listserv@psuvm.psu.edu
Article Submission: c18-l@psuvm.psu.edu

C18-L is an international, interdisciplinary forum for discussing all aspects of 18th-century studies. The primary language is English, but correspondents in other languages are welcomed. Subscribers can expect to receive frequent bulletins of professional interest (notices of conferences, grants, fellowships, calls for papers, etc.). There are usually two or three active discussions going on, and subscribers who send queries (identification of quotations, recommendations for reading, research support, etc.) report they have received answers within 24 hours, and sometimes even within minutes. Other conversations abound, so that the tone of the discussion is something like a particularly stimulating coffee room discussion or seminar. More information on the list is available at: *http://cac.psu.edu/~bcj/c18-l.htm.*

Listname: classicists
Moderator: Stephen Clark at srlclark@liv.ac.uk
　　　　　　　Alan Thew at Alan.Thew@liv.ac.uk
Subscribe: listserv@liv.ac.uk

Classicists is primarily intended to permit classicists in the British Isles to pass on information about conferences, posts, important discoveries, and the like. The original membership was drawn from amongst members of the Classical Association. Subscriptions from overseas are welcome. Archives of classicists can be reached on the web, at *http://listserv.liv.ac.uk/archives/classicists.html.*

Listname: epicurus
Moderator: Erik Anderson at ea@c-zone.net
Subscribe: majordomo@cluon.lake-shasta.ca.us
Article Submission: epicurus@cluon.com

This list is dedicated to discussions of epicurean philosophy.

Listname: history
Moderator: Kent Palmer at palmer@think.net
Subscribe: listserv@think.net
Article Submission: history@think.net

A Thinknet BBS philosophy list facilitating the discussion of issues relevant to the philosophy of history.

Listname: history-ideas
Subscribe: mailbase@mailbase.ac.uk
Article Submission: history-ideas@mailbase.ac.uk

A discussion forum for issues relating to the history of ideas.

Listname: h-rhetor
Moderator: Gary Hatch at garyhatch@byu.edu
Subscribe: listserv@uicmb.uic.edu
Article Submission: h-rhetor@uicvm.uic.edu

H-rhetor is an international electronic discussion group based at the University of Illinois at Chicago (UIC). It provides a forum for scholars and teachers of the history of rhetoric, writing, and communication. There are no geographical or chronological boundaries. The primary purpose of the list is to enable historians to communicate current research and research interests; to discuss new articles, books, papers, approaches, methods, and tools of analysis; and to test new ideas and share comments and tips on teaching.

Listname: medsci-l
Moderator: Joshua Brandon at brandon@gauss.math.brown.edu
Subscribe: listserv@brownvm.brown.edu
Article Submission: medsci-l@brownvm.brown.edu

This list was created to facilitate discussion on medieval and renaissance science. It is open to all.

Listname: philofhi
Moderator: Nikolai Rosov at ROZOV@cnit.nsu.ru
Subscribe: listserv@yorku.ca
Article Submission: philofhi@yorku.ca

The list is open to all subjects and information connected with philosophy of history, metahistory, futures studies, global projects, etc. At the same time it will focus mostly on philosophical understanding of history based on comparing and bridging the paradigms and results of various theoretical and empirical approaches.

Listname: sophia
Moderator: Stephen Clark at srlclark@liverpool.ac.uk
Subscribe: listproc@liverpool.ac.uk
Article Submission: sophia@liverpool.ac.uk

This list is for the discussion of issues in the interpretation and discussion of ancient philosophers from Thales to Iamblichus, Palestine to Spain.

Listname: xenophon
Moderator: Lance Fletcher at <u>lance.fletcher@freelance.com</u>
Subscribe: <u>listserv@freelance.com</u>
Article Submission: <u>xenophon@freelance.com</u>

This list is devoted to a slow reading of the work of Xenophon, with discussion being lead by Elizabeth Janairo of Loyalo University Chicago. Archives of the list are available at *http://www.freelance.com.*

Mailing Lists: Logic & Philosophy of Science

Listname: astronomy
Moderator: Kent Palmer at <u>palmer@think.net</u>
Subscribe: <u>listserv@think.net</u>
Article Submission: <u>astronomy@think.net</u>

A Thinknet BBS philosophy list facilitating the discussion of issues relevant to the philosophy of astronomy.

Listname: biology
Moderator: Kent Palmer at <u>palmer@think.net</u>
Subscribe: <u>listserv@think.net</u>
Article Submission: <u>biology@think.net</u>

A Thinknet BBS philosophy list facilitating the discussion of issues relevant to the philosophy of biology.

Listname: chaosphil
Moderator: Peter Turland at <u>peter.turland@VIRGIN.NET</u>
Subscribe: <u>Majordomo@hhobel.phl.univie.ac.at</u>
Article Submission: <u>chaosphil@hhobel.phl.univie.ac.at</u>

Ths mailing list is provided to facilitate a discussion of the philosophical implications of chaos theory.

Listname: colorcat
Subscribe: <u>listserv@brownvm.brown.edu</u>
Article Submission: <u>colorcat@brownvm.brown.edu</u>

Colorcat is a forum for the discussion of colour categorisation. The list explores how the colour continuum is partitioned into categories by various human processes. The approach taken on the list is multi-disciplinary and draws from colour studies in anthropology, linguistics, philosophy, psychology, and cognitive science.

Listname: darwin-l
Subscribe: listproc@listproc.cc.ukans.edu
Article Submission: darwin-l@listproc.cc.ukans.edu

This list facilitates a discussion of the history and theory of the historical sciences.

Listname: ga-list
Moderator: William M. Spears at gadistr@AIC.NRL.Navy.Mil
Subscribe: ga-list-request@aic.nrl.navy.mil
Article Submission: ga-list@aic.nrl.navy.mil

This mailing list facilitates a discussion of genetic algorithms and related issues. Back issues of the list are available at: *http://www.aic.nrl.navy.mil/galist*.

Listname: hopos-l
Moderator: Don Howard at einphil@ukcc.uky.edu
Subscribe: listserv@lsv.uky.edu
Article Submission: hopos-l@lsv.uky.edu

This list has been established in conjunction with the new History of Philosophy of Science Working Group (HOPOS) as a forum for the exchange of information, ideas, queries, job notices, course syllabi, conference announcements, and other news of interest to scholars.

Listname: hpsst-l
Subscribe: listserv@qucdn.queensu.ca
Article Submission: hpsst-l@qucdn.queensu.ca

The broad purpose of the History and Philosophy of Science and Science Teaching list is to foster collaboration in exploring ways in which the 'social studies' of science, including history, philosophy, psychology, and sociology of science has, and can contribute to the preparation of science teachers, the development of curricula, the enhancement of science education, and the development of a more scientifically literate community by making science and technology more accessible and attractive not only to young people, but also to the public at large.

Listname: l-math
Moderator: Anders Moen at anders.moen@filosofi.uio.no
Subscribe: l-math-request@math.uio.no
Article Submission: l-math@math.uio.no

The purpose of this list is to facilitate exchanges on the history and philosophy of mathematics and probability. It has no particular bias to any philosophy, and is open to all civilised exchanges on the topic.

Listname: logic
Moderator: Kent Palmer at palmer@think.net
Subscribe: listserv@think.net
Article Submission: logic@think.net

A Thinknet BBS philosophy list facilitating the discussion of issues in logic.

Listname: logic-l
Moderator: Frank Wilson at fwilson@coral.bucknell.edu
　　　　　　　Ted Chappen at chappen@coral.bucknell.edu
Subscribe: listserv@bucknell.edu
Article Submission: logic-l@bucknell.edu

The primary purpose of this list is to provide a forum for the exchange of views, experiences, techniques, and professional information pertaining to the teaching and study of elementary logic. 'Elementary logic' refers to the areas of logic customarily taught up through the undergraduate level, and including the concerns of both deductive and inductive logic, with special emphasis upon the apparatus of first-order predicate calculus. The intent of the list is to have a strong pedagogical emphasis, though this is not to be regarded as exclusive of discussions of a theoretical character.

Listname: medsci-l
Moderator: Joshua Brandon at brandon@gauss.math.brown.edu
Subscribe: listserv@brownvm.brown.edu
Article Submission: medsci-l@brownvm.brown.edu

This list was created to facilitate discussion on medieval and renaissance science. It is open to all.

Listname: mersenne
Subscribe: mailbase@mailbase.ac.uk
Article Submission: mersenne@mailbase.ac.uk

This list provides for a discussion of science, technology, and medicine studies.

Listname: meta
Moderator: William Grassie at grassie@voicenet.com
Subscribe: listserv@templeton.org
Article Submission: meta@templeton.org

Meta is an edited, moderated, and public listserv dedicated to promoting the constructive engagement of science and religion and to sharing information and perspectives among the diverse organizations and individuals involved in this interdisciplinary field. The list may be used for conference announcements, book reviews, job and grant opportunities, as well as general discussion.

Listname: new-physics
Moderator: Kent Palmer at palmer@think.net
Subscribe: listserv@think.net
Article Submission: new-physics@think.net

A Thinknet BBS philosophy list facilitating the discussion of issues relevant to the philosophy of new physics.

Listname: philsci
Moderator: Kent Palmer at palmer@think.net
Subscribe: listserv@think.net
Article Submission: philsci@think.net

A Thinknet BBS philosophy list facilitating the discussion of issues in the philosophy of science.

Listname: physics
Moderator: Kent Palmer at palmer@think.net
Subscribe: listserv@think.net
Article Submission: physics@think.net

A Thinknet BBS philosophy list facilitating the discussion of issues relevant to physics and the philosophy of physics.

Listname: relativity
Moderator: Kent Palmer at palmer@think.net
Subscribe: listserv@think.net
Article Submission: relativity@think.net

A Thinknet BBS philosophy list facilitating the discussion of issues in relativity.

Listname: relevant-logic
Moderator: Geoff B. Keene at g.b.keene@exeter.ac.uk
Subscribe: contact the moderator
Article Submission: relevant-logic@exeter.ac.uk

The relevant-logic forum aims to provide an opportunity for people working in the field of relevant logic to exchange ideas and information on conferences and publications. It is sponsored by the University of Exeter, Devon, England.

Listname: scifraud
Subscribe: listserv@cnsibm.albany.edu
Article Submission: scifraud@cnsibm.albany.edu

A fairly active discussion group covering a wide range of topics loosely tied to scientific fraudulence. Discussion of academic funding and grants is also included.

Listname: sci-tech-studies
Subscribe: listproc@kasey.umkc.edu
Article Submission: sci-tech-studies@kasey.umkc.edu

A list to facilitate the discussion of science and technology studies.

Mailing Lists: Philosophy of Law

Listname: ail-l
Moderator: David R. Warner, Jr. at warner@austin.onu.edu
Subscribe: listserv@austin.onu.edu
Article Submission: ail-l@austin.onu.edu

This conference is focused on the discussion of topics related to artificial intelligence and law.

Listname: cjust-l
Subscribe: listserv@cunyvm.cuny.edu
Article Submission: cjust-l@cunyvm.cuny.edu

This conference facilitates a discussion of criminal justice issues.

Listname: h-law
Subscribe: listserv@msu.edu
Article Submission: h-law@msu.edu

This is the H-Net and ASLH Legal History discussion list.

Listname: femjur
Moderator: Mark Folmsbee at zzfolm@acc.wuacc.edu
Michelle Rabouin at zzrabo@acc.wuacc.edu
Subscribe: listserv@assocdir.wuacc.edu
Article Submission: femjur@assocdir.wuacc.edu

The list provides a forum for discussing theories and issues regarding feminism and women and law. It is also a good place to share research questions, scholarship, calls for papers, job announcements, and provide support for people working in this area of law.

Listname: hislaw-l
Moderator: James A. Cocks at jacock01@ulkyvm.louisville.edu
Subscribe: listserv@ulkyvm.louisville.edu
Article Submission: hislaw-l@ulkyvm.louisville.edu

This is a forum for debate, discussion, and the exchange of information by students and scholars of the history of the law (Feudal, Common, Canon). Sponsored by the University of Louisville.

Listname: legphil
Moderator: Max Steinbeis at max.steinbeis@jura.uni-muenchen.de
Subscribe: majordomo@lists.lrz-muenchen.de
Article Submission: legphil@lists.lrz-muenchen.de

This mailing list is for discussion of academic legal philosophy: law and ethics, methods of law, history of legal philosophy, and related topics.

Listname: psylaw-l
Subscribe: listserv@utepa.bitnet
Article Submission: psylaw@utepa.bitnet

This is a discussion list for issues related to psychology and law.

Listname: unt-lpbr
Moderator: Neal Tate at Neal_Tate@unt.edu
Subscribe: listserv@unt.edu
Article Submission: not permitted, this is a distribution list only

This list is for the distribution of book reviews in law and politics. Archives of the reviews can be found at: *http://www.unt.edu/lpbr/*.

Mailing Lists: Philosophy of Mind, Psychology, & AI

Listname: artificial-intelligence
Moderator: Kent Palmer at palmer@think.net
Subscribe: listserv@think.net
Article Submission: artificial-intelligence@think.net

A Thinknet BBS philosophy list providing a forum for the discussion of AI and related topics.

Listname: brain-l
Subscribe: listserv@vm1.mcgill.ca
Article Submission: brain-l@vm1.mcgill.ca

This mailing list is for the discussion of mind-brain issues.

Listname: cognition
Moderator: Kent Palmer at palmer@think.net
Subscribe: listserv@think.net
Article Submission: cognition@think.net

A Thinknet BBS philosophy list facilitating the discussion of issues relevant to cognition.

Listname: cognitive-science
Moderator: Kent Palmer at palmer@think.net
Subscribe: listserv@think.net
Article Submission: cognitive-science@think.net

A Thinknet BBS philosophy list facilitating the discussion of issues relevant to cognitive science.

Listname: cognitiv-1
Moderator: Maria Elisa Sayeg at memsayeg@usp.br
Subscribe: listproc@net.usp.br
Article Submission: cognitiv-1@net.usp.br

This list was initially for Portuguese language discussions, but is now open to posts in English. It is primarily for the discussion of concepts from the point of view of Cultural Psychology. Philosophical topics invited for discussioin include: concepts, definitions, formal vs. informal thought, and philosophy of cognitive science.

Listname: cogsci-hum
Moderator: Anne Jaap Jacobson at ajjacobson@uh.edu
               Cynthia Freeland at cfreelan@uh.edu
Subscribe: listserv@listserv.uh.edu
Article Submission: cogsci-hum@listserv.uh.edu

This list is for the exchange of information regarding topics at the intersection of cognitive science and the humanities and social sciences. Cognitive science challenges some of the traditional models of explanation in the humanities and social sciences. In addition, cognitive science includes research on matters of importance to many disciplines not formally part of it. Furthermore, areas of the humanities and the social sciences include critiques of concept, theory, and model building that may provide fruitful issues for cognitive science. Hence, there are many topics the list may cover.

Listname: consciousness
Moderator: Kent Palmer at palmer@think.net
Subscribe: listserv@think.net
Article Submission: consciousness@think.net

A Thinknet BBS philosophy list facilitating the discussion of consciousness and related topics.

Listname: 1brain-list
Moderator: Scott Stirling at sms9@acsu.buffalo.edu
Subscribe: listserv@listserv.acsu.buffalo.edu
Article Submission: 1brain-list@listserv.acsu.buffalo.edu

The 1brain-list mailing list was formed to serve as a vehicle for (1) scientific and philosophical discussion of topics related to language, linguistics, and the brain and (2) collection of any information related to these topics and related areas such as psychology, neurophysiology, and cognitive science.

Listname: mind-l
Moderator: John Romkey at romkey@asylum.sf.ca.us
Subscribe: mind-l-request@asylum.sf.ca.us
Article Submission: mind-l@asylum.sf.ca.us

This list provides for a discussion of mind altering techniques, and mind machines (light and sound, TENS/CES, electromagnet pulse, flotation), and biofeedback equipment in particular. Back issues of this list are available via anonymous FTP to: *asylum.sf.ca.us* in the directory */pub/mind-l.*

Listname: mindbody
Moderator: Kent Palmer at palmer@think.net
Subscribe: listserv@think.net
Article Submission: mindbody@think.net

A discussion list focusing on the mind-body problem in philosophy. A Thinknet BBS and DialogNet philosophy list.

Listname: nl-kr
Moderator: Al Whaley at al@sunnyside.com
　　　　　　　Christopher Welty at weltyc@cs.rpi.edu
Subscribe: nl-kr-requests@sunnyside.com
Article Submission: nl-kr@sunnyside.com

This list is open to discussion of any topic related to the natural language (both understanding and generation) and knowledge representation, both as sub-fields of AI. The moderator's interests are primarily in knowledge representation, natural language understanding, discourse understanding, philosophy of language, plan recognition, and computational linguistics, but other related topical areas are welcome.

Listname: psyche-a
Moderator: George Buckner at metacom@mindspring.com
Subscribe: listserv@listserv.uh.edu
Article Submission: psyche-a@listserv.uh.edu

PSYCHE-A is the list for distribution of abstracts of articles published by the ejournal *PSYCHE*, a scientific journal of research on the nature of consciousness and its relation to the brain.

Listname: psyche-b
Moderator: George Buckner at metacom@mindspring.com
Subscribe: listserv@listserv.uh.edu
Article Submission: psyche-b@listserv.uh.edu

PSYCHE-B is the moderated list for scientific discussion of the nature of consciousness and its relation to the brain, with an emphasis on biological and psychological issues.

Listname: psyche-d
Moderator: George Buckner at metacom@mindspring.com
Subscribe: listserv@listserv.uh.edu
Article Submission: psyche-da@listserv.uh.edu

PSYCHE-D is the moderated list for scientific discussion of the nature of consciousness and its relation to the brain, with an emphasis on theoretical issues.

Listname: psyche-l
Moderator: George Buckner at metacom@mindspring.com
Subscribe: listserv@listserv.uh.edu
Article Submission: psyche-l@listserv.uh.edu

PSYCHE-L is the list for distribution of articles published by the ejournal *PSYCHE*, a scientific journal of research on the nature of consciousness and its relation to the brain.

Listname: psychology
Moderator: Kent Palmer at palmer@think.net
Subscribe: listserv@think.net
Article Submission: psychology@think.net

This is a DialogNet philosophy list devoted to discussions in the area of philosophy of psychology.

Mailing Lists: Political Philosophy

Listname: austral-ecopolitics-l
Moderator: Dr Kate Crowley at Kate.Crowley@polsci.utas.edu.au
Subscribe: majordomo@coombs.anu.edu.au
Article Submission: austral-ecopolitics-l@coombs.anu.edu.au

This list is for anyone working on, or interested in the study of environmental politics; green movements policies, strategies, origins and history; public opinion and media coverage of environmental issues.

Listname: austral-socpol-theory-l
Moderator: Prof Philip Pettit at pnp@coombs.anu.edu.au
Subscribe: majordomo@coombs.anu.edu.au
Article Submission: austral-socpol-theory-l@coombs.anu.edu.au

This forum was established by the Research School of Social Sciences at the Australian National University in Canberra to provide a world-wide communications vehicle and a central electronic archive for anyone working on, or interested in the study of social and political theory.

Listname: casid-l
Subscribe: listserv@vm1.mcgill.ca
Article Submission: casid-l@vm1.mcgill.ca

This list is the Canadian Association for the Study of International Development mailing list.

Listname: childri-l
Subscribe: listserv@nic.surfnet.nl
Article Submission: childri-l@nic.surfnet.nl

A United Nations list for the discussion of the rights of children.

Listname: clspeech
Moderator: Eugene Volokh at volokh@law.ucla.edu
Subscribe: listserv@ftplaw.wuacc.edu
Article Submission: clspeech@ftplaw.wuacc.edu

A list on free speech law, intended mainly for legal academics, but open to academics in allied disciplines who specialise in free speech.

Listname: cope
Subscribe: listserv@shsu.edu
Article Submission: cope@shsu.edu

The Cyberchronicle of Political Economy is a list facilitating discussions of political economy and related issues.

Listname: disarm-l
Subscribe: listserv@cnsibm.albany.edu
Article Submission: disarm-l@cnsibm.albany.edu

This list is for the discussion of issues relating to disarmament.

Listname: fastnet
Moderator: Loka Institute
Subscribe: majordomo@igc.apc.org

Article Submission: fastnet@igc.apc.org

Fastnet, sponsored by the Loka Institute, is dedicated to promoting a more socially responsive and democratically informed politics of science and technology. The list is aimed at strengthening cross-issue awareness and alliances among activists, organizations, and activist-scholars who are concerned with specific substantive areas (such as telecommunications policy, environmental racism, defense conversion, biotechnology, health research, civil rights, etc.). This list is also aimed at promoting a more democratic politics of science and technology within the United States. For a discussion of issues beyond the U.S., see pol-sci-tech.

Listname: fpi-d
Moderator: Freedom Press at freedom@tao.ca
Subscribe: majordomo@tao.ca
Article Submission: fpi-d@tao.ca

This list, run by Freedom Press International is for anarchists, libertarian socialists, and other radicals. Discussion themes will be varied but it is hoped that the discussion will center on practical anarchism and its role in the wider political community.

Listname: frankfurt-school
Moderator: Spoon Collective at spoons@jefferson.village.virginia.edu
Subscribe: majordomo@jefferson.village.virginia.edu
Article Submission: frankfurt-school@jefferson.village.virginia.edu

This list, sponsored by·the Spoons Collective, is for the discussion of the thought of Frankfurt School political theorists.

Listname: h-pol
Subscribe: listserv@ksuvm.ksu.edu
Article Submission: h-pol@ksuvm.ksu.edu

This list is for the discussion of political history.

Listname: hrights
Moderator: Margarita Lacabe at marga@derechos.org
              Mike Katz-Lacabe at mike@derichos.org
Subscribe: hrights-request@lists.best.com
Article Submission: hrights@lists.best.com

This list is designed for discussion of human rights issues, including: civic, political, economic, and social rights as defined by international law. More information on the list is available at: *http://www.derechos.org/human-rights/hrights.html.*

Listname: hr-law
Moderator: Margarita Lacabe at marga@derechos.org

Subscribe: hr-law-request@lists.best.com
Article Submission: hr-law@lists.best.com

This list is designed for discussion of human rights legal issues, particularly focused towards law students studying human rights law and related issues. Further information on the list can be obtained at: *http://www.derechos.org/human-rights/law/list.html.*

Listname: hrs-l
Subscribe: listserv@bingvmb.cc.binghamton.edu
Article Submission: hrs-l@bingvmb.cc.binghamton.edu

This list is for the discussion of the scientific study of human rights.

Listname: industrial-relations-research
Subscribe: mailbase@mailbase.ac.uk
Article Submission: industrial-relations-research@mailbase.ac.uk

A forum for academic discussion on industrial relations, broadly conceived. It covers current research, methods, results and theories on employment relations, collective relationships, trade unions, human resource management, and employment law.

Listname: int-law
Subscribe: listserv@tc.umn.edu
Article Submission: int-law@tc.umn.edu

This list provides for a discussion of international law, and related topics.

Listname: int-rel-nat-sovereignty
Subscribe: mailbase@mailbase.ac.uk
Article Submission: int-rel-nat-sovereignty@mailbase.ac.uk

This list is open to international relations researchers interested in how the concept of sovereignty has changed since the end of the Cold War. The list will study how the questions of human rights, environment, globalisation and political legitimacy have impacted upon the nation-state and the concept of intervention.

Listname: ipe
Moderator: Lev Gonick at lgonick@mach1.wlu.ca
Subscribe: listproc@csf.colorado.edu
Article Submission: ipe@csf.colorado.edu

International Political Economy is a list that facilitates discussion of topics such as NAFTA, regional trading blocks, trade regimes, women and development, indigenous persons and ipe, international debt, long cycles, historical world systems, EEC, currency and market crises, democracy and governance in Latin and South America, Africa and Asia, and commodity negotiations.

Listname: isafp
Moderator: Frank Beer at beer@spot.colorado.edu
           Barry Balleck at balleck@osiris.colorado.edu
Subscribe: listproc@csf.colorado.edu
Article Submission: isafp@csf.colorado.edu

International Studies Association sponsored discussion of foreign policy.

Listname: marxism
Moderator: Bryan Alexander at bnalexan@umich.edu
Subscribe: majordomo@lists.village.virginia.edu
Article Submission: marxism@lists.village.virginia.edu

Marxism is an electronic forum for discussion and experimentation informed by the work of Karl Marx, and more generally, the tradition(s) that work has inspired since. Clearly, this field encompasses a diversity of different traditions and figures, from Lenin to Luxemburg, to Williams and West; the complete A to Z from Althusser to Zizek. It is not the intention of the moderators of this list that any particular tradition or orthodoxy should receive more attention or more 'allegiance' than another. The list is open to all interested parties.

Listname: marxism2
Subscribe: majordomo@lists.village.virginia.edu
Article Submission: marxism2@lists.village.virginia.edu

Marxism2 is a list for the discussion of Marxian-related thought, politics, production, action, history, etc. The list emphasises productive, creative, non-sectarian, cross-occupational and interdisciplinary discussion. Relations with other liberatory thought is included, and interest in historical process, change, transition, and application of Marxian thought to current problems is strong.

Listname: moderndemocracy
Moderator: David Hwang at dhwang1@midway.uchicago.edu
           Vivake Gupta at vgupta1@midway.uchicago.edu
Subscribe: *http://www.onelist.com/subscribe.cgi/moderndemocracy*
Article Submission: moderndemocracy@onelist.com

This list will explore the fundamental challenges that confront democratic states as we approach the new millenium and strategies for increasing citizen participation as our political world becomes increasingly complex. In a world where political decisions are complex, many citizens find their voice in their government diminishing. This list will provide students, scholars, and ordinary citizens with a forum to discuss many of the fundamental challenges facing democracies today.

Listname: nyslux-l
Moderator: Munroe Eagles at psceagle@acsu.buffalo.edu

Subscribe: listserv@acsu.buffalo.edu
Article Submission: nsylux-l@acsu.buffalo.edu

This list is a discussion forum for those with an interest in the European Community and in particular those interested in the New York Consortium for Model European Community Simulations.

Listname: peace
Moderator: Robin J. Crews at crews@csf.colorado.edu
Subscribe: listproc@csf.colorado.edu
Article Submission: peace@csf.colorado.edu

Peace is a discussion group hosted by Communications for a Sustainable Future (CSF), at the University of Colorado at Boulder. Peace is a part of a larger project that integrates the discussion group with a peace studies database. Together, the list and database provide those interested in peace studies and its subject matter with the opportunity to access and contribute to the literature, read current work in the field, and discuss it with colleagues and friends.

Listname: pofp-l
Moderator: William Chittick at chittick@uga.cc.uga.edu
Subscribe: listserv@uga.cc.uga.edu
Article Submission: pofp-l@uga.cc.uga.edu

This list is for the discussion of the electronic journal, *Public Opinion and Foreign Policy*, but strays into general discussions in this area as well.

Listname: polcom
Subscribe: listserv@vm.its.rpi.edu
Article Submission: polcomm@its.rpi.edu

This list is for the discussion of political communication.

Listname: pol-econ
Moderator: George D. Greenwade at bed_gdg@shsu.edu
Subscribe: listserv@shsu.edu
Article Submission: pol-econ@shsu.edu

Political Economy is an unmoderated list to providing an environment where issues, questions, comments, ideas, and uses of political economy as a logical framework can be discussed.

Listname: polirhet
Subscribe: listserv@tamvm1.tamu.edu
Article Submission: polirhet@tamvm1.tamu.edu

This list focuses on discussion on the topic of rhetoric in politics.

Listname: political-islam
Moderator: Joseph Roberts at joseph.roberts@m.cc.utah.edu
Subscribe: political-islam-request@lists.utah.edu
Article Submission: political-islam@lists.utah.edu

This is a mailing list for the scholarly discussion of all aspects of political Islam. Requests for subscriptions must include a biography and agreement to abide by the terms stated in the guidelines for the list. These can be found at: *http://www.cc.utah.edu/~jwr9311/MENA/ Religion/polislam.html.*

Listname: politics
Moderator: Jim Ennis at jim@ucf1vm.cc.ucf.edu
Subscribe: listserv%villvm.bitnet@listserv.net
Article Submission: politics%villvm.bitnet@listserv.net

The politics discussion list is sponsored by the University of Central Florida and covers all aspects of politics, political philosophy, political science, and so on. The list has quite a heavy traffic flow, so be prepared for an overflowing mail box!

Listname: politics
Moderator: Kent Palmer at palmer@think.net
Subscribe: listserv@think.net
Article Submission: politics@think.net

A Thinknet BBS philosophy list facilitating the discussion of issues relevant to political philosophy.

Listname: pol-sci-tech
Moderator: Loka Institute
Subscribe: majordomo@igc.apc.org
Article Submission: pol-sci-tech@igc.apc.org

Pol-sci-tech is dedicated to promoting a more socially-responsive and democratically-informed politics of science and technology. It is especially concerned with strengthening cross-issue awareness and alliances among activists, organizations, and activist-scholars who are concerned with specific substantive areas (such as telecommunications policy, environmental racism, defense conversion, biotechnology, health research, civil rights, etc.).

Listname: pol-toc-l
Moderator: Andrew Gleeson at jrnl@coombs.anu.edu.au
Subscribe: majordomo@coombs.anu.edu.au
Article Submission: no submissions

This list provides periodic mailings of the tables of contents of journals dealing with social and political theory. This special service is provided by the Coombs Computing Unit, RSSS, Australian National University, and is available to researchers and scholars in Australia and New Zealand who subscribe to aphil-l.

Listname: poscim
Subscribe: listserv@vm.gmd.de
Article Submission: poscim@vm.gmd.de

The political science mailing list is intended as a forum for those studying, researching, or teaching the subject, as well as for practitioners of politics.

Listname: psrt-l
Subscribe: listserv@mizzou1.missouri.edu
Article Submission: psrt-l@mizzou1.missouri.edu

This is the Political Science Research and Teaching discussion list.

Listname: pubpol-d
Subscribe: listserv@tc.umn.edu
Article Submission: pubpol-d@tcs.umn.edu

This is the Public Policy Discussion list, a forum dedicated to open, serious, and substantial discussion of public policy issues, and for extended comments on items posted in pubpol-l. Pubpol-l is not an appropriate forum for general discussion. Summaries of research findings or digests of pubpol-d discussions are appropriate for pubpol-l.

Listname: pubpol-l
Subscribe: listserv@tc.umn.edu
Article Submission: pubpol-l@tcs.umn.edu

The Public Policy List is a forum for graduate students, professionals, faculty, and staff in the fields of public policy, public administration, planning, and other related areas. The topics covered in postings include current public policy issues, events and conferences, research, teaching, curriculum and courses, employment and career opportunities, activities of public policy practitioners, and other topics of interest. The list encourages the electronic posting of newsletters, conference notices, and other text normally distributed in paper form by public policy schools and their centers or programs, government agencies, or public-sector oriented organizations.

Listname: social-policy
Moderator: Pauline Hammerton
Subscribe: mailbase@mailbase.ac.uk
Article Submission: social-policy@mailbase.ac.uk

This list has been set up to facilitate and encourage discussion across a board range of social policy themes and services among social policy specialists: academics (teaching and researching in universities, colleges, schools, and reserch bodies), policy makers, and service providers. The list is linked to the Social Policy Association, and has three basic purposes: a means of informing members and others about the activities of the Social Policy Association; a forum for the discussion of social policy issues; a general social policy bulletin board for the placement of announcements, job advertisements, calls for conference papers, research initiatives, and so on.

Listname: social-theory
Subscribe: mailbase@mailbase.ac.uk
Article Submission: social-theory@mailbase.ac.uk

This list facilitates discussions relevant to social theory.

Listname: unt-lpbr
Moderator: Neal Tate at Neal_Tate@unt.edu
Subscribe: listserv@unt.edu
Article Submission: not permitted, this is a distribution list only

This list is for the distribution of book reviews in law and politics. Archives of the reviews can be found at: *http://www.psci.unt.edu/lpbr/*.

Mailing Lists: Religion & Eastern Philosophy

Listname: andere-l
Moderator: J. Shawn Landres at 6500land@ucsbuxa.ucsb.edu
Subscribe: listserv@ucsbvm.ucsb.edu
Article Submission: andere-l@ucsbvm.ucsb.edu

This is the official mailing list of the Department of Religious Studies at the University of California, Santa Barbara. It serves as a forum for discussion of theories, methods, and approaches to the study of religion, including but not limited to history of religions, sociology of religion, and interdisciplinary methods.

Listname: asi-philosophy
Moderator: Peter Turland at peter.turland@VIRGIN.NET
Subscribe: majordomo@asi.org
Article Submission: asi-philosophy@asi.org

This list facilitates a discussion of the cosmological, philosophical, and religious implications of the human colonization of space.

Listname: bible-l
Moderator: Paul Bellan-Boyer at pbb@fw.gs.com
Subscribe: bible-l-request@lists.wku.edu
Article Submission: bible-l@lists.wku.edu

Bible-l is devoted to discussion of topics broadly related to the Bible: history, texts, culture, reference sources, philosophy, religious practice and meaning.

Listname: buddha-l
Moderator: James Cocks at jacocks@ulkyvm.louisville.edu
Subscribe: listserv@ulkyvm.louisville.edu
Article Submission: buddha-l@ulkyvm.louisville.edu

The Buddhist Discussion Group is directed at those interested in the exchange of information and views regarding Buddhist studies. It is hoped that the list will function as an open forum for scholarly discussion of topics relating to the history, literature and languages, fine arts, philosophy, and institutions of all forms of Buddhism.

Listname: buddhist
Subscribe: listserv@vm1.mcgill.ca
Article Submission: buddhist@vm1.mcgill.ca

This list is devoted to an academic discussion of Buddhism.

Listname: buddhist-philosophy
Moderator: Kent Palmer at palmer@think.net
Subscribe: listserv@think.net
Article Submission: buddhist-philosophy@think.net

This is a Thinknet BBS and DialogNet philosophy list devoted to the discussion of all aspects of buddhist philosophy.

Listname: chinese-philosophy
Moderator: Kent Palmer at palmer@think.net
Subscribe: listserv@think.net
Article Submission: chinese-philosophy@think.net

A Thinknet BBS and DialogNet philosophy list devoted to the discussion of all aspects of Chinese philosophy.

Listname: confucius
Moderator: Todd Thacker at thacker@peacenet.co.kr
Subscribe: thacker@peacenet.co.kr
Article Submission: thacker@peacenet.co.kr

Confucius is a manually-operated list, and focuses primarily on "pure" Confucianism; that is, the text 'The Analects' and its relevance, application, or direct influence in ancient China or modern times. Questions about the accuracy of certain well-known translations are also encouraged.

Listname: dharma-talk
Subscribe: majordomo@saigon.com
Article Submission: dharma-talk@saigon.com

This list is a forum for discussions, information, and announcements relating to Buddhism.

Listname: ecotheology
Moderator: Marshall Massey at ecotheology-owner@.lists.best.com
Subscribe: bestserv@lists.best.com
Article Submission: ecotheology@lists.best.com

The focus of this list is the academic and professional discussion of religion/theology and ecology/environment. The list exists to serve the needs of theologians and philosophers, religious and environmental organizers, social and environmental scientists, and others with a serious, work-related interest in the connection between religion/theology and ecology/environment.

Listname: god
Subscribe: majordomo@hlms145.colorado.edu
Article Submission: god@hlms145.colorado.edu

This mailing list is for anyone who wishes to discuss or debate issues that relate, directly or indirectly, to the existence or nature or character of God. Past topics have included: the problem of evil, the relation between God and morality, the nature of morality, free will and determinism, omniscience and free will, the kalam cosmological argument, etc. An archive of posts to the list can be found at *http://hlms145.colorado.edu/god/archives/*.

Listname: hindu-d
Subscribe: listserv@listserv.nodak.edu
Article Submission: hindu-d@listserv.nodak.edu

This list provides for discussions relating to Hindu dharma, as followed by over 650 million people in the world. Various Hindu doctrines, and their application to day-to-day life are discussed here.

Listname: islam
Moderator: Kent Palmer at palmer@think.net
Subscribe: listserv@think.net
Article Submission: islam@think.net

A list for the discussion of Islam. A Thinknet BBS and DialogNet philosophy list.

Listname: islam-l
Moderator: James Cocks at jacocks@ulkyvm.louisville.edu
Subscribe: listserv@ulkyvm.louisville.edu
Article Submission: islam-l@ulkyvm.louisville.edu

Islam Discussion Forum is a non-sectarian forum for discussion, debate, and the exchange of information by students and scholars of the history of Islam.

Listname: jain-list
Moderator: Raphael Carter at jain-list-admin@ddb.com

Subscribe: jain-list-request@ddb.com
Article Submission: jain-list@ddb.com

This list is for discussion of Jainism, a non-Vedic religion of India. Jainism is one of the world's oldest religious traditions, with more than three million devotees in India and throughout the world. Jainism is best known for its emphasis on 'ahimsa', or non-violence toward all beings. Further information on Jainism and this list can be found at: *http:// ddb.com/~raphael/jain-list/*.

Listname: liberal-judaism
Moderator: Daniel Faigin at faigin@aerospace.aero.org
Subscribe: faigin@aerospace.aero.org
Article Submission: liberal-judaism@nysernet.org

This list provides for a non-judgemental discussion of liberal Judaism (Reform, Reconstructionist, Conservative, Secular Humanist, etc.) and the liberal Jewish issues, practices, and beliefs.

Listname: meta
Moderator: William Grassie at grassie@voicenet.com
Subscribe: listserv@templeton.org
Article Submission: meta@templeton.org

Meta is an edited, moderated, and public listserv dedicated to promoting the constructive engagement of science and religion and to sharing information and perspectives among the diverse organizations and individuals involved in this interdisciplinary field. The list may be used for conference announcements, book reviews, job and grant opportunities as, well as general discussion.

Listname: pagan
Moderator: Stacey Greenstein at uther@drycas.club.cc.cmu.edu
Subscribe: pagan-request@drycas.club.cc.cmu.edu
Article Submission: pagan@drycas.club.cc.cmu.edu

Pagan Religion and Philosophy is a forum for the scholarly discussion of paganism.

Listname: rambam
Moderator: Project Genesis at genesis@shamash.nysernet.org
Subscribe: listproc@shamash.nysernet.org
Article Submission: rambam@shamash.nysernet.org

Rambam is a Project Genesis mailing list devoted to the study of Maimonides' famed Mishneh Torah, or 'review' of the entire body of Jewish law.

Listname: religion
Moderator: Kent Palmer at palmer@think.net
Subscribe: listserv@think.net
Article Submission: religion@think.net

A list for the discussion of the philosophy of religion. A Thinknet BBS and DialogNet philosophy list.

Listname: religious-studies
Moderator: Kent Palmer at palmer@think.net
Subscribe: listserv@think.net
Article Submission: religious-studies@think.net

A list for the discussion of religious studies. A Thinknet BBS and DialogNet philosophy list.

Listname: taoism
Moderator: Kent Palmer at palmer@think.net
Subscribe: listserv@think.net
Article Submission: taoism@think.net

A list for the discussion of the philosophical aspects of Taoism. A Thinknet BBS and DialogNet philosophy list.

Listname: theology
Moderator: Kent Palmer at palmer@think.net
Subscribe: listserv@think.net
Article Submission: theology@think.net

A list for the discussion of theology. A Thinknet BBS and DialogNet philosophy list.

Listname: theosci
Moderator: Gary Mann at remann@augustana.edu
Subscribe: mxserver@alpha.augustana.edu
Article Submission: theosci@alpha.augustana.edu

A forum for the discussion of religion and science. The goal of the list is to enable academic discussion of issues involved in the dialogue between the sciences and theological-religious studies. The list is open to anyone with a serious academic interest in this integrative area of study, and from any discipline.

Listname: wmsprt-l
Subscribe: listserv@ubvm.acsu.buffalo.edu
Article Submission: wmsprt-l@ubvm.ascu.buffalo.edu

This list is an open discussion list for women and men interested in goddess spirituality, feminism, and the incorporation of the feminine/feminist idea in the study and worship of the divine.

Listname: womenrab
Moderator: Ann Plutzer at plutzera@ujafedny.org
Subscribe: listserv@jtsa.edu
Article Submission: womenrab@jtsa.edu

This is a multi-denominational, international discussion group for and by women rabbis and women rabbinical students, and is designed to provide supportive, accessible sanctuary in cyberspace to list members in which to discuss personal, professional, familial, emotional, spiritual, halkhic, and educational issues pertinent to women in the rabbinate.

Listname: zen
Moderator: Kent Palmer at palmer@think.net
Subscribe: listserv@think.net
Article Submission: zen@think.net

A list for the discussion of the philosophical aspects of Zen Buddhism. A Thinknet BBS and DialogNet philosophy list.

Newsgroups: Atheism & Humanism

Newsgroup: alt.atheism
A newsgroup providing an unmoderated, and so sometimes unruly, discussion of atheism.

Newsgroup: alt.atheism.moderated
A newsgroup providing a moderated discussion of atheism.

Newsgroup: soc.atheism
This newsgroup discusses atheism in society.

Newsgroup: talk.atheism
This is another miscellaneous group focusing on atheism.

Newsgroup: talk.philosophy.humanism
This newsgroup discusses humanism and philosophy.

Newsgroups: Environmental Philosophy

Newsgroup: sci.bio.ecology
Discussion of various aspects of ecology.

Newsgroup: sci.environment
A newsgroup devoted to the discussion of environment and ecology.

Newsgroup: talk.environment
A discussion of environmental issues.

Newsgroups: Ethics & Bioethics

Newsgroup: alt.soc.ethics
A newsgroup for the discussion of ethical issues.

Newsgroup: soc.rights.human
A newsgroup for the discussion of human rights issues.

Newsgroup: talk.abortion
Discussions and arguments on abortion.

Newsgroups: Feminism & Women's Studies

Newsgroup: alt.feminism
A discussion of various issues relating to feminism.

Newsgroup: alt.politics.sex
For the discussion of the politics of sex and gender.

Newsgroup: comp.society.women
This group discusses the issues of women and computing.

Newsgroup: soc.feminism
This is a moderated newsgroup for the discussion of issues relevant to feminism. Some useful resources are produced by this newsgroup (including bibliographies, definitions and discussions of various kinds of feminism, and so on), and are posted regularly to the newsgroup news.answers as well as to soc.feminism.

Newsgroups: General & Miscellaneous

Newsgroup: alt.culture.theory
This newsgroup discusses cultural theory.

Newsgroup: alt.philosophy.basism

Newsgroup: alt.philosophy.debate
A newsgroup for debates with a philosophical focus.

Newsgroup: alt.philosophy.jarf

Newsgroup: alt.philosophy.objectivism
This newsgroup discusses topics such as objectivism in science and math, emotions, rationality, and Ayn Rand.

Newsgroup: alt.postmodern
A newsgroup for the discussion of postmodernism.

Newsgroup: sci.philosophy.meta
This general philosophy discussion forum covers such topics as induction, chaos theory, foundationalism, holism, meta-ethics, consciousness, and Ayn Rand.

Newsgroup: talk.philosophy.misc
A forum for the discussion of philosophy, ranging widely in content and quality. Topics include atheism, abortion, politics, determinism, quantum mechanics, and Zen.

Newsgroups: Logic & Philosophy of Science

Newsgroup: comp.ai.fuzzy
A forum for the discussion of fuzzy logic.

Newsgroup: sci.logic
A forum for the discussion of logic: math, philosophy, and computational aspects.

Newsgroup: sci.philosophy
A forum for general discussion on the philosophy of science.

Newsgroup: sci.philosophy.tech
A forum for the discussion of technical philosophy: math, science, logic, etc.

Newsgroup: sci.physics
A physics discussion group.

Newsgroup: sci.physics.fusion
A newsgroup facilitating the discussion of fusion.

Newsgroup: sci.skeptic
A forum for the sceptical discussion of 'pseudo science'.

Newsgroup: sci.systems
A newsgroup dicussing philosophy of science.

Newsgroup: talk.origins
A newsgroup which focuses on a debate between evolution and creationism.

Newsgroups: Philosophy of Law

Newsgroup: misc.legal
This newsgroup provides for discussion focusing on law and legal research.

Newsgroup: misc.legal.moderated
This newsgroup facilitates a moderated discussion of a range of legal issues.

Newsgroups: Philosophy of Mind, Psychology & AI

Newsgroup: alt.consciousness
This discussion of consciousness covers spirituality, enlightenment, mind control, hypnosis, and linear thinking.

Newsgroup: comp.ai.neural-nets
This newsgroup includes discussions gated from the mailing list neuron, listed in the associated mailing list section.

Newsgroup: comp.ai.philosophy
The discussion focuses around consciousness with respect to computers, humans, and animals. Topics include animal consciousness, functionalism, materialism, complexity and emergence, and the computational metaphor.

Newsgroup: sci.cognitive
The discussion on this newsgroup focuses on cognitive science and related issues.

Newsgroup: sci.psychology.consciousness
This newsgroup discusses consciousness and pyschology.

Newsgroups: Political Philosophy

Newsgroup: alt.censorship
A newsgroup for the discussion of censorship and freedom of speech.

Newsgroup: alt.individualism
This newsgroup focuses on discussions of individualist and libertarian philosophy.

Newsgroup: alt.politics.economics
This newsgroup facilitates a discussion of economics, economic theory, and political economy.

Newsgroup: alt.politics.equality
This newsgroup focuses on discussions relating to equality and egalitarianism.

Newsgroup: alt.politics.libertarian
A newsgroup for the discussion of libertarian political philosophy.

Newsgroup: alt.politics.org.un
The discussion of the United Nations and related issues is provided for on this newsgroup.

Newsgroup: alt.privacy
A forum for discussion of issues relating to privacy and government policy/legislation which potentially infringes.

Newsgroup: alt.society.civil.liberty
                        alt.society.civil.liberties
These newsgroups focus on civil liberty and related issues.

Newsgroup: alt.war
A newsgroup supporting discussions relating to war.

Newsgroup: comp.society.privacy
A discussion forum on issues relating to computer security/privacy.

Newsgroup: soc.politics
This is a moderated group devoted to the discussion of political issues.

Newsgroup: soc.politics.arms.d
This is a moderated newsgroup devoted to the discussion of issues relating to arms.

Newsgroup: soc.rights.human
A newsgroup for the discussion of human rights issues.

Newsgroup: sci.military
This newsgroup is for the discussion of military science and current world military events.

Newsgroup: talk.politics.theory
A forum for the discussion of political theory and political philosophy.

Newsgroup: talk.politics.misc
Miscellaneous issues in politics are covered in the discussion on this newsgroup.

Newsgroups: Religion & Eastern Philosophy

Newsgroup: alt.christnet.philosophy
A newsgroup discussing Christianity and philosophy.

Newsgroup: alt.meditation
This newsgroup focuses on the discussion of meditation and Eastern Philosophy.

Newsgroup: alt.pagan
The discussion of pagan philosophy is the focus of this newsgroup.

Newsgroup: alt.philosophy.taoism
A forum for the discussion of taoist philosophy.

Newsgroup: alt.philosophy.zen
A forum for the discussion of zen philosophy.

Newsgroup: alt.religion.buddhism.tibetan
A newsgroup facilitating discussion of Tibetan Buddhism.

Newsgroup: alt.zen
This newsgroup provides for discussions of Zen Buddhism.

Newsgroup: soc.religion.bahai
A moderated discussion of the Baha'i faith is facilitated in this newsgroup.

Newsgroup: soc.religion.christian
This is a moderated newsgroup discussing issues relating to Christianity.

Newsgroup: soc.religion.eastern
A moderated discussion of issues pertaining to eastern religion and philosophy is provided in this newsgroup.

Newsgroup: soc.religion.islam
This newsgroup facilitates a moderated discussion of issues relating to Islam.

Newsgroup: talk.origins
A newsgroup which focuses on a debate between evolution and creationism.

Newsgroup: talk.religion.buddhism
A forum for the discussion of buddhism.

Newsgroup: talk.religion.misc
A newsgroup for the discussion of religious, ethical, and moral topics not covered elsewhere.

Newsgroup: talk.religion.newage
A forum for the discussion of new age religion and philosophy.

Section 5: Miscellaneous

Conferences & Calls for Papers

APNet Conference Information

http://www.arts.su.edu.au/Arts/departs/philos/APS/conferences/conferences.html

Maintained by Hugh Clapin Hugh.Clapin@anu.edu.au for the Australian Philosophy Net, this page provides information on conferences in philosophy all over the world.

Calls for Papers

http://www.english.upenn.edu/CFP/

This site provides a compilation of calls for papers for a range of conferences (some of the subject headings under which calls for papers are announced include: Medieval, Renaissance, Theory, Gender Studies and Sexuality, and Ethnicity and National Identity), located both in the US and internationally. It site is maintained by Jack Lynch jlynch@english.upenn.edu.

Conferences and Calls for Papers

http://www.udel.edu/apa/opportunities/conferences/

This is the American Philosophical Association's extensive list of philosophy conferences and calls for papers.

Conference Announcements

http://www.liv.ac.uk/Philosophy/meetings.html

This extensive list of links to philosophy conferences and meetings is from Stephen Clark's srlclark@liverpool.ac.uk philosophy guide.

Current Events in Legal Theory

http://www.legaltheory.demon.co.uk/currinfo.html

This site, from Deborah Charles Publications, provides information on current events and conferences in legal theory.

Philosophy Events

http://users.ox.ac.uk/~worc0337/phil_events.html

This is Peter King's peter.king@philosophy.ox.ac.uk page on events in philosophy, including conferences, seminar series, and lecture series.

Yahoo: Philosophy Conferences

http://www.yahoo.com/Arts/Humanities/Philosophy/Conferences/

This is the famous Yahoo net directory's listing of conferences in philosophy. Automated as it is, not all links are current.

Courses, Syllabi, & Teaching Resources

Aesthetics & Electronic Imaging
http://wwwfaculty.mccneb.edu/commhum/aesthetics/aeiph_1.htm

This site provides access to a syllabus for an interdisciplinary course which seeks to establish a dialogue between the new electronic technologies and the traditional fine arts by re-examining the basic questions of art and aesthetics. This page is maintained by Frank Edler fedler@ne.uswest.net.

Aesthetics Teaching Materials
http://www.indiana.edu/~asanl/teaching/syllabi.html

This site, from Dominic Lopes dlopes@indiana.edu, provides links to materials useful for those teaching aesthetics. It includes online courses, syllabi, and miscellaneous aesthetics resources.

Agricultural Ethics
http://www.public.iastate.edu/~rudge/ageti.html

This site, from David Rudge rudge@iastate.edu, provides a syllabus for this course which focuses on a number of moral dilemmas raised by the issue of world hunger. The first half of the semester surveys several extant political/ethical theories of justice; the second half examines specific applications of these theories to ethical problems associated with world hunger.

Art, Language & Cultural Studies: Syllabus
http://www.panix.com/~squigle/alcs/syllabus.html

This site provides an online syllabus for this course taught by T. R. Quigley squigle@panix.com at the New School for Social Research, New York.

Bioethics Syllabi
http://ccme-mac4.bsd.uchicago.edu/CCMEDocs/Syllabi

This page provides links to a collection of syllabi in bio-ethics-related fields. It is maintained by J. Hughes j-hughes@uchicago.edu as part of the MacLean Center for Medical Ethics site.

Biomedical Ethics
http://humanitas.ucsb.edu/~portmore/outlines.htm

This page, from Doug Portmore portmore@humanitas.ucsb.edu, provides access to a course in biomedical ethics, with lecture notes, links to additional resources relevant to the course, exam questions, topics for papers, and more.

Classroom Resources
http://www.epistemelinks.com/Main/MainClas.htm

This page is part of Tom Stone's trstone@rpa.net Episteme Links guide to philosophical resources online at *http://www.epistemelinks.com/* and provides access to a collection of teaching and study-related resources.

Cognitive Science at the CUNY Graduate School

http://web.gc.cuny.edy/dept/cogit/cs.htm

This site, from David Rosenthal drosenth@email.gc.cuny.edu, provides a syllabus and web resources in cognitive science.

Contemporary Moral Issues

http://www.public.iastate.edu/~rudge/cmi.html

This site, from David Rudge rudge@iastate.edu, provides a syllabus for this course which surveys a number of ethical issues that arise in the conduct of personal and social life, issues having to do with basic concepts of right and wrong.

Course Materials

http://www-philosophy.ucdavis.edu/phildept/gjmattey.htm

This page provides access to course materials developed by G. J. Mattey gjmattey@ucdavis.edu, of UC Davis. Most of the material on these pages consists of lecture notes, but you will also find notes on texts, examination questions, and some other background materials.

Course Materials in Philosophy

http://socrates.berkeley.edu/~phlos-ad/pedagogy.html

Edited by Andrew Carpenter phlos-ad@socrates.berkeley.edu, Course Materials in Philosophy is a systematic collection of syllabi, handouts, and other course materials which will prove useful to those teaching philosophy.

Cthink: The Critical Thinking Community

http://www.sonoma.edu/cthink/

This site is sponsored by the Center for Critical Thinking CCT@sonoma.edu, the Foundation for Critical Thinking, the International Center for the Assessment of Higher Order Thinking, and the National Council for Excellence in Critical Thinking. The site divides into sections on primary and secondary education, and on college or university education and provides a collection of critical thinking articles focused on the background and theory of critical thinking, guidelines and lessons for integrating critical thinking into the curriculum, and an archive of the critical thinking e-mail discussion group. It also provides information on critical thinking seminars, in-services, and conferences.

Current Continental Philosophy: Syllabus for PHIL 419.500

http://www-phil.tamu.edu/~sdaniel/419sy97.html

This course, from Stephen H. Daniel sdaniel@unix.tamu.edu, examines themes developed by French and German philosophers in the last 40 years. Major movements to be studied include structuralist psychoanalysis, deconstruction, Neo-Marxist critical theory, semiotics, philosophical hermeneutics, poststructuralism, and postmodernism.

Darren Brierton's Teaching Resource Page

http://www.cogsci.ed.ac.uk/~ddb/

For teaching resources in philosophy of mind, click on the link to Darren Brierton's ddb@cogsci.ed.ac.uk "Documents" section. From this page you will also find a glossary for philosophy of mind. Darren promises further resources will be added soon.

Discourse, Self, & Social Relations

http://www.panix.com/~squigle/dssr/syllabus.html

This page provides a syllabus for a course which examines, in historical context, concepts and discourses of knowing, subjectivity, and social formation that structure and inform contemporary cultural life. Material is drawn from a variety of sources including philosophical and literary texts, music, and the visual arts. Western forms of subjectivity are compared with non-western conceptions of self as questions of identity and difference are raised. The course is taught by T. R. Quigley squigle@panix.com at the New School for Social Research, New York.

Dr Z's Philosophy Page

http://www.fred.net/tzaka/phil.html

This page, maintained by Gordon Ziniewicz tsaka@fred.net, provides links to lecture notes which he has produced over the years to introduce students to philosophy. Plato, Aristotle, Epicurus, Epictetus, Medieval Philosophy, Descartes, Hobbes, Kant, Nietzsche, Kierkegaard, Dewey, Buddhism, Confucianism, and Taoism are represented. Dr Ziniewicz also includes some summaries of the ethical principles of a variety of philosophers, some works on the philosophy of John Dewey, and a number of other short papers that may prove useful to students of philosophy.

Dynamic Semantics: Online Course

http://turing.wins.uva.nl/~pdekker/ECDS/

The Electronic Course Dynamics Semantics is an initiative of the Institute for Logic, Language, and Computation (ILLC, University of Amsterdam). It is a forefront activity both with regard to teaching method and research contents. Teaching takes places at the Internet in the form of an electronic classroom. People attend the classroom on-line at home, and students from different countries work together on various themes and exercises through electronic communication. With regard to content, the course is concerned with the theme 'dynamic semantics', which is considered of great importance in the study of formal semantics and logic in general. The course is led by Paul J. E. Dekker and David I. Beaver who can be contacted at ecds@illc.uva.nl.

An Email Introduction to Philosophy and Philosophical Thinking

http://www.scott.net/~hmwkhelp/Philosophy.html

This page represents an experiment by Rick Garlikov hmwkhelp@scott.net, to see if he can teach philosophy on the net, via email. A number of questions are set out and Rick asks visitors to respond. Interesting responses will be displayed on the page, together with comments from Rick.

Ethics OCSE
http://wings.buffalo.edu/faculty/research/bioethics/osce.html

This site provides access to standardised patient scenarios for teaching and evaluating bio-ethics. Scenarios include confidentiality, truth-telling, decisions to forego treatment, and more. An accompanying video may be ordered. The site is maintained by Jack Freer JFreer@acsu.buffalo.edu.

Ethics Resources for Teachers & Trainers
http://condor.depaul.edu/ethics/ethc1.html

This site provides links to a range of ethics-related syllabi, lists of articles, texts and trade books used by ethics faculty, and more. The site is maintained by D. Thies dthies@wppost.depaul.edu.

Feminist Curricular Resources Clearinghouse
http://www.law.indiana.edu/fcrc/fcrc.html

The Clearinghouse provides access to a number of resources related to teaching about feminism and law. It offers syllabi, reading lists, and bibliographies from courses taught in law schools and other departments. All materials deal with legal or jurisprudential issues of concern to women. The site is maintained by Susan Williams SusanWilliams@law.indiana.edu.

Great Ideas Homepage
http://ernie.bgsu.edu/~skrause/Great_Ideas.html

Great Ideas is an interdisciplinary course offered through the College of Arts and Sciences at Bowling Green State University that is a survey of several fundamental ideas which have shaped modern culture in general and Western culture in particular. This page provides access to course-related resources and is maintained by Steve Krause skrause@bgnet.bgsu.edu.

History of Ancient Philosophy
http://weber.u.washington.edu/~smcohen/phil320.htm

This page, from Marc Cohen smcohen@u.washington.edu, provides a course syllabus, lecture notes, and links to ancient philosophy resources.

History of Ideas Online
http://www.msstate.edu/Dept/PR/H-Ideas/

History of Ideas Online is a team-taught online interdisciplinary course designed by a historian of philosophy and a Renaissance scholar where students explore ideas of space--literal and metaphorical—which are transformed in the 16th and 17th century. For information on course content, contact: Lynn Holt dlh4@ra.msstate.edu, Steven Shelburne sshelbur@beta.centenary.edu, or Bruce Avery bavery@sfsu.edu.

History of Western Philosophy: 1497-1776
http://www.orst.edu/~uzgalisw/302/

This page, from Bill Uzgalis uzgalisw@cla.orst.edu, provides access to a syllabus and materials for a course he teaches at Oregon State University.

The Internet Academy of Philosophy
http://www.mc.maricopa.edu/academic/philosophy/ic/main.html

From the Philosophy Department of Mesa Community College, comes this site for online courses in philosophy. So far, only one course is online (Intro to Philosophy), but three additional courses are planned: Intro to Logic, Intro to Ethics, and Intro to Bioethics. The site is maintained by Barry Vaughan vaughan@.mc.maricopa.edu.

Interquest Odyssey
http://iq.orst.edu/odyssey/

This site offers an introductory course in philosophy. It is maintained by John Dorbolo dorboloj@ucs.orst.edu. Past versions of the course can be accessed at: *http://iq.orst.edu/03phl01.html.*

Introduction to Ethics
http://humanitas.ucsb.edu/~portmore/phil4f97.htm

From Doug Portmore portmore@humanitas.ucsb.edu, this page provides an overview of an introductory course in ethics, with links to useful resources for students.

Introduction to Logic
http://www.public.iastate.edu/~rudge/206a.html

This site, from David Rudge rudge@iastate.edu, provides a syllabus for this course which aims to teach students to (1) be able to identify arguments from other forms of persuasion; (2) be able to evaluate arguments in accordance with principles of reasoning reviewed in class; and, (3) gain some insight into the "logic of science," or how scientists develop and test claims about the world.

Introduction to Philosophpy: PHIL251
http://www-phil.tamu.edu/~sdaniel251.html

This course, from Stephen H. Daniel sdaniel@unix.tamu.edu, uses Thomas White's *Discovering Philosophy* as text. The website provides extensive notes on each class, as well as over 700 true-false and multiple choice questions on all aspects of philosophy.

Introduction to Philosophy: Syllabus for PHIL 251.200
http://www-phil.tamu.edu/~sdaniel/251sy97.html

This is the syllabus for Stephen H. Daniel's sdaniel@unix.tamu.edu intruductory philosophy course at Texas A&M University, based on *Introducing Philosophy* (6th ed.) by Robert Solomon.

Introductory Philosophy: PD100
http://www.uq.edu/au/philosophy/pd100.html

This page, from William Grey wgrey@cltr.uq.edu.au, provides a syllabus for an introductory course in philosophy, complete with links to online texts and other relevant resources.

ISEE Syllabus Project
http://forest.bgsu.edu/ISEE/index.html

This site aims to identify all the courses in environmental philosophy and ethics at every institution of higher learning—from two-year community college courses to four-year state university courses, and to private liberal arts colleges and universities to master's- and doctorate-granting universities—who teaches them, what is being taught, and what texts are used. The site is maintained by Robert Hood rhood@bgnet.bgsu.edu.

Law, Philosophy, and the Humanities
http://www.csulb.edu/~jvancamp/452.html

This is an online course which provides a comparison of how the law is considered by various disciplines. The primary focus is on philosophical methods and legal methods, with some consideration of other humanities disciplines, such as literature. The principal aim of this course is to understand the ways in which various methodologies consider the law. The principal focus will be comparison and contrast of philosophical methods with legal methods. Some consideration will be given to how the law is treated by other methodologies in the humanities. Contemporary work on the law which stresses interdisciplinary perspectives will be introduced. The course will afford ample opportunity for the development of oral and written skills in argumentation and in clarity of communication. The course is conducted by Julie Van Camp jvancamp@csulb.edu, Assoc. Prof of Philosophy at California State University, Long Beach.

Mind and Cognition (PHL341)
http://suze.ucs.usl.edu/~isb9112/dept/phil341/

This page is maintaned by István S. N. Berkeley istvan@USL.edu for students of his Mind and Cognition course. The page provides a course description and syllabus, plus documents explaining connectionism, some advice on writing papers in philosophy and citing resources from the net.

Mission: Critical
http://arachne.SJSU.EDU/depts/itl/

Mission: Critical is an interactive tutorial for critical thinking, in which the user will be introduced to basic concepts through sets of instructions and exercises. Formal instructional materials have been kept to a minimum, in order to take advantage of Mission: Critical's interactive format. Through immediate reinforcement for right and wrong answers to a series of increasingly complex exercises, users will begin to utilise the essential tools of intellectual analysis. The site is maintained by D. Meshser mesher@email.sjsu.edu.

Pathways to Philosophy
http://www.shef.ac.uk/uni/projects/ptpdlp/

Run in conjunction with The Philosophical Society of England, Pathways offers a number of courses in philosophy in distance education mode. This site, maintained by Geoffrey Klempner G.Klempner@sheffield.ac.uk, provides details of the six Pathways courses currently available, and the Philosophical Society of England Associate and Fellowship Diploma.

Philosophical Debates

http://www.mindspring.com/~mfpatton/debates.htm

This page, compiled by Cheryl and Michael Patton mfpatton@mindspring.com and part of their Patton's Argument Clinic site, provides a growing bibliography on central philosophical questions such as: What is Knowledge? What is the nature of Reality? What is the relationship between the Mind and the Body? Is there a God? How can Science tell us anything? Links to primary texts available online are also included.

The Philosophical Institute

http://www.machtec.com/philoinst/

The Philosophical Institute provides online teaching of a range of philosophy courses. The courses currently on offer include: Nothingness: A Comparison of Eastern Religion and Existentialism; The Turning Point: A Change in the Mindset of Western Civilization; Biography: A Journey into the life of Simone deBeauvior; and more. The Philosophical Institute is not a University. The students must register and gain credit for the courses through their own University or College. The site is maintained by Karen Olesch-Williams g13693@email.mot.com.

Philosophy Courses, Syllabi, Teaching, & Learning Resources

http://www.earlham.edu/~peters/philinks.htm#courses

Links to a vast range of resources, this page is part of Peter Suber's peters@earlham.edu extensive guide to philosophy online.

Philosophy of Art and Beauty

http://www.csulb.edu/~jvancamp/361.html

This is an online course in aesthetics. Students should learn what philosophy of art (aesthetics) is, and what it means to think philosophically about art. They will learn how to ask philosophical questions and construct well-formed philosophical arguments about art. Students will be introduced to several major philosophical theories of art, including representation, expression, formalism, and contemporary approaches. Students will also be introduced to the range of on-line resources in philosophy and the arts and how to assess their value and possible use in their own work and future careers. The course is conducted by Julie Van Camp jvancamp@csulb.edu, Assoc. Prof of Philosophy at California State University, Long Beach.

Philosophy of Biology

http://www.public.iastate.edu/~rudge/philbio.html

This site, from David Rudge rudge@iastate.edu, provides a syllabus for a course that surveys several issues in contemporary philosophy of biology.

Philosophy of Natural Science

http://www.public.iastate.edu/~rudge/philsci.html

This site, from David Rudge rudge@iastate.edu, provides a syllabus for a course that surveys several topics pertaining to the nature of science: (1) What distinguishes science from other sorts of inquiry? (2) What is the nature of scientific explanations, scientific laws? (3) What is/are the relationship(s) between evidence and theories in science? and, (4) How are claims in science justified?

Philosophy Online
http://www.arts.monash.edu.au/phil/online.htm

Philosophy Online is a collection of philosophy courses offered by Monash University in multiple delivery modes with course materials provided online. The site is maintained by Dey Alexander dey@silas.cc.monash.edu.au.

Radical Philosophy Association's Teaching Resources
http://www.phil.indiana.edu/~jmusselm/RPA.html#teaching

This page provides links to syllabi and other teaching resources, and is maintained by Jack Musselman jmusselm@phil.indiana.edu.

Rethiking Society: Justice, Diversity, and Social Transformation
http://www.panix.com/~squigle/rs.syllabus.html

This site, from Timothy Quigley QuigleyT@newschool.edu, provides a syllabus for a course which examines controversial issues of social justice and equality in contemporary U.S. society.

Stephen's Guide to Logical Fallacies
http://www.assiniboinec.mb.ca/user/downes/fallacy/fall.htm

The point of an argument is to give reasons in support of some conclusion. An argument commits a fallacy when the reasons offered do not support the conclusion. These pages, by Stephen Downes downes@adminnet.assiniboinec.mb.ca, describe the known logical fallacies, and are an excellent teaching resource.

Syllabi in Ethics
http://ethics.acusd.edu/syllabi.html

From Lawrence Hinman hinman@acusd.edu, this page provides access to syllabi in contemporary moral issues, computer ethics, and courses taught by Dr Hinman.

Syllabus for Ancient & Medieval Philosophy
http://www.smcm.edu/users/mstaber/anc.htm

This page, from Michael Taber mstaber@osprey.smcm.edu, provides a syllabus for a 3rd year philosophy course in ancient and medieval philosophy.

Syllabus for Ethical Theories
http://www.smcm.edu/users/mstaber/eth430.htm

This page, also from Michael Taber mstaber@osprey.smcm.edu, provides a syllabus for a later year course in ethical theory.

Syllabus for Values Inquiry: "Self and Others; Friends and Lovers"

http://www.smcm.edu/users/mstaber/inqf97.htm

This page, from Michael Taber mstaber@osprey.smcm.edu, provides a syllabus for a later year course in value theory which aims "to examine some important aspects of the role of the self in some meaningful human relationships. Each of us exists in a variety of nested sets of communities, and people from different cultures may organize and experience some of those communities in very different ways, but each culture has some central role for love and for friendship."

Teaching Philosophy

http://socrates.berkeley.edu/~phlos-ad/teaching.html

This page, from Andrew Carpenter phlos-ad@socrates.berkeley.edu, provides access to course syllabi in Ancient & Medieval Philosophy, Early Modern Philosophy, Epistemology and Metaphysics, Ethics, Minds and Persons, and the Philosophy of Biology. It also includes a writing guide for students, plus links to books on writing in philosophy, and assorted links to study-related resources.

Teaching Your Child Philosophy

http://www.ozemail.com.au/~jpascal/intro.htm

This site, maintained by Jane Pascal jpascal@ozemail.com.au, provides resources to aid in the teaching of children by means of Socratic dialogue techniques. Dialogues accessible on the page relate to teaching children about truth, logic, faith, ethics, and the foundations of mathematics. A bibliography is also provided.

Teorias Éticas

http://www.economia.ufm.edu.gt/teorias.html

This is the syllabus for Ethical Theories, an introductory level course taught at the School of Economics of University Francisco Marroquín (Guatemala). The site contains multiple links to texts and sites related to the subject matter of Ethical Theories and is maintained by M. Polanco mpolanco@ufm.edu.gt. The site is in Spanish only.

A Virtual Classrooom: The Electronic Agora

http://www.valdosta.peachnet.edu/~rbarnett/phi/phicyber/

"In the so-called Marketplace of Ideas, a standard metaphor for depicting philosophical dialogue and participants' give-and-take, it is generally assumed that an open, critical thrashing-out of viewpoints enhances the pursuit of truth and the level of communication between the parties. Yet we all realise how personal bias, subjective presumptions (conscious and unconscious), based largely on another's physical presence (age, race, gender, demeanor, body language, or what have you), affects the tone and direction of such dialogue. In short, we all tend to bring to discussion with others attitudes based on how we perceive one another. What would happen if a group of interactive university classroom participants met and engaged in dialogue without each others' physical presence, only through personal identification based on computer exchanges? How would only the domain of mental thoughts, as represented through electronic dialogue, affect the dialectical development in this new cyberspace version of the marketplace of ideas, where one's ideas and expressed reasons are the class members' only points of contact?" Find out in this online course offered by Ron Barnette rbarnett@grits. valdosta.peachnet.edu from Valdosta State University.

World Lecture Hall: Philosophy
http://www.utexas.edu/world/lecture/phl/

The World Lecture Hall (WLH) contains links to pages created by faculty worldwide who are using the Web to deliver class materials. For example, you will find course syllabi, assignments, lecture notes, exams, class calendars, multimedia textbooks, etc. The site is maintained by Team Web www@www.utexas.edu at the University of Texas.

WWW Philosophy for Children Server
http://www.deakin.edu.au/arts/SSI/p4c/home1.html

"The idea behind establishing this server is to provide a way to enhance that sense of community which is pivotal to philosophical inquiry in Philosophy for Children; a way to extend community of inquiry beyond the space-time bounds of the classroom; and a way to participate in inquiry on a multitude of levels." The site provides information on the organizations and individuals which make up this community, as well as links to discussion forums, text resources and related web sites.

Directories of Individual Philosophers

APA Directory of Women Philosophers
http://www.ruf.rice.edu/~krist/APA/

This site houses a database developed by the Committee on the Status of Women of the American Philosophical Association. Search online for women working in philosophy by name or specialisation.

APA Members: Email Addresses
http://www.udel.edu/apa/membership/e-mail/

This is a directory of members of the American Philosophical Association, sorted into alphabetical order.

APA Member Homepages
http://www.udel.edu/apa/membership/homepages.html

This is an alphabetical list of links to APA members' home pages.

Email Addresses of CPA Members
http://www.uwindsor.ca/cpa/phones.html

This is a searchable directory of email addresses of members of the Canadian Philosophical Association. It is maintained by R. C. Pinto pinto@uwindsor.ca.

International Registry of Phenomenologists

http://www.fau.edu/divdept/schmidt/carp/registry.htm

This site, maintained by Embree@acc.fau.edu, is a database of information on phenomenologists—living and dead—providing information about their work and publications as well as contact details for those still working in the field.

List of Philosophers Working in Australasian Universities

http://LUFF.latrobe.edu.au/~PHIAJP/philoslist.html

This site provides a listing of philosophers working in Universities in Australia and New Zealand, and provides email addresses and/or other contact details. Enquiries about the page can be directed to phiajp@lure.latrobe.edu.au.

Philosophers' Home Pages

http://users.ox.ac.uk/~worc0337/phil_pages.html

This is Peter King's peter.king@philosophy.ox.ac.uk listing of philosophers' home pages. According to Peter "some of these people are professional philosophers, some are graduate students of philosophy, some undergraduates. All of them have personal web pages of some sort, of which the type of content varies tremendously." Peter adds to this page regularly, so if you're looking for someone in particular, keep checking.

Professors & Graduate Students of Philosophy

http://www.epistemelinks.com/Main/MainProf.htm

From Tom Stone trstone@rpa.net, this site provides links to home pages of professional philosophers and graduate students of philosophy.

Real-Life Philosophers

http://www.rpi.edu/~cearls/real.philosophers.html

This is an alphabetical index of people working in or studying philosophy who have homepages on the web. It is maintained by Sean Cearley cearley@matrix-media.com.

Theistic Philosophers on the Web

http://www.chass.utoronto.ca:8080/~davis/phil.htm

This site, maintained by Richard Davis davis@chass.utoronto.ca, provides a list of individuals who classify themselves as both philosophers and theists. They are working in such diverse areas as metaphysics, epistemology, logic, action theory, ethics, aesthetics, philosophy of language, philosophy of logic, philosophy of science, philosophy of religion, philosophical theology, existentialism, phenomenology, political philosophy, and the history of philosophy.

Job Vacancies in Philosophy

Academic Employment Network
http://www.academploy.com/

This site is a national clearinghouse of job vacancies. Job vacancies can be added to the database, or those looking for work can provide their details for prospective employers. Further information on the site can be obtained from info@academploy.com.

AI Job Posting Archives
http://www.cs.cmu.edu/Groups/AI/html/other/jobs.html

This site provides access to an archive of job postings from various AI-related mailing lists. It includes sections covering pre- and post-doctoral scholarship positions.

APNet Jobs Page
http://www.arts.su.edu.au/Arts/departs/philos/APS/jobs/jobs.html

This page, maintained by Huw Price huw@extro.ucc.su.oz.au as part of the Australasian Philosophy Net group of web pages, provides information on jobs in philosophy, with a focus on Australasia, but with links to other jobs-related sites.

Chronicle of Higher Education: Job Openings
http://thisweek.chronicle.com/.ads/.links.html

This is the job vacancy section of the US Chronicle of Higher Education, updated weekly.

Grants and Fellowships
http://www.udel.edu/apa/opportunities/grants/

This is the American Philosophical Association's page listing links to information on grants and fellowships such as the Fullbright, the National Endowment for the Humanities, and others.

Grants, Fellowships, and Academic Positions
http://www.uwindsor.ca/cpa/jobse.html

This is the Canadian Philosophical Association's job page, with links to job-related sites such as those listed elsewhere in this section. It also lists Canadian positions vacant.

H-Net's Job Guide
http://h-net2.msu.edu/jobs/

The H-Net Job Guide, updated weekly and maintained at the Michigan State University, provides listings of job vacancies in the humanities and social sciences.

International Academic Job Market
http://www.camrev.com.au/share/arts.html

This is the Arts and Humanities section of the Campus Reviews' International Academic Job Market site, providing listings of vacancies which are updated daily.

Jobs in Academe
http://www.jobtrak.com/jobguide/academe.html

This is the Riley Guide to Jobs in Academe, listing sites which provide information on opportunities for teaching and research positions with colleges and universities all around the world. The site is maintained by M. F. Riley mfriley@jobtrak.com.

PhilNet: Jobs for Philosophers
http://www.sozialwiss.uni-hamburg.de/phil/ag/jobs/

Maintained at the University of Hamburg by V. C. Mueller vmueller@informatik. uni-hamburg.de, this site aims to be the most comprehensive site for providing information on job vacancies for philosophers worldwide. It includes sections covering Europe, North America, and Asia/Africa/Australasia, and is available in English, French, German, and Spanish languages.

Philosophy Jobs
http://www.earlham.edu/~peters/philinks.htm#jobs

This is the comprehensive job section from Peter Suber's peters@earlham.edu excellent guide to a vast range of philosophy resources. Peter provides links to numerous sites where jobs-related information can be found.

Miscellaneous Sites

Alexandria: Cosmology, Philosophy, Myth and Culture
http://cosmopolis.com/

In ancient Egypt, the city and Library of Alexandria was the meeting place where philosophical, spiritual, and cosmological teachings flowed together to create vital new syntheses and a flourishing cultural environment. This website, maintained by David Fideler phanes@cris.com, aims to replicate, in electronic form, the cultural and philosophical space of Alexandria, providing a meeting place for people interested in ancient and modern cosmological speculation and what the humanities have to contribute to contemporary life.

APA: Software
http://www.udel.edu/apa/resources/software.html

This is the American Philosophy Association's page providing links to sites from which philosophy-related software can be downloaded.

Ariadne
http://www.arte-media.de/cgi-win/ariadne.exe

Ariadne is a limited-area philosophy search engine, in German language format, maintained by Stefan Müller SMueller@public.uni-hamburg.de. It is also mirrored at: *http://homehobel.phl.univie.ac.at/cgi-win/ariadne.exe.*

Australasian Philosophy Net

http://www.arts.su.edu.au/Arts/departs/philos/APS/APS.home.html

This site, maintained by Huw Price huw@extro.ucc.su.oz.au, provides links to the Directory of Australasian Philosophers, Departmental web servers in Australia and New Zealand, White pages of Australasian universities, a jobs page, and other Australasian-based web services for philosophers.

Brad McCormick's Home Page

http://www.cloud9.net/~bradmcc/

This is Brad's bradmcc@cloud9.net personal page, devoted to reflective thinking. Of particular interest is the text of Brad's doctoral dissertation, which engages the philosophy of communication in a critique of communication about communication in a socially significant (and power charged) situation, psychotherapy supervision. Brad employs a case study in psychotherapist education, to explore the dialogical construction of the social world from a perspective of Husserl, Habermas, Gadamer, et al.

Guidebook for Publishing in Philosophy

http://www.smith.edu/~jmoulton/guidebook/

This site houses most of the text from this 1986 publication devoted to providing information and advice on publishing in philosophy. The site is maintained by Janice Moulton jmoulton@smith.edu.

The Meaning of Life

http://www.access.digex.net/~hess/meaning/

This site houses a collection of opinions on the meaning of life. Email hess@digex.net to add your view.

Philosopher All-Stars

http://www.worldmedia.com/manucon/cards/CARDS.HTM

Philosopher All-Stars provides a small gallery of philosophers in trading-card format, with pictures and a brief biography, and maintained by Jeremy Allaire.

Philosophers' Gallery

http://watarts.uwaterloo.ca/PHIL/cpshelle/Gallery/gallery.html

Sure, you've read their books, but what did they look like? Now you can see your favourite philosopher's mug shot. This site is maintained by cpshelle@watarts.uwaterloo.ca.

Philosophers' Image Gallery

http://www.epistemelinks.com/Main/MainImag.htm

This page provides access to an online collection of images of philosophers. It is maintained by Tom Stone trstone@rpa.net, with new additions appearing regularly.

Philosophical Calendar

http://w3.one.net/~bzimov/tod/calendar.html

The Philosophical Calendar presents a philosophical thought for the day (an issue from contemporary Western metaphysics or epistemology) from Bruce Zimov bzimov@one.net.

Philosophical Discussions

http://www.visitweb.com/philosophy

This site provides a place where undergraduates or those with a general interest in philosophy can discuss philosophical issues suggested by the site's maintainer, James Petts petts@geocities.com. There are currently nine issues for consideration, centerd on metaphysics and sociological issues.

Philosophy Crossword Puzzles

http://www.fred.net/tzaka/cross.html

From Gordon Ziniewicz tzaka@fred.net, print out and solve crossword puzzles on general philosophy or philosophers by name.

Philosophy for Everyone Forum

http://207.226.249.105/cgi/webforum/others/get.cgi/ryanbreedon_philosophy. html

This is a small philosophy discussion forum taking the form of a public web-based message board, hosted by Ryan Breedon eco@sympatico.ca.

Philosophy is Everybody's Business

http://www.npcts.edu/~mj_adler/

Designed to "help awaken citizens from their moral and intellectual slumber," M. J. Adler mjadler@xsite.net and M. Weisman have created this site and the "Center for Study of Great Ideas." This page outlines the Center's activities, membership details, and provides links to resources.

Philosophy Miscellany

http://www.earlham.edu/~peters/philinks.htm#miscellany

A collection of links to miscellaneous philosophy-related sites, compiled by Peter Suber peters@earlham.edu.

Philosophy SIG

telnet://tso.cin.ix.net

This is a philosophy discussion bulletin board accessible by telnet (login as a visitor and follow the prompts until you reach the main menu, then type 'go philos'). There are five discussion areas: metaphysics, ethics, theology, technology, and epistemology. The SIG is hosted by Bruce Zimov bzimov@one.net.

Place des Débats

http://home.worldnet.fr/~erogue/Philosophie/Debats/Phildebat.html

This site provides a means for online discussion of philosophical topics via a web interface. Discussions are in French, and the topics currently include 'Is history a science?' and 'Can machines think?'. The site is maintained by Evelyne Rogue erogue@worldnet.fr.

Real-Time Talk for Philosophers

http://www.bris.ac.uk/Depts/Philosophy/VL/talk.html

This page contains information and links to multi-user environments where philosophers can generally be found, as well as listing Internet Relay Chat channels where people talk about philosophy. There will also be a few general links to Web sites which describe the various methods of live (real time) communication across the Internet, including audio and videoconferencing as well as text based systems. Please email Dan Brickley philosophy-vlib@bristol.ac.uk if you know of any established sites.

Thought Experiments

http://astro.ocis.temple.edu/~souder/thought/index.html

Galileo once introduced an invented scenario, saying, "But even without further experiment it is possible to prove clearly, by means of a short and conclusive argument, that a heavier body does not move more rapidly than a lighter one." He went on to describe a case where two stones of different weights are tied together and allowed to fall. Thereby Galileo successfully argued against Aristotle in what became one of the most famous thought experiments. Since then thought experiments have appeared often in both scientific and philosophical arguments. This site is an attempt to collect some resources for studying them. Although the emphasis is on philosophical thought experiments, many of the materials included here relate to the field in general. The site is maintained by Lawrence Souder souder@astro.ocis.temple.edu.

Zeno's Coffee House

http://www.valdosta.peachnet.edu/~rbarnett/phi/zeno.html

This interactive site, produced by Ron Barnette rbarnett@grits.valdosta.peachnet.edu, features logic and critical thinking puzzles. Participants can check back on results of puzzles run earlier in the year. Ron also includes a link to a prisoner's dilemma game from Serendip's Playground at: *http://serendip.brynmawr.edu/playground/*.

Zombies on the Web

http://ling.ucsc.edu/~chalmers/zombies.html

Very few people think that zombies could exist in the actual world (i.e., that they are naturally or nomologically possible), but many people think that they are at least logically possible—i.e., that the idea of zombie is internally consistent, and that there is at least a "possible world" where zombies exist. This logical possibility is sometimes used to draw strong conclusions about consciousness (e.g., in the book *The Conscious Mind*, and elsewhere). This site, from David Chalmers chalmers@paradox.ucsc.edu, brings together a range of resources and information on zombies, and their use in philosophical argument.

Other Guides to Philosophy

Sites in English

Bjorn's Guide to Philosophy

http://www.knuten.liu.se/~bjoch509/

This site is maintained by Bjorn Christensson bjoch509@knuten.liu.se, and is a well-designed guide with links to a range of philosophy resources. The subsections of the guide include: philosophers, journals, departments, library, and other links.

Blackwell's Guide to Online Philosophy Resources

http://www.blackwellpublishers.co.uk/PHILOS/philres.htm

Blackwell's guide contains a range of links to philosophy resources, divided into a number of categories including: Philosophy Departments, Conferences, Jobs, Reading List, Electronic Texts, Journals, Bibliographies, and specialist subject areas.

Chris's Philosophy Page

http://www.geocities.com/Athens/Forum/5507/

With a focus on US-related information, and on philosophical thinkers, this small but useful guide to philosophy is maintained by Chris Furlong chrisfurlong@mail.utexas.edu.

Episteme Links

http://www.epistemelinks.com

Episteme Links is a new guide, maintained by Tom Stone trstone@rpa.net and promises to be quite comprehensive. The feature unique to this site is its link to the bookstore Amazon.com, offering a range of philosophy titles for purchase online.

Factasia

http://www.rbjones.com/rbjpub/philos/index.htm

This site is maintained by Roger B. Jones rbj@campion.demon.co.uk and has links to science, mathematics, logic, and general philosophy resources, including a glossary of philosophical terms.

Galaxy: Philosophy

http://galaxy.tradewave.com/galaxy/Humanities/Philosophy.html

This philosophy resource is part of a range of subject-oriented resources from Galaxy galaxy@tradewave.com. The philosophy page includes links to resources in aesthetics, epistemology, ethics, logic, and metaphysics. It also provides access to a range of philosophy directories, academic organizations, and electronic journals.

Giacobazzi's Philosophy Links

http://www.kirtland.cc.mi.us/honors/fgphil.htm

Another guide to philosophy resources, broken into three sections: 'general philosophy links', 'philosophers', and 'branches and fields'. It is maintained by Frederic Giacobazzi giacobaf@k2.kirtland.cc.mi.us.

Guide to Philosophy on the Internet

http://www.earlham.edu/~peters/philinks.htm

Compiled by Peter Suber peters@earlham.edu, this extensive guide provides links to philosophy resources compiled into the following sections: General Guides to Philosophy; Philosophers and Philosophies; Philosophical Topics; Philosophy Associations and Societies; Philosophy Journals; Philosophy Teaching Resources; Philosophy Etexts; Philosophy Bibliographies; Philosophy Mailing Lists; Philosophy Newsgroups; Philosophy Projects; Philosophy Preprints; Philosophy Jobs; and Philosophy Miscellany. Peter attempts to steer users in the direction of the better resources available by red-starring those sites he feels are more worthwhile.

Hopkins Philosophy Pages

http://www.jhu.edu/~phil/philhome.html

This site is maintained by Dennis Des Chene deschene@jhunix.hcf.jhu.edu, and provides links to philosophical organizations, electronic texts, electronic journals, information on philosophy publishers, and resources compiled by subject area (ethics, aesthetics, logic, and so on).

Humanities Hub—Philosophy and Philosophers

http://www.gu.edu.au/cgi-bin/sitedb.cgi?search1=philosophy&url=http://www.gu.edu.au/gwis/hub/hub.hsearch.html&list=hub.hub.html

This site, part of a larger humanities resource index, links to all the main philosophy guides, and a database of researchers in the field of philosophy. It is maintained at Griffith University by Anita Greenhill A.Greenhill@hum.gu.edu.au and Gordon Fletcher G.Fletcher@hum.gu.edu.au.

HUMBUL Gateway

http://info.ox.ac.uk/departments/humanities/international.html

From the HUMBUL Gateway you can access pages providing extensive links to resources for philosophy, religious studies, and classics. The site is maintained by Chris Stephens christopher.stephens@oucs.ox.ac.uk.

Index of Philosophy Resources on the Internet

http://www.freenet.calgary.ab.ca/~kyasench/philosophyindex.html

This site provides an alphabetically-arranged index to a range of philosophy-related resources. It is maintained by Ken Yasenchuk kyasench@freenet.calgary.ab.ca.

Infinite Ink's Philosophy Page

http://www.ii.com/philosophy/

Compiled by Nancy McGough nancym@ii.com, this page specialises in philosophy of science, mathematics, and religion, while also providing more general links.

Internet Services for Philosophers

http://www.phil.ruu.nl/philosophy_services.html

This site provides a compilation of resources and information of particular use to philosophers new to the net. Maintained by Arno Wouters Arno.Wouters@phil.ruu.nl, access is provided to mailing lists, newsgroups, FAQs, information on Thinknet and the Spoon Collective, electronic texts, and more. From this site, a link to Arno's Philosophy on the Web can also be accessed.

LSU Libraries Webliography: Philosophy

http://www.lib.lsu.edu/hum/philos.html

Compiled by Stephen Harris notsrh@unix1.sncc.lsu.edu, as part of a larger subject-oriented guide, this site provides links to philosophy resources guides, journals, bibliographies, mailing lists, philosophy organizations, and texts.

My Virtual Encyclopedia: Philosophy and Religion

http://www.refdesk.com/philos.html

This site, part of a larger subject-oriented guide maintained by Bob Drudge rbdrudge@ www.refdesk.com, provides a listing of philosophy resources sorted into alphabetical order.

Net Resources in Philosophy

http://www.univie.ac.at/philosophie/phr/philres.htm

Located at the University of Vienna, this site provides links to canonical philosophers' works and discussions, online bookstores, philosophy-related projects, research and teaching departments, journals, philosophical events, and usenet newsgroups.

One Window to Philosophy

http://info.lncc.br/filosofia/index-e.html

A comprehensive guide to philosophy, grouping resources into these sections: journals; papers and works; departments; contemporary philosophy; past philosophies; research projects; philosophers; online bookstores; and lists and newsgroups. The guide, compiled by Sandro Reis Sandro.Reis@pobox.com, is also available in Portugese.

Paul Wong's Home Page

http://www.sfu.ca/~wongas/

This page from Paul Wong wongas@sfu.ca, provides extensive links to logic and related resources, as well as more general philosophy links. The page can also be found at *http://arp.anu.edu.au/wongas/*.

Philosophy

http://www.nerdworld.com/cgi-bin/page.cgi?PHILOSOPHY/950

This site is part of a larger subject-oriented resource guide from NerdWorld nerds@ nerdworld.com, and featuring a list of philosophy resources arranged alphabetically.

Philosophy

http://wwwstud.uni-giessen.de/~s1925/philosophy.htm

Compiled by Prakash Arumugam Prakash.Arumugam@med.uni-giessen.de, this page provides meta-links to philosophy resources, divided into two main categories, Eastern and Western philosophy.

Philosophy

http://www.uni-leipzig.de/~logik/wiedemann/philweb/

This site, from Uwe Wiedemann U.Wiedemann@link-c.cl.sub.de, provides links to a range of philosophy resources, including a small German philosophy lexicon.

Philosophy and Theory

http://www.muohio.edu/~phlcwis/philosophers/

From J. Purcell jpurcell@frank.mtsu.edu, this site provides links to general information on philosophy, as well as to sites on specific philosophers.

Philosophy Around the Web

http://users.ox.ac.uk/~worc0337/phil_index.html

This site provides links to a wide range of resources divided into various categories: departmental pages, institutions and commercial organizations, journals, individual philosophers, discussion, events, philosophers with web pages, philosophy jobs, and papers by the site's maintainer, Peter King peter.king@philosophy.ox.ac.uk.

Philosophy at Large

http://www.liv.ac.uk/Philosophy/philos.html

This extensive resource guide is compiled by Stephen Clark srlclark@liverpool.ac.uk of the University of Liverpool. It provides links to mailing lists, newsgroups, bibliographies, electronic texts, electronic journals, electronic classes and teaching tools, and other directories of philosophical resources. A French version of the site is now available at *http://agora.qc.ca/textes/sclark.html*, maintained by Josette Lanteigne gagnonc@cam.org.

Philosophy Collections Page

http://nervm.nerdc.ufl.edu/~blaland/phil.html

This site was formerly known as Blake's Internet Guide to Philosophy. Compiled by Blake Landor blaland@nervm.nerdc.ufl.edu, it is now part of the University of Florida's subject-oriented guides.

Philosophy/Ethics/Religious Studies

http://www.asahi-net.or.jp/~IS8K-NGSK/index-e.html

Maintained by K. Nagasaki s955006@ipe.tsukuba.ac.jp, this site provides links to philosophy of religion, ethics, and general resources from sites located in Japan. A Japanese-language version of the site is available from the main page.

Philosophy for Everyone

http://www.geocities.com/Athens/Delphi/2795/philinks.htm

This is a small, annotated guide to some of the better philosophical resources online, and is maintained by Ryan Breedon eco@sympatico.ca.

Philosophy Guide at Chinese University of Hong Kong

http://www.arts.cuhk.edu.hk/Philo.html

This extensive guide provides links to Chinese philosophy resources, philosophy department pages, other philosophy resource guides, artificial Intelligence and fuzzy logic resources, mailing lists, and a broad range of religious studies resources including Buddhism, Christianity, and Islam. The maintainers of the page can be contacted at twkwan@cuhk.edu.hk.

Philosophy: Hall of Minerva

http://www.nobunaga.demon.co.uk/htm/phil.htm

This is a collection of links to a variety of philosophy resources, with a growing section on individual philosophers. The site is maintained by Shine and Ian Jordan ian@amgmps.com.

Philosophy Links

http://soli.com/philo.htm

This site provides links to a range of philosophy resources divided into four main categories: Ancient Greek, Ancient Roman, Medieval, and Modern Philosophy. It is maintained by SOLI, the System of Life Institute, who can be contacted at robertj@soli.com.

Philosophy Links on the Net

http://www.webcom.com/duane/philom.html

This site, maintained by Duane Bristow oldky@webcom.com, is a small compilation of links to philosophy resources, in two sections: most interesting links, and other links.

Philosophy Sites on the Internet

http://spinoza.tau.ac.il/hci/dep/philos/links.htm

This page houses a nicely-organised list of links maintained at the philosophy department at Tel Aviv University.

Philosophy on the Web

http://www.phil.ruu.nl/philosophy-sites.html

This site is maintained by Arno Wouters Arno.Wouters@phil.ruu.nl, and contains links to a wide range of web-based philosophy resources in subject groupings such as: Directories,

Bibliographies, Departments, E-journals, E-texts, FAQ's, Gophers, Journals and Societies, Philosophy in the Netherlands, Preprints and working papers, Projects, Publishers, Regional Servers, and Software.

Philosophy Resources on the Network

http://blair.library.rhodes.edu/philhtmls/philnet.html

This site includes links to general resource guides, philosophy texts, journals, mailing lists, preprints, and philosophy resources by subject. It is maintained as part of the Blair Library Blair@rhodes.edu project at Rhodes College.

Philosophy Sources on the Internet

http://www.ed.ac.uk/~ejua35/phillink.htm

Maintained by Fiona Steinkamp f.steinkamp@ed.ac.uk , this site provides links to philosophy resources divided into the following categories: departments, journals, texts, jobs and software, German language links, mailing lists, 'just for fun', and general sources.

Philosophy Web Sites

http://www.cc.ukans.edu/~philos/guestbook/links.html

Leslie Jones lejones@falcon.cc.ukans.edu has compiled this site which intends not to provide exhaustive lists of links, but focuses on meta-links to those sites which do.

Polyhymnia's List of Philosophy Resources

http://web.syr.edu/~dhoracek/netphil.html

This site provides access to an extensive list of mailing lists, electronic texts, resources in philosophy, science and technology, links to sites on individual philosophers, and a list of other online guides. It is compiled by David Horacek david.horacek@student.uni-tuebingen.de.

Portmore's Annotated Guide to Philosophy on the Internet

http://humanitas.ucsb.edu/~portmore/links.htm

A richly annotated and select guide to the premium philosophy resources on the Internet, compiled by Doug Portmore portmore@humanitas.ucsb.edu.

Public Sphere Philosophical Resource Center

http://www.alphalink.com.au/~pashton/index.htm

This site, from Paul Ashton pashton@alphalink.com.au, aims to provide links to philosophy-related resources grouped into six areas: philosophers and philosophies, electronic texts, student essays (as submitted by visitors to the site), student resources, essays, and general links.

Religion and Philosophy Gopher, Rice University

gopher://riceinfo.rice.edu:70/11/Subject/RelPhil

This gopher provides access to a wide range of religion and philosophy resources, including mailing lists, electronic texts, Christian, Jewish, and Buddhist resources, and electronic and print journals.

Resources for Philosophers

http://www.arts.ubc.ca/~irvine/rfp.htm

Compiled by A.D. Irvine irvine@unixg.ubc.ca, this page provides a comprehensive list of links to a range of general philosophy resources as well as links to materials on AI, computability, and mathematics.

Resources in Philosophy and Women's Studies

http://billyboy.ius.indiana.edu/WomeninPhilosophy/Resources.html

This guide to resources in both philosophy and women's studies provides a range of links in the following categories: philosophy in general; academic philosophy; philosophical topics; conferences; women on the web; women's studies; mindwalk; libraries; personal pages; directories and search engines. The site is Maintained by Noel Parish Hutchings nhutchin@ius.indiana.edu, and updated regularly.

Routledge's Guide to Philosophy Resources on the Internet

http://www.thomson.com/routledge/philosophy/rprcmain.html

This site provides links to the major philosophy guides, as well as to Routledge-specific information. Enquiries about the site can be directed to philosophy@routledge.com.

Rutgers University Libraries Guide to Philosophy Resources

http://www.scils.rutgers.edu./~mpmeola/phil1.html

Compiled by Marc Meola mpmeola@scils.rutgers.edu and Michael Craven craven@scils.rutgers.edu, this site provides links to electronic texts, journals, departments, archives, online catalogues, bibliographies, and other philosophy resources.

Taiwan Super Logos Philosophy Web

http://taiwan.iis.sinica.edu.tw/~dasein/ame/index_a.htm

This site provides a guide to Taiwanese and general philosophy resources, and is available in English and Chinese versions.

The Source: Philosophy

http://hakatai.mcli.dist.maricopa.edu/smc/ml/phil.html

This page is part of a larger subject-oriented guide, and is maintained by Mary Long long@smc.maricopa.edu. It provides links to range of philosophical resources arranged by subject including, ethics, metaphysics, aesthetics, logic, epistemology, bioethics, and cognitive and psychological sciences.

The Tanner Philosophy Library

http://www.umich.edu/~philos/tanner.html

This website of the University of Michigan's Philosophy Library provides links to philosophy resources including a range of online resource guides, electronic texts, and electronic journals. It is maintained by Sara Memmott smemmott@umich.edu.

The Telsun Spur: Philosophy

http://www.islandnet.com/~pjhughes/sci.htm#Philosophy

Part of a larger subject-oriented guide maintained by PJ Hughes pjhughes@islandnet.com, this page provides a list of philosophy links sorted in alphabetical order, and focusing mainly on meta-links.

The Ultimate Philosophy Page

http://www.rpi.edu/~cearls/phil.html

Compiled by Sean Cearley cearls@rpi.edu, this page links to a vast range of resources including philosophy departments and projects, journals, guides to philosophy resources, home pages for living philosophers, and much more.

The Window: Philosophy on the Internet

http://www.trincoll.edu/~phil/philo/

The Window is maintained by Chris Marvin cmarvin@trincoll.edu and Frank Sikernitsky fsikerni@trincoll.edu, and provides biographical information on over 50 major philosophers. It also provides links to journals, departmental pages, electronic texts, and assorted resources.

Voice of the Shuttle: Philosophy

http://humanitas.ucsb.edu/shuttle/philo.html

This is part of a group of web pages for humanities research, and is compiled by Alan Liu ayliu@humanitas.ucsb.edu. The philosophy page provides access to general philosophical resources, philosophers and their works, mailing lists and newsgroups, departments and programs in philosophy, and philosophy course syllabi.

WWW Virtual Library: Philosophy

http://www.bris.ac.uk/Depts/Philosophy/VL/

Maintained by Dan Brickley philosophy-vlib@bris.ac.uk, this page provides links to a range of philosophy resources including philosophy guides, journals, electronic texts, mailing lists, philosophy departments, philosophy sites on the net, and real-time Internet talk for philosophers.

Yahoo: Philosophy

http://www.yahoo.com/Humanities/Philosophy

This page is the philosophy resource index from the net directory, Yahoo. Given that it is automated, some links may be out of date.

Sites in Other Languages

Annette's Philosophenstübchen

http://www.thur.de/philo/

This is a German language page providing searchable links to other German philosophy-related sites, and maintained by Annette Schlemm annette.schlemm@t-online.de. Some of Annette's writings are now included.

Camillo Schrimpf Pages

http://www.schrimpf.com/philosophie.html

This is a German-language collection of resources focusing on philosophy, literature, and psychoanalysis, maintained by Camillo Schrimpf Camillo.Schrimpf@t-online.de.

Centro Telemático de Filosofía

http://blues.uab.es/filosofia/esvincles.html

This is a Spanish-language collection of philosophy resources on the net, compiled by Jesús Hernández Reynés ilff1@blues.uab.es, and including a range of electronic texts, bibliographies, editorials, links to philosophy departments, and to other guides.

Choix de Sites Philosophiques

http://peccatte.rever.fr/

This guide is written in French and maintained by Patrick Peccatte peccatte@club-internet.fr. It provides links to other guides, journals, and resources related to: astronomy, astrology, Marx and Engels, Wittgenstein, electronic texts, cognitive science, history of science, and mathematics, plus some miscellaneous links.

Deutscher Philosophie-Knoten

http://www.sozialwiss.uni-hamburg.de/phil/ag/knoten/main.html

This site provides links to a range of good-quality German-language philosophy resources.

Filosofi

http://www.hedbergska.sundsvall.se/amnen/fs/fsgrs.html

A Swedish-language guide to philosophy resources, maintained by Ylva Holm ylva.holm@hedbergska.sundsvall.se.

Filosofia in Italia

http://venus.unive.it/~fasolo/FilosofiainItalia.html

This is a comprehensive Italian-language guide to philosophy resources from David Fasolo fasolo@unive.it.

Filosofiaa Internetissä

http://www.helsinki.fi/~pylikosk/flinkit.html

This site provides a Finnish-language guide to philosophy on the net maintained by pylikosk@cc.helsinki.fi.

Filosofie

http://www.xs4all.nl/~gerdeg/4-filo.html

Maintained by ger.de.gooijer@fgz.hva.nl, this site houses a small Dutch guide to philosophy.

La Philosophie sur Internet

http://WWW.CAM.ORG/~lanteign/

This site hosts a French-language guide to a range of philosophy resources online, maintained by Josette Lanteigne lanteign@CAM.ORG.

PhilNet

http://www.sozialwiss.uni-hamburg.de/phil/ag/internet.html

This is a German-language guide to philosophy on the net, focusing on local resources, located at the University of Hamburg, and maintained by internetag@www.sozialwiss. uni-hamburg.de.

Philosophie im Internet

http://www.uni-konstanz.de/ZE/Bib/zs/zsph.html

This is a German-language guide to philosophy, compiled by Karsten Wilkens Karsten. Wilkens@uni-konstanz.de.

Philosophie-Seiten

http://www.rzuser.uni-heidelberg.de/~dkoehler/philo/ihvz.htm

Primarily in German but with sufficient English to be navigable to non-German speakers, this guide to philosophy resources was compiled by Dieter Koehler dkoehler@ix.urz. uni-heidelberg.de, and provides links to philosophy departments, projects, associations, journals, bibliographies, and other general resources.

Philosophy at Large

http://www.liv.ac.uk/Philosophy/philos.html

This is the French version of an extensive resource guide compiled by Stephen Clark srlclark@liverpool.ac.uk of the University of Liverpool. It provides links to mailing lists, newsgroups, bibliographies, electronic texts, electronic journals, electronic classes and teaching tools, and other directories of philosophical resources. The French version is maintained by Josette Lanteigne gagnonc@cam.org.

Philosophy/Ethics/Religious Studies

http://www.asahi-net.or.jp/~IS8K-NGSK/index.html

Maintained by K. Nagasaki s955006@ipe.tsukuba.ac.jp, this site provides links to philosophy of religion, ethics, and general resources from sites located in Japan.

Proyecto Filosofía en Español

http://www3.uniovi.es/~filesp/

This is a well-designed Spanish-language guide to philosophy resources. It is maintained by filesp@dana.vicest.uniovi.es.

Red Filosofia Peruana
http://www.geocities.com/Athens/Acropolis/7214/

This site is a guide to philosophy resources, philosophical organizations, and activities in Peru. The site is maintained by redfilo@iname.com.

Richerche Filosofiche
http://www.forminform.it/filosofia/ufiloso.htm

An Italian-language guide to philosophy resources, maintained by P. Redondo redondo@mail.nexus.it.

SWIF: Sito Web Italiano per la Filosofia
http://lgxserver.uniba.it/lei/swif.htm

This site houses an extensive Italian-language guide to philosophy resources, and is maintained by Luciano Floridi luciano.floridi@philosophy.oxford.ac.uk.

Taiwan Super Logos Philosophy Web
http://taiwan.iis.sinica.edu.tw/~dasein/

This site houses a Chinese-language guide to Taiwanese and general philosophy resources.

Uma Janela para a Filosofia
http://info.lncc.br/filosofia/index.html

This is the Portugeuse version of One Window to Philosophy, a comprehensive guide to philosophy, grouping resources into these sections: journals; papers and works; departments; contemporary philosophy; past philosophies; research projects; philosophers; online bookstores; and lists and newsgroups. The guide is compiled by Sandro Reis Sandro.Reis@pobox.com.

Philosophy Humor

Biotechnology Code of Ethics
http://www.compbio.caltech.edu/~dliney/ethics.html

A few hints to help us create "a brighter world with trees and everything."

Comic Relief
http://www.webcom.com/~ctt/comic.html

"For the pathologically philosophical," the humor on this site includes Philosophy Lightbulb Jokes, Weightless Philosophy, Husserl's Seventh Cartesian Meditation, Make Tenure Fast, Monolithic Biavicide, the Teleology of Chicken and the Road, and reader submissions. It is maintained by Glen Miller gmiller@netcom.com.

Jean-Paul Sartre Cookbook
http://icemcfd.com/wayne/sartre-cookbook.html

"We have been lucky to discover several previously lost diaries of French philosopher Jean-Paul Sartre stuck in between the cushions of our office sofa. These diaries reveal a young Sartre obsessed not with the void, but with food. Apparently Sartre, before discovering philosophy, had hoped to write 'a cookbook that will put to rest all notions of flavor forever.' The diaries are excerpted here for your perusal."

A Non-Philosopher's Guide to Philosophical Terms
http://coombs.anu.edu.au/Depts/RSSS/Philosophy/People/Henry/gloss.html

A humorous guide to philosophical terms, from Henry Fitzgerald.

Philosopher Jokes
http://www.miami.edu/phi/jokes.htm

Maintained by Howard Pospesel pospesel@miami.edu, this page presents 'Top 10 Things Not to Say at an APA Job Interview', 'Causes of Death for Some of the Great Philosophers', and more.

Philosophical Humor
http://ling.ucsc.edu/~chalmers/phil-humor.html

From David Chalmers chalmers@paradox.ucsc.edu, this page presents an array of links to sites that would have made Aristotle giggle. And in case philosophically-induced humor isn't enough for you, David also supplies links to funnies in maths, economics, religion, psychology, physics, and science.

Philosophical Kisses
http://www. epistemelinks.com/Humo/KissHumo.htm

Do you know what an Aristotelian kiss is? How about a Wittgensteinian or Nietzscheian kiss? Don't miss this complete guide to philosophical kisses, from Trygve Lode tlode@nyx.cs.du.edu.

The Philosophical Lexicon
http://www.blackwellpublishers.co.uk/lexicon/

Edited by Daniel Dennett, the philosophical lexicon is a tongue-in-cheek guide to philosophy-speak, containing over 150 terms devised by those who've spent way too much time pondering philosophy.

Philosophy Comix
http://members.aol.com/lshauser/phlcomix.html

From Larry Hauser lshauser@aol.com, this site is a collection of scanned comic strips with philosophical content from a variety of sources: Dilbert, Doonesbury, Calvin & Hobbes, and many more.

Philosophy Humor

http://www.epistemelinks.com/Main/MainHumo.htm

This page, from Tom Stone trstone@rpa.net, presents an assortment of philosophical laughs collected from around the web. Choose from: Proofs that P, More Proofs that P, Monty Python's Philosophers' Song, Why did the Chicken Cross the Road?, Causes of Death, Non-Philosopher's Guide to Philosophical Terms, No One Ever Wants to Play Golf with a Philosopher, and more.

Philosophy Light Bulb Jokes

http://www.epistemelinks.com/Humo/BulbHumo.htm

Ever wondered how many cultural constructivists does it take to change a light bulb? Or how many Kantians or creation scientists it takes? Glenn Miller gmiller@netcom.com provides all the answers!

Philosophy Songs

http://www.manitowoc.uwc.edu/staff/awhite/phisong.htm

This page, maintained by V. Alan White awhite@uwc.edu, provides the lyrics to philosophy songs he has written: Solipsism's Painless, We Didn't Start Inquiry, Poppycock, Readin' Kripke, Reichenbach's Methods, Hume on the Brain, This PHD, and Antinomy.

Postmodern Essay Generator

http://www.cs.monash.edu.au/cgi-bin/postmodern

The Postmodern Essay Generator was written by Andrew C. Bulhak, and generates a new and meaningless essay with each click of the button.

Religious & Philosophical Humor

http://www.intermarket.net/laughweb/religion/

Maintained by joeshmoe@world.std.com as part of a larger humor site, this page provides a load of laughs including 'Christianity for Dummies', 'Confucian Jokes', and 'Top 10 Philosophical Questions Answered'.

Student Howlers

http://users.ox.ac.uk/~shil0124/jokes/howlers.html

From Peter King peter.king@philosophy.ox.ac.uk, this page houses a collection of howlers from students in philosophy as collected by Peter and submitted by others.

Valdosta Philosophy Humor

gopher://catfish.valdosta.peachnet.edu:70/11/ccr/subjv/phi/humor

This gopher site at Valdosta University houses some philosophy-related humor from Monty Python, including Bruce's Philosophy Song, the Argument Clinic, and the Meaning of Life.

The View From the Clouds: Philosophical Humor

http://www.olemiss.edu/depts/philosophy/humor.html

Featuring 'Top 10 reasons for majoring in philosophy'. 'Contemporary Football Philosophies', 'An Insurance Policy for Philosophers' and 'International Society of Solipsists', this site is from the University of Mississippi philosophy graduate students.

Student Resources

Postgraduate

Environmental Ethics Graduate Programs

http://www.cep.unt.edu/other.html

This page provides links to a range of graduate programs offered in the US, UK, and Australia. It is part of the Center for Environmental Philosophy site, maintained by Eugene Hargrove hargrove@unt.edu.

Graduate Programs in Asian Philosophy and Religion

http://www2.gol.com/users/acmuller/GradStudies.htm

Maintained by A. Charles Muller acmuller@gol.com, this site provides information regarding graduate studies programs in the field of Asian philosophy and religion (including Buddhism, Hinduism, Confucianism, or Taoism).

Graduate Studies

http://www.essex.ac.uk/ejp/gradua.htm

This page, from the *European Journal of Philosophy* website, carries a listing of graduate courses on offer at various universities, along with links—where available—to the homepages of the host departments, and email links to the relevant person (e.g., Director of Graduate Studies) in them. The aim is to build up a comprehensive resource for prospective students. The full list will be published in hard copy once a year, in the December issue of the *EJP*.

The 'Hartmann Report'

http://www.geocities.com/Athens/1575/report.html

On this site, John Hartmann at hartmajr@bigvax.alfred.edu, provides a ranking of US Graduate Programs in continental philosophy.

The Philosophical Gourmet Report

http://www.nyu.edu/gsas/dept/philo/leiter/

This site provides a ranking of US graduate programs in analytic philosophy for 1996/7. It is maintained by Brian Leiter bleiter@mail.law.utexas.edu.

UMI Dissertation Services
http://www.umi.com/hp/Support/DExplorer/find/

With more than 1.4 million entries, UMI's Dissertation Abstracts database is the one central, authoritative source for information about doctoral dissertations and master's theses. Graduate students customarily consult the database to make sure their proposed thesis or dissertation topics have not already been written about. Students, faculty, and other researchers search it for titles related to their scholarly interests. The database includes citations for materials ranging from the first U.S. dissertation, accepted in 1861, to those accepted as recently as last semester; those published from 1980 forward also include 350-word abstracts, written by the author. Citations for master's theses from 1988 forward include 150-word abstracts. Of the 1.4 million titles listed, UMI offers over a million in full text. The database represents the work of authors from over 1,000 North American graduate schools and European universities. Some 55,000 new dissertations and 7,000 new theses are added to the database each year. Search the database online from this site.

Undergraduate

The Argument Clinic
http://www.univnorthco.edu/philosophy/clinic.html

The folks at the Argument Clinic invite visitors to submit pieces of reasoning for evaluation. See what others have submitted to the site, and access information on arguments and issues to consider in evaluating them. The site is maintained by tkrelo@bentley.unco.edu and is an excellent resource for students of philosophy.

Arguments and their Evaluation
http://www.univnorthco.edu/philosophy/arg.html

From the authors of the Argument Clinic, this page considers the nature and structure of arguments and their evaluation, aimed at first year philosophy students.

A Brief Guide to Writing Philosophy Papers
http://www.nwmissouri.edu/~rfield/guide.html

This site, part of a collection of resources by Richard Field rfield@acad.nwmissouri.edu of Northwest Missouri State University, provides some sound advice for students writing philosophy papers. It considers framing your topic, standards of evidence, citation, quotation, footnotes, plagiarism, use of primary and secondary sources, and more.

Constructing a Logical Argument
http://www.infidels.org/news/atheism/logic.html

This page gives an overview of the structure of good arguments, and provides an extensive list of fallacies in arguments. An excellent teaching resource, it is maintained by meta@pobox.com.

Critical Thinking Core Concepts

http://www.kcmetro.cc.mo.us/longview/ctac/corenotes.htm

From Longview Community College, this site provides an excellent introduction to basic logic, including a short history of logic, a discussion of symbolic vs. informal logic, and an introduction to logical vocabulary.

An Email Introduction to Philosophy and Philosophical Thinking

http://www.scott.net/~hmwkhelp/Philosophy.html

This page represents an experiment by Rick Garlikov hmwkhelp@scott.net, to see if he can teach philosophy on the net, via email. A number of questions are set out and Rick asks visitors to respond. Interesting responses will be displayed on the page, together with comments from Rick.

Good & Bad in Philosophy Essays

http://www.cogsci.ed.ac.uk/~ddb/vade-mecum/sections/section4/4-1.htm

This page provides some useful insights into what is required in an undergraduate philosophy essay.

Guide to the Study of Philosophy

http://people.delphi.com/gkemerling/sy.htm

This site provides information on reading philosophy texts, writing philosophy papers, writing exam essays in philosophy, and more. It is maintained by Garth Kemerling gkemerling@delphi.com.

Guide for Writing Papers in Philosophy

http://www.uq.oz.au/~pdgdunn/watessay.htm

From Ellen Watson, this page provides a general guide to writing philosophy essays.

How to Write a Philosophy Paper

http://www.cariboo.bc.ca/ae/php/phil/mclaughl/courses/howrit.htm

From István Berkeley, this page provides a guide to writing essays in philosophy, with notes on style, quotations, and referencing.

Identifying the Argument of an Essay

http://wwwfaculty.mccneb.edu/commhum/argument/summary.htm

This page, from Frank Edler fedler@ne.uswest.net, provides a tutorial on critical reasoning. It begins with the most basic sense of what an argument is and then builds up to the practice of identifying conclusion and reasons. Finally, it concludes by going through a sample newspaper editorial step by step in order to identify the argument structure of the editorial.

Informal Fallacies

http://www.drury.edu/faculty/Ess/Logic/Informal/Overview.html

From Charles Ess DRU001D@vma.smsu.edu, this site provides a guide to logical fallacies, grouped into three sections: fallacies of relevance, fallacies of presumption, and additional fallacies. It is written as a guide for undergraduate students.

Logic

http://people.delphi.com/gkemerling/lg/

The treatment of elementary logic on this site, from Garth Kemerling gkemerling@delphi.com, closely follows the structure, content, and nomenclature of Copi and Cohen, *Introduction to Logic* (9th Ed.) (New York: Macmillian, 1994). It includes discussion of: Logical Arguments, Language and Logic, Informal Fallacies, Definition and Meaning, Categorical Propositions, Categorical Syllogisms, Syllogistic in Ordinary Language, Symbolic Representation, Proving Validity and Invalidity, Quantification Theory, Analogical Argument, Causal Reasoning, Scientific Explanation, and Probablity.

Paper-Writing Strategies

http://hampshire.edu/~jlcCCS/writingpage.html

From J. Hernandez Cruz cruz@hampshire.edu, this site provides a tutorial for writing introductory philosophy papers. The tutorial "is designed to explore one way of making sure that your writing does not obfuscate your philosophical views," and involves a series of links which explore each stage of the writing process.

The Philosopher's Assistant: A Research Guide for Students

http://www.bluemoon.net/~harrsnow/

Compiled by W. Gordon Snow harrsnow@bluemoon.net, this site aims to aid philosophy students in their research. More specifically, the intent is to provide, in a simple and clear format, high quality Internet resources that will be valuable for student research. Some of the resources available here include the following: instructions on how to write a research paper in philosophy; links to classic philosophic texts that can be saved to a disk, printed, or even read on-line; a dictionary; and a manual of style. Perhaps, the most useful resource is the small but growing library of annotated texts. These annotations, written by professional philosophers, can be thought of as classic texts coupled with class lecture notes that clarify the most important issues addressed in the texts.

Philosophical Debates

http://www.mindspring.com/~mfpatton/debates.htm

This page, compiled by Cheryl and Michael Patton mfpatton@mindspring.com and part of their Patton's Argument Clinic site, provides a growing bibliography on central philosophical questions such as: What is Knowledge? What is the nature of Reality? What is the relationship between the Mind and the Body? Is there a God? How can Science tell us anything? Links to primary texts available online are also included.

The Philosophy Major

http://www.udel.edu/apa/publications/texts/major.html

This site, presents a statement concerning the nature of the philosophy major, prepared under auspices of the Board of Officers of the American Philosophical Association.

So You Want To Pass Your First Philosophy Course?

http://www.arts.ubc.ca/~irvine/sywtp.htm

From Andrew Irvine irvine@unixg.ubc.ca at UBC, this page provides a (partly tongue-in-cheek) guide to writing philosophy papers, and offers advice to students on avoiding plagiarism.

Stephen's Guide to Logical Fallacies

http://www.assiniboinec.mb.ca/user/downes/fallacy/fall.htm

The point of an argument is to give reasons in support of some conclusion. An argument commits a fallacy when the reasons offered do not support the conclusion. These pages, by Stephen Downes downes@adminnet.assiniboinec.mb.ca, describe the known logical fallacies, and are an excellent teaching resource.

Tips on Writing a Philosophy Paper

http://humanitas.ucsb.edu/~portmore/tips.htm

With sections on argumentation, clarity, criticising an argument, style and layout, and more, this guide from Douglas Portmore portmore@humanitas.ucsb.edu provides useful advice on writing philosophy essays.

Vade Mecum: A Survival Guide for Philosophy Students

http://www.cogsci.ed.ac.uk/~ddb/vade-mecum/

An excellent site aimed at students of philosophy at the University of Edinburgh, but useful to students anywhere with an overview of the study of philosophy, information on how to read logical notation, and a lexicon of philosophical terms. Maintained by Darren Brierton ddb@cogsci.ed.ac.uk.

What Can You Do With a Philosophy Degree?

http://www.philosophy.ilstu.edu/philosophy/whatcani.htm

If you're wondering how a major in philosophy can be useful for your career, consider the information on this page, provided by the Philosophy Department at Illinois State University.

Why Major in Philosophy?

http://www.yorku.ca/dept/philo/whystud.htm

On this page, Michael Gilbert Gilbert@Yorku.ca considers the practical value of studying philosophy.

Writing Argumentative Essays

http://cougar.vut.edu.au/~dalbj/argueweb/contents.htm

From Bill Daly BillDaly@vut.edu.au, this site provides comprehensive advice to students on writing argumentative essays.

Writing in Philosophy

http://www.chass.utoronto.ca:8080/philosophy/phlwrite/index.html

Having good philosophical ideas is one thing; communicating them effectively to someone else is another. Both tasks are important parts of an education in philosophy. The resources included here are designed to help students, especially undergraduates, to improve their skills in saying what they mean. An advice section includes handouts prepared by faculty and instructors at the University of Toronto for use in their courses. This section will be expanded as time permits. The site was created by Will Buschert buschert@chass.utoronto.ca.

WWW Resources for Student Philosophy Writers

http://www.ualberta.ca/~gbarron/write/

This site collects links to a range of sites offering advice and guidelines for student writing in philosohy. It is maintained by Guillermo Barron gbarron@gpu.srv.ualberta.ca.